Snida McKinnish Bridges
2001

D0712211

Religion in the South
John B. Boles, Series Editor

William Louis Poteat

A Leader of the
Progressive-Era South

✢

Randal L. Hall

THE UNIVERSITY PRESS OF KENTUCKY

Publication of this volume was made possible in part by a grant
from the National Endowment for the Humanities.

Scholarly publisher for the Commonwealth,
serving Bellarmine College, Berea College, Centre
College of Kentucky, Eastern Kentucky University,
The Filson Club Historical Society, Georgetown College,
Kentucky Historical Society, Kentucky State University,
Morehead State University, Murray State University,
Northern Kentucky University, Transylvania University,
University of Kentucky, University of Louisville,
and Western Kentucky University.

Editorial and Sales Offices: The University Press of Kentucky
663 South Limestone Street, Lexington, Kentucky 40508–4008

04 03 02 01 00   5 4 3 2 1

Library of Congress Cataloging-in-Publication Data

Hall, Randal L., 1971-
    William Louis Poteat : a leader of the progressive-era South / by Randal L. Hall.
        p. cm.
    Includes bibliographical references and index.
    ISBN 0-8131-2155-8 (alk. paper)
    1. Poteat, William Louis, 1856-1938. 2. Social reformers—North Carolina—
Biography. 3. Biology teachers—North Carolina—Biography. 4. College
teachers—North Carolina—Biography. 5. Baptists—North Carolina—Biography.
6. Evolution—Study and teaching—North Carolina—History. 7. Evolution—
Religious aspects—Baptists. 8. Wake Forest College—Faculty—Biography. I.
Title

HV28.P67 H35 2000
378.756'55—dc21
[B}
                                                                    99-049444

The author affectionately dedicates
this work to his wife,
Naomi J. Hall.

Contents

Illustrations

Acknowledgments

I would like to thank the staffs and archivists at the special collections departments of Wake Forest University and Duke University and at the Southern Historical Collection at the University of North Carolina at Chapel Hill. Particularly helpful were John R. Woodard and everyone in Special Collections at Wake Forest. Their assistance enabled my research to proceed quickly. Also of great help was the interlibrary loan department of Fondren Library at Rice University. Generous research funding obtained from Rice University with the help of History Department chair Thomas Haskell made my research trips possible. I would also like to thank Keith Smith and Bill Owens for graciously providing lodging during my research, and Paul Escott, James Barefield, Howell Smith, and Thomas K. Hearn for taking an interest in this project and for making my research visits to North Carolina more enjoyable. Diana P. Hobby and Sylvia S. Lowe provided papers and journals held by William Louis Poteat's family and also offered their hospitality at Forest Home on more than one occasion. The late Arthur S. Link generously shared a draft of his book on the history of medical study at Wake Forest.

Professor John Boles has my gratitude not only for setting a good example as a historian but also for the encouragement that his deep-seated optimism provides. Allen Matusow and Dennis Shirley offered invaluable advice after closely reading the manuscript, and Thomas Haskell provided a helpful reading of a difficult chapter. Evelyn Thomas Nolen, Patricia Bixel, and Patricia Burgess provided advice and collegiality during the drafting of this work. Carlos Blanton, David Dillard, Charles Israel, Melissa Kean, and Steve Wilson shared their ideas on many occasions. Nancy S. Midgette provided helpful critiques of the material about science.

My parents, Ernest and Mary Hall, and siblings Michael, Kathy, and Becky encouraged my work. My debt is greatest to my wife Naomi for sharing me with this project for several years, and this book is dedicated to her.

Introduction

✟

From his lair on the South's northern border, Baltimore journalist and critic Henry L. Mencken pounced on the region's absurdities and intellectual sterility throughout the early twentieth century. On rare occasions, however, he observed someone worthwhile trekking through the cultural aridity of the southern Sahara. One such person he identified was William Louis Poteat, president of Wake Forest College in North Carolina, whom he included on a list of "a few hard-boiled and heroic men, their veins filled with manganese, [who] manage to hold out" as intellectuals in the South.[1]

Poteat was born in 1856 on a large plantation in Caswell County, North Carolina, and attended Wake Forest College from 1872 until 1877. In 1878 he returned to the school as a tutor, then professor of biology, and finally president from 1905 until 1927. In 1881 he married Emma James Purefoy (1857–1939), and they had a son, Hubert McNeill (b. 1886), and two daughters, Louie (b. 1889) and Helen Purefoy (b. 1896). Poteat's knowledge of biology was gained from his own study, with the exception of brief summer classes in Germany and Massachusetts, but he gained fame in the South as a believer in evolution. Poteat's prolific writing reflects his struggle to accept a liberal theology that could reconcile his scientific understanding with the Southern Baptist mores that formed him. He was involved in numerous denominational activities and Progressive-Era campaigns but achieved lasting notoriety when his educational and religious teachings clashed with conservative ideas in the evolution controversy of the 1920s. He remained active as a teacher until his death in 1938.

Poteat was quite familiar to the acerbic Maryland journalist because "Mencken's two leading Southern apostles" worshiped Poteat for helping to create and legitimize their critical attitudes.[2] Gerald W. Johnson and Wilbur J. Cash both came of age in North Carolina and found intellectual liberation at the state's Baptist college, nestled in its namesake town of Wake Forest, a few miles north of Raleigh. Two of the leading southern liberals of the first half of the twentieth century, Johnson and Cash both gained early inspiration from Poteat and eulogized him soon after his death in 1938. In a bit of hagiography from 1943 titled "Billy with the Red Necktie," the imaginative Johnson depicted a young Poteat in the 1880s as he "returned to this country with glowing testimonials from his instructors in the Zoological Institute of the University of Berlin, where he had been doing graduate work in biology." The budding scientist, however, "threw his life away, sacrificing not wealth and ease only, but also reputation and that greater thing, the joy of extending the boundaries of knowledge in his own field." Poteat supposedly relinquished these opportunities in order "to introduce a little gleam of light into some thousands of young minds that went darkling" at the struggling religious college. Along the way, he contributed "to saving the intellectual honor of his State."[3]

W.J. Cash echoed Johnson's sentiments in his 1941 classic *The Mind of the South,* a starting point for all historians of the region since its publication. By teaching biology and the theory of evolution, Poteat allegedly provided "the first wholly honest and competent instruction of the sort in a Southern evangelical school" and with few exceptions "the first in Southern schools of any sort. . . ."[4] With Harry W. Chase and Frank P. Graham of the University of North Carolina at Chapel Hill, he then helped to save these glimmers of intellectual development from assault by Fundamentalists in the 1920s when the three chose to "come boldly out in defense of academic freedom. . . ."[5] Elsewhere, Cash summarized his romantic view of Poteat more succinctly: "Dr. Poteat has an almost uncanny way of being right. And I believe no man in America better understands more clearly what Jesus, the most misunderstood figure of all times, teaches."[6] Cash's biographer concludes that Poteat had a lasting influence on Cash. For the troubled writer "the modern mind was his mind, . . . the mind he had started to acquire at Wake Forest."[7]

One hallmark of the modern mind is a critical spirit, the willingness to test sacred assumptions. Ironically, in examining Poteat, Johnson and Cash suspended the operation of that modern outlook and lapsed into worship. Their lack of analysis and their unquestioning praise for Poteat as a forward-looking, twentieth-century liberal has been echoed in virtually all subsequent writing about him. Suzanne C. Linder's 1966 study of Poteat (with a foreword, incidentally, by an aging Gerald Johnson) hails Poteat as a "prophet" whose major contribution was his "work of interpreting progress" to the people of North Carolina.[8] He "had a formative influence on the most outstanding forces for social progress of his day." Further, "in his work as college president," Poteat "recognized the opportunity not only to aid society in the interpretation of progress but also, through his influence on the lives of future leaders, to help shape the progress of the South."[9] For Linder, Poteat's effort to reconcile science and religion and his related battle against anti-evolution laws in the 1920s were his most important legacies. He "led the people of the South to a more enlightened religion, and in so doing, he helped to insure freedom of teaching and a reverence for truth that would last far beyond his lifetime."[10]

Willard B. Gatewood Jr. also praises Poteat's role in the anti-evolution controversy, though he too fails to push his analysis far enough. He caricatures Fundamentalists, obscuring the stakes in their fight against liberal theology. His work pictures a Manichaean battle between "zealots . . . waging a righteous war" and "a few academicians, journalists, and clergymen who considered such statutory restrictions as by-products of ignorance, intolerance, and bigotry."[11] He contends, "Evolution happened to be the issue on which protagonists decided to wage their major struggle" in this "collision between two states of mind that occurred during the first major intellectual confrontation with the twentieth century by North Carolinians." In Gatewood's analysis, Poteat and Chase are the victorious proponents of open-mindedness and twentieth-century ideas. They "refused to relinquish the freedom of the academic cloister or to surrender the college to the control of the mass meeting. Despite the personal vilification by their adversaries, they stood fast against the rising tide of anti-intellectualism."[12] In their search for a forward-looking liberal southerner in the early twentieth century, these and other writers have oversimplified William Louis Poteat's life and thought as well as the significance of his actions in such critical historical events as the evolution controversy.[13] This biography analyzes Poteat in a more comprehensive and nuanced way, while reinterpreting his significance in the broader context of the South.

The period in which Poteat lived was a dark time in the South, marked by intolerance, outbreaks of extreme violence, desperate poverty in rural areas, and a corrupt political system that worked against meaningful democracy. Lynchings of blacks increased dramatically in number and savagery, beginning in the 1880s and continuing through the rest of Poteat's life. Sharecropping spread among blacks and whites after the Civil War, keeping the agricultural economy mired in low productivity and its farmers hopeless. At the ballot box political elites violently overcame dissent by the lower orders of society, and the most impoverished whites seldom saw blacks as potential allies, even during the brief moment in the 1890s when the Populist party tried to somewhat democratize southern politics. Beginning in the 1880s, industrialization in such areas as the North Carolina Piedmont benefited the owners of textile mills, but for the workers, moving to a mill job often meant trading the exploitation and exhaustion of sharecropping for an equally hopeless and brutal existence in unregulated factories. Times were similarly benighted for southern intellectual activity. An extremely conservative, individualistic form of religion dominated southern thought between the Civil War and World War II. Until the twenties literary creativity was typified by the romantic stories of plantation life by Thomas Nelson Page and the racist diatribes in which Thomas Dixon Jr. supported the Confederacy, the Ku Klux Klan, and the Lost Cause mythology. And public education at all levels remained so poor as to assure that each new generation could hardly hope to overcome the region's intellectual sterility.

Poteat's long life encompassed this brutal period in the South. He was born into and remembered fondly the orderly world of the antebellum plantation and slavery, and he was educated in the classical tradition, both by tutors and then at Wake Forest College. Yet he also avidly read the Victorian moralists popular during his early adult life. Poteat combined these sources with the evangelical Baptist faith that surrounded him like the very air of central North Carolina to produce a worldview that imbued every aspect of life with moral meaning. He sought to bring order to the violence and chaos of southern life by advocating that the superior people in society must lead and uplift the rest along Christian lines. Education was to provide those natural leaders with refinement, high culture, and moral principles. The underlying goal of most of his life's work was to bring about change within orderly Christian channels. Poteat spoke as a member of the elite, but his was a voice of gentleness, of nurturing concern, of quiet reasonableness in a harsh age of exploitation and insensitivity. He believed he could identify the reasoned and obvious path for the South to follow in negotiating the treacherous waters of the late nineteenth and early twentieth centuries, without losing either the benefits of genteel leadership or Victorian moral absolutes.

Despite the sometimes conservative sources and goals of his ideas, Poteat ranked as a leading liberal among southern intellectuals for much of his life, a fact that reveals a great deal about North Carolina and the South during this tempestuous time. In the Baptist denomination, Poteat was relatively unusual in stressing the social duties of Christians, and he actively supported or led many of the campaigns of the Progressive Era. He closely followed the development of modern biology and was exceptionally frank in teaching evolution. Further, his defense of intellectual liberty in the twenties placed him among the foremost liberals of his time. Nonetheless, even the most active proponents of Progressive change during Poteat's life drew from southern tradition. Poteat maintained throughout his life a remarkably consistent set of core beliefs that centered around the moral absolutes of religion, respect for high culture and learning, the need for elite leadership, and a love of order and hierarchy. Into this matrix he absorbed dramatic modernizing disruptions such as evolutionary biology, professionalization and specialization, mass political campaigns, racial unrest, and the moral relativity of the twentieth century. That he successfully maintained a foundation of Victorian values from the nineteenth century does not minimize the struggles he faced as he encountered conflicts with modernity.

The ever-astute Mencken—more than Poteat's many later admirers—recognized in 1925 the compromises made by the South's first generation of liberal intellectuals. Poteat's "argument seems to be that modern man should continue to accept all those parts of the Bible that have not yet been disposed of by science," while seeing the rest as symbolic or literary. Mencken saw this as "nonsense" and contentiously, though perhaps truthfully, identified Poteat as less a scientist than "primarily a good Christian—more, a good Baptist." Thus, Poteat "stuck valiantly to such curiosities of the Baptist sorcery as total immersion and Prohibition. . . ." On the other hand, Poteat's liberal efforts led Mencken to admit, "The fact that North Carolina is now the most intelligent of all the Southern States is largely due to him."[14] Analyzing the paradoxes, compromises, and tensions that Poteat faced yields a deeper understanding not only of his life, but also of the history of religion, education, reform, and intellectual dissent during a critical period in the South.[15]

1

Genesis of a
Southern Reformer

✦

The Poteat family began a long relationship with North Carolina in the mid-1760s when John and Ann Miles McComas Poteat, along with her father, apparently moved from Baltimore County, Maryland, to the frontier portion of Orange County, North Carolina, that later became Caswell County.[1] The early Poteats chose an excellent area for settlement. Caswell County is nestled in the Piedmont region of North Carolina and borders Virginia to the north. Land was granted there as early as 1745, and Caswell County was formed in 1777, only a few years after the Regulator uprising against the royal administration brought this region of the state to the governor's attention. The county grew steadily thereafter on the basis of agriculture; one historian concludes that "during the period between the American Revolution and the Civil War Caswell County was the scene of a flourishing society typical in the popular imagination of the antebellum South." Its soils are a rich sandy loam with a stiff red clay underneath, and the gently rolling hills provided fertile fields for the various crops that drove the antebellum economy. Population climbed from a total of 5,193, with 1,076 blacks, in 1786, to 16,215, of whom 9,355 were slaves, in 1860. Corn and wheat were popular products, and there were the usual activities of millers and various artisans. Tobacco, though, overshadowed all else.[2]

Caswell growers initially depended on a dark, heavy-leaf variety of tobacco and marketed it in Petersburg, Virginia. In 1839, however, a Caswell slave first discovered the curing process that produced the coveted bright-leaf tobacco. By the 1850s the process was perfected and routinized, and the high prices that the leaf brought launched a golden age in Caswell in the years preceding the Civil War.[3] The soils "where the finest bright leaf is raised" were limited to a few counties in southern Virginia and Piedmont North Carolina. The Poteat family was situated to benefit from this development, and tobacco became their key cash crop.[4]

Soon after the arrival of the first Poteat in Caswell County, the family slowly started to build a prosperous plantation and to acquire local influence. Upon John Poteat's death in 1788, his holdings in land and slaves passed to his sons, among them Miles and John. The younger John gradually accumulated a substantial estate in the early decades of the nineteenth century, while Miles found more modest success. Miles's son James Poteat began to achieve distinction in the 1830s. In 1838 he owned at least 216 acres of land, and he purchased land aggressively over the next two years. In 1840 he was chosen as a patroller for his portion of the county, and the county court's confidence in him grew enough by 1846 that he was elected standard keeper.[5] He continued to perform local duties such as "leveling the grounds around the Court House" in 1849 and rebuilding a neighborhood bridge in 1854.[6] His community contributions in the 1850s included service as a tax lister and evaluator, an election judge, guarantor of the bond of the county clerk, and foreman of the grand jury.[7] This list of activities in a rural antebellum county defined him as a member of the local gentry. The crowning mark was his election as a captain in the area's militia.[8]

Captain Poteat, as he was typically known even by his son eighty years later, married Isabella G. Roberts on October 14, 1837, and her father advanced some money to the couple.[9] The death of James Poteat's father, Miles, and the division of his estate in 1842 probably aided their progress.[10] Their family grew quickly to include four children in 1850, three sons and a daughter, all residing at a hotel they operated in Yanceyville. A fifth child, another daughter, had died in infancy.[11] Events of the early 1850s then radically altered the life of James Poteat. His wife died at some point after 1850, leaving him the children to raise. On the side of good fortune, his uncle John—who died in November 1852—left his entire estate, real and personal, to his nephew.[12] When in January 1853 the will was proven in court, this inheritance vaulted James Poteat to the level of southern aristocracy.[13]

John Poteat's estate included 61 slaves valued at $26,645; 2,104 acres of land worth $8 per acre; a lot with a house in Yanceyville worth $2,500; and half-interest in the town's grocery valued at $900.[14] With his new resources, the middle-aged Captain quickly restored direction to his life. By 1855 he had completed an imposing home in the Greek Revival style of the time, situated near Rattlesnake Creek two miles from Yanceyville and complete with a two-story entrance porch topped by a Doric pediment.[15] On November 17, 1855, he married Julia A. McNeill and proudly brought his 21–year-old bride to their "Forest Home."[16] She came from a leading family that, like the Poteats, had been in Caswell County since before its creation in the 1770s, and her father had frequently been involved in local government. Julia McNeill had secured an education at the seminary that the Baptist State Convention had opened in July 1851 at Oxford, North Carolina. In addition to such subjects as English, piano, drawing, painting, and needle work, her education had emphasized the "quiet and lady-like deportment" expected of "young ladies." She likely had a major role in raising the two youngest children from James's first marriage as well as their own four children and was the refined, educated example for both sets of offspring.[17]

The Captain proved his business acumen, and the couple profited from the booming economy of the 1850s. In 1860 the 53–year-old Captain Poteat had real estate worth $45,000 and personal estate worth $100,000. This included 94 slaves, giving him the county's third-largest holding of slaves.[18] The plantation consisted of 1,200 acres of improved land and 800 acres of unimproved land. It supported 109 sheep, 15 horses, and 10 mules, along with other livestock, and farm implements worth $650. In 1860 Poteat produced 4,000 bushels of corn, 1,800 bushels of wheat, and the money crop of 40,000 pounds of tobacco, outranking even the county's largest slaveholder on that crucial score.[19] In 1863 during the Civil War, Poteat's holdings of slaves reached 105, placing him among that select few in the Old South for whom reality approached the later legends about antebellum prosperity and refinement.[20] In the young and unstable world of southern plantation aristocracy, the Poteat family's standing had begun to acquire the patina of age by 1856, when William Louis Poteat was born on October 20 and entered an arena of wealth and privilege as the first child of James and Julia Poteat.

In addition to starting a second family, James Poteat's second marriage occasioned another major change in his life. Julia had grown up in a strongly religious family, and she had studied at a Baptist institution. Her influence converted James Poteat (and the children to follow) to the cause of North Carolina's evangelical Baptists. He joined the Baptist church in Yanceyville after their marriage, perhaps as part of an "out-pouring of the Holy Spirit" that frequently occurred in Caswell County during revival season. He was baptized along with his two older sons in 1858. Poteat rapidly assumed a prominent role as clerk and deacon,[21] and by 1861 he was a trustee of the church.[22] William Poteat's youth was filled with religious activities and people, including preachers such as the tireless home missionary Elias Dodson who never "passed without turning in to refresh himself at 'Sister Poteat's' hospitable board."[23]

As a workhorse, and a generous one, within his church and the organization of Baptist churches in the area, the Beulah Association, James Poteat served in various capacities. He was a member of the executive committee of the prosperous Beulah Association and in four instances was elected moderator of their annual meeting.[24] On many other occasions he led the meeting of the ministers and deacons of the twenty-seven churches then part of the association.[25] During Reconstruction, James Poteat was one of "the old familiar faces" among area Baptist leaders, and he was rewarded for his diligent services since the mid-1850s with appointment in October 1866 as trustee of Wake Forest College.[26] However, his leadership within the denomination did not reach beyond his association. Influence on the statewide level, the Baptist State Convention, waited for his sons, and their father's regional prominence gave them a good start.

James Poteat also embraced the fledgling social concern of the Baptists, a corollary of the universal Christian appeal to charity. His understanding of religious duty is manifest in his appointment to help formulate "a plan for taking care of super-annuated ministers" and in his "essay on Systematic Benevolence."[27] He argued that "without System in every thing failure is the result" and called for churches to appoint committees to encourage "a course of liberality on the part of church members. . . ."[28] This sort of earthly stewardship fit in with concerns long established among nineteenth-century evangelicals. Within the antebellum South, the evangelical churches created the beginnings of a limited southern reform tradition, and James Poteat was a progressive within Baptist circles of the time. His interests ranged from denominational education to benevolent activities, and this sentiment within the household undoubtedly influenced young William Poteat, who later pursued many of the same progressive goals.[29]

Like many southern planters, the elder Poteat tried to reform slavery to be more in accord with Christian paternalism. He built a two-room chapel on the plantation to be used by his slaves and "supplied preaching for the place." At least some of the slaves accepted his religion, for William Poteat remembered that soon after the war the slave cooper and carpenter "Uncle Morris" would sit in front of his house each Sunday with a Bible always open to the third chapter of John. The biracial Yanceyville church likely included some Poteat slaves, constituting the only institution in which young Poteat would have seen any semblance of unforced interracial activity.[30]

The slave chapel also represents a second interest of Captain Poteat that became his son's life work—education. In summer, the elder Poteat conducted a Sunday school there to teach the neighborhood's white children, and possibly some adults, how to read. In winter the activity moved inside the big house. William Poteat later recalled, "In that Sunday School I made my first and only contact with Webster's 'Blue Back.'"[31] As William grew up during Reconstruction, his father especially favored Sunday schools as a "great work" in education through which the church could improve southern society. He and his wife operated the Sunday school at their church, and he was a vice-president of the denomination's Sunday School Association, as well as Sunday school superintendent for the Beulah Association.[32] Like his son to follow, the Captain focused on childhood as the time to shape the next generation along proper principles (though the younger Poteat had a broader vision of proper education). In the insecurity, unrest, and perceived moral laxity of the Reconstruction Era in North Carolina, Sunday schools were an offensive for order. He hoped to save young southerners "from the many and imminent perils that threaten their moral ruin."[33]

The Civil War and Reconstruction left the Poteat family to adjust to many other challenges in addition to those of a moral nature. Perhaps because of his care for his land and his diversified interests, James Poteat did not lose everything at the end of the war. His worth declined, though, to $14,000 in real estate—still among the county's highest figures—and $12,000 in personal property, making him one of the wealthiest men in Caswell.[34] Unlike many planters, he remained able to pay in cash and always to top or at least match the highest donations in church collections.[35] Nonetheless, the war did take from the family two of Poteat's sons from his first marriage. Felix Lindsey

Shown here at about age ten, Poteat enjoyed an idyllic childhood until the end of the Civil War, but then faced adolescence during the violent turmoil of Reconstruction in North Carolina. (All photos courtesy of Special Collections, Reynolds Library, Wake Forest University, Winston-Salem, North Carolina.)

Built in 1855, Poteat's childhood home was an antebellum showplace, but it decayed after the Civil War. It was then used for many years as a home for tenants and even in part a storage area for cotton. Poteat's daughter and son-in-law, Helen and Laurence Stallings, enlarged and restored Forest Home to pristine condition in the 1920s.

died from a wound received in battle in 1864 and was brought back from Richmond by his father, while John Miles contracted consumption while in the army and returned home to die soon after the war's end. Their graves in a little grove only yards from Forest Home would have been a constant reminder to James as well as young William of the cost of civil conflict.[36] James seemingly moved beyond wartime animosities quickly; in nearby Danville, Virginia, he took the oath of amnesty to the United States on August 17, 1865. Apparently because they expected to benefit economically, the family moved to Yanceyville after the war, when William was fourteen. On the public square they opened a hotel, a field of business in which James had worked earlier in his life.[37] Tenants were secured for the old plantation. Though operating a hotel undoubtedly required a humbler outlook than commanding a force of slaves on the plantation, money must not have been too tight because ex-slave "Uncle Morris" remained as the family's "carriage driver."[38]

William Louis Poteat seldom wrote or spoke about the family's Reconstruction experiences operating the hotel; however, he treasured his plantation childhood. Later in life when he was "thinking much of the past," he reminisced about the plantation world that instilled in him many of the values and assumptions that he carried throughout life.[39] Poteat noted fondly, "The plantation, it is interesting to recall in this day of specialization and exchange, was a self-sufficient social unit." His lifelong dislike of specialization originated in his memory of the organic unity of Forest Home. The plantation supplied everything but hats, he remembered, including active intellectual engagement.[40] He accepted part of the Lost Cause view of the Old South, lamenting "the passing away of the social and intellectual life which in some sense had its material basis in slavery. . . ." The region "gave its ample leisure to the amenities of social intercourse, to the enrichment of the religious and the intellectual life." Planters "cultivated the higher ideals" such as "candor, charity, and hospitality, and the graces of an elegant simplicity blossomed out in natural beauty in its country homes."[41]

Poteat firmly believed that plantation life at Forest Home included a sincere sense of paternalism toward the black slaves. The slaves were part of the family in that the Poteats called the domestic servants "Uncle Jerry," "Aunt Chanie," and "Uncle Morris." William Poteat recalled that in turn "the slaves called my father 'Marse Jim.'" Their respect was expected: "He was not unlike the centurion of Scripture who reported that he had instant, unquestioning obedience from those under him. . . . He was imperious but kind." Further, "he was solicitous for the bodily comfort and the religious needs of the slaves." Poteat's mother also had a role in this drama; she directed the household production of cloth and went into "the cabins to minister personally to" sick slaves. In the ultimate statement of faith in antebellum paternalism, Poteat noted that the image of his mother supervising slave women "always raises in my mind the question, Which after all was the greatest slave of the group?"[42]

Poteat, given the lifetime nickname Bud Loulie as a youngster, had his own childhood classroom in slavery and paternalism. He recalled the experience frequently and with relish throughout his life: "Nat was black as Egypt. His mother died at his birth, which occurred about the same time as my own. He was admitted to the superb abundance of the same white fountain from which I drew my infant nourishment,—my turn then Nat's. With that start we grew up all the way together. Papa gave him to me. He was mine and in a very real sense I was his. Wherever 'Loulie' went Nat was sure to go, and when Nat led out into the yard or garden or grove Loulie trailed faithfully after."[43] Poteat vowed, "I shall never forget our boyish frolics in the oak-grove back of my country home and how, when the fried chicken had been taken up, we sopped the gravy in the wide skillet on terms of perfect friendship and equality." With this as evidence, he refused "to be imposed upon by misrepresentation of the kindly relation which existed between master and slave."[44] Because he was only a child when slavery ended, Poteat did not have to endure that wrenching moment of realization experienced by most planters when they discovered the emptiness of paternalism and became aware that their slaves really did want freedom.

Poteat's childhood was idyllic, and it gave him a lifelong appreciation for the values of the country. He henceforth distrusted urban influences. He developed the aesthetic appreciation for manual labor found only in those never forced to engage in it: on the plantation, "the cutting of the wheat was beautiful to see,—a half dozen men singing to their swinging cradles, the strongest man in front, the others following each a little behind his fellow and a swath's breadth to the right of him, all pushing together, a sort of stairway across the field of gold." His childhood was filled with images of spinning, weaving, killing hogs, the blacksmith shop, the mills, and of course the animals. Like any country boy, he could name the bays, Bill and Pete, and the old ox Rock decades later. Skating, fishing, or swimming in the mill pond, alternately by season, occupied much of his time. Nonetheless, he was not isolated, taking "many an early morning trip to Danville," the neighboring town in Virginia that was "the big city" of Poteat's youth.[45]

His early education followed the pattern typical of the antebellum elite. After learning some rudiments of reading in Sunday school, he and his younger siblings had the benefit of a governess. His family was growing in numbers. A sister, Ida Isabella, arrived in 1859, and a brother, Edwin McNeill, followed in 1861. Like William, both would become influential educators. They were joined soon after the war's end by a sister, Emma Lindsay, who died in 1888.[46] "I seem not to have played much with my brother and sisters," Poteat recalled, because Ida had such passions as dolls and his "habits were set before my brother reached the level of coincident play interests." Further, "there was Nat on my hands. I had to attend to him." The much older children of James Poteat's first marriage stayed in Poteat's memory principally because of the visits home of the two brothers who fought in the war, though he remained in occasional but cordial contact throughout his life with his surviving half-brother and half-sister and their families. The children's first governess was a distant cousin by marriage, who was succeeded by a young woman from the neighborhood. Joined at times by a young cousin, the little group of children studied informally, occasionally on the roof of the back porch. After learning the basics at home, Poteat walked two miles to "a sort of boys' school" in Yanceyville for five months and also received some instruction from Miss Lizzie Lowndes, who operated the Yanceyville Female Academy. From her, Poteat learned the Latin needed to pursue the classical education still prevalent in most of the state's institutions of higher education.[47] Though North Carolina ostensibly supported a system of common schools, the only options for secondary education in Caswell County were private schools that dotted that part of the state. For Poteat to receive academy training elevated him into the educational elite.

Julia Poteat became the guiding force for the family after the move to the county seat of Yanceyville. In Poteat's fond memory she "was a better man than" his father, perhaps because she retained more vigor of youth than her aging husband. In the large, old home they owned there, they opened a hotel despite living in the midst of Reconstruction unrest that rivaled the worst in the South. In 1870 James Poteat's son Preston was living with them and working as a clerk at the local store, and William, Edwin, and Ida were attending school. Crucial years of Poteat's adolescence were spent at this village business. If surviving registers from a few years later are any indication, the hotel was a successful venture, especially when the court was in session at the imposing classical courthouse building just across the town square. Preparing and serving meals and caring for horses and mules would have made the work a challenge, but according to one traveler, the accommodations were "tolerable good." The children would have met visitors from throughout the North Carolina Piedmont region and the neighboring areas of central Virginia. Occasionally, people might arrive from places farther away, big cities such as Richmond, Baltimore, and even New York, but the heart of the business was regional.[48]

During the uncertainties of this time both in his life and in Reconstruction North Carolina, one force for order in William Poteat's developing world was his church in Yanceyville. Following the end of the war, the church disciplined its members to restore morality, a practice almost absent during the conflict. For example, in January 1867 the deacons investigated two women members for reportedly dancing. One asked the church's forgiveness, and James Poteat and a Brother Lea visited the other to "reclaim her if possible." Perhaps in this way women received the message that their enlarged activities of the war period were no longer acceptable. The biracial church also struggled to adjust to Emancipation. In July 1865 a committee was appointed to investigate the "unchristian character of three of the colored members," but the charges were dismissed at the next meeting. Rules were tightened in April 1866. After the acceptance of a white applicant into membership, "a colored woman . . . also presented herself for the purpose of connecting her self with this church and after some conversation with the members it was thought to be best for all parties to waive her reception for the present. A resolution was then offered and carried unanimously that hereafter a certificate of character as formerly be required of colored applicants for membership in this Church."

The racial tension only worsened. In August 1866 the church took the radical step of recommending "to the colored members of this church the propriety of withdrawing and organizing themselves into a separate church" that "for the present" could share the church's building. This represented the vanguard of deciding the racial question in North Carolina's churches. The following June the Baptist State Convention faced the issue and after a hot debate recommended "that our colored brethren be encouraged to form separate Churches and Associations," the reverse of the situation in most of the South where blacks took the initiative in separating after the war. The resolution's proponents recognized that in some cases blacks wanted to form separate churches, but the motivation for the recommendation was white inability to face black equality. A supporter summarized, "One of two courses is left open to us: either to form separate organizations for the two races; or to gather both, without distinction in point of privilege, into our churches." He continued, "The latter course is not to be thought of."[49] The new whiteness of the Yanceyville church allowed an instance of disregard for black humanity in September 1867. The minutes record that "Bro. L. F. Mason reported (through Pastor) that he had had a difficulty with a freedman which resulted in his shooting freedman. But that he did not justify himself for so doing though the circumstances were of the most aggravating character." Since he had acknowledged his sin and asked forgiveness, the church easily forgave Mason (apparently the pastor's son Louis for whom young William Louis Poteat was named) despite the severity of his offense.[50] With the decrease of biracial interaction in the churches, the only forum for ameliorating racial tension disappeared. As the Poteats clung to the church, Caswell County sank deeper into a morass of racial violence.

Swirling throughout Caswell County was a whirlwind of racial problems that were among the most bitter in the South. Trouble began in North Carolina after the passage of the Military Reconstruction Act in 1867 allowed a viable Republican party to form and to challenge the Conservative organization in the Old North State. When the biracial Republican coalition triumphed in 1868 and the newly enfranchised freedmen helped to ratify a progressive state constitution, the threatened Conservatives struck back in hope of regaining political control. The political terrorism of the Ku Klux Klan made a few tentative strides in the state leading up to the 1868 elections, and by the end of that year the violence was whipped into full frenzy.

The Piedmont area of the state, where Conservatives and Republicans were most nearly equal in strength, became the core of the unrest. In testimony in 1871 to the Select Committee of the Senate to Investigate Alleged Outrages in the Southern States, Joseph W. Holden explained, "The counties of Alamance, Orange, Moore, Caswell, Lincoln, and Cleveland are the counties in which the most of these outrages have been committed, though they have been committed in a greater or less degree in at least two-thirds of the counties of the State." The result by mid-1869 was "a series of beatings, cuttings, shootings, and other outrages, usually against Negroes."[51] Prominent young Caswell citizen John G. Lea organized the Klan in the county, with "a den in every township. . . ."[52] In Caswell County, local commissioners, officers of the law, and various officials were loyal to the Conservatives, but a strong Republican organization drew strength from the black majority of the county. Between 1868 and the approach of the state elections of 1870, Republican strength grew.[53]

James Poteat was not visible in the political fighting in Caswell County. He devoted himself to denominational leadership for the Beulah Association. The younger Poteat followed suit in turning to the church during this troubled period. His mother "was the ruling spirit of the home, and . . . she ruled it by a sort of graciousness."[54] Poteat recalled that her "gentle, sometimes tearful, insistence, reinforced by her life of sweetness and light awakened in me early the wish to be a Christian." On the Saturday before the fourth Sunday of August in 1869, at the church's monthly business meeting, Poteat continued, "I presented myself and was received into the membership of [the] village church. I recall no profound eruptive experience, only the passing of embarrassment and anxiety and the coming of a cool deep peace." As the church clerk, Poteat's father recorded in careful handwriting in the church minutes the conversion of his twelve-year-old son to the religion he was to serve the rest of his life. The following Sunday, Poteat was baptized along with sixteen others.[55]

Poteat's conversion was part of an outpouring that "thoroughly revived" the church that summer and fall. The minister reported fifty conversions and noted that "the whole community is alive." In the only important revival in the church between the war and the state's return to Conservative rule, membership continued to grow in September and October.[56] Not only for the Poteats, but for a significant portion of the white community, the church was a haven of reassurance in troubled times.[57]

The following year, 1870, was the worst for Caswell. In neighboring Alamance County in February, the Klan assassination of a black political leader climaxed a renewed campaign of terror across the state. Attempts to reach a moderate compromise also failed in Caswell, and the result was the assassination of the county's leading white Republican, state senator John W. Stephens. The Klan had secretly "tried" Stephens in absentia, convicted him of arson, and ordered his death. On May 21 a group of the county's leading Democrats and Ku Klux Klan members lured Stephens to a basement room of the courthouse and murdered him. Governor William W. Holden declared Caswell and Alamance Counties to be in a state of insurrection. Courts were not functioning because officials were often Klan members and juries would not bring convictions. Holden noted that the Klan "has had absolute control for the last twelve months" of the two counties. Therefore, he gathered a militia force under the command of Colonel George W. Kirk that was sent to restore order.[58]

The result was the so-called Kirk-Holden war. In the two counties, Kirk's forces arrested approximately a hundred men suspected of criminal activity as part of the Klan conspiracy. Nineteen men were detained in Caswell; some were bound over by a court in Raleigh for local trial; but none were ever punished.[59] Nonetheless, the summer's events were a major disruption to all citizens of the county, even those not directly involved. After joining the church, the always dutiful young William Poteat became a regular along with his father at the monthly business meeting. He would have felt "the state of confusion and alarm produced by the military sent in our midst" that in July 1870 forced the church to cancel an association meeting there.[60] The disorder further intruded into the Poteats' lives because "of the arrest of several of our beloved Brethren" in the church, recorded by clerk James Poteat though that reference was later crossed through in the minute book.[61] In addition, during Poteat's youth, his home swarmed with visitors. His parents "seemed to keep open house to friends of the neighborhood including Yanceyville,—the Williamsons, the Womacks, the Graveses, the Leas, the Robertsons. . . ." From these families, some related to the Poteats, came members of the group that killed John Stephens and many of those suspected of making up the county's powerful Ku Klux Klan. Among the arrested was Poteat kinsman and former Congressman John Kerr, who succeeded James Poteat as moderator of the Beulah Association. Kerr testified to the Senate that he was arrested along with "twenty others of the best men of the county" though he "did deny the existence" of the Klan in the county. After all, blacks had "been very kindly and generously treated by the whites" of the area.[62]

William Poteat could hardly have remained unaffected by the events of Reconstruction in Caswell, but the destruction did not lead him to completely repudiate his neighbors and regional tradition. In the hotel, endless conversations about politics and violence would have occurred during court sessions. His family's acquaintance with the families of leading Klan members and their presence in the church would have made a close identification with the chaos inevitable. The overwhelming tradition of violence and racism of the time marked him deeply, and throughout his life he worked against war and on behalf of various peace organizations. However, just as polite company covered over the violence by leading citizens of the county, Poteat never dredged up or recorded his thoughts about those times. His faith in the guidance of the best of respectable society was not shaken, just as he retained a great respect for John Kerr. Further, the loyalty of the southern elite to the Democratic party, a faith that grew during Reconstruction, also remained with Poteat, and with occasional lapses he was a lifelong Democrat.

Conflicting elements were present, though. The removal of blacks from Baptist churches came with the additional directive that whites must help them form their own churches because, in the words of the editor of the *Biblical Recorder,* "we can not allow the heathen to grow up at our doors without manifest departure from the christian duty."[63] This formula translated antebellum paternalism toward slaves into the postbellum environment and became the justification of a minor tradition of racial paternalism that endured in the South.[64] Poteat never really saw beyond this paternalism to perceive the equality of blacks, but as the doctrine took its postbellum form, it was the progressive option because many whites of the time were supporting or conducting violent attacks against blacks.

The Reconstruction period essentially ended in North Carolina with the successful impeachment of Republican governor Holden in March 1871. He was unseated for allegedly abusing his power as governor when he challenged the Ku Klux Klan's imposition of white supremacy by using the militia to suppress the group's violence. Soon after the state settled into uneasy quiet, William Louis Poteat left Yanceyville for Wake Forest College, a world that would finish shaping his young mind. The Poteats' relationship with Wake Forest had begun in the 1850s when James Poteat started donating money to the college after he became a Baptist. After being appointed a trustee in 1866, the elder Poteat sent Preston, a son from his first marriage, to Wake Forest for a time, though he soon left school. A few years later, the little college, seventy miles southeast of Forest Home, was a natural next step for William, not yet sixteen, once he had exhausted the educational possibilities of Yanceyville. Even though the college was nearby and well known to the family, the move was scary for Poteat. He recalled, "I was really not very eager to go to school. . . . When I got to Wake Forest, I begged to go back with the gentleman who brought his son and me down."[65] Poteat nonetheless soon felt at ease in his new home, for Wake Forest College grew out of the same influences and intellectual environment that had shaped Poteat's family and childhood.

The higher education of ministers was a principal objective of the Baptist State Convention at its formation in 1830; of the denomination's four college-educated preachers at the time, three—Samuel Wait, Thomas Meredith, and John Armstrong—had migrated from the North. As with the creation of the convention itself, these three men were pivotal in implementing the 1832 decision of the group to solicit funds and to found a manual labor institute that would encourage the education of preachers. The founders intended to combine formal education and hands-on work for the students on a scientifically managed farm. They, along with William Hooper, chose Wait to be principal of the Wake Forest Institute, named after the 615–acre plantation bought from Dr. Calvin Jones to house the facility. Situated sixteen miles north of Raleigh, the school opened in February 1834 after surviving a determined effort by antimissionary Baptists to block its legislative charter. The antimissionary group opposed the charter because of their concern for the separation of church and state and their belief that the denomination's role did not extend to education. The institute became Wake Forest College in 1838 and endured a variety of growing pains during the 1840s and 1850s.[66]

By 1860 the college was on solid footing. Its debt was paid, an endowment of $46,000 was invested, and alumni had replaced outsiders in the presidency and on the faculty. A number of preachers had been educated with the aid of the convention, and the list of alumni included lawyers, teachers, and planters.[67] The Civil War, however, derailed this progress and nearly destroyed Wake Forest. The college closed after May 1862, and Confederate bonds digested all but $14,000 of the endowment when the upstart nation collapsed and could not repay its creditors. Classes resumed in January 1866, but students returned only gradually. The majority of students (34 of 51 in the first postbellum term) were placed in a reopened preparatory department that Wake Forest, like most southern colleges, relied on for decades after the war to remedy students' poor preparation. The college appealed to new geographical areas, gaining patronage from Piedmont counties such as Caswell and others farther west rather than from the eastern plantation districts that had dominated the antebellum college. Further, the closure for several years of the competing University of North Carolina helped "in no little degree. . . ." Nonetheless, most students came to Wake Forest for only relatively short periods. Graduates were few, and the situation remained grim into the 1870s.[68]

In a strategy that underscores the flow of philanthropy between American regions during Reconstruction, the college leaders turned to the Baptists of the North to rescue their faltering enterprise. In early 1874 the trustees sent Reverend James S. Purefoy on a mission to raise $10,000 from northern churches, and he crisscrossed the area from Baltimore to Boston for much of the next two years. He attended all manner of church services, conferences, and meetings about education and social issues, as well as pursuing individuals. The trips netted close to the desired $10,000 for the endowment, and the college gradually gained a sense of permanence in the recovering South.[69]

Poteat entered the college in September 1872 and graduated in June 1877, remaining at home during the 1873–74 school year while he spent seven weeks in bed with typhoid fever.[70] The college's history would have been instinctive knowledge to him after growing up in a religious home amid a steady current of denominational visitors. The successful struggle to preserve the college, undertaken during Poteat's student years, could only have strengthened his awareness of the power of organized religion, the benefits of unity with the moral forces of the North, and the lack of educational opportunities for most North Carolinians. These concerns, however, would blossom only with time. As with most college students, Poteat's immediate concerns were the social and academic life of the college.

Poteat faced a rather inflexible curriculum of courses categorized into six schools. Of three bachelor degrees offered, Poteat sought the bachelor of arts, the only one requiring four years of study. The college catalog reflected the post–Civil War attempt by educators to reorganize the curriculum in the style of a modern university; however, for Wake Forest that meant nothing more than rearranging old classes into so-called schools. The B.A. degree "involved completing the work of the Latin, Greek, and Mathematics Schools, and doing the English part of the Modern Language School, the Chemistry, Physics, and Astronomy parts of the Natural Sciences School, and the Logic, Rhetoric, Mental and Moral Science, Political Economy, and History parts of the Moral Philosophy School." As an old man, Poteat remembered fondly those days when "we did not scatter over so much ground. We had three years of English, three years of Greek and history, philosophy and science. . . . We went into a subject and went on through it." He did note that "I think our science teaching was very deficient. One professor of science taught all the sciences and we had no laboratory work; it was all recitation." His study of physics was largely mathematical, and chemistry involved "verbatim recitations out of a horrid thick book." He took none of the offerings in natural history. Poteat did quite well in this varied regime of courses and was a diligent student, being "absent from no duty" during his second year.[71]

The Wake Forest that Poteat knew as a student was a small and personal place. He was "a timid little boy of sixteen away back in 1872" when he was "pushed off to college. . . ." The new atmosphere and respect pleased him nevertheless, "I went down to college and Dr. Taylor called me 'Mr. Poteat.' . . ." The hundred students and six professors all knew each other intimately, for the presence of only "one train a day in each direction and a horse and buggy trip to Raleigh requiring a whole day, severely restricted outside contacts, and pressed the little group in upon themselves." Sheltered in room number twenty of the college building for almost his whole time as a student, he came of age in "what may be called the social education of personal contacts. . . ."[72]

A significant part of that social interaction was the moral influence of the professors upon the students. As a Poteat family friend and college trustee noted, "The moral element of this college ought to be more appreciated" because "mental without moral cultivation is frequently a great curse." Another booster believed that the college's "superior corps of instructors" trained students in a "higher and better moral culture" that fitted them for glorious duty.[73] The services at Wake Forest Baptist church were routinely conducted by President Wingate, a superb preacher, and in addition a major revival occurred near the end of Poteat's first year. Probably at this revival, at a meeting conducted by F.M. Jordan, Poteat reaffirmed his religious beliefs. Though he had joined the Yanceyville church at age twelve, he wrote of the revival service in his first year away from home, "a vivid experience brought me face to face with [the] earlier experience." The result was Poteat's "questioning its validity. Was I not too young? Was I quite free under constraint of positive Christian surroundings?" His new conversion left him with no doubts: "I wept my heart out as I said to my Lord that the experience which I had at the age of twelve might have been genuine or not, one thing was certain now, that He was mine and I was His forever." As with most evangelical southerners, Poteat found the event beyond description, but his reliance on it was unshaken thereafter.[74]

In addition to religion, another important feature of Wake Forest from its beginning was the activity of the two literary societies. They structured the social—and to a great extent the intellectual—exercises of the students. The students began a debating society in Wake Forest's first session, and, at the opening of the second year, students formed two literary societies, the Euzelian and the Philomathesian. Every student belonged to a society, and each participated in the debates, declamations, and dissertations (essays) that occupied the students at their meetings. Each society had its own plush hall and its own library, and the rivalry between the two was intense, at times to the point of disruption.[75]

The object, according to the societies' identical constitutions, was "the intellectual improvement of its members." They met twice each week, on Friday night to hold a debate and on Saturday morning for the reading of essays and for general business. The writing, reading, and criticizing of essays was a crucial opportunity since Wake Forest provided little instruction in English composition, given its emphasis on classical education. The paramount activity, though, was the weekly debate. After the principal debaters presented, the question was opened to all members. Poteat recalled, "We would sit up there in the Euzelian Society until one o'clock in the morning debating questions, and that was in the winter time when we had no fire. The hall was so beautiful that we did not want to smoke it up. We would wrap our feet in over coats."[76]

A perceptive chronicler of Wake Forest's history summarized the tributes that former members paid to the societies: "They speak of skill in public speaking, . . . learning to argue logically, intellectual enlargement, development and training of all the powers that make for effective public speaking, and interest in the great problems of life."[77] Poteat excelled among the Euzelians. The societies incorporated new students into their activities almost immediately, and Poteat took full advantage of his opportunities. At various times he served as door keeper, recording secretary, corresponding secretary, treasurer, and president for two terms. His first year there he replaced Amzi Clarence Dixon as the society's librarian, perhaps sparking his interest in the college's libraries (and libraries in general) that lasted a lifetime. He sharpened his skills in debates with fellow society members such as Richard T. Vann and Dixon, both of whom would eventually have an important impact on North Carolina and Baptist history. He addressed such questions—most of which concerned issues of morality and some of which would engage him for life—as "ought war, under any circumstances, to be engaged in?" and "Is the existence of political parties beneficial to a state?"[78]

The great chance to display oratorical skills as a debater or an orator came at the anniversary celebration, an honor accorded to the societies' best speakers. In 1875 Poteat introduced the Euzelian orator and in 1876 was chosen to argue the affirmative in publicly deciding whether "the career of Oliver Cromwell [is] more to be condemned than admired?" As a senior in 1877, he was given the ultimate honor as the Euzelian orator. These displays, along with the three required public senior speeches, gave Poteat ample opportunity to develop the oratorical ability that enabled him to be a leader of public opinion in a southern culture that prized oral expression.[79]

The editor of the *Raleigh Biblical Recorder* often attended events at Wake Forest, and he affirmed that a senior speech by Poteat was "of the highest order and worthy of any audience." Another notable Baptist and later college president echoed the praise that Poteat's speaking was as good as he had ever heard from a student. At his graduation in June 1877 Poteat gave the Latin salutatory and followed with an oration titled "Ripples on the Sea of Life." This speech and two other addresses from Poteat's college years survive.[80]

At five feet, six inches tall and with a receding hairline even in his college years, the diminutive Poteat did not make an immediate impression from the rostrum. Nonetheless, a large mouth, broad nose, and penetrating gray eyes gave him a strong face, and his Euzelian training and robust, controlled voice served him well before the crowds by the time of his commencement.[81] Though but twenty years old, Poteat had imbibed deeply at the fountains of rhetorical lushness, and the ideas expressed in "Ripples on the Sea of Life" indicate that he also embraced the intellectual dispositions of the time. He stated, "The great end of all the accidents, labors, wants and intercourse of life is the ripening and exercising of character." The result of an individual's bad character might snowball until "what once was civilization is now barbarism. . . ." Self-control and discipline were the keys in this Victorian mindset, in that "the manner in which commonplace things are done grows up by [the] power of habit into the dignity of a principle which governs life." Southern evangelicalism blended seamlessly into his Victorian intellectual musings. For the "young pilgrim" searching for the way, "the one path becomes a shining highway through the desert, and grows brighter and brighter with the radiance of the 'City of Gold.' . . . The other is dark, leading ever downward." Thus, the wrong step as a young man could lead the individual to damnation, and society to barbarism.[82]

Poteat marveled in another college speech that "voluntary human actions are either *right* or *wrong*. The impulses to the actions are of *two* classes, selfish and benevolent, those which tend to the absorption of happiness and those which urge to its diffusion." One's character reflected the choice between the two. The goal should be to "*live for God and for your fellow-men;* let your better, higher nature be the winner in the heart struggles and battles of life." This struggle, "fought in the solemn stillness of the soul," must eventually be won by truth and good. Despite "depravity" in each soul, it was "the grand, the beautiful plan of Providence that the great end of individual life should be the weal of others; happiness is dependent upon benevolence."[83]

In his zeal for duty, Poteat manifested the paternalism that held together the Forest Home plantation, and his advocacy of benevolence reflects the particular religious influence of the missionary Baptist doctrine that his parents instilled in him. His time in college broadened these early influences. By his senior year, his writing was peppered with classical allusions, and his overall intellectual and social views about human nature and social interaction, though tempered by evangelical religion, fit easily within the broader Victorian world. The general training of Wake Forest's classical education, combined with the oratorical ability ingrained by the Euzelian society, left Poteat poised to be a southern reform leader—yet still in search of his life's work.

Poteat returned to Yanceyville after graduation and cast about for a calling. He considered opening an academy in Yanceyville for boys, preparing a flyer declaring that he had "noticed the need of such a school, and during the last years of his course at college, had an eye to this work." Whether it ever opened is unclear. During his first year after college he also started to read law, preparing to enter a profession that had vaulted many bright young men into local prominence.

In that same year, he also began the activity for social reform that would characterize his life. In a letter to the editors of the *Biblical Recorder,* Poteat turned his beliefs about religion and individual character toward the fight against alcohol—a social and moral evil long targeted by the state's evangelical reformers and one that would interest Poteat for the rest of his life. He especially attacked ministers who engaged in drinking. "There is but one standard for all Christians, ministers and laymen," he argued, "and every man is equally bound to conform to it." Preachers should not "encourage by association and participation so blinding and blasting a sin as intemperance in drink" because "the minister's mission is to lift up men. . . ."[84] Poteat's career of exhortation had begun.

2

Separate Spheres—Personal, Professional, Religious

✟

In 1878, only a year after graduating, William Louis Poteat returned to Wake Forest College as a lonesome tutor, but he gradually established himself as a popular professor of biology and a vital part of the college's administration and religious life. By 1905 he had achieved statewide intellectual eminence, and his alma mater eagerly elected him president. He rose to prominence as an educator, scientist, church statesman, and intellectual by participating in the nationwide trends of Victorian America, and he led a family based upon notions of nurture and self-control. However, Poteat never fully accepted the overriding devotion of the Victorian middle class to professional advancement and material progress. His classical education and religious heritage led him to scorn such narrow development in favor of an older tradition of cultivating broad, liberal learning. Further, in his coming to terms with science and evolution, he retained a great deal of traditional evangelicalism in his celebrated reconciliation of science and religion. He remained within acceptable boundaries while becoming widely known as a liberal southern intellectual.

Poteat had opportunities to consider new and old ideas because of the dynamic and unstable intellectual climate in the late nineteenth-century South. Innovations in science and education that had earlier swept the rest of the country began to enter the region. In this era of unsettling social and economic conflict, new ideas such as evolution and critical biblical study could be offered as options for a time. Liberal thought gained relatively few followers, but the comparative freedom with which intellectual ideas were presented reveals at least a moment of possibility when somewhat more cosmopolitan theological and scientific beliefs were options even for southern Victorians. For example, some modernizing change did occur as colleges belatedly, and sometimes not wholeheartedly, adopted the structural and curricular changes that altered higher education throughout the country.[1] Further, though the study of the history of science in the New South is in its infancy, it is already clear that the region's scientists also followed new developments closely but at times ambivalently.[2] Southern scientists imported many of the national norms of the period, although they did not participate fully in the growth of research and disciplinary specialization. In this exciting time in the South and in his own life, Poteat explored the boundaries of intellectual innovation acceptable to his society as well as to his own developing understanding.

Professor at a Changing Wake Forest

In the last two decades of the nineteenth century and the first decade of the twentieth, southern colleges and universities faced a rapidly changing educational world that affected schools across the nation. In the South at the century's end, about half of the region's 26,000 college students attended institutions affiliated with a religious denomination, making denominational education a major factor in the region.[3] Wake Forest and similar schools embraced many of the dynamic trends occurring around the country, including broadening the curriculum, hiring professors with graduate degrees, instituting the elective system, creating or strengthening admissions requirements, and teaching the sciences by a new approach that emphasized laboratory investigation. As a result the intellectual atmosphere of the time was an inquiring one in which professors and students could test the limits of learning, stretching southern traditions. Poteat took part in all aspects of this exciting yet challenging period in higher education, when a college degree became the central means for the advancement of the Victorian middle class.[4]

On June 13, 1878, the board of trustees of Wake Forest College, with his father among the members present, elected William Louis Poteat to be a tutor in the college beginning that fall. In his first year the faculty included only five professors and one other part-time tutor (a student), with 117 students enrolled for at least one semester. Like most small colleges throughout the South until the 1890s and after, Wake Forest continued to admit students unprepared for college classes, and a principal role of the tutors was to teach the rudiments of Latin and Greek to the less competent incoming students. Poteat also served as "keeper of rolls," monitoring grades and attendance for the reports sent to parents at the close of each semester.[5] At the end of the year the chairman of the faculty reported to the trustees that "Mr. W.L. Poteat has made us a very efficient tutor on a salary of Four Hundred Dollars per annum." The board reappointed Poteat as tutor for the following year and increased his salary to $500. In Poteat's second year as tutor, enrollment surged to 171 students. Thomas A. Pritchard, president of the college, responded by asking the trustees to expand the faculty, and in June 1880 Poteat was appointed assistant professor of science with an increase in salary to $600 per year.[6]

The new title brought tough challenges. Natural science was one of the seven so-called schools into which the curriculum at Wake Forest was divided in the early 1880s. Professor W.G. Simmons, with Poteat's help, taught chemistry, physics and astronomy, and natural history using "oral instruction and experimental illustrations" in addition to hearing student recitations of material learned from textbooks. Though Wake Forest offered more science training than some southern schools, its choice to continue to lump the sciences together under one category reflected the extent to which such schools had slipped behind the times, and a tutor of languages with only a bachelor's degree could not likely have won an appointment as a professor of natural science at a more modern university. Northern schools and emerging southern research universities such as Vanderbilt and Johns Hopkins, formed in the 1870s, offered a curriculum reflecting the specialization that marked the growth and professionalization of the American scientific community in the late nineteenth century. Teachers in small southern schools struggled to gather the equipment and knowledge needed to introduce the new learning to their students.[7]

Poteat's duties did not end with the classroom, however, and he impressed everyone at the little school with his diligent approach toward the many chores he faced at an understaffed institution. President Pritchard reported in 1882 that "Prof. W.L. Poteat is recommended to the Trustees as meriting a larger salary than he has heretofore received. He is a very accurate scholar, a careful, painstaking and enthusiastic teacher, and one of the most valuable members of the Faculty. He has taught four regular classes in college, and as Keeper of the Rolls, and Alumni Editor of the College Magazine, has performed duties equal to the teaching of two other classes. . . ." Poteat also filled a variety of other roles in the college. In 1879 the two literary societies agreed to combine their respective holdings of books to create a college library of eight thousand volumes. Perhaps reviving his not-too-distant interest in the Euzelian society's library as a student, Poteat for a while devoted Monday and Wednesday afternoons and Saturday mornings to classifying books in the collection and to procuring donations of new material. He and Simmons subsequently composed a standing committee on the library.[8]

The small faculty gathered each Friday in the face-to-face world of college governance at Wake Forest, and Poteat joined his colleagues in managing the details of the institution through ad hoc committees appointed for such chores as arranging hospitality for commencement, compiling the annual catalog, purchasing books, keeping order at chapel, and awarding commencement medals. The principal discipline problem was students assembling without permission to watch the arrivals and departures of the trains, a practice that could create a disorderly crowd of young men in the heart of town. Poteat served his time along with the other professors in assuring that the students were not at the depot seeking vicarious thrills from the excitement of travelers and the powerful machinery. Poteat's attention to detail soon earned him the assignment of serving as secretary for faculty meetings.[9] The workload almost overwhelmed him, and at the end of the 1882–83 session the chairman of the faculty recommended that Poteat's class load be lightened in order to retain him as editor of the impressive college magazine. To continue performing all his chores, the chairman reported, Poteat had realized was "impracticable."[10]

For the 1883–84 session, as Wake Forest celebrated its fiftieth anniversary, the faculty rearranged the curriculum to place more emphasis on the sciences, a process occurring throughout the South as colleges sought to remain abreast of national trends in education. The school (as a department was then called) of natural science separated to become the schools of physical science, chemistry, and natural history. For the moment Simmons retained both chemistry and physical science, but Poteat was named professor of natural history, with an attendant raise in salary to $1,200 per year.[11] Perhaps in anticipation of his new duties, Poteat spent much of the summer of 1883 in a tour of northern universities, visiting Brown, Yale, and Harvard, leaders in many of the educational innovations of the time. Significantly, he purchased a microscope to aid in the teaching of the courses that would now be his to design. He took his enhanced teaching duties quite seriously. To improve his skills and supplement his bachelor's degree with additional instruction, he attended a course of lectures at the Martha's Vineyard Summer Institute, a pioneer summer school for teachers on the pleasant Massachusetts island. Poteat studied with Edward S. Burgess, a northern botanist.[12]

Poteat had already been responsible for the natural history courses under Simmons, but Poteat's description of his courses in the new school of natural history reveals his own method of teaching the sciences, a pedagogical approach only recently popularized by Harvard zoologist Louis Agassiz and likely brought back by Poteat from his northern travels. Unlike the previous emphasis on recitations, lectures, and demonstrations by the professor, Poteat envisioned a hands-on approach. In the fall term he taught zoology and mineralogy and geology. The zoology class performed dissections, utilized specimens deposited in the college museum (a vital teaching resource throughout the nation at the time), and used a compound microscope to analyze slides, some purchased from Germany and some prepared by Poteat. The mineralogy and geology class similarly demanded that students analyze specimens of minerals and participate in field work. Classes meeting during the spring term were human physiology and botany. Again Poteat stressed laboratory activity, including use of the microscope on both animal and plant tissues. Botany captured Poteat's interest most strongly: "The importance of Botany as a branch of Biology is recognized, as well as the superior opportunities which it affords for the cultivation of the reasoning and observing methods."[13]

He sought the same goal in all his teaching: "The text-book is subordinate to the direct study of nature itself, the student being encouraged to find out for himself by personal observation the structure, properties, history, and relations of the objects studied." Lectures, rather than recitations, provided "much of the instruction" by 1886, with "the text-book being used chiefly as a guide."[14] His purchase of the microscope in 1883 enabled him to make the changes in teaching strategy and "added new interest to the study of Natural History" among the students. The purchase of additional microscopes in 1887 aided Poteat's teaching, and the same year a visit to Johns Hopkins University with its recently opened biological laboratory perhaps inspired him with its world-class facilities. He found that "the most impressive thing about the University is the air of original investigation which one encounters on every hand."[15] Laboratory work did more for students than just teach science, in Poteat's opinion. He enumerated its effects to show that modernization could support traditional southern values. He praised its effects in cultivating "a wholesome self-reliance" by forcing students to observe for themselves and in developing "the freedom and confidence of independent thinking." In the religious world of Wake Forest, Poteat even envisioned for laboratory classes a moral goal, to gain respect "for what is natural as opposed to what is merely formal and artificial."[16]

The college as well as Poteat thrived in the quiet town that had gradually formed around the campus. In the 1880s and 1890s Poteat regularly wrote brief news reports from Wake Forest to the *Raleigh News and Observer.* He took the opportunity on one occasion to reveal the characteristics of the town: "A news-letter from this quiet, busy village is almost a paradox. . . . A newspaper man would find it dull at Wake Forest. No courts, no crimes, no drivelling gossip, every man on Thursday going early to the same work which engaged him on Wednesday, and sticking to it late. . . . Our people seem somehow to have learned the dignity of labor, certainly the importance of labor, for they keep at it." He rejoiced that "this characteristic of the village is thought to exact a wholesome influence on the students who flock hither." The catalog of the college also stressed the moral benefits of the town: "The proximity of the College to the capital of the State affords many of the advantages, without the moral dangers, of city life."[17] Poteat's columns included such information as, "Several of the boys have looked a little droopy since last Tuesday. A number of the girls of the [town] went off on that day to Murfreesboro institute." Notices of frequent public lectures at the college, news of local businesses, the activities of area women's groups, and even updates on the health of the campus's young magnolia trees filled Poteat's postings.[18]

As in other southern colleges, constant campaigns for the endowment made possible the expansion of the faculty, the student body, and the campus in their quiet village. A frenetic campaign conducted largely by the soon-to-be president Taylor raised the endowment from $53,400 in November 1882 to $100,000 by January 1, 1884. Poteat aided the campaign by helping to conduct Taylor's classes during his frequent trips to raise the funds. Jabez A. Bostwick of New York City, a wealthy investor and Baptist, gave the largest donation, $10,000 of stock, to the 1883 campaign, and in early 1886 he added stock worth another $14,000. Bostwick contributed an additional $50,000 in late 1886 and $14,000 in matching funds for a campaign in North Carolina in 1890 and 1891. The relationship with Bostwick—which would benefit Wake Forest even more in the 1920s—enabled the college (under Taylor's presidency beginning in 1884) to raise the endowment to $189,302.50 by May 1892. By 1905 the endowment had grown incrementally to a total of $286,932.87.[19]

The college continued to expand through the 1890s because, as Taylor believed, "not to move forward will be to go backward." He contended to the trustees in 1894 that "we are probably at a turning-point in the history of the College. Before many years have passed, it will be decided whether it is to have the opportunity to expand naturally into a great institution, or whether it is destined to become a small institution, whose work will be largely confined to the education of the ministry." Taylor clearly believed that the Baptists of North Carolina needed more than a seminary. Competition for students in the 1890s was stiff, and many of Wake Forest's peer institutions expanded their professional offerings during that decade of change. Wake Forest followed suit. Under Taylor's guidance the trustees approved the addition of schools of law in 1894, the Bible in 1896, pedagogy in 1900, and medicine in 1902.[20] In 1905, 313 students received instruction in fifteen schools from eighteen professors. The faculty acknowledged the increased number of choices available to students by loosening the elective system beginning in the fall of 1896, giving students more freedom in choosing their electives and eliminating the various tracks to the bachelor of arts degree in favor of a single set of requirements. A bachelor of laws degree was created in 1894–95 for students completing the offerings in law, and in 1902–3 the faculty approved a bachelor of science degree for those students completing the two years of medical study that Wake Forest offered as a prerequisite to advanced entrance into four-year medical schools.[21]

Poteat assumed more significant leadership roles in the growing college in the late 1880s and the 1890s. The use of ad hoc committees for a variety of purposes continued throughout this period, and Poteat served on a number of them, from one to set out trees and improve the campus grounds to one recommending a course of classes to prepare students for medical school. These committees of two to three professors continued to have an important role in governing the college, but in 1893 the faculty created an array of standing committees in recognition of the growing complexity of the institution, an innovation forced on other expanding colleges as well. Poteat kept to his old interests through membership on the library and lecture committees and as curator of the library beginning in 1887, but he resigned as keeper of the rolls in 1886, as secretary of the faculty in 1888, and as alumni editor of the student magazine in 1890. He increasingly devoted his work outside the classroom to the administrative duties of the college.[22]

President Taylor frequently left the college on extended trips to raise funds, and, as at similar colleges, in the president's absence the chairman of the faculty led the administration. Poteat first acted as chairman in the fall of 1888, a role that included such chores as presiding over weekly faculty meetings, making announcements after morning prayer, and hearing excuses of students absent from class. The faculty once more selected Poteat as chairman in 1890 in Taylor's absence and again in 1892, 1894, and 1895. The students, Taylor, and the trustees all praised the administrative ability of the college's future president. The student magazine reported Poteat's new office in 1888 and noted that "just as everything else he attempts to do, [he] fills it well." Taylor verified to the trustees that Poteat "served as Chairman of the

As a young professor of biology in the 1880s, Poteat acquired most of his knowledge of science on his own. He read diligently in both the sciences and humanities, and, by his willingness to lecture in many forums beyond the classroom, he quickly acquired a statewide reputation as a budding intellectual.

Faculty with marked ability. . . ." Poteat "discharged with universal satisfaction the executive duties of the institution." The job entailed "no little of responsibility and labor," and the trustees recognized him for his efficiency.[23]

Poteat's course offerings changed little for almost his first full decade as professor of natural history, but in 1892–93 he became professor of biology and geology. He reshaped the classes in his renamed school as well. While Poteat continued to teach geology and physiology, he combined zoology and botany into a class on general biology, in recognition of the developing understanding of life science, along with offering upper-level semester-long courses to address zoology and botany separately. Both the use of the term *biology* and the creation of a general biology class represented a cutting-edge understanding of his field, despite lacking the resources to participate fully in the research side of the discipline. The concept of biology was just then on the rise as a way of developing a unified vision that would combine the competing fields of zoology, botany, and physiology and that would define development and heredity as topics of importance to both of the older pursuits. Even some of the leading universities of the country failed to make biology function in practice, however, as botany, physiology, and zoology remained distinct and often rival departments.[24]

Poteat's "popular and very important School" continued to improve under his new guidelines. Entrance requirements for students wishing to study under Poteat were in place for the 1892–93 session, mandating an introductory knowledge of one of the component subjects. Admissions requirements were new to southern colleges and tended to be casually observed. Nonetheless, the creation of standards, and in 1895 the standardizing Association of Colleges and Preparatory Schools of the Southern States, represented major steps toward betterment of the region's education. For the 1894–95 session Poteat made each of his upper-level courses—botany and zoology—into two-semester courses taught in alternating years. He was also able that year to hire a lab assistant for the first time, selecting John Kerr Jr., the son of the former Caswell County congressional representative. In the 1901–2 session Poteat's growing knowledge and the increasing complexity of the sciences enabled him likewise to make his human physiology and his mineralogy and geology courses into year-long courses taught in alternating sessions. When the medical school was added in the fall of 1902, medical students swelled the numbers of Poteat's introductory biology and physiology courses when they were incorporated into the medical curriculum. The following year, however, Poteat was able to turn physiology over to a specialist hired for the medical faculty.[25]

Poteat was a creative and popular teacher who instantly charmed students. Writer Thomas Dixon Jr. recalled his first contact with Poteat upon his arrival in 1879 as a student at Wake Forest: "I liked him from the moment we met. He was the youngest member of the teaching force. If he was a sample of the teachers I was going to work under, I was in luck."[26] Poteat worked constantly to improve the natural history museum holding the specimens that were so vital to his teaching. At the annual state fair he scouted the exhibits, seeking donations of teaching material. He took the zoology class to visit the circus when it performed nearby, in order to illustrate points about animals, a commendable way of coopting a morally questionable institution into denominational education. He and his students trekked the fields and woods about Wake Forest ever in search of specimens. Rufus Weaver, later president of Mercer University, recalled that during his days as a student at Wake Forest in the 1890s, Poteat trained him in such "methods of thought" as "the freedom from tradition, the enthusiasm in making investigation, [and] the abiding faith in God's revelation of Himself through Nature. . . ."[27] Poteat's doors were always open to students, and he enjoyed their company. He recorded in his diary in 1896, "Last night . . . one of the students, called to get some suggestions for his thesis on the widespread departure from nature. . . . He staid [sic] two hours . . . and yet the interview was not unpleasant to me. I was introducing a young and sympathetic mind into a new world of thought and beauty."[28] Poteat's involvement with students extended to renting rooms to students in the cottage in the corner of his yard.[29]

In addition to his teaching, research, and administrative work, Poteat took an active part in directing the religious life at Wake Forest that was so important to him and his family. He lectured to the group of aspiring ministers on campus, spoke often in the college chapel, spoke to student missionary groups, actively encouraged the campus YMCA after its formation in the early 1890s, and served a year as president of the Wake Forest Missionary Society.[30] In the late 1870s Poteat began to teach Sunday school at the Wake Forest Baptist Church and continued to do so until shortly before his death six decades later. In addition, he led the singing at chapel services and in the church from the 1870s until 1903 and filled the position of clerk in the church at times. In 1893 Poteat helped to create a successful summer course of study at the college for pastors. He also directed and helped to teach a series of classes on the Bible in the 1894–95 session, taught by various professors each Sunday morning, and he organized a number of biblical study groups among the students.[31]

The Wake Forest Baptist Church regularly sent Poteat as a delegate to the annual meetings of the Central Baptist Association. He served on association committees that investigated the education of ministers and wrote reports on colportage, state missions, and foreign missions. In 1886 and 1887 the delegates selected Poteat as moderator of the meeting, and in 1888 he served on the association's executive board.[32] Poteat treated his affiliation with the Wake Forest Baptist Church as an extension of his work at the college. As he explained in trying to convince their minister not to accept a job offer elsewhere, "More than two hundred young men, gathered from all parts of the country, are regular members of the congregation. They are to be leaders in the churches and in society hereafter, and it is difficult to overestimate the far-reaching influences which may be exerted through them."[33]

An important component of Poteat's climb to leadership in North Carolina also involved his work in the religious life of the denomination at the state level. From 1878 to 1880 much of Poteat's time as a tutor was specifically devoted to helping students who were studying for the ministry to improve their academic qualifications at a time when the presence of educated ministers was an aid in enhancing the respectability of ambitious Baptist churches. The Board of Education of the Baptist State Convention provided financial assistance for the room and board of ministers (who also received free tuition), and the board funded Poteat's position as tutor. He was appointed a member of the board in 1878 and became its president in December 1884, continuing in that capacity until 1914. This position gave the young professor a special attachment to the ministerial students at Wake Forest as well as a starting point toward obtaining prominence in the state convention. Beginning in 1885 he served as treasurer of the Baptist Historical Society formed at the convention's meeting that year and over the years served on such committees as periodicals and credentials. In 1895 the convention added him to the Board of Missions and Sunday Schools. The delegates from across the state expressed their confidence in Poteat's leadership skills by electing him one of three vice-presidents in 1898.[34]

Poteat's leadership credentials in the college and the denomination earned him an appointment to the board of trustees of the Baptist Female University soon after the state convention suggested the new school. In 1888 the convention named a committee to investigate the feasibility of opening such an institution. The next year the delegates approved the idea, a board of trustees was named, and they subsequently selected Raleigh as the site of the college. The legislature approved the charter of the Baptist Female University in 1891. Wake Forest relaxed its fundraising activities within the state to make room for a campaign on behalf of the proposed school. Funds trickled in slowly, however, and after the 1892 opening of the state's Normal and Industrial School for Women in Greensboro, there was discussion among Tarheel Baptists in 1894 that, in lieu of forming a college for women, Wake Forest should become coeducational. In the fluid atmosphere of the 1890s, coeducation received its first major hearing in the South. This was due in part to the need to enhance revenue possibilities by increasing the student body and in part to the Victorian middle-class emphasis on expanding opportunities for the refinement of women. A number of the region's schools debated admitting women. The discussion of coeducation made little progress among North Carolina Baptists, however, especially once the financial crises of the 1890s passed. The plan gained relatively few followers at Wake Forest, despite the failure of a premature attempt to procure a president and open the Baptist college for women in 1894. Financial limitations and lack of a proper structure doomed the first attempt. Construction on a college building began in 1895, and under mounting debt, delays plagued the project until the college opened in its still unfinished quarters in September 1899.[35]

Poteat joined the board of trustees in 1891 and served as the board's chairman for much of the 1890s. He fought throughout the decade to ensure that the education provided would be of a high quality. He served on the committee in 1893 and 1894 that ended up naming a president before there was a realistic possibility of opening the school, and the lack of financial support from the state's Baptists may have led him to support coeducation. Poteat's views challenged Baptist conservatives; he was "not in hearty accord with the brethren at all points" by 1897 because he would have preferred to divert the money that would be used in Raleigh, using it instead to expand the Wake Forest campus and "open its doors to women." Poteat found it "not only expensive, as dollars and cents go, but unnatural also to educate our sons and our daughters in separate institutions."[36] Despite such hesitations Poteat served on the nominating committee named in December 1898 to again select a president. In March 1899 the committee settled on James C. Blasingame, president of a teacher's college in Tennessee. Poteat had reservations about Blasingame from the beginning. On the positive side Blasingame had "a devout mind and a near sense of the leadership of God," but Poteat declared, "I do not take him to be a man of extraordinary mental power or culture."[37]

Discord erupted at the women's college within two weeks of its successful opening in September 1899. According to Poteat, nearly the whole faculty opposed the president's intention to adopt a system of three terms each school year and supported instead a semester system similar to Wake Forest's plan, which Poteat had suggested to Blasingame "as a working basis until they could mature their own system." At a meeting in mid-October, the trustees mandated the same scheme of studies required at Wake Forest as graduation requirements for the women. Poteat and Blasingame were appointed to work out the details.[38] The two never found grounds for cooperation. Poteat was "afraid we shall not agree" for "he is persistent in his view that a girl should not have over 15 recitations per week and should not have more than three subjects at a time." In view of Blasingame's disagreements with the faculty, Poteat considered him "deficient" in "administrative qualities." By February 1900 Poteat and other influential trustees concluded that Blasingame needed to be replaced, and in April the trustees accepted Blasingame's resignation. After declining the offer of the presidency for himself, Poteat again helped select the college's leader.[39]

The trustees chose one of their own this time, Richard T. Vann, a friend of Poteat since their days together in the Euzelian society at Wake Forest. Vann appointed Poteat, another trustee, and J.L. Kesler (a professor of biology at the women's college who had studied under Poteat at Wake Forest) to shape the curriculum and prepare the catalog. This time there was no opposition to making the entrance requirements and the curriculum at the women's college equal to those at Wake Forest rather than a weakened substitute. Poteat's stand for the equality of women's education meant that, in the words of the college's historian, he "did more than any other one person in putting the curriculum of the Baptist Female University on a sound basis."[40] Poteat thus participated in some of the latest liberal educational trends during the 1890s, in regard to equal education for women, as well as in his own teaching methods and his influence on Wake Forest's curriculum and its increasingly stringent standards.

Science in the South

Despite his varied and unceasing teaching, administrative, and denominational duties, Poteat found time to participate in the national and international world of science. Joseph M. Stetar has argued that following the Civil War, the slowness of change in southern culture meant that higher education developed differently in the region than in the nation at large. He explains that outside the South in the postbellum era "research and utility dominated higher education and relegated mental discipline, piety, and liberal culture to marginal positions." In contrast, in the South "the contest was much closer," and "discipline and piety joined with liberal culture and Christian education to create a potent, viable educational philosophy. . . ." As a result, "the concept of research met with little enthusiasm in the South." It violated the old belief that specialization, so necessary for research, would deprive the mind of development of all its varied faculties and upset balance in one's thinking.[41]

To some extent, Poteat's career choices support this generalization. Science emerged nationally as a powerful force in education by 1876, but the South lagged behind. Nonetheless, as historian Nancy S. Midgette has shown, a substantial number of southern scientists in the late nineteenth century sought to acquire professional identities to the greatest extent possible, despite their relative isolation from the national scientific mainstream. Poteat was at the vanguard in the formation of the scientific societies vital to professional maturation. He found scientific research interesting and recognized national trends in scientific pedagogy and scholarship. For practical and cultural reasons, however, he refused to make the overriding commitment to research that would have been necessary for him to achieve excellence as a scientist in the national arena. He chose instead to devote a great deal of time to the balanced refinement of his literary and religious capacities.[42]

Poteat evolved slowly as a scientist; he had not studied biology as a student and reported that he "had to learn these courses as I taught them." He read avidly the most current scholarship simply to master the basics for teaching. Beginning in the college magazine's premier issue in 1882 and for the rest of the decade, Poteat wrote "Science Notes," a column in which he reported striking scientific facts, technological innovations, and various oddities from the world of science. The sources for these articles indicate that Poteat not only read monographs and textbooks but also searched for science news in current scientific and popular periodicals such as *Scientific American, Science,* New York newspapers, magazines from London, and reports of the meetings of both the American and the British Associations for the Advancement of Science.[43]

In his science column in 1883, Poteat reported the formation of the Elisha Mitchell Scientific Society at the nearby University of North Carolina. By May 1886 Poteat had earned the respect of enough Tarheel scientists to be elected a member of the pioneering organization. The society sought "the arousing of an increased interest in scientific work, the building up of a spirit of research, the encouraging of those already at work and the advancing of our knowledge of the State and its resources." As always, Poteat excelled in organizational leadership; in May 1887 he was elected a vice president of the society. In December 1887 he presented a public lecture for the society on ditch water, and in the summer of 1888 he published in the *Journal of the Elisha Mitchell Scientific Society* his first scientific paper, a catalog of the varieties of desmids (a unicellular algae) found in the vicinity of Wake Forest. The paper reflected the older natural history approach of classifying and determining geographical dispersion of species rather than the newer experimental methods of emerging universities, but the very publication of research set Poteat apart from many southern teachers.[44] That other scientists, many with graduate degrees, readily accepted Poteat as a colleague despite his lack of credentials underscores the openness and fluidity of the early stages of professionalization within the region.

With his appetite for laboratory work and research whetted by his visits to Johns Hopkins and his own beginning endeavors through the Elisha Mitchell Society, Poteat visited the University of Berlin in the summer of 1888 in search of knowledge and perhaps of legitimation as a scientist. He was accompanied by his brother Edwin and Charles Lee Smith, a Wake Forest graduate of 1884, both of whom had just been studying at Johns Hopkins. The three sailed on May 31 and visited several other countries in addition to Germany. Poteat spent at least eight days in late June, however, studying at the Zoological Institute at the University of Berlin. He recalled later that he "went mainly to get some inside information about the method of teaching." His surviving notes confirm that most of his activity centered around the preparation of specimens for the microscope, a field in which the Germans were regularly making innovative discoveries that led the scientific world. He remarked in the 1930s that "the slides I made in 1888 in Berlin are still useful in my classes."[45] Likely as a result of the respect accorded anyone studying in Germany (and perhaps to avoid the embarrassment of having a faculty member in science with only a B.A. at a time when Ph.D.'s were the mark of progress), Wake Forest awarded Poteat an honorary master's degree at the recommendation of the faculty at the next commencement.[46]

Poteat's visit to Berlin accelerated his scholarly involvement, but he still faced significant obstacles to his success as a researcher. In the fall of 1888 he prepared a report for the Elisha Mitchell Society about the advances made in the field of bacteriology, stressing the construction of specialized laboratories and the promised opening of the medical school at Johns Hopkins. In 1889 in his most extensive published scientific paper (sixteen pages), Poteat analyzed notes from observations he had made of a particular variety of spider over the past three years. Though again his research strategy was not the latest experimental method, he had mastered the form of scientific papers, a substantial step toward professional achievement: he surveyed the existing literature from both America and Europe on the tube-building spider, utilized footnotes, pointed out the paucity of knowledge about the particular variety under investigation, and presented his own observations and sketches. However, Poteat faced handicaps in addition to the obvious difficulties of finding time for extended research amid his many unrelated duties at the college. He mentioned that he did not have access to the journals in which some relevant research had been done, and in the identification of the exact species of the spider that he was scrutinizing, Poteat had asked for assistance from a biologist at distant Cornell University.[47]

Despite the challenges, Poteat continued to seek professional development. In 1891 he organized some observations made in 1886, presenting the results to the Mitchell Society and publishing the brief paper in their journal. The Mitchell Society recognized his progress in 1892 by electing him first vice-president. Poteat applied the benefits of his involvement with the Mitchell Society to an endeavor closer to home. Schools across the country in the last two decades of the nineteenth century sought to keep abreast of changing times by forming scientific societies, and Wake Forest had one of the few that appeared in the South. At the organizational meeting of the Wake Forest Scientific Society in the spring of 1891, Poteat was chosen to be president. Its founders intended for the society "to promote interest in the progress of science and to encourage original investigation," but it functioned largely in service of its first goal. Throughout the 1890s and at least as late as 1908, the society met under Poteat's guidance, monthly at first and less regularly later, and professors from Wake Forest and occasionally visitors from Chapel Hill or other area colleges made presentations. The lectures seldom presented original research. Presenters rather offered demonstrations, performed illustrative experiments, or lectured on new ideas in their various fields, although in 1892 Poteat did present a paper about his "observations on the sensitive briar" that reflected some original work.[48]

Occasionally the Wake Forest group met jointly with the Mitchell Society from Chapel Hill, perhaps as a result of Poteat's joint membership. The society helped to introduce Wake Forest faculty and students to the latest ideas in particular fields in addition to offering a passing acquaintance with a wide variety of scientific topics. Its creation may have contributed somewhat to the declining participation in the Mitchell Society by those outside the University of North Carolina. That lagging interest led the Mitchell Society in 1892 to restrict membership to the faculty and students of its home university in formal recognition of its failure to become a broader forum for scholarly exchange.[49]

In 1893 Poteat expanded his professional scientific activities beyond the boundaries of North Carolina. In the spring, *Science* magazine published Poteat's discussion of science in the curriculum of colleges in North Carolina. Building on that achievement, he applied to take part in the sixth session of the prestigious Marine Biological Laboratory (MBL) at Woods Hole, Massachusetts, to be held for six weeks beginning in early July. The Marine Biological Laboratory opened in 1888 with the support of the Boston Society of Natural History and the Boston Woman's Education Association; it served as a research facility for major scientists and as a school to enhance the knowledge and skills of teachers of biology. Students such as Poteat in the MBL's early years were required to possess some qualifications and experience in their work, and the scientists at the MBL then led them in studies that included techniques "such as using microscopes, staining, fixing of specimens, and collecting materials to use in teaching." No more stimulating place for an aspiring biologist could be found in the 1890s; the leading life scientists of the country congregated there.[50]

Poteat was a student in the MBL's first class on vertebrate embryology. The course that year was taught by Charles O. Whitman, director of the MBL and head of biology at the new University of Chicago, who was a major figure in establishing the intellectual justification for biology as a discipline comprising various specialties. Embryology in the 1890s represented a major area in which biologists moved away from older observational methods toward more experimental approaches in their studies, and men and women prominent in guiding this evolving definition of the discipline surrounded Poteat for this one invigorating summer. Poteat also attended lectures on invertebrate zoology, another MBL specialty. He seems to have been pleased with his summer work; he proudly reported to his wife on one occasion that he had perfected a particular method "which many seemed to have been unable to do."[51]

The summer session helped Poteat to develop in several ways. Whitman's commitment to creating the overarching field of biology undoubtedly affirmed Poteat's decision of the previous year to rename his department (from natural history to biology) at Wake Forest. Further, the practical side of the work helped Poteat to improve the skills he had acquired on his own and during his visit to Berlin. The summer of work solidified Poteat's commitment to teaching his students by the laboratory method. While at the MBL he made a pilgrimage to the island of Penikese; it had been home to the pioneering Anderson School of Natural History in 1873 and 1874, a model from which the founders of the MBL drew inspiration. The Penikese school had been operated by Harvard zoologist Louis Agassiz, who had spread the idea that students should study nature and not books, a motto later adopted by the MBL. Poteat's summer resulted in the publication not of scientific research but of an essay describing his meaningful visit to Penikese on a collecting trip. He mentioned "the far-reaching influence of [Agassiz's] forerunner of summer schools of science in America," an appropriate tribute since Poteat's own teaching methods drew directly from Agassiz's tradition.[52]

Spending a summer in the company of research scientists roused Poteat to do some additional research of his own once he returned to the South. In May 1894 Poteat queried the readers of *Nature* for citations to literature about a form of amoeba he was investigating, his way of ameliorating the lack of journals and colleagues in his own region. At least three scientists corresponded with Poteat on the matter, and in 1898 he presented the resulting paper at the Boston meeting of the American Association for the Advancement of Science (AAAS), his most significant professional activity with a national organization. Poteat argued that the genus *Ouramoeba* was invalid; he believed that the form in question was just a normal amoeba with a parasitic fungus attached. The article appeared in the journal *Science* in December 1898; it represented the peak of Poteat's scientific research.[53] The difficulties of securing professional literature, the heavy teaching duties that meant a simple original project would be an extended endeavor, and his own varied intellectual and social interests soon led Poteat away from research.

His summer at Woods Hole also inspired in Poteat a lifelong interest that affected not only his teaching but also the social reform activities that occupied him more fully later in his life. In 1893 and throughout the early 1890s, a dominant topic of debate at the MBL and among biologists nationwide was the murky processes of embryological development and heredity. At the MBL a series of evening lectures instituted in 1890 allowed leading biologists each summer to discuss the major unresolved problems of their still inchoate discipline. In 1893 nearly a dozen lecturers—among them several leading young scientists—discussed their own work and the controversial claims of others such as Frances Galton, Wilhelm Roux, and August Weismann. Poteat attended these lectures and took detailed notes, and this work deepened his interest in theories of the transmission of characteristics.[54]

Although the mechanism of genetic transmission was not understood fully until many decades later, a major step toward comprehending genetics occurred in 1900 with the rediscovery by Hugo de Vries and others of the results of experiments made in the 1850s and 1860s by the Austrian monk Gregor J. Mendel. By 1903 Poteat had enthusiastically adopted the new understanding of genetics; he presented a paper on it to the newly formed North Carolina Academy of Science, and undoubtedly incorporated the new ideas into his teaching.[55] The pathbreaking discoveries enabled scientists to begin to discern that the inheritance of individual traits depended upon the combination of dominant and recessive genes contributed by the parents. The findings quickly gained acceptance and cleared the way for research that later led to the modern understanding of genetic material and its role in the formation of new species. Poteat did not apply his grasp of genetics to any scientific research, instead eventually using his scientific knowledge to bolster social agendas such as eugenics. Nonetheless, studying at the University of Berlin and Wood's Hole, along with his limited research and professional activity gave Poteat statewide visibility as a scientist of note. He had joined the AAAS at least as early as 1891, and in the 1890s he was part of a small number of southern scientists who took part in the organization.[56] At the state level, he was even more active in a new professional organization.

In 1902 Poteat's reputation as a scientist resulted in his election as the first president of the North Carolina Academy of Science. With the exception of a short-lived organization in Texas in 1892, the North Carolina academy was the first in a southern state and for its first decade the only one in the region. In the ten years since the closing of the dwindling Mitchell Society to scientists not affiliated with the University of North Carolina, other scientists across the state were without a broad, organized means to encourage research and to overcome the isolation that hindered their professional development. The idea for the academy originated in Raleigh among several biologists employed in state government positions. They invited a number of scientists, mostly other biologists, from both academic and government posts to meet in Raleigh. One organizer outlined his hopes for the academy in an invitation requesting Poteat's presence at the organizational meeting: "It seems desirable from every point of view to form some sort of permanent organization which will bring the scientists of the State into closer contact with each other and stimulate research and the study of local scientific features." On March 21, 1902, Poteat attended the gathering, and his peers chose him as one of fourteen charter fellows, named him to the executive committee, and on the second ballot elected him president of the new group.[57]

The effectiveness of the academy in its early years was somewhat limited. It initially sought to publish its own journal, but for lack of financial support soon arranged that the *Journal of the Elisha Mitchell Society* would become its official publication. Membership remained low, with only ninety-four people having joined for any period between 1902 and 1909, most of them for only a brief time; but in its second decade the academy grew in membership and became more stable. Poteat was active in the formative period of the academy, as well as much later in life after he retired from a long administrative career.

The highlight of his involvement was his presidential address at the first annual meeting of the academy in November 1902, a lecture he repeated to many audiences over the succeeding few years. In part Poteat used the occasion to call for a reversal of the trend toward specialization among scientists and scientific societies. He noted the existence of the state's chapter of the American Chemical Society, the Audubon Society of North Carolina, and the North Carolina Physical Society and complained, "Unchecked divergence of lines of research from one another cannot fail to attenuate and warp the workers and infuse into their work the tinge of error and extravagance. Specialists need the catholicity, the sobering of judgment, and the sense of proportion which come from contact with workers in other fields quite as much perhaps as they need the stimulus and criticism of their fellows in the same field." He urged scientists not to forget the "essential unity" of all fields of science at a time when the separation into disciplines had reached "a dangerous extreme" of subdivision. Poteat's critique of the growth of specialization and professionalization marked his alienation from the direction of science in higher education. His activity as a scientist had peaked. Whether he would have continued to participate actively in scientific research is unclear because soon his administrative duties expanded to the point that the pursuit of science became secondary in his varied intellectual repertoire.[58]

Poteat's commitment to science was limited by his aversion to specialization, his devotion to religion and church activities, and his great belief in cultivating classical and literary learning. He always left biology "at the Laboratory and cultivated other matters at home." He recognized in 1896 the cost of that habit: "I did a little microscopic work at the Laboratory this morning on an interesting *Rotifer*. I am fond of such work and might achieve some success and reputation in it, but it requires more time than I am willing to give to it. My evenings might be so used, but in that case I should be compelled to forego the refreshment and culture of the great books of the world. These I cannot surrender, since myself is more to me than my reputation in science circles."[59] Three years later he observed almost metaphorically, "This morning I came upon a remarkable *Amoeba*. . . . I had no opportunity to observe him in the afternoon on account of my obligation to lead the choir in practice." He bemoaned, "This circumstance has brought up afresh the limitations which the conditions of my life here set to any independent work which I might put my hand to. The leisure which the night brings I devote religiously to maintaining myself, in intellectual interest and outlook, above my pursuit. And so it falls out that this and that and the other bit of science work which drops into my hand commonly drops out before it gets itself done."[60] Poteat prepared all his lectures at the college and even left his textbooks there. When he arrived home at nights he "was a man and not a man of science."[61]

A Victorian Home

Poteat had plenty to occupy himself outside the laboratory, and he approached all his obligations with zest. Upon his return to Wake Forest as a tutor in September 1878, Poteat had not yet turned twenty-two years old. After a privileged early childhood and the transition to living in town as an adolescent, he now faced the challenge of establishing an independent life in the town of Wake Forest. He rapidly embraced aspects of the middle-class pattern of the late nineteenth century. In this period education became a profession that brought the highest levels of social respect, and science too gained an air of authority that extended well beyond the campuses. As a scientist and a professor Poteat received deferential regard and was well paid relative to salaries in other occupations. He further enhanced his community standing in the South through his religious and social activities. He sought always to serve society for religious reasons, to develop his character toward moral ends, and to refine his appreciation of literature and other formal cultural achievements. More importantly, though, he devoted himself to his wife and children, fulfilling the duties of Victorian manhood by leading the household in a moral and cultured fashion. Poteat's commitment to liberal learning and his evangelical aversion to materialistic motives prevented an all-encompassing focus on career, which some historians posit as vital to the formation of the middle class. Nonetheless, he achieved a measure of the middle-class, Victorian domestic ideal that revolved around character, discipline, self-control, intellectual community, and cultivation of social stability.[62]

Amid his teaching burdens, the young man found time to read widely, and he started a lasting habit of recording in notebooks the quotations and ideas he found most striking. His interests found free rein, and he jotted down material from such diverse sources as Edward Gibbon, the novels of George Eliot, Johann W. Goethe, Robert Burns, John Ruskin, Alfred Tennyson, John Milton, contemporary periodicals, and a variety of Christian apologists. Occasionally he sprinkled his own poetry among the notes, and these lines reveal that a sense of loneliness plagued the young teacher. On New Year's Day of 1879 he mourned "the year is gone, / But leaves no shining track or fragrance sweet / To recompense its loss, or light the gloom. / In all the jumbled plunder of my life." The arrival of spring brought better spirits to his poetry; he "wandered in the woods" where "the spring-time buds are bursting and blossoming from death, / And surprise the soul with sweetness with perfume-laden breath."[63]

Poteat eventually cut back on his ill-advised attempts to write poetry, but he found a lasting source of happiness in Emma J. Purefoy (1857–1939), the only child of Addison F. and Araminta Allen Purefoy of Wake Forest, and part of a Baptist family influential in governing the college from its beginning. It is likely that Poteat knew Emma, only eleven months and three weeks younger than he, during his student years in the close confines of the little town. He seems to have acted as a tutor of some sort for Emma soon after he began teaching at the college, and the two were engrossed in their friendship before January 1880 despite some possible objections from her mother. By January 1881 Emma was quite attached to Poteat's "pure, noble self," though in expressing her emotions she meant to "never tempt" her beau to neglect his "duties."[64] Their growing closeness cheered Poteat during his early years of teaching, and his poem for New Year's Day in 1881 expressed more optimism than that of two years before. He hoped that the new year would bring all the "joys the older ones have given; / And ope a new and deeper fount." The two were married on June 24, 1881. "Mr. Poteat," as his homesick wife referred to him to her parents, and Emma spent the summer in Yanceyville before returning to Wake Forest. Poteat found marriage quite agreeable; he later advised a young friend that "a man is not quite a man until he has bowed his neck to the yoke of a good woman's love."[65]

At some point the couple moved into a home built in the southern colonial style with nine rooms and four baths that was owned by Emma's family. Near the campus, the spacious house with its detached two-room cottage and large grounds accommodated Emma's parents as well. The couple's first child, son Hubert, was not born until December 12, 1886, suggesting that William and Emma practiced the birth control methods that relieved a growing number of middle-class parents from large families beginning in the Victorian era. They sought some advice in *Babyhood,* a magazine for mothers that offered scientific wisdom on all aspects of parenting, but they also relied on Julia, a black servant, and Emma's mother for more traditional help for many years. Poteat wrote his father in 1888, "Emma is singing . . . to Hubert. . . . We are bringing him up on the same songs you and Mamma used to sing me to sleep with, some thirty or more years ago." A daughter, Louie, followed on February 12, 1889, and a second daughter, Helen, was born April 6, 1896.[66]

Befitting the self-control and desire for domestic privacy of the Victorian middle class, Poteat spoke only circumspectly of his relationship with Emma. For example, news of Emma's pregnancy with Helen does not enter Poteat's journal until shortly before the birth: "This evening I had a pleasant walk with Emma. We talked mainly about preparations for the little visitor who is looked for some six weeks hence." Poteat also mentions "Emma's room" on at least two occasions, indicating that perhaps the two had separate bedrooms, at least for a significant time after Helen's birth.[67] Nonetheless they were close, enjoying time together with the children, singing and reading aloud at home, discussing literature, and even bicycling together in pursuit of the physical fitness that was a middle-class fad at the end of the century. Poteat often left home for speaking engagements and conventions, and, amid news of her frequent illnesses, Emma's letters to him gushed with sentiment. As she noted, "I seem not to *live* here when you are gone."[68] William's restrained style permitted only brief declarations of love, but he mentioned many times that he eagerly awaited her letters. Their correspondence reveals little but a stable marriage, ensconced in the social life of the small town and revolving around family and other professors, and bits of sage advice such as "keep your dear self warm and your feet dry."[69] Each maintained conventional gender roles. Poteat wrote home from an extended trip in 1900, "I have no directions to give about the conduct of affairs at home. You and Mother are so much more efficient in those lines than I am even when at home. I know things are going on all right." Emma fulfilled her role by offering to do such things as "go up to the Laboratory and get your bottles wiped off and things put in place" before he got home on another occasion.[70]

Poteat showed a strong interest in the development of his children. Even before the first was born he had concluded that his era was "the children's hour" because "the wide prevalence of the principles of the Christian religion" had created the positive "sentiment of the modern world about childhood."[71] By the 1890s he was aware of the "greatly intensified" energy being devoted to the study of childhood by such educators as psychologist G. Stanley Hall, and Poteat recorded approvingly the conclusion that "the child is not a man in miniature." He proclaimed that "today men of all political and religious beliefs and of all social grades submerge their differences in a hearty and unanimous tribute to the little child."[72]

Poteat tried to nurture his own children in a systematic way. Perhaps following the recommendation of *Babyhood,* he kept a detailed record of Hubert's early childhood and resumed the habit for Helen, jotting in his journals notes on her physical growth, milestones in her mental development, and simply the many charming insights and activities of a young child. While the more arduous aspects of raising a family were left to the servant and the cook, Poteat devoted considerable time to his children. They regularly visited him at the lab, helping him with various chores there once they were old enough.[73] Poteat was particularly attached to the infant Helen in the late 1890s, bragging about her to friends across the state like any proud father. He rejoiced, "I enjoy her greatly, especially after supper at night, when she sits perhaps a half hour on my lap and plays."[74] It took an absence from the children of only one day for him to declare, "How I miss Hubert and Louie!" The little family epitomized in many ways the Victorian archetype of genteel domesticity: "We had music in the parlor tonight after supper. Emma was at the piano, and she and Hubert and I sang a number of . . . ballads. After the 'Torpedo and the Whale,' we did not hear from Louie, who, already dressed for bed, made a pretty picture as she lay asleep on a long-haired black rug on the floor. When we were tired singing, Hubert played, and more than once his mother and I exchanged expressions of pleasure and surprise across the room as he executed some difficult or delicate movement. . . ."[75]

Through their education Poteat sought to equip his children for similar refinement. Though the trend in southern education was toward hierarchical and competitive class environments in graded schools, the town of Wake Forest had not yet created a public graded school. Therefore, Poteat educated his children in a way far removed from the drive for material progress characteristic of the public school movement. Emma's mother, who had operated a private school in the town for twenty-eight years, taught Hubert and Louie at home, and Poteat also had a large part in their education, particularly for Hubert.[76]

Before Hubert's ninth birthday, he and William were memorizing poems of Shakespeare and Wordsworth, and even then William found that his son's memory was "the quicker and more reliable." In 1896 at age nine, Hubert was committing to memory, with his father's coaching, not only parts of the Bible but also works by Robert Burns and other major poets. During that summer, William recorded, "Hubert and I resumed a habit of last vacation. We went to the woods where the water runs over a big rock and read the *Iliad*. I read aloud while he waded in the water." At summer's end, they had completed the *Iliad* and "at Hubert's suggestion" moved on to the *Odyssey*. Hubert's education included more than literature, though. By 1896 the bright young child had spent enough time around his father's laboratory that when William gave Hubert exams using the microscope on certain animal forms, Hubert's scores were nearly perfect. Already Hubert tagged along "with the Botany class tramping in the woods for plants" and helped in the lab as his father taught. Emma contributed to the children's learning by teaching music to them. Hubert's skill advanced so rapidly that he was but nine years old when William noted, "For the past half hour or more Hubert has been improvising at the piano, while Emma, Louie, and I have been reclining on the sofas."[77]

William was less close with Louie, but he noted around her seventh birthday that "she has seemed lately to grow more fond of me, and when I am at home she is usually on my lap."[78] He tried to inculcate in her the love of learning as well. At age six she was reciting poetry along with Hubert to William and Emma, and by age seven she was studying music and was "industrious in her reading and anxious to get on, often reading a number of pages at night of her own motion." Nonetheless, Louie soon began to slip toward the separate sphere. At seven years old she was learning to sew, and for her eighth birthday "she was particularly delighted with a tea-set with large pieces given her by her mother, who preserved it from her own childhood." Poteat fretted in 1897, "Louie came up stairs this afternoon with a certain dress and said to her mother, 'Do you object to my putting on this dress? I want to look sweet this afternoon.' I had hoped to bring her up with a juster estimate of the place of clothes in the sum of life than most girls have, but the atmosphere of opinion counts for more than individual training." She had "no love for study or books" and around kids was already "a perfect little mother." Her occasional efforts toward intellectual attainment were a ploy to get attention in competition with Hubert. She tried on one occasion to memorize a poem that Hubert had mastered quickly, and William pondered, "I think her ambition is aroused to recite the poem for me as her brother does. . . ." Her father could scarcely conceal his disappointment when she was nine, "Louie reads nothing and does not care to be read to. She is the girl for the bicycle and to go visiting among her little girl friends."[79] As Poteat's advocacy of equal educational opportunities for women indicated, his view of women's role included a broad education, even if it were used principally within the household, as in his wife's case.

Poteat not only tried to raise learned children, he also sought to instill in them conscience and rigorous self-control. He began the lessons early; Helen was barely two when Poteat "punished her with a switch for the first time." He elaborated, "Her mother has found it necessary several times before. She 'gives herself away' when she 'panks' her dolls: it is in every case for one of two offences,—'eatin' dirt' or 'peepee in di'per.' I can see that she has no conscience. If I tell her to stop biting her finger-nails, she will sometimes hide her mouth and immediately begin again the suspended action, with the remark, 'Tan't see me now!'" In addition to spanking her dolls, two-year-old Helen on other occasions commanded birds to hush their noise. Helen's discipline of toys and animals in imitation of her parents perhaps reflects the offenses for which William and Emma punished her. They expected a high level of self-control for one so young, as well as recognition by Helen of the immorality of deceit.[80] Their childhood socialization led the children to accept Christianity quite actively as they had been exposed constantly to church activities since birth. Because the student body included no pianist, Hubert began playing the piano daily for the college chapel service at age ten. Only a few months later he enthusiastically joined the church. At age seven Louie too already "insisted profusely . . . that she loved Jesus."[81]

The internalization of such high expectations of childhood discipline perhaps resulted in an obsession with order, particularly in Hubert. Poteat explained the actions of ten-year-old Hubert:

> For a number of years Hubert, on opening a biscuit at the table, has taken a pinch of crumb out of each half and put it in his mouth before doing any thing else. When his mother mentioned the habit, I asked him why he did it. He looked up and smiled, saying, 'I have rules for doing things.' No matter in how great a hurry he is when he opens his mother's sitting-room door to go out in the hall, he invariably turns the key, although he has no need to unlock the door. He has ever been methodical about certain things; for example, he takes off his clothes at night in the same order and places them carefully on a chair, and is greatly upset if he finds them disturbed next morning; at a certain stage in his preparation for bed he long insisted upon a drink of water. Some time ago he told me he had got into the habit of counting his steps as he walked to a given place and it troubled him.[82]

Hubert's love for ceremony and structure would later inspire him to support fraternities and to become a national lodge leader.

His discipline also brought rapid success. In 1898 Hubert began taking violin lessons at Peace Institute in Raleigh, and a year later he switched his musical studies to the Baptist Female University. In January 1900 he enrolled for one class, Latin, at Wake Forest College, and that fall he entered full-time study there at age thirteen. By the end of his first year he had already decided that he wanted to be a teacher of Latin, a goal he would fulfill at Wake Forest as his life work.[83] Hubert's time as a student at Wake Forest was hindered only by a vicious bout with typhoid fever in 1903. Overall his college career was marked by near-perfect grades and plaudits from all sides.[84] He graduated in 1906 and remained two years at the college as an instructor of Latin, continuing his musical leadership of the college's religious life during that time. In 1908 he went to Columbia University and returned in 1912 with a doctorate and an appointment as professor of Latin at Wake Forest.[85]

Poteat's daughters found disparate ways of building satisfying lives. In 1902 Louie and Helen both entered the Wake Forest Public School when it opened.[86] In 1905 Louie registered at the Baptist University for Women (as the Baptist Female University was renamed), where she compiled a mediocre academic record. In 1912 she married Wheeler Martin. They lived in the eastern North Carolina town of Williamston where Martin worked as an attorney and Louie took care of their son Wheeler Jr. (born 1917). Louie did volunteer work with the church, and at some point learned typewriting and taught the skill to secretarial students.[87]

Helen went on from Wake Forest's public school to do well in preparatory classes at Meredith Academy in Raleigh and then to attend Meredith College (as the Baptist University for Women became more lastingly known). She became engaged to Laurence Stallings, a native of Macon, Georgia, who attended Wake Forest, during his time at the college. He began newspaper work in Atlanta in 1915, but the couple were not married until March 1919, after an injured Stallings returned from fighting in World War I.[88]

William Louis Poteat's family life included more than just his wife and children; his parents and siblings visited frequently and were welcome guests. His sister and brother had developed liberal tastes and understandings similar to his own, all having fled their plantation background for the greener pastures of life in towns and cities. Poteat's sister Ida had attended the Raleigh Female Seminary in the 1870s, possibly along with their younger sister Emma who died in 1888 at age twenty-two. After graduation, Ida studied art in New York. She taught at a women's school in Oxford, North Carolina, before being hired as professor of art when the Baptist Female University opened in 1899 in Raleigh. Poteat's mother Julia lived with Ida, who never married, in Oxford and Raleigh most of the time after James Poteat's death in 1889. Julia and Ida frequently visited William and Emma in nearby Wake Forest. William found delight in his sister's visits: "It is a great pleasure to me to have her here. She is interested in the religious questions which interest me and holds very much the same attitude; and she enjoys the same great poetry which I enjoy." Julia remained in good health until a stroke three years before her death in 1910 limited her activity, and she treasured William and every opportunity to see him.[89]

Edwin, William's younger brother, added a challenging perspective to the family circle. He graduated from Wake Forest in 1881 and from the Southern Baptist Theological Seminary in 1885. In 1886 he briefly taught ancient languages at Wake Forest but left for graduate study in philosophy and psychology at Johns Hopkins University from 1886 to 1888. He spent the next ten years as pastor of Calvary Baptist Church in New Haven, Connecticut, and took advantage of the location by attending some classes at Yale. He then moved to Memorial Baptist Church in Philadelphia for five years before his selection as president of the Baptists' Furman University in Greenville, South Carolina, in 1903. Though Edwin's visits to Wake Forest were relatively rare after he moved to the North, the brothers supported each other's intellectual inquiry. Edwin did not completely abandon all of the orthodox notions that he learned in the South, but he had an inquisitive, open mind and seems to have encouraged William also to examine liberal ideas and to seize leadership opportunities in the worlds of thought and reform. William consulted him for suggestions about which of the latest books on religion were worthwhile, asked Edwin for help in getting his own work published, and benefited from Edwin's declaration that North Carolinians were filled with "timidity" in comparison to northern reformers in pressing for such changes as better education. William expanded his own horizons somewhat by visiting Edwin in his urban pastorates, and he sought on more than one occasion to secure Edwin as pastor of the Wake Forest Baptist Church.

Edwin was more cosmopolitan than William in his life experiences, but both Edwin and William tried to lend an uplifting hand to Preston, their older half-brother from their father's first marriage who still lived in Caswell County. Preston was an intelligent man and he briefly edited a newspaper in a town in their old home county, but financially he seems to have been something of a failure. William had recently paid "a considerable debt" for Preston when, in the summer of 1896, Edwin proposed that the two of them rescue Preston's son Ernest "from a narrow and ignorant life" in the depressed countryside by helping with his education. Edwin offered to pay his nephew's tuition to a preparatory academy in Wake Forest if William would provide room and board for Ernest. William agreed, and Ernest studied there for at least three years.[90]

Though William did not have the advantages of a big city, he did enjoy a very active intellectual life while living in the little town of Wake Forest. He sometimes traveled to events of national importance, including the New Orleans Exposition of 1885 and the 1893 World's Fair in Chicago.[91] More frequently, though, his participation in the national intellectual world was at a distance. One outlet for study enjoyed by a number of the professors beginning in the early 1890s was the literary circle that met at a participant's home each Friday evening for readings, music, and discussions of major literary figures from a variety of periods. Both he and Emma, and in time their children, actively took part. In addition to enjoying the social aspects of the gatherings, Poteat took the studies seriously. On one occasion as English professor Benjamin Sledd was describing why Wordsworth "never would be a popular poet and quoting from that flippant Frenchman Taine, my pulse rose slightly and I felt for my shooting iron. But . . . I was quite calmed and satisfied when he came to the positive" aspects of Wordsworth's poems.[92]

Poteat read voraciously virtually every night. Though he read many books on religion, literature was his true love, and the English poets ranked the highest. When summer vacations brought a "comfortable sense of relief and liberty," he had a great deal of freedom to read, but even during the school year, Poteat devoted his evenings to a wide variety of material. A typical diary entry recounts, "It was past twelve last night before I could lay down my books. I read the first chapter of Brooks Adams' *Civilization and Decay* and the first chapter of Nash's *Genesis of the Social Conscience.* That reading I took up rather than *Mill on the Floss,* of which I have read some 80 pages." Poetry, however, represented the peak of literary achievement: "Homer was worth more to the Greek world than Demosthenes; Tennyson is worth more to the English people than Gladstone. The rise of a new poet is an event of importance."[93] The poems of Robert Browning had a special appeal. "Surely one cannot be the same after the discovery of Robert Browning as before," Poeat wrote, and on more than one occasion reading Browning moved him to tears.[94] Novels were of less interest to Poteat, with one often taking him months to complete. Such fiction did not attract him because "much of it that I undertake . . . is trivial." Poteat's reading was directed instead toward moral and intellectual refinement.[95] His friend Sledd indicated that Poteat's writings aimed at "moralizing" as well. Poteat recorded, "Sledd says that what I write is for the reader somewhat like a diet all cheese. If he might have his way with me, he would make me read light fiction a year on a stretch."[96]

Poteat's deep love of literature had a social function. Even at age twenty-five the young professor had developed the sense of social crisis that would follow him throughout his life. He professed this sense in the flowery language that he had not yet set aside: "The excellence and perpetuity of our social institutions, as well as the beauty and blessing of individual life, depend upon the health of human sentiments—veneration, for what is holy and noble, patriotism, compassion, hope, love. . . . A tide of iniquity, with brazen irreverence on its crest, threatens to sweep out of our nature the last vestige and germ of nobleness and purity; and a fierce brigand called Caricature . . . stalks triumphantly through the land blackening and destroying all in our humanity that is holy, inspiring and beautiful."[97]

In Poteat's opinion, society faced decline if citizens lacked reverence for older religious attachments and a deferential respect for traditional values with their attendant stability and order. When political and economic turmoil created social unrest in the 1890s, Poteat began to show even more fear, but as of the mid-1880s he believed that refined, elevated learning could check the degeneration that he described. He announced, "Thank God for good books! that instruct our ignorance, that kindle imagination, that lead our weaker thought over heights we could never know without them, that strengthen the pillars under character, and lift up our trailing affections to what is pure and beautiful and good."[98]

Public lectures also served grander purposes in Poteat's view, and he was quite adept at this form of spreading knowledge. "We are not sure," he mused early in his career, "that any other institution can so combine entertainment and instruction as [the] system of lectures" found in some New England towns only a few years before. In opposition to the New South rhetoric of material progress, he concluded, "There can be no doubt that much of the intelligence of New Englanders is attributable to this one thing. . . . In our eagerness to develop our material resources, let us not neglect our intellectual resources." He recommended that more North Carolinians take the lectern before their fellow Tarheels.[99] "I have long believed that the possession of serviceable information imposed the obligation to impart it," he wrote in 1896, and as his career developed Poteat followed his own dictates.[100] In 1901 the *Wake Forest Student* reported that "Professor Poteat has gained for himself a wide reputation . . . as a lecturer. . . ." Two years later the *Christian Index* echoed this evaluation, "Prof. W.L. Poteat . . . has made many charming addresses at picnics, educational rallies, and district associations during the vacation period. . . . He can make an address on missions, education, the Orphanage, Sunday Schools—well, just any subject you may suggest."[101]

Two lectures that aided the spread of his reputation, each delivered a number of times, addressed the writings of Dante and Lucretius. In beginning the Dante lecture to the Randolph-Macon Reading Club, he explained his endorsement of the purpose of the club: "In a time like the present, such aims are in need of especial cultivation. Our period stands up to its ears in the sea of business, which threatens to submerge all else, all that is really worth while in life." The study of literature offered an alternative to more worldly pursuits. He adopted in these literary studies much the same approach he used in study of the Bible, evaluating the work by understanding the historical period and place of the author. His critical standards were reminiscent of his emphasis on unity and harmony in other aspects of his life: "A poem is to be judged, not by the proportion of prosaic content which it carries, nor by successes or infelicities of detail, but by the single impression which it makes considered in its totality."[102]

Science and Religion

In the early and mid-1890s Poteat faced something of a crisis as he contemplated what he had accomplished as his life reached its midpoint. In 1891 he reflected to his brother Edwin that perhaps he was "outgrowing" his environment at Wake Forest. On his thirty-ninth birthday in 1895 he mused: "I am surprised to find myself so old. The years add themselves up by seconds, and we are not prepared for the totals. The increments follow one another like the quiet settling of imponderable snow-flakes. Besides, my life stream has been for the most part a smoothly flowing current, without the sharp contrasts of plunging cataracts, narrow rapids, and lake-like expansions. It lacks 'events' and is monotonous." Yet, in spite of the extreme stability of his small-town life, he was "unwilling to barter away that steadyness and reposefulness of movement for the dash and exhilaration of a mountain torrent." He saw no need for a radical break with his past. Still, he wondered if his life had brought the service to others that he desired. Though his friends told him he was of "influence upon the religious and intellectual life of the College," Poteat declared, "The retrospect looks mean beside my early ambitions. I can point to no 'achievement,' to no beneficent mark which I have made on the face of the world's thought. And that is what my youth dreamed of." Nonetheless he mused, "I think I can discern a real movement, particularly in the last four or five years. I am conscious of a wider outlook and of what may perhaps be called some enrichment of my nature." Despite his misgivings he looked to the future with hope: "I have to confess that the pride of that ambition is not, even yet, wholly dead."[103]

A few days afterward he resolved to edit and add to some of his old speeches in order to put together a book on "the influence of Biology upon some of the higher questions of life" as an aid to "those who have got only enough of the new thought to perplex them. . . ." He hoped "it might facilitate their transition and save a wreck here and there."[104] A year later his birthday again spurred Poteat to work on the book, which was still in the planning stage. Noting that his life was over half completed by most averages, he sought even greater discipline: "Let me be up and at it from now on! Procrastination, with many a month of mine in thy bag, put no foot henceforth on my demesne upon pain of death! God and all good influences support me in the concentration of time and energy upon the service of man and the enrichment of my nature to that end." By the following year, 1897, Poteat's birthday caused less trauma for him as he settled into middle age; however, the desire to spread his ideas about science and religion stayed with him and proved to be his main contribution to the world of letters in the South.[105]

For several years Poteat had been writing articles and lecturing about religion and its relation to new scientific findings, and it was on this subject that he most fully accomplished his ambition to make a lasting mark in the intellectual arena. As a leader in religious, scientific, and educational circles, Poteat had ample opportunity to influence a wide range of North Carolinians. He seized every chance to direct his fellow Tarheels toward a more liberal view of Christianity, an acceptance of modern science, and a degree of comfort about the intermingling of religion with science and the theory of evolution. By the end of his first decade as a teacher of natural history, Poteat had in large measure accepted the theory of evolution without displacing his religious faith. Many prominent American scientists such as Harvard's Asa Gray, University of California professor and southern native Joseph LeConte, and South Carolina botanist Henry W. Ravenel had achieved a similar reliance on the argument that God had chosen evolution as the means to create the world. Thus, Poteat had many guides through the wilderness of doubt that he faced, and in turn he hoped to help others along the same safe path.[106]

In *The Mind of the South,* W.J. Cash memorably posited that "Darwin, Huxley, Ben Butler, Sherman, Satan—all these came to figure in Southern feeling as very nearly a single person." As a result, supporters of evolution such as James Woodrow and Alexander Winchell were dismissed in the 1870s and 1880s from Columbia Theological Seminary and Vanderbilt University, respectively. However, as historians C. Vann Woodward and more recently Bruce Clayton have shown, some critical thought and alternative viewpoints appeared in the South despite the "savage ideal," Cash's theory that southern uniformity crushed dissent. Much less dramatic than—but certainly as meaningful as—the handful of highly publicized instances of dissenting intellectuals being pressured to leave the South are the many instances in which southern society tolerated slightly less radical versions of liberal or dissenting thought.[107] The reign of the so-called savage ideal was far from universal in the region during the liminal years of transition before and just after the turn of the century. As Poteat struggled to reconcile religion and evolution, he could take comfort that even in 1884, according to Woodrow in his dismissal hearing, evolution was being taught at the University of Virginia, Wofford College, the University of Georgia, Southwestern Presbyterian University, and Kentucky's Central University, among others. By the 1890s Guilford College had joined the list, and Woodrow himself simply moved to the University of South Carolina and resumed teaching. As in Poteat's case, many of these teachers faced relatively little opposition as they tested the boundaries of southern thought.[108]

Late in life, Poteat recalled that in 1880 "I was called to teach the most revolutionary of the sciences in the period when the biological revolution was taking shape. . . . And I had to make some adjustment for my own comfort, don't you see? I was learning that what I knew in biology was in direct conflict with what I had been taught in the field of religion." He was under "a cloud of doubt." As Poteat began his preparations to teach natural history, which he had not studied in college, he immediately confronted the theory of evolution.[109] He quickly encountered the writings of Thomas Huxley, the English scientist who energetically promoted Charles Darwin's theory of evolution from the 1860s to the 1890s. Poteat set about reconciling his religious and scientific views. In December 1880 he noted in the *Biblical Recorder* that even "so prominent a name in the materialism of to-day as that of Huxley belongs in the catalogue of thinkers who discard the idea of chance in the phenomena and government of the world." Huxley instead believed "that all things take place according to invariable natural laws." Poteat added another layer to the thought of the famously agnostic Huxley: "But the Christian goes further to say, that these laws are but the expression of the Creator's modes of action in his constant, minute, and universal superintendence of the works of his hands."[110]

Poteat remained cautious about the most important of the new scientific findings, Darwinian evolution. He reported Darwin's death in 1882, noting that "the popular opinion of Mr. Darwin is grossly inaccurate" but warning that "we say nothing here of the correctness or incorrectness of his theory," only that it was "much misunderstood." Reflecting his own doubts, he claimed, "Whether the theory is to be received wholly or not, scientific men have not yet decided." Poteat, though, struck his own characteristic note that if it were true there must nonetheless "have been an intelligent and beneficent Cause at the starting point of this progress upward."[111] He seemed a bit taken aback by the rush of ideas in his new field. In October 1882, in reaction to a statement that evolution was accepted throughout the field of biology, he reflected, "We were aware that the doctrine of evolution was fast gaining ground among scientists, but must confess that we have here an item of news in the statement that it is received by all scientific workers in biology."[112] In March 1883 he still resisted belief in evolution. He argued that neither "Atheistic" nor "Agnostic Evolution" constituted science; they "leaped the bounds of science proper, and have striven to account for all natural phenomena without recognizing divine power in it." Poteat was not yet ready to offer a theory of theistic evolution.[113]

By June 1884 Poteat had read more widely in science but still waffled on the question of evolution. He "repudiated" the image of Darwin as "the monkey man" but carefully noted that "this tribute to the man, however, means no sympathy with his account of the origin of different kinds of animals and plants." Nonetheless, Poteat argued in this same address that many of the leading scientists of the time "see in nature the manifestation of God; recognize the laws of nature as divine laws, among which there can be no conflict because the lawgiver is one and all-wise." Among the examples he named were evolutionists Asa Gray, James D. Dana, and Joseph LeConte; and Poteat mentioned that in reading Herbert Spencer's *First Principles* he had surprisingly found that even Spencer acknowledged that religion expressed "some eternal fact" and was in "fundamental harmony" with science.[114]

In the fall of 1884 Poteat stepped closer to full acceptance of evolution. In a glowing review of Henry Drummond's *Natural Law in the Spiritual World,* Poteat noted that "the natural laws which modern science has brought to light, are traced into the spiritual world" with the result that "the unbelieving scientist must now surrender or keep silent." Poteat seemed unbothered that Drummond "assume[d] the evolution hypothesis."[115] Though it seems that he did not publicly advocate evolution during the 1880s, Poteat was certainly close to accepting, and probably had accepted, the doctrine by the latter years of the decade. In 1887 he wrote that man "may not deny the close resemblance of his own physical organism to that of the humble creatures. . . ." By that year he had also accepted that the earth was considerably older than conservative Christians had acknowledged. "The subject-matter of Geology," he explained, covered "the natural history of the earth and of the tribes of animals and plants that successively peopled it during those long periods when it was growing into its present form and condition. . . ."[116]

By May 1888 he felt confident enough to publish his general views of science in the *Biblical Recorder,* reaching beyond the limited readership of the college magazine that had contained most of his earlier writings on the topic. In a three-part series titled "Religion in Science," Poteat demonstrated that he had enlarged his conception of religion sufficiently to encompass his scientific understanding. "The progress of science," he claimed, modified human understanding of God by "making more and more untenable the Augustinian conception of the transcendency of God, and necessitating our return to . . . the biblical conception,—namely, that God is immanent in nature and vitally connected with man." The connection between God and nature occurred through "the universality and immutability of natural laws." Poteat reiterated that "science and materialism are quite distinct," using as evidence a quotation from LeConte and Darwin's statement that belief in evolution could coexist with belief in God. Poteat's views on evolution remained muffled, though: "It will probably be agreed that if evolution is not materialism and atheism, then certainly science is not."[117]

In order to clear his way to bring God back into nature Poteat had to dispense with the orthodox evangelical conception of God and the Bible. To do this he formulated a distinction between religion and theology that drew on traditional evangelical emotionalism yet discredited the conservative understanding of the Bible. He hinted that God was immanent in natural processes, but his refusal to relinquish all of his conservative religious training meant that he had to maintain the transcendent truth of biblical morality, by fiat if necessary. He noted that the perceived conflict between science and religion so prevalent in the 1880s resulted from "the misconception of the purpose of the Bible by its accredited interpreters. They were not content to regard it as the guide to duty and the revelation of spiritual truth, which is beyond the reach of man's investigation. . . ." Instead, Poteat argued, "they supposed that in the Bible they had a complete natural history of the earth. . . ." The biblical interpretation was accepted in place of scientific demonstrations to the contrary, thus divorcing "the Creator from his handiwork." Poteat concluded, "Their mistake lay in not seeing that God had made in natural forms and processes another record, supplementary to that in the Book and equally authoritative with it, and that contradiction between these records would cast doubt upon both." On the other hand, scientists who felt they discredited religion when they disproved a portion of the Bible also erred, according to Poteat. They equated "two things that are quite distinct, namely, theology and religion." He explained: "Religion, considered in Christianity its final and highest expression, is fundamental and absolute; theology, being merely the systematic view of human interpretation of its facts and teaching, is derived and partial, noble in its aim indeed, but limping with human infirmity and confused with human ignorance." The conflict, then, was "between the expounders of religion and the expounders of science, not between religion and science."[118]

This formula, which Poteat elaborated later and held the rest of his life, viewed religion as nonrational and emotional, unaffected by the findings of scientific errors in the Bible. The poetic language of the Bible could help one's search for spiritual truth, but its primary purpose was to serve as a way to become acquainted with the moral teachings of Jesus. Poteat believed that religious conviction resulted from a deep emotional encounter with Jesus, rather than by the acceptance of doctrinal subtleties and a literally interpreted Bible. His somewhat muddled half-acceptance of liberal theology left the way clear for Poteat to embrace evolution.

In 1895 Poteat made two speeches that left no doubt that he accepted

Darwinian evolution and that evolutionary concepts had affected his understanding of religion and of society. At the invitation of secretary Walter Rauschenbusch and the executive committee, Poteat spoke at the meeting of the Baptist Congress (a group of liberal educators and ministers that had convened annually since 1883) in November 1895 in Providence, Rhode Island, on the topic of "The Physiological Basis of Morality." Using several evolutionists as authorities, in his paper he sought to outline a foundation for morality in light of the latest scientific and philosophical thought. He explained that "a system of morals, if it is to guide the life of the new time," has to realize that "humanity grows . . . , overflows from very exuberance of vitality into new channels, and acquires fresh complexities of structure and function with the consequent emergence of new needs and new problems." As a result, "the formal theorizing of an earlier time, having no such possibilities of progress, is left behind" and in the new period becomes "dogma and prejudice to contest the further progress of life." From "the fragments of truth" of old ideas would come "new systems which incorporate the special phenomena and reflect the complexion of the thought of the time."[119]

Poteat outlined the two new theories of moral nature that had "grown up under the scientific impulse" of his time. After assuring the audience that "an intellectual account of the moral nature" does not "impair or imperil the binding force of its decrees in the practical guidance of life," he explained the thesis of morality that Charles Darwin presented in *The Descent of Man* in 1871. Darwin had argued "that man's bodily structure was derived by descent from animals below him, under the laws of variation and natural selection acting thro' the struggle for existence" and then extended those "general laws . . . to the sphere of the higher and distinctive faculties" such as morality. "The moral sense," Poteat elaborated, was traced by Darwin "to the social instincts of savages and gregarious animals, which became progressively more assured of survival in proportion to the perfection of these instincts of obedience, mutual dependence, cooperation, and sympathy."[120]

Poteat could not accept evolution quite so brazenly, however; he had to combine the ideas of Darwin with religion. He asserted "that we are prepared now to recognize the strength and the weakness of the materialistic evolutionists' account of the origin of morality." Poteat contended that "its value consists in having sketched the history—not of morality, but—of the physiological basis of morality" and that the physical theory had to be supplemented by a "Neo-Christian theory of ethics [that] is a restatement of the Christian conception from the point of view of evolution." He clarified, "According to it, conscience is still conscience speaking with the authority of the voice of God, and tho' it is the result of a process of development, it is still, for the modern man at least, innate and intuitive." This theory conceded that man developed by evolution and that morality grew from the same process, but went further to argue that such material development was "simply the vehicle of the moral nature, which is, on its part, able to take on higher forms and increasing definiteness of organization as these occasions for its exercise become ampler and more adequate." In short, "God's hand is on the physiological process, and as with his energy and nourishing it rises into higher planes, he can put into it more and more of ethical and spiritual significance. . . ."[121] No matter how manifest God was in the world, for Poteat the deity had to retain simultaneously a traditional transcendent authority accessible only through a nonrational experience. Poteat never moved beyond this tempered version to a fully modern view.

The paper was well received by the Baptist gathering; Poteat "was particularly pleased by the warm commendation of Dr. [C.B.] Crane, President Andrews of Brown, and Mr. Leighton Williams."[122] Upon his return to North Carolina Poteat presented the paper as a public lecture at Wake Forest. He celebrated the opportunity as evidence of the "quickened and enlarged" state of "the intellectual life of the College" in recent years. "The paper contains ideas," he discerned, "as for example the doctrine of evolution applied to man's body and the derivative theory of the moral nature, which I certainly would not have ventured to express here ten years ago."[123] Poteat's confession to his diary raises the question that he may have adopted the doctrine of evolution more quickly and firmly in the late 1880s than his published comments on science reveal, but if so he certainly felt that restrictions on his thought had loosened a bit by 1895.

His ideas did meet some protest, however. Earlier in 1895 he had delivered a commencement address to the alumni in which he glorified scientific learning. Science had "pressed upward sustained by undivided love of truth and unwavering faith in the intelligibility of the universe," and in light of such "devotion to a high ideal" Poteat challenged conservatives to "cry depravity and materialism till the stars die out of the sky!" The "spirit of inquiry" had spread into art, literature, philosophy, and religion, he argued, and "the age of criticism was come." He showed no regret that "the spread of the critical spirit was inevitably accompanied by the decay of authority and emancipation from traditional discipline," despite "the chaos which to some extent has reigned in the sphere of religious beliefs and of practical morality." In sum, "many a brazen absurdity has survived by virtue of the appeal to its age."[124]

He urged his audience to take advantage of the new outlook to broaden their understanding of religion, calling science "the open gateway into a larger development of spirituality and power." Religious faith had gained new perspectives "from the so-called 'destructive criticism'": "the resurrection and rehabilitation of the life and thought of ancient Israel, which had been obscured by generations of spiritualizing interpreters," "the reconstruction of the human life of Jesus," and "a living Scripture in the room of a mechanical mosaic of texts." Faith had shown its "power to incorporate and assimilate" the fresh ideas of science, and Poteat was not daunted by the necessary changes in theology. He proclaimed:

I do not fear a theoretical skepticism. The only fatal skepticism is—not the questioning of abstract propositions about the existence and personality of God, but—the denial of his living presence in the world of physical nature and of man; . . . that derogatory dogma that the Infinite Father spoke ages ago his last word of tenderness to man, and that for the enlarging capacity and craving of the race he has never a syllable more of answering revelation; that selfish fear lest the divine Goodness and Truth, in a boundless and exultant inundation, shall sweep over and obliterate the pitiful barriers which our systems of theology have presumed to build against them.[125]

Poteat frankly recommended that the conservatives among his listeners adopt a faith based on their direct experience of religious truth and leave behind their outmoded doctrines.

The bold statements in Poteat's address to the alumni did not go unnoticed. Even before his address, the president of the board of trustees had received at least two letters of protest against the college's "position on Darwinism": "The school that teaches Darwinism ought to be blasted with a curse, for we must judge the tree by fruit, and the fruit of Darwinism is *agnosticism*." A popular minister in the town of Oxford objected to "teachers of science . . . instilling into the minds of our youth the *unproven* theories of science" as well as to "the fact that Wake Forest is *in* sympathy with the University of Chicago, and *not* in sympathy with the Southern Baptist Theological Seminary."[126] Just after Poteat delivered his controversial speech, the head of the trustees sent the letters to Poteat with the disclaimer that he did not agree with the attacks but that he wanted to alert Poteat to "one danger to which we are exposed through the honest views of some good brethren. . . ." Poteat did not compromise the views expressed to the alumni; he responded that the address "was first and foremost designed to be helpful to just such brethren" as his critics. His "purpose was a religious purpose. . . . to present the new *modus vivendi,* the new friendly relations between science and Christianity."[127] This round of criticism availed little but foreshadowed later bouts.

His critics accurately measured Poteat's approach to religion. His approach to Bible study reflected to some extent the critical methods of liberal nineteenth-century students of Christianity. In late 1893 and early 1894 Poteat published in a Baptist newspaper, the *Raleigh Biblical Recorder,* a series of articles titled "A Layman's Studies in the Life and Letters of Paul." He depicted Paul as a cosmopolitan and learned Roman whose canonized writings must be viewed in the context of the fierce struggle among early Christians about whether Christianity was open to all peoples or first required conversion to Judaism. Difficulty in understanding Paul's advice to the early churches resulted from the "inability to transport ourselves into the midst of the precise historical conditions out of which it sprung," Poteat argued.[128] The contents of the letters "were determined by the circumstances of the writer and of the church addressed" and could only be understood by "an open-minded reader who is not searching for a syllabus of systematic theology." In short,

Paul was "not concerned with metaphysics, but true to his unvarying practical aim of religious edification and the preservation and extension of the supremacy of Christ."[129]

Rather than regarding Paul's letters, which make up much of the New Testament, as transcriptions of "the verbal dictation of the Holy Spirit," Poteat urged readers to read them in chronological order and to see them as springing "out of his dramatic experience. . . ." They were "transcripts of his mind and heart under the stress of varying external conditions and at different stages of his progress in the 'apprehension' of Christ" and were therefore "unintelligible apart from his personal history. . . ."[130] The use of historical context and the abandonment of a literal interpretation of scripture indicate that Poteat had been influenced by the tenets of higher criticism, the technique of critical scholarship in the late nineteenth century that applied historical and literary methods to the Bible. In the late 1880s and early 1890s Poteat read a number of works of formal theology, some suggested by his brother. In his alumni address in 1895 he praised higher critics such as David Friedrich Strauss, Joseph Ernest Renan, and James Martineau, all of whom Poteat's conservative attackers would have considered very unorthodox. Poteat found Renan particularly appealing, quoting him often in later writings.[131]

In 1894 Poteat extended his critical religious study to the life of Christ and debuted his thoughts on "The Thirty Silent Years" of Jesus, an address he presented to dozens of churches and church groups over the next two decades. Similar to his study of the writings of Paul, Poteat's look at Jesus' early life was an "effort to reproduce the environment, the atmosphere in which Jesus grew to manhood" in order to explore the "foundations" of Jesus' teachings as they evolved in his period of "*normal* human development" in Galilee. Poteat sought to "guard against reading western and modern standards into the oriental life of that remote period" and argued that Jesus grew up in a stable, economically secure, learned family and lived in a vibrant, cosmopolitan region.[132]

In 1898 Poteat defended critical study of the Bible: "The method of a reverent biblical criticism must be allowed. . . . If the Scriptures are too sacred to be examined in their origin, method, and contents, they are too unearthly to affect the course of human life." However, Poteat hesitated to accept all the findings of biblical scholars, noting that the results of critical study "at this stage of it may be questioned."[133] Criticism that questioned the divinity or existence of Jesus would have been unacceptable to Poteat, for it would have destroyed the foundation that he sought to uncover beneath the centuries of theological obscurantism.

Poteat's insistence that both Jesus and Paul underwent a dynamic process of growth and development and did not reflect a static ahistorical truth also guided his work on a speech for the Baptist Congress meeting in Richmond in 1900. Poteat explicitly applied his biological understanding to a discussion of the Christian doctrine of atonement, the orthodox conservative Baptist belief that Christ had secured forgiveness for the sins of humanity by taking their place on the cross to appease God. Poteat argued that scientific understanding had rendered untenable such old theological doctrine from the time of John Calvin. He explained that, just as "the law of evolution unifies the totality of nature," there were laws and an "inner life and consistency" in spiritual and moral matters. "The community of nature necessitates one law" in spiritual matters, and it had to be consistent with both spiritual and scientific knowledge.[134]

Poteat reconfigured the atonement in a way that brought Jesus into the historical process through a quasi-scientific analysis of the family. He argued that humans, the children of God, had caused a breach with their father by disobeying him through sin and thus threatening "the security of the family." This breach could be overcome only by "the change of man's attitude to God" because God would naturally welcome humans back into the family if they rejected sin. Jesus' role, therefore, was to help change man's attitude by demonstrating "the injurious quality of sin" and by revealing God's love. In "standing by our side," Jesus exposed himself "to the natural operation of historical forces which got their tragic triumph at Calvary." Thus Jesus served his purpose in that his death focused "upon sin a light which displays its irrational and monstrous character" and inspired Christians since "to escape its sway. . . ."[135] In this liberal interpretation humanity represented erring children returning to the family fold in order to further family stability, and Jesus was a facilitator of human spiritual evolution, rather than man's supplicant to a harsh God. This particular speech would return to light two decades later as the basis of conservative attacks on Poteat's orthodoxy.

Poteat's application of scientific and historical analysis to spiritual and social questions peaked with the publication in book form of two series of lectures that he delivered in 1900 and 1905. In 1899 Edgar Y. Mullins of the Southern Baptist Theological Seminary invited Poteat to deliver the Gay lectures at the seminary in the spring of 1900. After considering discussing his other favorite religious theme, the application of Christianity to social problems, Poteat chose to address "the attitude of the pulpit toward science." He fully realized that the question was an old one by the turn of the century: "Reconciliation books are out of date for thoughtful and reading people, but many editors and preachers, particularly in the South, are still either hostile to science or uneasy about its effects upon religious beliefs."[136] These three lectures delivered in March 1900 in Louisville incorporated the major ideas that he had developed in his various speeches over the past decade and disseminated his views of science and religion more widely than ever before.[137]

Before the aspiring ministers and the faculty, Poteat identified the time as "a period of transition, more distinctly so, perhaps, in our conservative South" and urged them to break willingly the "protecting shell" of "old habits" in order to face "the inevitable transition" with a progressive spirit.[138] His first lecture, "The Biological Revolution," accurately described the history of biology in the nineteenth century and stressed the unifying intellectual effect of the cell theory and the theory of evolution. He prominently declared his view of evolution: "There is no single object or phenomenon which is independent of the process of evolution. That process is not rightly conceived as an agent; it is only the method of God's operation. It is the method of becoming." Evolution moved with an "upward tendency to a foreseen goal," he argued, and "religion itself has developed out of rude and germinal beginnings" as well. Citing liberal scholars Andrew Lang, Max Muller, and Edward Caird as authorities, he explained, "The revelation of God has been of necessity progressive as being conditioned by the stage of culture which received it."[139] Darwin's influence extended beyond science and religion, though. Articulating even more clearly points made in some earlier addresses, Poteat briefly mentioned evolution's impact on thought in psychology, sociology (through Herbert Spencer), ethics, and literature.[140] His brave endorsement of the doctrine occurred at a time when seminary classes discussed evolution and, in the words of a student there, recognized it "as a possible theory until it touches some so-called orthodox doctrine, and then it is vigorously opposed."[141]

The second lecture, "The New Appeal," discussed science's effect on theological questions, and in trademark style Poteat reiterated the heart of his religion, the factor that freed his intellect to roam freely. His analysis of theology's shortcomings could not affect his faith because "religion is emotion; theology, reason. Religion is the response of the heart; theology, the logic of the head. Religion is the inward experience of God; theology, the intellectual account of it."[142] Poteat noted that "Christianity is absolute, our apprehension of it is progressive." Changing interpretations of religion were to be expected, he attested, as scientific knowledge grew. But he comforted his audience, "The theological ferment and confusion of this end of the century is but the effort to restate the doctrine of God and man in conformity with the new knowledge." In the new intellectual order, science required "that God reside within the natural order" rather than being "a rare visitor from inaccessible depths outside nature, whose laws he must violate or suspend in order to get in." Understanding God's position thus increased awareness of the possibility for "fresh, immediate, and personal communication" that would aid in understanding God.[143] The new knowledge made survival impossible for the "absurdities" of literal interpretation of the Bible but made God an immediate presence. His final lecture further encouraged the future ministers at the seminary not only to welcome science but to maintain a broad openness to secular literature in general.[144] Retaining the necessity of a nonrational encounter with God—a conversion experience—left Poteat firmly in touch with evangelical tradition, even as he tried gently to shove the students forward to a more expansive view.

The denomination received the lectures with mixed reviews. Poteat had tested the first of the lectures on a North Carolina audience, and subsequently was roundly attacked in a Hendersonville paper.[145] For the most part, though, printed reactions expressed support for Poteat's position. One report acknowledged that "some were not prepared, to accept all the ideas advanced" but concluded that "they were generally well received" by the Louisville audience. In response, one Louisville Baptist donated a thousand dollars for the seminary to use in purchasing scientific books. The *Greenwood South Carolina Baptist* believed Poteat's ideas to be "far from what the denomination believes," but the *Greenville (S.C.) Baptist Courier* countered that the lectures were evidence "that a man may believe in modern biology and in Christianity at the same time. . . ."[146] A level of suspicion about Poteat's orthodoxy endured among some, though. In 1902 he was singled out at the meeting of a Tarheel Baptist association in a discussion of "heresy among the teachers in our colleges."[147]

In December 1903 Poteat agreed to prepare a series of four lectures for the Hamilton Theological Seminary. After one postponement he delivered them in May 1905 and presented the same series in October and November of that year at Crozer Theological Seminary, Newton Theological Institution, Rochester Theological Institution, and the Divinity School of the University of Chicago.[148] This series, published as *The New Peace,* covered much the same ground as his 1900 lectures, enhanced somewhat by additional reading in so-called primitive religions and expanded to fill four lectures. He reaffirmed that "reason is not the only attribute of man nor the only faculty for the ascertainment of truth; that the moral and spiritual faculties are of no less importance." Even though "the Gospel in its origin was connected with a view of the world which the progress of science makes impossible for us," Poteat believed that "the Gospel itself does not thereby become impossible for us." The nonrational component of religion allowed "the persistence of faith in spite of the vanishing of many beliefs," and this lack of need for logical consistency again allowed Poteat to hesitate to define the limits of his ideas. He admitted, "I do not undertake to say how far one may go in the denial of intellectual propositions on religious subjects without losing the vision of God, which is the essence of faith." Intellectual rigor simply was not necessary in a religion of emotion, and Poteat's own ambivalence toward the intellectual conclusions of modern theology probably left him unwilling to investigate too far.[149]

In the introduction to *The New Peace* Poteat acknowledged that, like most of his earlier writings, "I seem to have done little more than bring together the thoughts of other men," a truthful admission of his lack of originality in the context of the national intellectual scene.[150] The value of his work lay in blending innovative thoughts from outside the South with the evangelical and emotional emphasis of his native region. With the 1905 lecture series, Poteat had achieved a comfortable understanding of science and religion. He believed that a dynamic process of development and change governed nature, man, social institutions, and religions; that to resist evolving was to embrace tradition. Ironically his own ideas reached their final form around 1900; he changed his views on religion and science relatively little the remainder of his life, instead devoting his creative intellectual energy to understanding the social implications of Christianity.[151]

Poteat's climb to prominence and leadership culminated in his election to the presidency of Wake Forest College in the summer of 1905. His labors in the denomination for two and a half decades had won him the confidence of most of the Baptist leaders represented on the board of trustees. He had gained a reputation as a scientist yet avoided significant criticism of his support of evolution by emphasizing publicly his belief that science and religion did not conflict. His widely varied learning and lecturing left no doubt that he was able to guide not only the scientific but also the classical and humanities portions of the Wake Forest curriculum. Further, his typical middle-class Victorian family life within the small college town gave no room for disapproval. Poteat had worked through the doubts brought on by encroaching middle age and had rededicated himself to productive cultivation of himself and service to others. His reputation had already reached Baptist circles outside North Carolina. In 1905 he had been given the honorary degree of Doctor of Laws from Baylor University, and in the late spring of 1905 the trustees of Baptist-affiliated Mercer University in Macon, Georgia, chose Dr. Billy, as he would become known as a result of his honorary degree, to be the school's president. The stunned Wake Forest trustees reacted by considering raising his salary in order to retain him, for they had no presidential vacancy. That soon changed, and their dilemma was solved two weeks later when President Taylor resigned his post as head of Wake Forest in order to take to the field to raise funds. On June 22, 1905, the trustees elected Poteat president with but one dissenting vote. Poteat was on his way to a Baptist meeting in London when the offer arrived, and upon reaching port he accepted.[152]

The *Biblical Recorder,* edited by a good friend of Poteat, trumpeted his election but hinted that there had been some opposition. The editor reported, "He is a Scientist who has devoted himself with open candid mind to that wedding of Science and Religion which the Creator intended. . . . There has been talk of his orthodoxy. Immature young men have charged up their half-baked notions to him. Like any other Scientist he has at times made utterances that were misread." However, Poteat had "entered the Dark Tower of Doubt, and he has come forth triumphant in the faith of his fathers," ready to lead others through similar trials.[153]

Poteat had managed to nourish a controversial belief in evolution for over two decades and to evangelize his scientific views by stressing his own Christian belief. He recognized the delicate balance: "I have tried . . . to keep to myself my own gropings after the truth in the dark; to speak of my findings only in response to inquiry or the demands of an actual situation. The relation I have sought to sustain between old and new is delicate and dangerous. My scheme has been to facilitate the transition in my small sphere, lifting the point of view and widening the outlook."[154] With his new position Poteat would have more visibility and a greater opportunity to influence the public, but there would also be more exposure to attack. Undaunted, Poteat used his prestige as professor and president to champion more than the marriage of science and religion. Beginning in the mid-1890s he worked incessantly to convince Tarheel Baptists that Christians had an obligation to take part in the social reform movements sweeping America.

3

Christian Progressivism in the South

✠

As historians have belatedly acknowledged, the American South participated actively in all aspects of the Progressive movement during the late nineteenth and early twentieth centuries.[1] North Carolina is often cited as one of the states most involved in reform activities, and an understanding of William Louis Poteat's role in the state's Progressivism is crucial to an understanding of the movement in the state and the region. From the 1880s to the 1920s, even as he labored diligently as a biology professor and then college president, he participated in numerous campaigns for change. Poteat's reputation as an educator and a leader in the Baptist denomination gave him his initial opportunities for important roles in reform organizations, and he then promoted a variety of causes with incredible zeal. He served in leadership capacities for several groups devoted to social improvement, ranging from the state Teachers' Assembly to the Conference for Social Service to the state Commission on Interracial Cooperation. His desire for change originated in his understanding of Christian teachings, and he applied those principles unswervingly to the myriad social problems that he identified in his slowly industrializing home state. More than perhaps any other person, William L. Poteat personified North Carolina Progressivism.

Historians have identified Poteat as one of the leading southern liberals during this period in regard to both social reform and religion. However, none have explored his ideas in adequate detail.[2] Scholars have also debated vigorously the nature of the relationship between churches and social activism in the South, and Poteat's activities and ideas offer insight into this broader question. In his investigation of the relationship between Baptists and social issues, historian John L. Eighmy singles out the formation of the Southern Baptist Convention's Social Service Commission in 1912 as among the most significant manifestations of the liberal religious viewpoint. He praises the choice of Poteat to head the initial commission and to write its first report because "Poteat advocated a liberal social philosophy fully in accord with the Progressive age that had produced the social gospel." He was "one of the earliest and foremost advocates of social Christianity" and "was destined to play a key role in introducing the new ideas to the denomination."[3] Because Poteat was at or near the liberal edge of southern thought on many issues throughout his life, a full exploration of his ideas reveals a great deal about the potential and the limits of liberal thought among Progressives in the South.

Historian Dewey W. Grantham has noted the existence of "a kind of moral-religious tone to much of the South's social reform" but cautions that "the influence of religious liberalism in the South during the progressive era should not be exaggerated." He argues that "two views frequently coexisted among southern white Protestants as to the church's social mission: that evangelism was 'the cure for social problems' and that it was sometimes necessary to support social reform programs."[4] An investigation of Poteat's tangle of reform ideas confirms this judgment. Poteat's experience also reveals the subtle ways that the various campaigns for change related and overlapped, and it underscores that religious and moral concerns could enter virtually every question facing southern Progressives. Like Progressives throughout the region, Poteat and the many organizations he led employed the same strategy for virtually every campaign, one of building public sentiment for change while often lobbying for direct legislative action.[5]

The late nineteenth century was a time of industrialization and rapid social change in America. For much of the century local democracy and independence characterized the "island communities" in which most Americans lived. In these provincial communities, mostly small towns or rural areas, the economy and political leadership depended on local initiative and decision-making, and the institutions of church, family, education, press, and civic life still centered around the concerns of the community. Late in the century, urbanization and industrial expansion began to destroy local bonds. A national economy controlled by distant corporations, the strengthening of national political power, and the anonymity of urban life produced a sort of national disorientation, and isolated communities were swept into a corporate order over which they had no control. To relieve their sense of crisis, around the turn of the century a growing middle class began to attempt to restore order and systematic control to society through Progressive reforms.[6]

Intellectuals coping with the sense of disorder of the 1890s had to acknowledge that interdependence marked America's industrial society. Although particular individuals might never meet in the anonymity of the booming cities, they were all linked. The integrated capitalist economy and the consequent growth of specialization meant that interdependence encompassed virtually everyone, and belief in self-sufficiency became largely obsolete. This change "devitalized the island community and simultaneously opened up the tantalizing promise of a grander community, one embracing the whole nation, or even all mankind," in the assessment of Thomas L. Haskell.[7] Poteat was among the intellectuals who discerned at least in part that the revolutions in communication, transportation, and economic organization had made society more interdependent. He observed in 1901, "The modern mind . . . discovers interdependence and unity where to the older conception there was isolation, if not discord." He, however, like all intellectuals of the time, conceived of the new community in a particular way shaped by his own regional context and personal biases. Just as nations are "imagined communities" whose boundaries—linguistic, racial, ethnic, or physical—can be conceived in different ways by competing thinkers, the boundaries of the new interdependent communities envisioned by Progressive reformers seldom encompassed all mankind.[8]

The limitations of Poteat's liberalism can be discerned by identifying the parameters he placed on the interdependent Progressive community that he imagined and advocated. Though he emphasized individual responsibility, he nonetheless saw the individual as part of a conglomerate society with a religious mission. His new community was to be the kingdom of God on earth; however, not everyone could be a full social member even in theory. Poteat remained hesitant about fully embracing an interdependent society, and he always maintained room for individualism in his ideas. He defined the members of the ideal Progressive society in terms of Christian morality and sought to exclude violators of a rather traditional moral code. The educated classes would take a predominant role in his ideal society, and further, he gladly omitted blacks from full citizenship, as did nearly all white southerners. Poteat's view was also limited by class bias as he failed, for example, to recognize fully the plight of sharecroppers and child laborers instead acknowledging a moral community membership for the cotton mill owners and, by implication, landowners. Hierarchy and moral conformity were the traditional assumptions behind his reform plan.

Poteat's conception of the Progressive community was not static. The unrest following World War I heightened his sense of crisis, and he correspondingly changed the boundaries of his ideal society. With the Commission on Interracial Cooperation, he and other southern liberals somewhat accepted the educated leadership of the black community into their own circle (though not as equals), and he welcomed women into a fuller citizenship with their new political rights. However, Poteat in turn wanted to police the boundaries more rigidly at other checkpoints, thereby excluding through marriage restrictions and eugenic proposals such as sterilization the right of a wide variety of defectives, including the insane, physically deformed, and alcoholics, to even exist. Despite recognizing societal interdependence, Poteat could not acknowledge that as a member of the same society he was dependent on the various groups he saw as inferior. Thus, he sought to uplift some and eliminate others in order to produce a kingdom of God within which he could feel comfortable acknowledging his link with all in an organic ideal society. The logical climax of Poteat's Progressive philosophy—eugenics—indicates that the traditional morality and hierarchical, elitist assumptions underlying the movement prevented reformers from sympathetically and realistically addressing the many ills of southern society.

Origins of Progressivism

Poteat's Progressive ideas grew out of his liberal interpretation of Christianity. His reform impulse was rooted in the belief that the message of Jesus had implications for social conduct. Encouraged by his younger brother Edwin, at the time a Baptist minister in New Haven, Connecticut, Poteat struggled with the question of Christianity's role in society at least as early as the unrest of the mid-1890s, a time when church leaders across the nation were debating the relative importance of social Christianity and traditional evangelism. In coming to accept evolution as a fact in the late 1880s and early 1890s, Poteat had adopted a nonliteral interpretation of the Bible and focused his religious study on the life and teachings of the human Jesus. This led to an emphasis on the program of Jesus for human life, rather than the more exclusive focus of conservative Christians on life after death. In 1895, he met and was impressed by Walter Rauschenbusch, Leighton Williams, and other social gospel figures while presenting a paper at the Baptist Congress in Providence, Rhode Island. On the same trip he attended a Christian Workers' Convention at his brother's church in New Haven. He commented, "What impresses me in the proceedings is the absence of the sermon element and the predominance of an enthusiasm for the practical work of saving the lost, the street arab, the disreputable and criminal classes." He was favorably struck by the "work for the tramps in New York" and believed as well that "the Christian impulse is beginning to be strongly felt in municipal administration. . . ."[9]

In his encounters, in person and in print, with leaders of the social gospel movement in the North, Poteat had discerned the outlines of an interdependent Christian community. While prominent social gospel proponents never discarded evangelism as a goal for churches, they did forge a new emphasis on the obligation for Christians to lead the way toward a just society. They saw the many ills caused by the industrialization and urbanization of America and for the first time recognized that the poor had little likelihood of leading a moral, Christian life when surrounded by depraved conditions. The social gospel never attracted a mass following, but leading clerics developed a strong critique of the economic structures that restricted and oppressed the lives of so many. Some, including Rauschenbusch, even advocated socialism as a remedy for economic exploitation, and most recommended that poor workers unionize. Most social gospel adherents saw the church's role as one of education and inspiration, rather than direct political involvement in implementing change, but many churches took something of a direct role by reaching out to the poor with settlement houses and institutional churches that offered charity or basic social services.[10]

Though the northern social gospel was far from radical for the most part, its counterpart in the South was more limited. Historian C. Vann Woodward recognized in 1951 that "the social-gospel movement that swept Protestant denominations in the North was not unknown to Southern clergymen, and even had a few spokesmen among them." Historians have since corroborated that claim by showing that in the South's growing cities, such as Atlanta and the industrial boomtowns of Alabama, a number of denominational leaders urged Christians to accept their obligation to apply Christian ideals to society. Educational missions to the Appalachian region, some urban settlement houses, and social service commissions appeared with denominational support; but they only slightly expanded the traditional goals of southern churches to provide education, charity, and moral guidance. However, spokespersons for this "mild regional variant of the Social Gospel" seldom critiqued the economic structures that produced the demoralizing poverty and loose morality against which they directed their jeremiads. Not until the 1930s did a group of radical southern churchmen question the basic economic arrangements of their region. Poteat and other southern advocates of social Christianity read and were inspired by the writings of the social gospel proponents but adapted it to a region without a strong tradition of critical intellectual inquiry.[11]

After more than a year of careful note-taking and composing drafts, in the spring of 1898 Poteat, gradually becoming widely known as a speaker on religion and education, delivered a "stirring address" to the American Baptist Education Society on "Christian Education and Civic Righteousness."[12] In endeavoring to define civic righteousness, he noted, "We must proceed from the known to the unknown. We know the features of individual righteousness in private life. What we require to know is its features in public life." He first rejected "that there are two standards of right, one for the individual, another for the corporation or trades union; one for private life, another for public life." Instead, righteousness "is independent of locality, time, or circumstance" and is identical in both public and private life. Ultimately, Poteat explained civic righteousness "as righteousness in that section of human relations concerned with the State." He elaborated, "It carries into the municipality and the State the same conscience that dominates the home, the farm, the shop. It contemplates not only the honest politician, the incorruptible public servant, but also the just arrangements of social relations, a regenerated social order."[13]

The renewed interest in ameliorating social problems owed its birth, according to Poteat, "to the present social distress." Primary among the problems he identified were "the extraordinary development of *party spirit*" in politics and the "closely related evil" of the spoils system. Partisanship "is corrosive of patriotism and disintegrates the solidarity of the community," and in insisting on "a particular interpretation, it quenches a healthful curiosity and manly independence, with the practical result of retiring to private life the best men and securing the field of public life for those who are willing to make the sacrifice." Already he saw corruption as damaging all members of an interdependent community. Poteat also singled out for criticism "the *party Boss* with his *party machine*" and "the *Lobby*" two other instruments of civic life that destroyed the unity that Poteat and other Progressive reformers sought. Much of this discord Poteat blamed on newspapers, which he criticized regularly throughout the Progressive Era. The press, "a tremendous engine for the creation and the dissemination of public opinion," was "largely responsible for the intensity and rancor of party spirit, for the perpetuation of the spoils system against the intelligence and patriotism of the country, and for the pettiness and self-seeking of the so-called servants of the people."[14]

The answer to the problems was in making "Christianity responsible for the realization of civic righteousness." Poteat's own deep faith led him to advocate religion as the cure for the ills of the threatened community. From it "must issue the . . . amelioration of social conditions. . . ." Realizing that the dominant understanding of religion in the South at the time, especially following the Populist political movement, was that the churches should have no role in political matters, Poteat countered that Christianity "is no brotherhood of pilgrims taking, indeed, transient lodgings in our work-day world, but marking a straight path across it to another world where all its aspirations and all its duties await it." Instead, the aim of Jesus "was primarily the progressive transformation of the present social order." Poteat declared, "The kingdom of heaven, as the organic expression of the will of God, is to come on earth," a post-millennial theological declaration that contrasted with the argument of many religious conservatives who believed that the transformation of earthly society would come only after a physical second coming of Jesus.[15]

In explaining the method by which the interdependent social order would be transformed, however, Poteat proved that he had not strayed too far from the generally conservative southern understanding of evangelical religion. Though he acknowledged that the impulse for socialism could be traced to Christianity, Poteat did not challenge the basic forms of southern economic and political structures, and expressly rejected all forms of socialism as a palliative for social distress. He scorned the effectiveness of "the reorganization of society by direct legislation" for "righteousness by law is impossible." "Law is merely a standard of conduct in the sphere of the outward life," he elaborated. "Law falls short of enforcement and avails nothing, unless it is supported by the consensus of opinion. If it is so supported, it is superfluous." Thus, in his projected community, a unanimity of opinion behind Christian ideals would assure consonance. Poteat explained "the method of Jesus" as simpler than legal proscription: "He propounded no sociological theory. He left no legislation for the systematic construction of his ideal social order. He was no iconoclast. . . . Nor was he a revolutionist. . . . Least of all did he seek his aim through political agencies." Instead, "the method of Jesus is, social regeneration by an inward spiritual ministry, civic righteousness through the leaven of individual righteousness. He renews all social life at its source in the human heart, and trusts the new life to take on the external embodiment which is appropriate to it."[16] In Poteat's view, one saved society by saving individuals, who in turn responded to Christian appeals to conscience. No institutional critique was necessary, just a stronger emphasis on the Baptists' old doctrine that social perfection would result from the natural actions of converted individuals. Poteat's uneasy combination of traditional individualism with social concern marked a liberal point of southern social Christianity and distinguished it from the somewhat more ambitious social gospel.[17]

Poteat conceived of Christianity's "creation of a just society" through "the regeneration of the social unit" as a very gradual process. A proper perspective on the evolution toward a Christian society required "just a little of the geologist's time-sense." Poteat chose a very telling biblical example to indicate how Christianity, "without violence to the existing social order, so renovates it that a new society emerges to which an anti-Christian institution, at home in the old, becomes alien and impossible." He argued that the letter of Paul to Philemon, in which Paul returns a slave to his owner but exhorts the owner to treat the slave well—despite the missive containing "no word against slavery"—"was the prelude to the protection of slaves under Constantine, the amelioration of their condition during the Middle Ages, and in our own time the abolition of slavery by the greatest nations of the world."[18]

Poteat took pains to develop his social views not only in conjunction with his religious beliefs but also in agreement with his understanding of science in a slightly altered version of the Social Darwinism of the time. As in all aspects of his life, he deftly modified the intellectual trends of his era to agree with his Christian beliefs: "The development and consummation of [the] Kingdom of God are a detail of the general sweep of evolution," thereby interlacing the anticipated sacred outcome of social developments with the broadest sanction of science. He explained further with optimism:

> I have great confidence in the arrangements of Nature as the expression of the mind of God. The struggle for existence, the law of competition, is universal; and tho' it wears a forbidding exterior, its issue is beneficent. It is the only condition of peace. Human society is no exception. The entrance of conscious intelligence upon the arena changed somewhat the sphere of the struggle, substituting refined for the gross methods of the animal stage. The introduction of the factor of Christianity initiated another period of transition and readjustment, the probable outcome of which will be, not the revocation of the law of competition, but the softening of the conditions of its applications mainly thro' the growth of respect for the rights of others.

He clarified that "we are still in this period of readjustment; hence the number of programmes for social amelioration." Not everyone had recognized their proper duties to benefit society. Poteat therefore expressed suspicion "of all schemes which proceed upon the assumption that 'social conditions, like our food, clothes, and shelter, are something to be thought out, planned, and systematically constructed' and not allowed to 'happen into shape.' The sociologists need to go to school to Jesus." A majority of individuals could not be coerced to acknowledge interdependence; the conversion of individuals had to lead the way toward a wider acknowledgment of mutual obligation.[19] The rapid basic modification of society was not even a goal for Poteat, unlike the social gospel leaders from whom he took some of his rhetoric.

Though Poteat repeatedly returned to these themes throughout the rest of his life, his understanding of the relationship between religion and social change altered little over time and remained at the heart of his desire for Progressive reform. He reaffirmed in 1905 to the Baptist World Congress in London that "the questions sprung by pauperism, vice, corporate wealth, education, public franchises, [and] the public service . . . all need to be brought down to the bottom principles of the Gospel. Their final settlement is there, or it is nowhere." He attacked socialists, singling out sociologist Lester Ward for criticism, because "they do not recognize the main fact in the case, namely, that moral evil is the root of all social unrighteousness. And that root, however severely legislation may prune the twigs above ground, will continue to send up its obnoxious shoots from below." He explained the cure in more detail, "The transformation of the social unit leads by natural processes to the creation of a Christian public opinion; and this Christian public opinion, in proportion to its strength and pervasiveness, will control any new expressions of the social life, and, without violence, first soften and ultimately eliminate any features of the existing order out of accord with it. In the end a new society emerges. . . ."[20] His views had changed little two decades later. In 1926 he defined the kingdom of God as the "will of God realized in all human relatio[ns]" and proclaimed that "as he revolutionizes individual[s] and establishes personal righteousness, so he will revolutionize society and establish social righteousness." As always, though, there could be "no secure and permanent reconstruction of society in fraternity and justice apart from inward renewal of the social units."[21]

Poteat's scheme for reform did not entirely diminish the role of legislation, however, and he spent much of the Progressive Era advocating various legislative enactments. He explained that "when the public conscience has been formed upon the Christian ideal, vested interests which grew up before and are found to be opposed to this ideal will never yield to the pressure of a public opinion which contents itself with nerveless entreaties or rhapsodic denunciations." Instead, "such pre-Christian survivals can only be dislodged when the public conscience takes practical embodiment in legislation" for "the only effective burial of them is beneath a heap of snowy ballots."[22] The interests that stood in the way of moral goals simply were not part of the community that Poteat was defining and were thus open to political force. In the interconnected citizenry that he saw emerging, any obstacle to a moral public conscience had to be eliminated for the benefit of community members, and Poteat expected that once enough Christians realized the imperative to shape a moral community for mutual welfare, the legislative embodiment of those expectations would occur naturally. Legislation was not the starting point, but it followed inherently.

Early Progressive Campaigns

Because in Poteat's prescription social change had to begin with individual choice, the spread of reform required changes in public opinion. Consequently, like that of many other advocates of the social gospel and Progressive reform, Poteat's method was hortatory. His initial targets as methods for changing opinion included education and the press; if those could be made more efficient and subordinated to the goals of the Progressive community, recognition of social interdependence could occur more quickly among the general populace. Early in the new century, he began to apply his new analysis by also arguing for reform of municipal government and rural life.

Poteat believed that the education of youth presented a crucial opportunity to advance his own social goals. Education was not just about learning facts, preparing for a trade, or for refinement; it was for developing the "whole personality." Because children were "unperverted by the hypocri[s]ies and artificialities" of adults, the school acted "as a manufactory of power."[23] It was therefore vital to "put in your school what you want in your civilization."[24] Like many reformers of the time, he located the "salvation of [the] New South in right education" because for the student the school "socializes his individualism and sets his aims and ideals," making it "the most important of social institutions."[25] Education should create in children "character and efficiency," and then their "higher intelligence and wider range of interests" would bring such benefits to society as an enhanced social consciousness and a devotion to public service. Specifically Poteat named good roads, good schools, and public health as causes that worthy graduates were likely to support.[26] Looking back in 1924 over a lifetime of advocating better education, Poteat felt this strategy had worked: "Schools have largely made sentiment for prohibition, law enforcement, good roads, public health, and public education." He celebrated, "what modernizers and civilizers are books! . . . In short, the school, with the indispensable aid of the church, lays the foundation of the better order of human life, efficient, cooperative, secure, and contented."[27]

Poteat began his support for rationalized and efficient public education very early in his own career as a science professor. In June 1884 the North Carolina Teachers' Assembly was formed by three hundred people at a mountain resort near Waynesville at the call of the editor of the recently formed monthly journal, the *North Carolina Teacher*. Poteat, probably remembering his own experience the previous summer at the Martha's Vineyard Summer Institute for teachers, signed up as a charter member. As a supplement to the summer sessions (offered around the state by the University of North Carolina) that many teachers attended, each subsequent year the group's members met for about ten days early in the summer for a chautauqua-style meeting to discuss ways of improving the quality of their teaching.[28] As one speaker noted, "Probably there has never been in North Carolina an interest in schools more generally felt than now."[29] In the late 1800s the distinction between college professors and secondary and primary teachers was not a great one because many colleges, including Wake Forest, offered preparatory courses and because often specialized training beyond a college degree was not needed to teach college classes. Nonetheless, the college professors quickly took a disproportionate share of the leadership positions of the assembly, and in its second year Poteat served as a vice-president along with fellow college educators Charles D. McIver and Edwin A. Alderman.[30]

Teachers in both colleges and secondary and primary schools used the recitation method of teaching, and the discusssions of the assembly could benefit all. However, the college professors received a great deal of respect from teachers statewide and taught many of the sessions at the yearly meeting that had grown by its third year to include in attendance seven hundred of the fifteen hundred total members.[31] In 1887 the assembly recognized Poteat's wide-ranging intellectual interests by appointing him to the Reading Circle Committee that "intended to organize and unite the profession in a steady march of improvement" by suggesting general reading matter. The resulting report reflected Poteat's biases for the classics and for English literature.[32] In March 1888 he was among the incorporators of the assembly as the group solidified its legal status in order to build its permanent meeting place at Morehead City on the coast.[33] Poteat also served on the executive committee from 1889 until 1892, but his principal contribution lay in his guidance to teachers on the teaching of science.[34] He addressed the group on "Biology in the Scheme of Education" in 1889 and along with Joseph A. Holmes, University of North Carolina professor and later state geologist, organized Natural Science Day in 1890.[35] Poteat advocated that teachers take a hands-on approach to science; on one occasion he distributed "to the audience several hundred grasshoppers which he had collected in the marshes in this vicinity. These insects he used in illustrating his remarks by carefully analyzing them in every way, clearly showing all their habits and wonders of construction."[36] Poteat even outfitted a laboratory at the permanent meeting hall and in some years supplied a microscope to aid the teachers' understanding.[37]

In 1896 Poteat was elected president of the Teachers' Assembly for 1896–97, a position that had already been held by the distinguished educators Edwin A. Alderman, Charles D. McIver, and James Y. Joyner.[38] In Poteat's presidential address in 1897 he hailed the role of the assembly in "the recent intellectual awakening of our State" and outlined his view of the importance of education in an address titled "The Child As Teacher."[39] He used the occasion to idealize the potential of children, highlighting their innocence, purity, simplicity, and originality. Poteat lamented that "practical" education was so much emphasized and worried that "our very systems of education are ingeniously contrived means for the suppression of intelligence and originality." As a result, students became "only one grain in the great democratic sandheap of modern society." He called for fresh critical thinking about traditional society: "If you dare express an opinion of your own, you are suspected, you are dangerous. It is time for teachers and all intelligent people who care for the future of our country to resist such domination and censorship of individual initiative." Teachers should "put a living child into the social structure which we are building" by fostering children's creative and critical thought.[40] The child was to be a thinking part of a broader social project, the Progressive community. As with Poteat's understanding of Christianity and social reform, he was torn between maintaining creative opportunities for the individual and subordinating him or her to the needs of a new society. Philander P. Claxton, editor of the *North Carolina Journal of Education,* assured Poteat that his addresses were "very helpful to the teachers."[41]

State superintendent of public instruction Charles H. Mebane served on the assembly's executive committee during Poteat's presidency, and Poteat joined him during the 1896–97 and 1897–98 school years as one of four members of the State Board of Examiners, with Mebane as chairman.[42] The board's responsibilities each year included writing new questions for and grading examinations of teachers applying for a lifetime certificate that would allow them to teach throughout the state, an attempt to replace the scattered issuing of renewable licenses. The board wrote the first set of questions in 1897 and following their use, published the wide-ranging, difficult questions from 1897 and 1898 to aid teachers in their preparation.[43] Further, in 1898 the examiners created a lengthy "course of study for teachers."[44]

Poteat had full responsibility for writing and grading the botany and the physiology and hygiene questions and for preparing the study guide on those subjects. He used the opportunity to extend to public education some of the pedagogical methods he had helped to pioneer at Wake Forest. On physiology and hygiene, the course of study recommended evenhandedly, "The best practical results for the pupil should be expected, not from exaggerated accounts and flaming pictures of abnormal conditions, but from a clear comprehension of the normal processes that go forward in the body." Here, "the text-book ought to be supplemented by demonstrations wherever possible."[45] Similarly, the standards for the study of botany emphasized that students should approach problems with an open mind and practical, individual experience, recommending use of specimens for "there can be no profitable study of plants apart from the plants themselves."[46] Likewise, Poteat recommended that students should have access to a school museum of rocks, plants, minerals, and animal specimens. The guide also encouraged reform in the conditions of schools: "One who is willing to teach where the window panes are dirty, the floor unswept, and the walls unsightly, should not be employed to teach our youth."[47] Overall, the examiners hoped "that our teachers may realize that they *must study* and keep up with their profession, or fall out by the way and make room for those who are progressive."[48] Education, such a vital element in creating a Progressive community, had to be efficient and in an environment conducive to Christian middle-class morality.

Poteat participated in a number of other groups designed to increase the professional capabilities of teachers and to advance the cause of public education in the South. Following the yearly adjournment of the Teachers' Assembly in 1890, Poteat joined a group from across the region meeting at the same place to form the Southern Educational Association. The association's constitution justified its creation because "the cause of education in the South is encumbered by problems that exist in no other section of the Union, and

. . . the workers in this field believe that by organization they may benefit the cause of education especially in the South. . . ."[49] Poteat later served a term as the Tarheel member of the association's executive committee.[50] In 1891 a committee of the Teachers' Assembly called for a meeting that Poteat attended and that resulted in the creation of the North Carolina College Association to bring the state's professors together. The originator of the idea, President Charles E. Taylor of Wake Forest, claimed that not only would higher education benefit by closer "union" but secondary education would as well "for each had a mutual beneficial effect on the other."[51]

Poteat also spoke at the annual meeting of black teachers in North Carolina.[52] He regularly attended the annual Conference for Education in the South, including the crucial 1901 meeting in Winston-Salem that was essential in catalyzing the subsequent crusade for better public education in North Carolina and across the South. The Winston-Salem gathering, he reported, was "a very enthusiastic and (it is to be hoped) profitable meeting."[53]

Philanthropy from the North was a crucial component of southern educational improvement, and Poteat welcomed the contributions of sympathetic and like-minded northern reformers. Speaking to a church audience in New York City in 1912, Poteat satirized those southerners who "with the jealousy and pride of exclusive proprietorship, insist that our problems are our own, and resent what they call outside interference, whether it comes in the form of Mr. [Robert C.] Ogden's conferences for Education in the South, or Mr. [John D.] Rockefeller's so-called subsidies to Southern Colleges." Interdependence obviously ignored the Mason-Dixon line. He insisted that most southerners did not hold such attitudes and instead recognized "the patriotic motives of the great agencies which are now occupied with the industrial and educational progress of the South. . . ." The regional reconciliation of the turn of the century was for the Progressives part of the recognition of a new type of community across the nation.

Southern reformers nonetheless expected their region to retain its traditional idiosyncrasies. One challenge Poteat identified for the South was the difficulties of separate school systems for blacks and whites, but he defensively noted that segregation in New York's schools had disappeared only in 1900 and that "the policy is established in the South." He declared, "I remind you, further, that the policy of certain states with reference to the franchise, criticised as discriminative and exclusive, is now discovered to be inclusive and constructive" because blacks in North Carolina received twice as much in spending on education as they paid in taxes. "White and colored are distinct and remain so," Poteat affirmed blindly, "but the corn and beans of our succotash are boiled in the same pot," the closest he could come to acknowledging that whites and blacks occupied the same social setting. He found optimism as well in the economic development he saw occurring rapidly in his region and looked to southerners to contribute to the national economy, but only "on condition of the *education of the people*." The North could help, for in the South's backward educational state "money appears to go so much farther with us, and the need of it appears to be so much more fundamental." He pleaded for the donation of money not only toward black education but also for white schools for "it is the right education of these white boys and white girls in the highlands and the lowlands that will determine the future of our tragic but hopeful Southland."[54] To his wife Poteat expressed hope that the address would "bear good fruit."[55]

Poteat maintained an ambivalent attitude toward the growth of professional specialization in teaching that reformers had helped to bring about in the public schools. Educational expertise was vital to the project of creating a cohesive Progressive community. He reiterated that "the problems of the social, as of the individual life, are settled in the right education; for where the social unit is just and capable, social problems resolve themselves and disappear." However, Poteat argued that the growth of specialization in education had become "extreme" by 1899. He recommended that teachers "be more than a specialist" in order to assure the best education for students, for their goal was to be "the building up of a complete human life, not the furnishing out of a special machine." Society as a whole could then benefit because "the only safe reform party consists of the promoters of the education of the whole people."[56] The citizens of his ideal Progressive society had to have old-fashioned moral and intellectual components as well as more specialized practical knowledge, and the teachers had to be capable of providing it all.

While education could help create an informed and Progressive public, a sensationalistic and defensive press could divert the public from the real social problems facing Progressives. Poteat believed that the press, by focusing on celebrities, murders, and trivial matters, often stood in the way of the debate and discussion that he felt was needed to bring attention to the underlying defects that ultimately threatened the state's citizenry. In 1903 he satirized the desire of the press to see "life's dregs and filth . . . brought out to the open sky."[57] The next year he urged journalists to fulfill their obligation "to solidify the community in the common struggle against all forms of social evil," for "it will hardly be denied that the free press is under some sort of moral bonds. . . ."[58] Writers should recognize their obligation to aid the "protection of public morals," Poteat believed. He recognized keenly the extent to which the press could aid his favored causes, noting that "every democracy is a monarchy, and Public Opinion is its king." Newspapers, he elaborated, "are the standard and guide of the popular feeling and the popular judgment, and not seldom the sole agent of the popular will." Therefore, the press "may rectify the moral judgments of the time, and set forward the general social progress as few other instruments of reform ever can."[59] Throughout the Progressive Era, though, he argued that "the modern newspaper drains the sewers of civilization and poisons the fountains of morality. . . ."[60] His remedy turned to the morality of individuals, as his Baptist heritage dictated: "it will be serviceable here as elsewhere to personalize the institution and to think not of the press, but of the editor."[61]

Not only did editors and their papers often offend the morality that

Poteat wished to spread, but newspapers stood in the way of social progress. He noted in 1916, "When the splendid campaign against hookworm in North Carolina was inaugurated a leading paper in the State resented the implied discredit and ignorantly denied the facts to save the reputation."[62] In 1927 Poteat still chafed under the savage ideal, under which critical discussion was discouraged in favor of chauvinistic loyalty to the South. He concluded from long experience, "It is quite possible for the press of the State to form public opinion and not merely express it; candidly to lay unpleasant facts before us in order that the situation may be corrected or improved. . . ." Instead, he gave as an example, "if one ventures the judgment that our agricultural methods and results are rudimentary and unsatisfactory as compared with European standards, one expects an opprobrious epithet like pro-German or pro-French." Further, "it is held to be improper and disloyal to 'parade' the fact that on the basis of what the school people call the educational index we rank five from the bottom in the sisterhood of states."[63] Even with all his attachments to older ideals, Poteat earned his reputation as a liberal by being willing to criticize the defects of his home state. Poteat sought to show the editors that everyone's welfare was at stake in the burgeoning society if a problem was not solved. Although Poteat's fulminations against the press failed to change its emphasis, overall the press served him well through its continuous coverage of his addresses on seemingly all conceivable topics.

Reforming schools and newspapers would bring public opinion in line behind the Progressive program in a general, indirect way. In the first decade of the twentieth century, however, Poteat began to agitate to change public opinion on specific social issues that lay at the heart of his imagined Progressive community. Poteat subscribed to an organic view of social life and often decried socialists for regarding society as a mechanism that could be taken apart and reassembled. In a speech to the Raleigh Chamber of Commerce in 1907 advocating reform in city administration, Poteat spelled out his views on the role of government in the community and the necessity for unity among citizens. Not surprisingly in view of his knowledge of science, he drew from biological principles to explain. The various groups of citizens are "interdependent," he argued, and "separation means death." Much like cells in a complex organism, they are "organized into a higher unity" in order to help the individuals to be "efficient" and to realize their "highest possibilities" as well as to handle specific duties such as water, lighting, protection from fire and disease, providing parks and schools, and maintaining order. The main obstacle to achieving this unified community life, according to Poteat, was political partisanship. "The work of city government is not government primarily," he pronounced, "but the conduct of a great business." Its duties "are in no sense political," and "they cannot properly be made the occasion of division into political parties." Therefore, Poteat supported the introduction of the "Texas idea" of commission government, in which elected officials both legislate and administer city departments in hope of added efficiency.[64]

Municipal government was not the only aspect of community life that

Both intellectually and socially, Poteat had an extremely productive and dynamic life after age forty. Beginning in the late 1890s, he acquired great visibility as a professor and after 1905 as president of Wake Forest College (as shown here early in his presidency). He used that recognition to forward many social reforms, including Prohibition, eugenics, and interracial cooperation.

concerned Poteat in the first decade of the twentieth century. He addressed rural life with similar concern in his presidential address in 1903 to the North Carolina Historical and Literary Association. This "address of power" by Poteat opened with a quote from Wordsworth and articulated a similar longing for a lost connection with things natural. Like the Progressive movement as a whole, Poteat discerned the sweeping changes that industrialization and urbanization were bringing and took a long look backward toward a simpler society, yet he could not reject the town life that he so actively enjoyed. He scored "the artificialities of city life" and fervently advocated that "the manhood and womanhood which we wish to grow and to brighten must be in the country and of the country."[65] His yearning description to his Raleigh audience of the advantages of rural life expressed the sense of rootlessness and drifting that afflicted many urbanites caught in the rapid change of the time: "The blessings of attachment to the soil are, that primary one of harmony with nature, which draws after it a bright retinue of dependants; the opportunity of self-realization in an atmosphere of independence and freedom and repose; exemption from the pettinesses and moral obliquities which swarm on the surface of a crowded and conventional life." He celebrated the renewed interest in nature and rural life that he discovered among city dwellers.[66]

Nonetheless, Poteat and his audience could hardly envision the real dreariness of much agricultural life of the time, just as most Progressives approached rural problems with no attempt to understand the perspectives of their objects of reform. Poteat blithely undercut his evocations of nature, "Of course, no one could be so simple as to wish for the reversal of the progress which modern days have made toward the elaboration, the refining, and the beautifying of life. The simple life does not involve the return to barbarism, nor does it require asceticism or poverty. . . . Neither is it incompatible with the highest industrial development." Instead, he argued, "simplicity is an inward attitude." He constructed a harsh list describing "the poverty of country life itself," including lack of good nutrition, proper clothing, adequate housing, and "the deepest poverty of country life," the lack of contact with the arts and sciences. He found hope for "the enrichment of the farmer's life," though, in bringing the advantages of urban life to the country. "The standard of comfortable living is spreading into the country," he claimed, aided by guidebooks on building and furnishing middle-class homes and making flower gardens. The further spread of good roads, transportation, and agricultural machinery would lighten the work of the farmer, as would the advance of scientific farming. Telephones and rural free delivery would end the isolation of rural citizens and create "new fellowships of country life," just as the rural school and the free rural library program advocated by the Literary and Historical Association would create "an intellectual fellowship" where none had existed. During Poteat's tenure as president, the association continued to lobby for increasing the rural library program begun by the state. All in all, he felt, the modernization of the countryside would relieve "the monotony of country life" by connecting rural dwellers more vitally to the rest of society.

Just as he thought certain modernizations would benefit the rural areas, Poteat likewise envisioned that cities could become more rural without destroying the essence of the natural life. "The city is trying to countrify itself," he gushed, through parks, gardening, and movement to the suburbs. "It really looks as if, in the city of the future, agriculture will join hands with trade and manufactures to enhance its prosperity and to preserve its physical and moral health," he foretold with an optimism that ignored the brutal reality of the South's sharecropping regime. "All this means a return to nature, to a simpler, saner, truer, life. It means the emergence of agriculture into a new dignity and respectability." He celebrated antebellum society in his evocation of modern changes, "It means for us in this agricultural region the recovery of at least some of the charm of the social life that crowned the prosperity of other days."[67]

Much of Poteat's Progressive activity revolved around the restoration of the moral health and social unity and stability that he believed characterized the simpler life of his rural past. However, his own attachment to life in town and his cosmopolitan intellectual wanderings gradually left him with only a caricature of rural life. His distance from the people of the countryside was evident in his propensity to make jokes about the ignorance and simplicity of mountaineers.[68] He continued to express interest in rural reform, though. In 1913 Poteat was still decrying the spread of urban "artificiality" and agitating for talented rural youth not to desert their homes for the city. Better rural services, such as roads and health, were his hope for making the countryside more appealing, making even the good roads crusade a moral issue.[69] Shortly before the United States entered World War I, he found the country school to be especially "strategic" in the campaign for better education and an improved life for young residents of rural areas. Improve such schools, he argued, and one could move the life of the state "to higher levels of efficiency and happiness."[70] Poteat's blind belief that modernizing change could occur without significantly modifying the essence of rural life was echoed in his support of the conservation movement. Speaking in 1916 he decried the abusive harvesting of forests and their lack of protection against fire. He called "for adequate appropriation by the General Assembly for forest wardens in our wooded townships and for the application of scientific forestry. . . ." The careful use of resources was his goal for "use is not waste." Rather, it served as "the best conservation, which may be defined as the business management of the people's capital with due regard to the claims of prosperity."[71] Though rural life and the environment were not Poteat's central concerns, his attitude toward them was consistent with his efforts to reform public opinion in other areas, and his approving references to business values in government and public management revealed an unwillingness to acknowledge the sins of elite businessmen, at the height of the Gilded Age.

Poteat could not imagine a Progressive community in which the intellectual life was as handicapped as it was in rural areas of the time. Yet his whole Progressive program in some way sought to recapture the sense of cohesiveness that the island communities of rural America had in retrospect achieved so naturally. He ignored the real problem facing the rural South, the poverty of sharecroppers caught in a hopeless cycle of work and debt, perhaps because sharecroppers still labored at his childhood plantation home. Further, denunciation of sharecropping would not only condemn his own family, but also the many rural elite landowners whom he considered the best possibilities for inclusion in the Progressive community once they had livened their intellectual activity. He looked longingly at the rural values whose loss and unfeasibility necessitated the whole Progressive search to define a new community. However, as the reform movement gained momentum, he began to look more exclusively toward other opportunities for change. After 1910 he sought to speed up the creation of a moral community by working with large, multi-issue groups.

Progressive Organizations and Religion

As his belief in the necessity of a Christian Progressive society became stronger, Poteat began to seek bigger and more influential venues for delivering his message. His own increasing prestige and notoriety as a college president, beginning in 1905, gave him the visibility to gain such opportunities. Organized religious groups offered a way to influence the outlook of large numbers of southern people, and Poteat sought diligently at both the state and regional levels to change the opinion of Baptists regarding their social obligations. Targeting the denominational public was an attempt to persuade those already converted to Christianity that social change had made it imperative for them to recognize their interdependence with, and consequent need to uplift, other parts of society. This soon led into his involvement with important secular reform groups in an ever-broader attempt to gain support in the individualistic South for a Progressive society based on at least a limited recognition of interdependence.

Poteat helped first to foster social awareness in the Baptist State Convention of North Carolina. In 1911 a letter from a concerned Tarheel to the convention delegates termed the growth in influence of Catholic churches "The Catholic Menace" and argued that "the great strength of this denomination which threatens us, lies in the fact that they are doing things for human beings, as human beings, and in that way they are strengthening their forces." Alarmed, the convention appointed Poteat to head a committee "to take into consideration social conditions in North Carolina. . . ."[72] Reporting in December 1912 for the committee, Poteat declared, "The time is full of humanitarian movements and schemes of social uplift and reform, and the need of them was never so great as now owing to the complications and more intimate contacts of modern life." He outlined the duties of the church at such a time if it were to maintain moral leadership: "Its mission is to relieve suffering and remove its cause, to forestall the increase of defectives and dependents, to check the terrible havoc wrought by disease among the effective agents of the kingdom, to clean out the nests of vice, to fight in a heroic and relentless war every enemy in the life of man, to pluck up moral evil, which is everywhere the root of social unrighteousness—in short, to make its community a little province of the kingdom of God." He cautioned nonetheless that "evangelism is primary and fundamental" because a religious approach to social problems could work only through the action of individuals.[73] With that caveat preventing any outright threat to Baptists' settled convictions, the report sufficiently interested the convention that in 1913 it appointed another ad hoc committee on social service that reported in 1914. This committee recommended that the convention "should take a deep and abiding interest in the complete welfare of our entire commonwealth." As a result, the state convention created a standing committee on social service.[74]

In 1913 Poteat became involved in the investigation of religion and social conditions at the regional level of the Baptist denomination. A resolution passed by the Baptist World Alliance in 1911 challenged affiliated groups to set up committees on social action, and in May 1913 the Southern Baptist Convention (SBC) followed several of the statewide organizations in appointing a Social Service Commission. Edwin C. Dargan, president of the SBC, chose Poteat to head the seven-man commission.[75]

Poteat wrote the report that was presented in May 1914 and that offered several "principles and policies" to guide the denomination. He opened with his oft-repeated social gospel belief that "the kingdom of God, which was the theme of Jesus' teaching and the aim of his ministry, is the organic expression of the will of God in human relations, an all-embracing social ideal to be realized in the reign of righteousness in the earthly life of man." He relieved conservative fears by noting that the kingdom "is not formal or institutional" but instead "a social spirit. . . ." He claimed boldly that "the Church imposes its standards upon all other social institutions" such as the family, the state, schools, the press, and business. It should, he believed, limit divorce and family impurity, insist that the state "suppress unrighteous practices," maintain religious schools and papers, regulate the labor of women and children, and "check private greed and compose class antagonisms." Further, the church must take responsibility "for the right solution of [the] social problems" of war, alcohol and drugs, vice, and public health. However, this work was to be accomplished primarily by the "work of individual renewal and inspiration," Poteat's longtime solution to his never-resolved mental struggle between individualism and interdependence, tradition and modernity.

In this instance, though, he struggled to envision a more direct role for the church as an organization, but his effort lacked specificity. Converting individuals to recognize social duties "does not discharge the full social responsibility of the Church," he admonished. Instead, the church should offer helpful criticism, support, and cooperation to "the distinctively social service departments of the municipality and the state" and "influence and direct legislation by memorial, protest, and petition, and by the creation of a Christian public opinion on the wrongs and perils, the duties and possibilities, of community life." Further, the church should endeavor "to provide for the poor, the sick, and the defective, and, what is more important, to provide against them."[76] This was Poteat's most radical statement on the social duties of Christianity, and even here the duties of the church as an aggregate body consisted in large measure of the traditional duties of caring for society's weaker elements and the vague requirement to change public and legislative opinion to favor Christian ideals, in essence an evangelical endeavor. He did not follow many northern critics in the additional step of criticizing the basic economic structures at the root of many of the problems. At his most liberal, Poteat's roots in southern evangelicalism could not be easily escaped, and his call for a Progressive community was ambivalent.

Arthur J. Barton replaced Poteat as head of the SBC's Commission on Social Service (CSC) after its first year (when it was merged with the Committee on Temperance that Barton had headed since 1910). Historian John L. Eighmy concludes that Barton "almost single-handedly" set the temper of the commission for over twenty-five years and that "Barton's more conservative treatment of the issues soon made him the accredited spokesman for the convention on all social questions."[77] Eighmy implies that Poteat was replaced as chairman because his views, even rooted in the past as they were, were too liberal. Under Barton the commission focused on the issue of Prohibition until ratification of the Eighteenth Amendment then broadened its scope in 1920 to include such issues as economic antagonism, race relations, and international peace.[78] Eighmy concludes that Barton led the commission to emphasize "individualism in religion" more than social Christianity, but Poteat's dictates concerning "the leaven of individual righteousness" as the way to reform indicate that even the liberal edge of Baptist thought that he embodied relied on individual conversion.[79] Poteat returned to the CSC in 1919 and served until his death in 1938, cooperating with Barton on many issues.[80] But his removal as head of the commission attests to the narrow range of thought considered acceptable for leaders in the region.

Poteat played a relatively minor role on the regional commission after its first year, but for a number of years he chaired the state Baptists' commission on social service that he had helped to inspire, and he often wrote its annual report to the Baptist State Convention. His ideas in the North Carolina reports in many aspects mirrored those that Barton presented year after year to the regional denomination. Poteat's state reports were in accord with those of the CSC in emphasizing the enforcement of Prohibition following its passage, and in expressing dismay at the general increase of lawlessness following World War I. The reports of both Poteat and Barton encouraged the U.S. to work for peace and disarmament, and expressed endorsement of cautious efforts for amelioration of racial unrest. Poteat's statements on the balance between evangelism and social Christianity remained cautious, reflecting his perception that vice and immorality were growing stronger. He asserted in 1921: "The community is composed of individuals and it, therefore, cannot be redeemed apart from the redemption of the constituent individuals. Accordingly, social service must wait upon evangelism, is hopeless without it, and its ministry merely palliative rather than remedial." He of course then went on to list the duty of Christians upon conversion "to form and guide a public opinion and sentiment before which industrial oppression, violation of the rights of childhood, and any type of social injustice and evil cannot stand."[81]

The limits of southern social Christianity can be contrasted with the northern social gospel by comparing Poteat's address at the 1913 Southern Sociological Congress with an address on the same program by Walter Rauschenbusch, prominent northern advocate of the social gospel. This assembly of social workers, educators, religious leaders, and government officials from throughout the region met annually between 1912 and 1919. The first gathering occurred in Nashville in 1912 at the behest of governor Ben W. Hooper with about seven hundred in attendance, but by 1919 the group had dwindled. Poteat was a member from the beginning; the governor of North Carolina appointed him to be one of the state's delegates to the formative 1912 assembly. The "social program of the congress" from the first meeting outlined the objectives of the group: prison reform and the end of convict leasing, extending juvenile courts, preventing alcoholism and prostitution, caring for the insane and handicapped, requiring school attendance, strong uniform laws on marriage, divorce, and vital statistics, and "equal justice to both races." Further, the congress declared support "for the closest cooperation between the church and all social agencies for the securing of these results."[82] This gathering included many of the small group of religious liberals from throughout the region, men and women who repeatedly encountered each other through various campaigns in the small world of the South's Progressive movement.

The group convened in Atlanta in 1913, and a number of speeches addressed the topic of "the church and social service." Among others, Poteat represented southern churches, and Rauschenbusch was one of several persons expressing the religious sentiment of some liberal northerners. Rauschenbusch exclaimed, "The Church should have the highest and bravest, the most far-reaching and revolutionary social program. It has such a program in the idea of the reign of God on earth." He went on to read approvingly the synopsis of social duties that the Federal Council of the Churches had passed in 1908 and revised and reapproved in 1912, arguing that it "comes nearest to being a definite social program of the Protestant Churches of America." It specified that "the Churches must stand" for its various initiatives, not that individuals must. The creed advocated such ideas as the prohibition of child labor, regulation of women's labor, protection of workers against workplace harm and unemployment, and a minimum wage. Rauschenbusch did not shy away from class conflict, either: "The ruling classes always and everywhere resent an increasing self-assertion on the part of the working class as if it were the beginning of evil, whereas it is really the beginning of virtue." He criticized those who would save souls but "pay them $3.50 per week [and] place them in slums. . . ." Rauschenbusch himself did not forget the importance of evangelism, and a southern liberal could have agreed with him that "all social questions are moral questions on a large scale." However, Poteat could not concur that class conflict could represent a positive step toward redeeming society.[83]

Poteat's presentation to the congress resembled his liberal report to the SBC in 1914. As usual, he refused to flesh out the implications of his ideas, instead evading some controversial points. He cautiously noted that while the realization of the kingdom of God on earth was the goal, "its exact place in relation to the functions and the apparatus of civil government we may hesitate to define with precision." However, "it is not a divine society set over against or supplanting the family, the State, or any type of industrial or political organization. It is rather a social spirit which will transfigure them all." Christian government would be "the humane and democratic government which recognizes the Christian standard of fraternity and justice. . . ." As to how to bring that about, Poteat could not resolve the contradictory pulls of social Christianity and southern evangelicalism. Poteat did, however, recognize that churches needed "a more elaborate organization" to carry out "its new ministry" and praised the commitment of some denominations "to specific social programs" for "this is the age of conference and cooperative association—scientific, educational, agricultural, industrial, political." He fully recognized the spirit of interdependence characterizing the intellectual era. His unresolved tension continued, though: "Social life is to be cleansed by cleansing the life of the social unit [the individual]; for moral evil is the root of all social wrong." He explained, "No factory inspection or minimum wage, no new scheme of election, of publicity, or of impeachment will correct the injustice or check the graft. New *people* are wanted, and nothing else will do."[84] Though he was in accord with the social gospel on many points, Poteat could not bring himself to see beyond certain limits.

Poteat continued his involvement with the Southern Sociological Congress by serving on the Committee on the Church and Social Service (along with his brother) in 1914 and the Committee on the Church and Health in 1915. He attended the 1915 session that met in Houston just before the opening of the Southern Baptist Convention there, and in 1917 journeyed to Asheville for the annual meeting. There he summarized his understanding of the congress's purpose in accord with his own motivation for many of the Progressive crusades; it was to "crystallize [and] consolidate Christian opinion and sentiment" and "supply [an] apparatus of cooperation for common ends." Overall, it would "secure in legislation [the] practical expression of [the] judgment and moral sense of [the] majority of [the] community for guidance and control of [the] minority, whether community unit be county, State, [or] nation." It would "suppress immoral practices [and] restrain evil men."[85]

After 1910 the Progressive movement cohered more than before, organized by multi-issue secular organizations.[86] Poteat was at the forefront of this change in reform strategy, not only by belonging to the Southern Sociological Congress but also through his activities with the North Carolina Conference for Social Service (NCCSS). The NCCSS was formed on September 17, 1912, by a group of North Carolinians inspired by the recent inaugural gathering of the Southern Sociological Congress. More than a dozen committees were created to address the whole range of social issues facing the state—from illiteracy to alcoholism, race to insanity, and so on. Committee chairmen spread the news of the group's creation, and at the first meeting of the NCCSS in Raleigh in February 1913, over three hundred members enrolled. Within three months more than five hundred people had joined the organization.[87]

The founders of the NCCSS invited Poteat to make the opening address at the conference's first meeting.[88] Drawing on ideas prevalent at the Southern Sociological Congress and among liberal religious leaders across the nation, he sounded a clarion call for interdependence among the various elements of the moral Progressive community that he envisioned. Discussing "The Correlation of Social Forces," Poteat drew together many strands of his reform interests and indicated that the NCCSS would weave them into a united reform strategy. He concluded:

> Here are some five different social forces which I have enumerated—the home, the school, religion, government, business—all independent, all working toward the social amelioration of the people. . . . Now, what we want is to correlate them, to make every one cognizant of the service every other one renders in securing the common aim, and, by thus uniting them, multiply their efficiency. Individualism has had its day. . . . We can come to the level of our individual capacity only as we share the common life and lead our own individual lives in harmony with the community life of which we are a part. So the impulse to correlation of these forces, the reason for it, is the greater efficiency of each, the larger results for all. Let us remember also that the energy which expresses itself in these several directions is definitely Christian.[89]

Reflecting the underlying link between religion and the NCCSS, the group's quarterly journal reprinted in its first volume Poteat's pioneering report to the Baptist State Convention on social conditions, and in 1916 the Baptists' Committee on Social Service endorsed the work of the NCCSS.[90] Poteat attested in 1916 that "'The Kingdom of Heaven' conception is dominant in the Conference."[91]

The annual meetings of the NCCSS featured speakers on a wide variety of social reform issues, and a committee on resolutions then expressed the sentiment of the group on the matters deemed most important, sometimes targeting their resolutions to influence the biennial sessions of the state legislature during which the NCCSS meetings were generally scheduled. Its statement of purpose articulated the desire "to insure here and now an environment of physical, mental, and moral healthfulness that will prevent human waste and make for the fullest development of every individual within its borders" by uniting "the now scattered forces of social service" for "investigating conditions," "awakening the people," and "securing the remedies."[92] Poteat took an active part in the organization. He closed the meeting with a short summary in 1914. The next year he preached a sermon on Christian service arranged by the conference in a local church, and in 1916 he addressed the opening session on "Christianity and Social Progress." He was elected third vice-president in 1916, and as a member of the executive council he approved of a plan being developed by the NCCSS for a state board of public welfare.[93] One of the most important accomplishments of the NCCSS in its early years was its role in the enlargement of the State Board of Public Charities into the State Board of Charities and Public Welfare by the state legislature in 1917. The agency was a major step toward the construction of a rational statewide system that acknowledged societal interdependence through taking responsibility for the most needy.[94] In 1917 Poteat presided over a session that included a talk by the governor, served on the resolutions committee, and introduced a resolution supporting a pending legislative bill mandating that makers of patent medicines be forced to publish their formulas. He was appointed to the executive council again that year.[95]

In 1919 the NCCSS elected Poteat president.[96] The group met in Goldsboro in 1920 (since the legislature was not in session that year), and Poteat's presidential address was titled "The Old Method for the New World." He made his usual point holding "individual renewal and inspiration," along with "indirect" influence on government and society, to be the key to Christian social change—again revealing the tension between individualism and social unity that he never resolved.[97] Poteat continued his activity with the NCCSS by working for change in the state's prison system. In 1922 the NCCSS appointed a committee to investigate penal issues, and the committee expanded into the Citizens' Committee of One Hundred on Prison Legislation, holding a special meeting in November 1922 under NCCSS auspices. Poteat served on the subcommittee formulating "a system of classification of prisoners." Overall, however, few of the committee's recommendations were taken seriously by the legislature.[98]

Strengthening the regulation of child labor was another of Poteat's reform interests in which the NCCSS took part. One historian has concluded regarding the curtailment of child labor that "the North Carolina campaign could claim few victories," in part because of "a nonconfrontational, even cozy relationship between the state committee and the cotton textile industry."[99] Poteat's involvement verifies that argument. As with the landowners on the sharecropping issue, he found it impossible to imagine that the mill owners who were his peers in social standing were not part of the moral Progressive community. He was a member of the North Carolina Child Labor Committee as early as 1907; however, an exchange with the state secretary Charles L. Coon in 1911 leaves doubts about Poteat's initial commitment to change. Poteat reported, "I confess that I think extravagant positions are sometimes taken on the subject of Child Labor in the factories. Not unfrequently the opportunity of such labor is a great blessing, and I think that in many cases the conditions under which children labor in factories are distinctly better than the conditions of their lives on the farms from which they come to the factories." He reiterated his views when an astounded Coon wrote in dissent, but Poteat did express support for the pending legislation providing for no work for children under fourteen years of age and no work at night for those under sixteen.[100]

Poteat remained a consistent advocate of a limited form of regulation of child labor. In 1913 as a member of the North Carolina Child Labor Committee he helped formulate proposed legislation, and in 1914 he introduced a successful resolution before the Baptist State Convention "that this Convention should endorse the principle of the regulation of the labor of women and children in the interest of the race, and commend to all the people a practical interest in this fundamental social problem."[101] In 1915 he addressed the Joint Committee on Manufactures of the state General Assembly regarding "Guiding Principles in Child Labor Legislation." Still having trouble attacking those of his own social class, Poteat maintained blindly, "The manufacturers with whom I have the honor to be acquainted are as good men as I know, intelligent, public-spirited, humane. They want their ten per cent, but I cannot think of them as securing it at the price of the health and character of little children." He praised some mill owners for supporting the legislation under consideration, and noted, "I crave their active co-operation in extending the present protection of working women and children up to the standard set by the most enlightened and experienced of manufacturing States." He urged that child labor reformers and mill owners "get together for the common good." This unifying, nonconfrontational approach was rooted in his view of the mediating role of Christianity, which "must impose its ennobling restraints upon private greed and class antagonisms. . . ."[102] Poteat returned to the legislature in 1919 as the chairman of a committee of the NCCSS to speak on behalf of a pending child labor bill.[103] In downplaying the harshness of children's working conditions, Poteat seems to have ignored his own commitment to first-hand observation in favor of following his biases.

In addition to mills in the South, some of the strongest and most enduring corporate powers were railroads, the regulation of which was a perennial for reformers. In 1913 the General Assembly of North Carolina passed regulations on freight rates within the state but provided that the governor, upon petition from railroad companies that found the rates too strict, could appoint a special commission to adjust the requirements. Governor Locke Craig named Poteat to the three-man commission in November 1913, and Poteat devoted much care to his role as mediator between corporate and public interests. He attended public hearings from January 12–15, 1914, in Raleigh and July 7–16 in Asheville. He remained in Asheville until July 24 in consultation with his fellow appointees to determine reasonable rates that would assure the companies a fair return. The commission recommended the use of the rates of the Southern Railway Company as the standard.[104] In this way they hoped to assure harmony.

Poteat's whole program of restoring community by recognizing interdependence faltered when antagonism toward the elite was introduced; he could not conceive of a high level of coercion for a social equal. In general he had a cautious attitude toward large corporations and business activity because their greed and self-interest could interfere with the spread of recognition of social obligations. In 1898 he declared that "the sea of business" of the period "threatens to submerge all else, all that is really worth while in life." Nearly two decades later he affirmed, "There are public dangers from great financial power in the hands of a few men who may be unscrupulous. Such power may block and control legislation and fix national policy in the interest of private persons. . . ."[105] Nonetheless, Poteat at various times was an investor both in cotton mills and railroads. In specific cases, he never took a harsh attitude toward corporations.Only the onset of world war caused Poteat to begin haltingly to question the role of business. He pondered, "When the aim of each is the good of all, then the success of each is the profit of all. Otherwise the network of economic relations becomes a net in which the few catch the many, and the kingdom of business is composed, not of brothers, but of vultures and their victims." The European war was an example: "The lurid tragedy which has wrecked civilization from the Baltic to the Aegean is witness." His forgiving outlook toward business evolved gradually into a suspicion of corporate motives by the time of his death over two decades later. He discerned in 1915 "in our own loved country, under the guise of a beforehanded patriotism, the germ of a like catastrophe, when business, losing the motive of common good, will employ the apparatus of justice itself to exploit the physical and personal resources of the country for private ends."[106] Though Poteat remained decades behind his reform counterparts in the North in even beginning to question the corporate economy, he remained ahead of most influential southerners. Business had ignored the need for social concern, but in producing the ultimate disaster they reaffirmed for Poteat the need for a society tied together for mutual interest in a new and smaller world.

War, Race Relations, Prohibition, and Eugenics

Poteat's initial apprehension of interdependence and his quest to conceive of a Progressive community emerged from a sense of crisis in the turbulent 1890s, but the effect of World War I was equally important in shaping his climactic understanding of the society he wanted. The brutality of war pierced his optimism somewhat, and the strife that swept America following the armistice represented a tremendous breakdown of the harmony required in an interdependent Christian society. Further, the discord made him aware that two decades of Progressives' cries had not shaped public opinion adequately. As a result he reimagined the ideal community by including in it the black elite, who in turn would influence the black community to recognize harmony (albeit always unequal) as a valued end. It was rather easier to conceive of white women, newly enfranchised, taking a more active role in a Christian community. Even other countries could become part of the kingdom if they followed a cooperative moral diplomacy.

However, he also sought to combat the moral deterioration that accompanied the end of the war by increasing the strictness of Prohibition and its enforcement. The moral majority could successfully use legislative force on this matter to bring into line the minority, who to him were without concern for the effects of their actions on the broader society. Other people, in contrast, he began to visualize as altogether unworthy of being part of the community. Though for many years he had had an interest in the possibilities of eugenics, not until after the war did he enthusiastically advocate that large classes of society not be allowed to exist beyond the present generation. These changes, he hoped, would restore to viability his vision of a Progressive community in a changed postwar era.

The problems of war and peace had long concerned Poteat, perhaps reflecting his own early memories of civil war. He spoke out against violence despite living in a society that historians have argued was dominated by a culture of violence; the Progressive emphasis on harmony and mediation was stronger than the southern military tradition for Poteat. As early as 1903, at the peak of Lost Cause glorification of the gallantry of Confederate soldiers, Poteat voiced his opposition to "the anachronism of the military tradition." He claimed, "The appeal of intelligence and conscience is to arbitration, to law" and believed that "the military spirit must give place to the industrial and co-operative."[107] In 1908 he was optimistic, even naive, in an address to the North Carolina Peace Society. He expressed a belief that bloodshed could be justified: "War has been the effective agency for the suppression of evil intrenched in backward stages of culture and for pushing forward the moral progress of the race." In addition, "war must be admitted as a last resort in the protection of the home territory and the national honor. . . . Here the moral code for the nation coincides with the moral code for the individual." Nonetheless, peace could be encouraged by educating "against the war spirit" and thus removing "the factitious glamour and romance of the military career." His second prescription, in retrospect filled with irony, echoed his Progressive solutions to other social problems: "We must extend more and more to public and national relations the moral code universally recognized in personal relations. Not a little progress is already made. The society of nations is developing an international conscience. . . . France and Germany could not fight to-day about the Spanish succession as they did forty years ago."[108]

War, Poteat argued in terms of science, resulted from a "fighting passion bred by natural selection," and conflict had become equated with honor because the "roots of honor" lay in "unselfishness" and willingness to die on the battlefield. He sought to redefine honor in the interests of peace, however, outlining a "new battlefield" where one need "not lose [the] ideal of manliness" yet did "not need to perpet[uate] war." Glory and honor should be recognized in peaceful pursuits such as physician, preacher, lawyer, and public official because honor grows "only in [the] generous soil of struggle for [the] life of others."[109] The battles should be against disease, vice, alcoholism, ignorance, and war. He called for a "new declaration of war against war."[110] In 1910 Poteat journeyed to Washington to attend a convention of the Association for the Judicial Settlement of International Disputes, and the following year he and his brother attended the Lake Mohonk Conference on International Arbitration in the state of New York.[111]

He maintained a certain optimism even when war broke out in Europe. Speaking in November 1914 on behalf of relief to Belgium, Poteat confirmed that "the position of our country today is unique and splendid" because of a "sane and righteous diplomacy" that brought the nation rapidly into a position of "leadership and responsibility. . . ." He welcomed the burden because "whether we wish it or do not wish it, the conditions of modern life make national isolation impossible," an early hint that he believed the interconnected new society would ultimately extend across national lines.[112] Nonetheless, a certain sadness is obvious in his musing in 1915 that the war woke the world "from its dream of [the] brotherhood of man" just as "provincialism and prejudice were giving way before the world-wide intercourse which science had made possible, just when the Christian standard of justice and brotherhood was everywhere respected, and humanity was beginning to feel itself one. . . ."[113]

In 1916 he lamented that "in these great days of intense national spirit and jostling sovereignties, a man can hardly address an audience anywhere in America except in the atmosphere of patriotism, no matter what his theme may be."[114] When the U.S. entered the fighting, though, Poteat supported the crusade and like many other intellectuals was caught up by the patriotism of the time. He argued, "We were justified in entering the World War. The motives and the effectiveness of our participation were as righteous as they were splendid."[115] During the war he spoke often in support of liberty bonds, and at one such event he attested that the war was a "holy war against autocracy and militarism" and would establish "moral law in state action" while offering a "new birth of freedom in all lands."[116] If the country could "preserve in clear relief [the] ideals and motives with which we entered [the] War," he declared in late 1917, it would "renew [the] moral and spiritual vitality of [the] Nation."[117] In his view, the performance of America's duty toward other nations could enhance the recognition of societal duties at home and perhaps even extend the moral, interdependent community to include other countries.

At the war's end Poteat welcomed home the returned soldiers and, like other Christian reformers, felt a great sense of potential.[118] Speaking on the "moral gains of war," he rejoiced that "we are governed by our ideals of liberty and right and unselfishness," standards that were triumphant because the nation "went into war for them." The mobilization had created "cooperation for common ends" during the fighting that could now be applied to "world brotherhood" in the battle of "nationalism versus internationalism." Furthermore, "physical and moral sanitation" had been "good in war time" and would be "good in peace time," and "moral reforms, once strongly in [the] public mind, may be hastened to consummation." He hoped for improvements such as Prohibition, sex hygiene, and individual and public health. He anticipated the war's "highest and best result"—the "practical application of ideals in [the] League of Nations."[119] Joining the league in "maintenance of law and justice in international relations" would be the "extension of [the] American ideal to [the] whole world."[120]

His hopes were bitterly disappointed. Only weeks after the armistice he reacted sharply to a "proposal to build the biggest navy in the world," calling it an insult to the nation's intelligence. He wondered, "Have we abolished the role of German militarism in order to take it ourselves?"[121] He urged people to "recall now and then" the horror of war "lest we slip into indifference and resign in favor of reactionaries and militarists."[122] He felt betrayed when the United States did not join the League of Nations, fuming that "partisan politics plunged" the U.S. into "national humiliation and disrepute" before the world.[123] As late as 1924 he urged joining the "cooperation of conscience and intelligence of mankind" that the league represented.[124] Poteat welcomed the Washington conference on naval arms limitation in 1921 and attended a conference on arms limitation there that year. He also wrote and secured the passage of a resolution in the Baptist State Convention supporting the negotiations in hope of "preparing the way for the earlier universal reign of righteousness in the earthly life of man."[125] In 1924 his report of the Committee on Social Service at the Baptist State Convention reiterated his futile belief that moral issues should guide diplomacy: "The churches . . . have a grave responsibility in the creation and spread of a public opinion which will require and enforce the settlement of international disputes in accordance with the law of Christ."[126] The expansion of the Progressive idea of community to include the world had not materialized.

In September 1919 the governor appointed Poteat as one of twenty-five members of the State Reconstruction Commission to investigate the problems caused by the war. The commission's statement urged that Congress prohibit the immigration of "ignorant foreigners," that citizens practice "rigid economy" and increase production, and that "all classes and conditions of people must work together in a spirit of mutual helpfulness."[127] For Poteat the national disorder in 1919 and 1920 struck especially hard. His goals throughout the Progressive Era included harmony, cooperation, and order, and the strife after the armistice threatened years of working toward widespread recognition of the modern interconnected social order. He struck a dramatic and foreboding note in March 1920 in addressing the NCCSS:

> This is a critical and decisive hour; the situation is astir with anxiety and hope. Problems thicken and deepen. Habitual restraints are grown lax. The fighting spirit which we built up in all our able bodied young men for the winning of the war refuses to be exercised [*sic*] over night on the signing of the Armistice. A crime

wave is over all the world. On the other hand, the social passion has mounted in temperature to a point never before reached. There is such a fact as the public conscience, and the movement toward cooperation in all the spheres of human life is pronounced and growing. Certainly, if never before, we are in need of the sober and open mind, clear vision, and aggressive heroic consecration. Is it the law of social progress which we seek? Then we stand at the parting of the ways, the issue goes to the roots of things. If we fall into error we shall but renew the old oscillation between progress and barbarism.[128]

He faced this challenge through his advocacy in Baptist circles of law enforcement and strict adherence to Prohibition, by advocating stronger marriage and divorce laws, and by working to "direct accumulated national energy in[to] sane channels—not *hate*."[129] Race relations was one such area of hate in the South that threatened any concept of a united community, let alone one fashioned around Progressive aspirations for harmony, morality, and social concern. Poteat stretched the limits of his imagination to include elite blacks, but the inability to go further and envision equality doomed Progressive hopes for racial peace.

North Carolina's racial situation had interested Poteat since before the turn of the century. Amid racial violence in the state during the elections of 1898, he concluded that the contest had ended "happily" with white victory, and he decided that the situation called for "the breaking of the solidarity of the negro vote, and an educational qualification upon suffrage," severe limitations upon the idea of community.[130] During the statewide discussion in 1900 leading up to the vote on an amendment that disfranchised blacks, Poteat was taken aback by the contrasting black viewpoint. On vacation in the eastern part of the state, he "talked politics and the amendment with a negro, who I confess silenced me when he said, 'If the amendment takes away voting from the colored man, it ought to take away his tax too.'"[131] The amendment passed, and his silence was short-lived. As on other topics, Poteat never relinquished his initial hierarchical assumptions about race.

His interest in the racial situation continued throughout the Progressive Era. He had done significant reading on race relations by October 1911 in preparing for an address to the New York Baptist Ministers' Conference in New York City on "The Negro of the South," and he never changed the conclusions he reached. He read the works of W.E.B. Du Bois accusing whites of exploiting blacks throughout the world and the path-breaking findings of anthropologist Franz Boas that intelligence did not differ among whites and blacks. However, he stubbornly rejected those viewpoints in favor of more conventional beliefs.[132] From various authorities considered scientific at the time he concluded that white traits included dominance, self-control, originality, and rationality and that blacks were submissive, emotional, imitative, and passionate. Caucasians were thus the "advanced race" and blacks the "backward race."[133] Community among members of the two races was hardly an option; in the South it seemed that interdependence could never be acknowledged to extend so far.

Drawing on his own past and historical wisdom, Poteat lectured his northern audience that race relations before the Civil War had been good but that during Reconstruction some northern teachers who came South had taught blacks to be aggressive and politically assertive. Southern race problems in all their "present gravity and difficulty" resulted from this "monstrous blunder of reconstruction" with its "train of surviving bitterness and acute race consciousness. . . ."[134] The intelligence of the South, Poteat verified, resented the North's superior attitude on this national problem, and the "religious, educational and political leaders" of the South opposed lynching and the demagoguery of bigoted southern politicians James K. Vardaman and Coleman L. Blease. The better people of the region instead had a "genuine sympathetic interest quickened by economic, often personal, obligations, enlightened by intimate knowledge of [the] needs and limitations" of blacks. Poteat put forth the origin of his own "long-standing interest" in blacks as coming from being "brought up with negroes" such as his childhood slave and friend Nat.

He acknowledged that American blacks were the "highest branch" of their race in the world, "but all that distinguishes it—its religion, culture, economic and political freedom—is not an achievement but a gift" from whites. Blacks possess merely the "symbols of culture, not culture; mere literacy not education." The recognition by whites of their own superior development, though, should evoke "a deeper sympathy, a larger tolerance, and a freer ministry" to aid blacks "who struggle forward under so tragic an inheritance." The Negro, for his part, "likes it where he is" and has no plans to move. After emancipation, Poteat argued, many blacks had used the "gifts of slavery" to achieve some success.[135] In 1916, Poteat "enjoyed 'Birth of a Nation'" while visiting Nashville with his brother "about as much as the first time" he saw it. His sentiment is hardly a surprise in view of his substantial agreement with the derogatory view of blacks during Reconstruction presented by the controversial film that was based on two novels by Poteat's friend and former student, Thomas Dixon Jr.[136]

As with child labor, sharecropping, and business exploitation, Poteat remained blind (perhaps willfully) to the full plight of blacks because he not only could not see them as equals but he also likely did not want to bring conflict into the harmony of the Progressive community by denouncing fellow paternalistic whites. However, he took a quite liberal stand for his time by encouraging whites to take seriously their paternal obligations to blacks by leading the way toward peaceful interaction. Because YMCA leaders took early action to encourage better race relations, he spoke often at the Wake Forest branch of the YMCA, various YMCA clubs throughout the state, and virtually every summer and many other times throughout the year at the YMCA's training facilities at Blue Ridge, North Carolina. In March 1911 he presented a version of his New York speech to the college YMCA, and over two hundred Wake Forest students engaged in a weekly class, as described by the *Wake Forest Student,* "for the study of negro life in the South, or, as certain of the Morally Stunted have termed it, 'Niggerism.'" The class used the textbook recently issued by the national YMCA and divided into discussion groups of about a dozen students; however, the description by the student magazine puts in doubt the effectiveness of the classes in encouraging a wider view of the membership of society.[137] Poteat, though, began to recognize the need of white leaders to communicate with the black elite. In organizing a conference for 1917 on the "State, County, Municipality, and Social Welfare," he invited a black educator, Simon G. Atkins, president of the Slater Industrial and Normal School in Winston-Salem, to share the program with such white academics as Chapel Hill sociologist Eugene C. Branson.[138]

After the end of World War I, Poteat cooperated with the YMCA in their work on the homefront. In October 1919, at the invitation of YMCA official John R. Mott, Poteat traveled to Atlanta to attend the United War Work Conference, and in early November he led war work conferences in five North Carolina cities. Also in November, he attended an international YMCA convention in Detroit at Mott's invitation and was made vice-chairman of a committee to consider future YMCA policy.[139] Poteat's relationship with the YMCA leadership may also have brought him into the effort by a group of southern liberals to ameliorate the racial problems that swept through the South after the war. Willis Duke Weatherford, head of the YMCA's training school at Blue Ridge, and Will W. Alexander of the YMCA's War Work Council obtained a grant from the War Work Council to hold a series of meetings to prepare both whites and blacks to deal with racial problems that might erupt following the war. In the early months of 1919, Weatherford directed the training of more than eight hundred white men at Blue Ridge, and Alexander led meetings for over five hundred black men in Atlanta. Three YMCA officials, including Alexander and Weatherford, were among the six or seven white men, mostly ministers, who met in Atlanta in January 1919 and began meetings that led to the formation of the Commission on Interracial Cooperation. This group built on the earlier plans of one of its members, Thomas Jesse Jones of the Phelps-Stokes Fund, and black educator Robert R. Moton to form an interracial group to ease the tensions. A slightly larger meeting that included Moton was held in March in Atlanta, and those in attendance created the Committee on After-War Cooperation. Additional meetings were scheduled for April, with Moton gathering black leaders at Tuskegee and whites assembling in Atlanta.[140]

At the invitation of chairman John J. Eagan, a Georgian who shared Poteat's commitment to social Christianity, Poteat became involved. He took part in the all-day conference on April 9 and endorsed its work:

Eighteen men and one lady were in the meeting at the Ansley hotel, Atlanta, . . . representing nine Southern states. Organization of the 'Committee of After War Cooperation' was effected. Its principal aim is to secure the right attitude of white people in the South to the negroes. A similar organization with like aim is to be effected among the colored people. . . . No publicity is yet to be given the movement. The financing is yet undetermined. We are asking for an appropriation from the War Camp Community Service Committee in N.Y. on the ground that the return of the Negro soldiers is the occasion which calls for the new movement. I am asked to be state chairman for North Carolina and to serve as a member at large of the Executive Committee.[141]

Poteat returned often to Atlanta for meetings of the Inter-Racial Committee (as it soon became known), and the YMCA-funded group began to conduct local meetings across the South. He attended a meeting on July 3 and another on July 24 in which he was among eight white men who agreed to be in charge, with YMCA help, of their respective states. Poteat reported to the committee that he "didn't think the trouble so acute in North Carolina as in some of her sister states." The strategy of organizing permanent local interracial committees was strongly recommended, and the group decided to expand its membership from sixteen to twenty. Four members were appointed to consult with Moton.[142] On February 17, 1920, Poteat attended the committee's meeting in Nashville when the members unanimously decided to invite some black leaders to join. By June blacks such as Moton regularly attended.[143] The slightly broader Progressive community was on its way to reality, as interdependence had demanded of whites who wanted to keep social peace.

In August 1920 the religious emphasis and the sharp limits of the interracial movement's aims became clear when a large group attended the three-day Christian Leaders' Conference on Inter-racial Cooperation held at Blue Ridge at the call of Poteat and two other "prominent churchmen" who belonged to the Commission on Interracial Cooperation. The statement drafted by the conference after vigorous debate received wide distribution both in the press and as a pamphlet. It began, "We a group of white Christian men and women of the South, absolutely loyal to the traditions and the convictions of the South, and especially to the principle of racial integrity, . . . do deliberately declare it to be our profound conviction that the real responsibility for the solution of inter-racial problems in the South rests directly upon the hearts and consciences of the Christian forces of our land." The goal was racial harmony within the context of segregation. The statement went on to endorse the organization of local interracial committees of Christians, to decry lynching, and to urge the improvement of conditions of black education and traveling facilities, but it closed with a reiteration of their "unalterable adherence to both the principle and practice of race integrity. . . ." Throughout the twenties and thirties the commission urged a so-called moderate solution and never moved beyond its adherence to the Jim Crow tradition.[144]

The commission always sought cooperation with religious groups. In

December 1920 Poteat journeyed to Florida "to present the question of Inter-Racial relationships" to the Florida Baptist State Convention. When in 1921 the Federal Council of Churches of Christ in America created an interracial committee on race relations, Poteat was among the one hundred appointees from across the country. Many of the hundred were deliberately chosen from the Commission on Interracial Cooperation, ensuring continuing close cooperation between the two and allowing the interracial movement to enter some northern cities.[145] Poteat remained active as a member of the executive committee of the regional commission through the twenties. At the state level he played an even more critical role.[146]

Several efforts were already underway in North Carolina after the war to improve race relations. Beginning in 1919 the state department of public instruction annually called together black leaders to discuss education, health, and welfare. Also, by early 1921 the state YMCA had organized an interracial department, and the state secretary of the YMCA, J. Wilson Smith, and the secretary of the interracial department, G.C. Huntington, were both active with the regional interracial commission.[147] C. Chilton Pearson, a professor at Wake Forest College, served as a field worker for the YMCA, and in the summer of 1920 he spent two months "seeking out and bringing into formal contact with each other white and colored leaders in North Carolina towns"— "liberal minded whites and careful though progressive negroes." The object in each town was "a standing joint committee of white and colored men working for the benefit of both races," and "the sponsors of the movement" specified that the organizer was not to discuss "political rights and 'social equality'" with blacks. Nonetheless, Pearson reported that some local committees sometimes actually succeeded in easing tensions. The work of the YMCA was treated as virtually synonymous with that of the regional commission at the commission's meetings. Thus, despite being among the last states to officially organize a state branch of the commission, North Carolina made about as much progress as any state in organizing local committees in 1919 and 1920.[148]

In March 1921 Huntington and Poteat invited "a few interested persons" to a meeting in Raleigh on March 25 with T.J. Woofter Jr. of the regional commission "to take steps in the organization of a State Commission on Inter-Racial Co-operation."[149] At this meeting it was arranged for a committee on personnel to select "right minded citizens of the state in every community."[150] Governor Cameron Morrison then commissioned "about 20 white and Negro people as the first Commission in North Carolina." On August 25 Poteat was named chairman.[151] The efficacy of the state and local committees is questionable, however. Will W. Alexander of the regional commission noted to Poteat, "I have been very much disappointed at the failure of a number of these local committees in North Carolina."[152] Nonetheless, the commission in the Tarheel State was one of the most active in the South during the 1920s.[153] By the summer of 1922 the state commission comprised twenty-eight men and seven women, including such notable liberals as Mrs.

T.W. Bickett, Clarence Poe, W.S. Rankin, Howard W. Odum, and Mrs. Josephus Daniels. At its annual meeting in October 1922 at Christ Episcopal Church in Raleigh, the state commission discussed black education, checked progress on the status of a proposed training school for delinquent black male youths, and appointed committees on the press, railroads, church cooperation, and health. The women's group met both separately and with the full commission, and Poteat was reelected chairman of the full assembly.[154]

In March 1922 Poteat led a "general conference on interracial cooperation" at the meeting of the NCCSS, featuring state and regional commission member Mrs. T.W. Bickett and South Carolina interracial activist Croft Williams.[155] Perhaps stemming from this meeting, Poteat conferred with NCCSS leaders in late 1923 about the state commission "becoming affiliated with the North Carolina Conference for Social Service as one of its standing committees." After stipulating that the interracial commission's black members "could be affiliated with the Conference in an advisory capacity, but could not be admitted to full Conference membership," the NCCSS executive committee approved the arrangement.[156] The limits of the Progressive community were clear even in its own house. In March 1924 Poteat presided over the interracial committee's meeting at the annual gathering of the NCCSS.[157] However, many members of the NCCSS opposed this arrangement: "there was opposition, misunderstandings as to the status of this group, difficulty experienced in scheduling meetings, etc., for a number of years."[158] These problems could only have hindered the effectiveness of the commission during the twenties, but the organization accomplished at least one tangible gain for blacks. In 1930 the state Supreme Court ruled—in a case that the commission had carried on for several years—that bus companies in the state could not refuse, as some wanted, to transport blacks (though a separate but equal status was of course acceptable).[159] Poteat apparently headed the state group as late as the 1926 meeting, but at some point before the 1928 gathering, perhaps too occupied with other challenges, he handed the reins of the state commission over to Walter C. Jackson of Greensboro.[160]

Poteat held an optimistic view of the state's racial situation in the early twenties. He believed that the limited concession of including the black elite in a Progressive community had worked: "I am happy to believe that the relations of the races in our State are exceptionally favorable. To the maintenance and extension of these relations the intelligence and the conscience of our citizenship are committed. . . . I dare to believe that we shall come thro[ugh] at length to permanent social peace, cooperation and an uncompromised racial integrity."[161] He continued to support his ideas with the authority of science, arguing in an address at a black school that "the racial varieties must be preserved for the good of a race depends upon its integrity. Race mixing is detrimental to the races themselves."[162] As he would later make clear, he felt that the breakdown of segregation would lead to social interchange and eventually a debilitating mixing of black and white blood. Through his report on social service to the Baptist State Convention in 1922, though, Poteat got that group to endorse the activities of the inter-racial commission.[163]

Further, he denounced the revived Ku Klux Klan in no uncertain terms: "The K.K.K. with its fe-fau-fum, mumbo-jumbo, thirteenth century mummery is an insult to the intelligence of the time, and an out-and-out slap at the existing apparatus of justice." Poteat verified that "its appeal to religious and racial prejudice marks it unchristian in its very principles," and he described it "as violating fundamental principles of American democracy and therefore threatening the security of social institutions the Klan proposes to protect."[164] To Poteat, the Klan's terrorism endangered not only racial harmony but also social order, both core values in the reform impulse. The Klan was antithetical to the carefully reconstructed Progressive community that mediated race relations.

As in virtually every Progressive organization, women were an active part of the Commission on Interracial Cooperation. Poteat seldom explicitly discussed the role of women in society, but in 1913 he depicted social reform as a particularly male endeavor. He posited that "Jesus' program of social regeneration makes special appeal to men, to their inbred fighting instinct." He explained, "Men love to fight evils, to attack problems. They are won by the Christ of a bold and daring leadership, who calls them to heroic and dangerous tasks." In contrast, "the religion of women is a religion of tender personal attachment" to "a suffering Savior of infinite love and sacrifice." In a South where manliness was a powerful ideal, Christian social reform had to be justified as a manly undertaking. Poteat's view seems to have changed after World War I. Once suffrage was won and the postwar tumult began, he welcomed the opportunity of working with devout women reformers. In 1923, as many women pondered what approach they should take in exercising their right to vote and participate fully in politics, Poteat called for them to bring their so-called superior morality—a traditional attribute that at times had previously isolated women in the home or on a pedestal—into the community on behalf of reform. He opposed a separate party for women, indicating, "I see no necessity in women having a political party. I do not think they should be a distinct sect, but, their sex should sprinkle over, as it were, and like silver, melt into the copper and thus improve the alloy."[165] Even though his own wife seems to have pursued only such activities outside the home as missionary groups and literary clubs, Poteat had no trouble imagining women as an active part of an interdependent Progressive community battling the postwar crisis.

World War I and the social change of the period also brought the climax of another Progressive cause—the fight for Prohibition. On this issue, Poteat sought to turn Progressive sentiment into social policy, mandatory even for transgressors who rejected the morals of the reform community. In the South reformers had battled for temperance and Prohibition since the antebellum period, and beginning in the 1880s the crusade for Prohibition was the campaign that premiered the methods used by activists for the whole variety of Progressive causes. Poteat had taken an active role on behalf of Prohibition as early as the failed state referendum on the issue in 1881. He was one of the speakers at a rally in Yanceyville in July 1881 and was "digging away at Prohibition."[166] Not until 1903 did North Carolina pass statewide Prohibition legislation, a ban on the sale of alcohol in rural areas. In July 1903 Poteat served the North Carolina Anti-Saloon League as a member "of a committee on law enforcement to make [the new law] more effective."[167]

Throughout the Progressive Era he continued to hold his belief regarding this issue that "good men" should "combine for righteous causes."[168] After the voters of North Carolina extended Prohibition to the cities in 1908, Poteat and others pressed constantly for strict enforcement and a national amendment. In 1914 he was appointed by the Baptist State Convention to travel to the national capital "in the interest of temperance legislation," and along with James Cannon of Virginia and the head of the national Anti-Saloon League, Poteat was among the most active, if unsuccessful, proponents of submitting the proposed constitutional amendment on Prohibition to the states for ratification. In January 1915 he was among the main speakers at the meeting of the North Carolina Anti-Saloon League.[169] At the 1915 meeting of the state's Baptists, Poteat presented a report on social service that labeled alcohol "one of the two most gigantic evils of modern times" and celebrated that "every organization and agency for the uplift of humanity unites in saying that the saloon must go."[170]

While he had supported Prohibition his whole life, Poteat took a much more active role during and after the war. On January 16, 1917, at its biennial convention that featured a speech by William Jennings Bryan, the Anti-Saloon League elected Poteat president. Poteat expressed his optimism to the convention, recognizing recent victories in various states but urging delegates to push for national legislation. He criticized current laws, though, that allowed small quantities of beer and alcohol to be procured: "The ground of our hope is the growing intelligence of the people. That intelligence will see the absurdity of such comp[rom]ises, and it will not be much longer in bringing all the people into practical co-operation to record in law the moral judgment of the community." He elaborated, "Society is impossible except on the understanding that its interests are paramount. The individual must surrender his liberty when the common good requires it. . . . The moral judgment and the intelligence of the community has [sic] outlawed the use of alcohol, and individuals who feel differently must of necessity and right submit to the will of the majority." Even more importantly, at issue was the health of future generations as well, Poteat pointed out, for "defective" children often resulted from alcoholic parents.[171] In an interdependent society, current immoral practices had ramifications not only for the living but for future generations. With that understanding of the stakes, the coercive nature of Prohibition laws did not bother Poteat. He was excluding from his imagined community an antisocial element that did not deserve membership.

Calling the manufacture of alcohol "moral and economic barbarism," Poteat took his message to the legislature as well in 1917, lobbying for strengthening of state laws to outlaw public drinking and drunkenness, advertising of liquor, and the transportation of liquor. He argued that allowing limited drinking in the state was an attempt "to appease a remnant of its perverted and decadent manhood." Reformers denied "the right of [a] tippling and drunken minority of our citizenship to set its standards and dictate its laws." Instead, the legislature should "dissolve the partnership of [the] State with the mother of inefficiency, poverty, and crime."[172] The effects of alcohol could not be isolated to the individual drinker, thus the evil had to stop.

Poteat worked with equal intensity after the ratification of the Eighteenth Amendment in 1919. As part of the league's legislative committee he pressured the legislature until it ratified the amendment, and he pushed unsuccessfully for the creation of laws that would have formed the office of Prohibition commissioner and allowed the removal of officials who did not enforce Prohibition. He served as president of the state Anti-Saloon League until 1923, including presiding at its 1921 meeting focusing on law enforcement; he helped to raise funds for the national effort by speaking in Tarheel churches; and he was appointed by the governor as a delegate from North Carolina to the International Congress against Alcoholism in Washington, D.C., in September 1920. He authored a resolution in support of Prohibition at the 1920 Baptist State Convention, as well. Continued advocacy was necessary, however. Not until 1923 did North Carolina strengthen its state laws to the point of being in accord with the national legislation.[173]

Even after relinquishing the presidency after 1923, Poteat remained active with the league. He headed its board of trustees in 1924 and 1925 and remained on the board throughout the twenties and early thirties.[174] In the context of what Poteat considered society's individualistic fragmentation after the war, alcohol's threat to society remained alive to him even after the passage of the Prohibition amendment: "The plain man, the average citizen, is the problem. If he is intelligent, social-minded, efficient, the group of which he is a member will be efficient and may be trusted with [the] largest democracy. If ignorant and debauched, no power can save democracy from anarchy and disintegration." Therefore, he concluded, "to make democracy safe, there must be compulsory education and compulsory abstinence from alcohol." He acknowledged that such laws take away from individual liberty, but he identified restrictions by the majority as "the essence of democracy" because "uncontrolled individualism is anarchy," the utmost breakdown of social unity and cooperation. In 1927 he echoed these sentiments to the Women's Christian Temperance Union convening in Raleigh: "Personal interest must yield to community interest, for no type of society is possible except on condition of its supremacy."[175]

Advocates of Progressive reform developed their goals of harmony and efficiency to an intellectual climax in dealing with a perceived decline in the population's mental ability, which they perceived to be an even broader social crisis than race relations or the use of alcohol. Both before, and more intensely after, the war, Poteat and other reformers believed that they saw an overall weakening of the mental capabilities of North Carolina's population.

Through heredity, such a trend would strew disorder and problems not only through their own generation but into future ones as well. Finding a solution to this problem would be the ultimate Progressive achievement because it would force society to recognize its links to the future as well as to other groups in the present. First, however, there was the question of what to do with the alarming (to reformers) number of mentally incompetent persons in the present. Just as the interracial commission had a significant relationship with the NCCSS and often overlapped in membership, several of the founders of the NCCSS also had important roles in the founding and early governance of an important organization through which Tarheels sought to influence social policy regarding insanity.

In a decade when the perception of a threat from mental disease was widespread across the country, the North Carolina Society for Mental Hygiene grew out of a conference on mental hygiene that was held in Raleigh from November 28 to December 3, 1913, under the sponsorship of the National Committee for Mental Hygiene. Poteat addressed the gathering at its closing session on the topic of "Americanitis." The founding meeting of the society was held in Raleigh the following day, a little over a year after the NCCSS was conceived, and shortly before the state opened one of the South's first institutions for the care of the feebleminded in July 1914. Though concern about supposedly declining mental capacity was widespread among the region's Progressives, North Carolina was the first southern state that had a committee on mental hygiene, and its members adopted the constitution and by-laws of an older Connecticut branch of the national group. The society's stated objectives were "the conservation of mental health" and "to help raise the standards of care for those suffering from mental disease or defect and those in danger of developing nervous or mental disorder." Poteat was elected to the board of directors at an organizational meeting on February 14, 1914.[176]

Similar to the NCCSS, in odd-numbered years the Society for Mental Hygiene scheduled its annual one-day meeting to coincide with the legislative session and conducted its program sessions in the evening in the state capitol to encourage legislators as well as the general public to attend.[177] After its organizational meeting, the society apparently met only four times, 1915, 1916, 1917, and 1921. Representatives of various state hospitals reported on their work, the group encouraged an educational campaign on mental hygiene in the eastern part of the state, and speakers exhorted the audience to a greater awareness of mental illness.[178] In January 1915 Poteat addressed the annual meeting in the chamber of the House of Representatives, harshly criticizing the historical tendency of Christianity to believe "that mental disease is caused by Satanic influence" and thus to punish the ill, rather than acknowledging them as part of the social web. "I find it hard to forgive them," he said, "Let us hope that God does not." He cautioned his audience to search out in themselves remnants of such medieval superstition. He closed, though, with an emphasis on education and religion: "If it be granted that, with the progress of knowledge, selective breeding may in the distant future be relied upon to weed out the inharmonious and inefficient factors in the life of the group, the fundamental demand for individual training would still remain; the fit social material provided by selective breeding would require to be brought up to the level of social efficiency by that artificial moulding of character and habits which we call education." He stressed, though, that it must be "the right education, or as may be said for clearness' sake, education plus religion."[179]

In January 1917 the members of the Society for Mental Hygiene elected Poteat president (within a week of his selection as president of the state's Anti-Saloon League).[180] In an acceptance speech, Poteat identified "an actual increase of insanity among us. It is due to the intense life conditions which prevail, to dissipation and drugs, to the continued absence of restraint by law or public sentiment upon the marriage eligibility of defectives." "Diversional therapy," or a strategy of preoccupying the patient with activities in "the field of the patient's dominant interest," offered the best possibilty for recovery but required extensive resources. He posited that, in view of the fact that inadequate facilities forced the state's hospitals to regularly turn away people needing care, the society and the state should focus upon the care of those known to be insane, rescuing them from confinement "in common jails under the care of ignorant and sometimes brutal men. . . ."[181] In January 1921 Poteat presided over the annual meeting and was re-elected president of the society, but the organization then lapsed until being re-formed in 1936.[182]

From caring for the insane, it was but a short intellectual step for Poteat to begin advocating ways to eliminate this disease that weakened the organic community. As with Prohibition, eugenics was an old interest that gained new importance for him following the war. He had closely followed the scientific debates about development and heredity beginning at least with his work at Woods Hole in 1893. In 1902 he hinted that advances in science gave "hope of some actual improvement in the race itself, in its substance and texture over and above the enhancing of its physical well-being."[183] At the YMCA retreat at Blue Ridge, North Carolina, he gave a week-long summer course on "The Physical Basis of Eugenics" in 1914, a class on "Eugenics and Sex Education" in 1916, and a two-week course on eugenics in 1920 and again in 1924.[184]

By 1914 he had developed an understanding that heredity, environment, and activity were the three controlling factors in human life, and he had an extremely optimistic view of their interaction in North Carolina. On heredity, he noted that North Carolina produced a large crop of white children "of a vigorous strain, now pure-bred and native." The various original immigrant groups "are now blended into one North Carolina type, sterling, self-reliant, frank, conservatively progressive, with one-fourth of one percent of foreign birth. Such a racial inheritance explains this splendid spectacle, is winning rapidly the prosperity and moral dignity of the State, and enriching all the currents of the national life." His almost chauvinistic paean about North Carolina praised the environment as well: "The wholesome conditions of the open country call out our inherited capacities, save us from the taint of artificiality, and conserve the native vigor which would wear down under the excitements of city life." The result was a spate of activity in the state with "a strong tide [that] is setting away from individualism toward collectivism." He continued, "Witness the rapid development of public opinion and public conscience on sanitation; corn clubs, canning clubs, and other associations for the heightened efficiency and happiness of country life; the growing co-operation of the churches in the practical ministry to the needs of men and in the common fight against all the enemies of human life." His conclusion was optimistic—"These modern Fates, weaving from month to month and year to year the web of destiny for North Carolina, look for all the world like three Graces under vows to enhance the beauty, the joy, and the strength of our beloved State for all coming days."[185]

By 1921, the turbulent reassertion of conflict and individualism over cooperation led Poteat to express less optimism about the racial future of whites without eugenic assistance. He sought particularly to interest other educators in his ideas, devoting both of his presidential addresses to the Southern Baptist Education Association to the themes of heredity and eugenics. His three factors became environment, training, and heredity, and his understanding of them became more subtle as he blended his social beliefs more thoroughly with science. Heredity he singled out as "of the greatest importance" of the three because it set the limits beyond which "no intelligence or assiduity of training, no passion of ambition, is ever able to transport us." He complained, "There has been a conspiracy of silence on this fundamental matter by all the agencies of enlightenment—the home, the school, the press, the church." However, "we have seen the peril of feeble-mindedness and insanity multiplying under the cloak of silence. . . . Probably 8 per cent of us are a burden on the back of the rest of us." As a result, "the progressive degeneracy of the race from mismatings and anomalies in early sex life presented a dangerous possibility before which no social convention could stand."

The new, more open discussion of eugenics had increased awareness of its implications for social development, Poteat believed, but "nevertheless, our knowledge is yet too limited and public sentiment too unfavorable and hostile for the practical application of what is known as positive Eugenics, that is, selective mating of the fittest for race improvement. We cannot go too fast. But there can be no doubt that we are ready for the application of negative eugenics, that is, restrictive mating for the elimination of the obviously unfit." His enumeration of groups to be eliminated revealed the implications of reimagining a whole society: "The feeble-minded, the insane, the epileptic, the inebriate, the congenital defective of any type, and the victim of chronic contagious diseases ought to be denied the opportunity of perpetuating their kind to the inevitable deterioration of the race." Though Poteat seldom outlined specific methods, presumably marriage restrictions or sterilization were to be the means of eliminating these categories of people. He easily blended science and religion in support of his beliefs: "the standard man," Poteat's goal, "will be well born, well conditioned, well trained, but also born again."[186]

The outline of his ideal community had grown considerably more confining in hopes of alleviating postwar upheaval.

In his 1923 presidential address to the same assembly, Poteat extended his earlier ideas and revealed his underlying fears more clearly. He asserted, "Levels of intellectual capacity in children, above which they cannot develop, are correlated with the social status of parents, that is to say, children of superior social status show the highest mental levels, children of unskilled laborers the lowest." His conclusion from that statement demonstrates the bias of Poteat and southern Christian Progressives. Rather than using that assertion to advocate improvements in the living conditions of laborers, Poteat went on to say, "In other words, the upper social strata contain a larger percentage of persons of superior natural endowments than the lower strata. Station is determined by capacity." This natural, hierarchical viewpoint carried Poteat further, "It is an easy and logical step from family traits to racial traits. . . . The inborn capacity for intellectual growth is possessed by different races of men in different degrees."

The change and unrest in society following World War I brought about much of Poteat's disquiet. "The most unreasoning and confirmed optimist will admit the menace of the present social situation," he warned, "There is widespread personal discontent and distress." Further, the harmony that Progressive legislation sought to create had disappeared; "the old antagonisms of the social classes and of the nations are reasserting themselves after their suppression in the common heroisms of the World War. Standards of conduct with the highest sanction are flouted. . . . Organized groups of men [such as the KKK] are taking the law in their own hands and with the avowed purpose of protecting our ordered society are in reality, perhaps unwittingly, digging into its foundations." He resorted to dire Victorian language that had virtually disappeared from his prewar declarations: "Civilization itself . . . is already tumbling about our ears." His estimate of those constituting a social burden had risen in only two years from 8 percent to "something like 10 per cent," and he envisioned no improvement because at the current birthrates "1,000 graduates of Harvard will have 50 descendants 200 years hence, whereas 1,000 Roumanians in Boston will have 100,000. Now, the enemies of society are recruited from this rapidly increasing lower section of the population. . . ."

His only solution was eugenics; by "assigning to each grade of ascertained intelligence tasks within its capacity and eliminating by negative eugenics the lowest 10 per cent, we should attain a degree of social efficiency and reduce individual maladjustment and distress to a minimum quite impossible on the present hap-hazard policy or want of policy." In short, tests that "scientifically ascertained" intelligence revealed that "a percentage of the population is handed to us as of too low mental capacity to participate in the privileges and activities of our social life." The fascist implications of this line of thought are revealed in Poteat's handwritten notes on a clipping of the address—"over-production of under-men," who would constitute a drain on everyone in a society that had to care for them. Poteat especially encouraged his audience of Baptist educators to take up their "heavy obligation" and "mould public opinion and, what is more important, public sentiment, on these fundamental matters."[187] That Progressive assumptions could lead directly to such a blatant disregard for the humanity of one in every ten persons is an indictment of the elitist groundings of Poteat's whole strand of liberal reform proposals.

Two themes united Poteat's diverse Progressive desires. All his goals grew out of a social Christianity in which individual believers were to apply Christian precepts to social questions in the pursuit of an earthly kingdom of God. Second, his method of bringing about change centered on changing public opinion, a variant of the evangelical missionary impulse. From education to reform of the press, from race relations to eugenics, Poteat's plan was to influence political and social decision-making indirectly. All issues had a moral base, and all social wrongs had a moral root, in Poteat's vision. Thus the key to change was a Christian public opinion. Poteat's widespread popularity and the constant calls for his leadership indicates substantial agreement on his goals and strategy among Progressive reformers. Almost every campaign or group that Poteat aided linked reforms to religious ideas or organizations, and oratory, discussion, and lecturing to the public and to state legislators were for many Tarheel activists the accepted ways of increasing awareness and accomplishing change. Nonetheless, assessing the concrete results of a reform strategy aimed at changing public opinion is difficult, as historian William A. Link has shown, for widespread public backlash against coercive measures of almost every kind undermined the effectiveness of a number of Progressive causes throughout the teens and twenties.[188]

By the mid-1920s, Poteat's imagined and eagerly anticipated community had broadened only a little beyond the citizenry that he originally envisioned in the 1890s—white, educated, at least partially modernized, and socially-minded religious liberals. He had admitted in addition only upstanding white women, elite blacks, and potentially other moral nations. Acknowledging interdependence with inferiors meant recognizing a degree of dependence on them, and Poteat's own elitism and individualism made that impossible. They had to be uplifted. However, he had a growing and ironic fear that the individualistic assertiveness of those inferior groups (blacks, the immoral, labor, etc.) following the war threatened the idea of harmony in an interdependent society, and he reacted by proposing further legal mandates to recreate the social bonds of a peaceful community. His vision was reaching its breaking point because it required more and more coercion, yet he still believed that only the religious conversion of individuals would provide a strong base for society. His Progressive concept of community began to stumble in the twenties; the intellectual climate of the thirties would finish it off and replace it by approving the political conflict of divisive interest groups. Throughout all the tumult of the era, however, Poteat labored diligently to educate the Baptist youth of North Carolina. The one hope he always sustained was that a cultured and religious leadership could bring into being the new community to replace the lost island worlds of the nineteenth century.

4

Wrestling New South Education

✠

Following the Civil War, one group of southern leaders advocated that the South should overcome its postbellum devastation by reconciling with the North and recognizing and exploiting its own rich resources. In their program, scientific techniques and diversification would improve agriculture, and industrial development would process the South's agricultural products and mineral riches and bring wealth to the region. Northern capital and skilled labor would be induced to move South to help implement this vision, which historians have labeled the New South Creed. The prosperity and regional salvation promised in the doctrine came to pass only in myths created by the advocates of economic development, but a significant degree of industrialization—especially in areas such as the North Carolina Piedmont—and urbanization driven by business interests did occur.[1]

Education was a major part of the creed of progress. Increased support for public schools would help to provide a larger portion of the population with the basic skills needed in industrial towns and cities. Further, the switch from locally controlled schools, with ungraded classes that emphasized oral interaction (the so-called one-room schools), to graded schools enmeshed in a rational, state-level bureaucracy, represented a crucial way of introducing the standardization and hierarchy required in the competitive world of business. New South boosters expected higher education in particular to contribute to their program of economic advancement in several ways: professional education of teachers for the graded schools, education and experimentation in scientific agriculture, and technical and engineering instruction. Public universities would be of practical service to the state by directing or supporting various Progressive reforms such as efficient government and good roads, changes that would aid economic development.

Many in North Carolina embraced the new ideas. The state spawned several prominent New South promoters, including Daniel Augustus Tompkins, Walter Hines Page, Josephus Daniels, and members of Raleigh's Watauga Club. In higher learning the exhortation for the spread of modern, practical education in the Tarheel State was led by Edwin A. Alderman, James

Y. Joyner, and Charles D. McIver. All were graduates of the University of North Carolina, which had been reorganized in the 1870s, moving away from the classical curriculum and widening its appeal to a growing middle class of professionals. These changes, along with the opening of the state agricultural and mechanical college in 1889 in Raleigh and a state normal school for women in 1892 in Greensboro, placed North Carolina at the forefront of the changes in education in the New South.[2]

William Poteat staked out a complex position in regard to education and the New South. Throughout the Progressive Era, from the 1880s to the 1930s, he actively supported the spread of public schools and lobbied for additional funds to increase the quality of the facilities and instruction and to provide for longer terms. In a time of social upheaval he viewed education as a means of not only preparing for economic progress but also of ensuring that the mass of voters would avoid supporting such extremes as the Populist party or demagogic politicians and would turn instead to a rational, restrained leadership. The development of critical, independent thought through education would, he believed, foster all the Progressive goals. In regard to higher education, however, Poteat, along with a number of educators across the South, decisively rejected the arguments of the New South reformers. He criticized the eclipse of classical studies and the introduction of technical education and practical industrial training as a betrayal of the real liberal education needed for regional maturation and progress.[3]

By the turn of the century, with more than two decades of classroom experience and years of lobbying for public schools behind him, Poteat's beliefs about education were largely fixed. However, his greatest opportunities for enacting and propagating those convictions lay in the future. From 1905 until 1927 he served as president of Wake Forest College. Given the extensive respect and deference accorded college presidents in this era, Poteat had a bully pulpit of wide influence, especially within the Baptist denomination that supported his growing college. He seized every opportunity to criticize the materialistic motives and intellectual inadequacy of New South educational reform and to propose an alternative course centered around liberal learning and religious tutelage. His path for the region's higher education emphasized the pursuit of culture, which in part he defined in the terms of English social and literary critic Matthew Arnold. Ironically, though, during Poteat's tenure as head of Wake Forest, the college continued trends initiated by Poteat's predecessor and in many ways evolved toward the ideal that Poteat loathed: specialized professional education. Compromises were necessary in wrestling with the New South proponents for the character of the region's future.

A Philosophy of Denominational Education

In 1885, at the height of industrial boosterism and the lobbying for technical and industrial colleges, Poteat announced his discontent with prevailing trends. He did not oppose material progress as such, for "there is wisdom and hope in this turn of the popular mind, that is, if it keep within proper channels and stop short of extremes." However, he expressed alarm "to hear in these practical and money-loving times the demand that education shall be made practical." Poteat recognized that "for the mastery of the details of any profession or calling, one must serve a sort of apprenticeship," whether it be studying plowing with a farmer or medicine at a medical school. All alike needed "the mental power to grasp those details when presented and so relate them as to evolve the highest success," and for this, Poteat argued, a broader curriculum needed to be retained. He asserted that even the most abstract learning is directed toward some end and that, regardless of intended vocation or profession, students should receive direction toward both moral and intellectual goals. Knowledge should do more than add "to a miser's hoard"; it should instead develop "the character and mind." Practical instruction could later provide vocational skills, "but let this industrial training keep its place and preserve its true relations to education; it is a supplement, not a substitute."[4]

Poteat's early objections to utilitarian schooling drew upon both religious and social concerns. Most markedly, the raw materialism of the New South repelled him on moral grounds. He could "conceive of the man of the future as 'specialized' into a wonderfully successful money-making machine, but he will be mostly machine, with small wisdom or righteousness" to supplement the wealth. In addition, Poteat's dawning Progressive ideology dictated in the 1880s that he consider the effects that a radical change in education would have on social and civic efficiency. "Man is more than the profession," he reminded educators, "He is a citizen under civic obligations; father of a family under the numerous and grave responsibilities of parenthood; a being possessed of intellectual and spiritual activities and sensibilities." In sum, "industrial training fits a man for his calling, but it does not fit a man for life."[5] Without the broader understanding that Poteat felt a traditional education delivered, citizens would become simply representatives of their profession, self-interested and ignorant obstacles to the greater good and civic harmony.

Denominational higher education required a steady supply of students with high school training, leading Poteat to support both state public schools and Baptist high schools. During the 1890s and early 1900s Baptist churches and associations opened over two dozen preparatory schools in the state, but, after the passage in 1905 of a proposal to create a system of state-supported high schools, their importance gradually faded. Initially Poteat did not see state high schools as a threat to the denominational academies, indicating in 1912 to the Central Baptist Association that such institutions faced "no peril from the multiplication of the rural high schools" because "for the high school period we have been unwilling as a people to trust our children to the secular guidance of the State." Even after the decline of Baptist high schools became apparent, Poteat still encouraged the spread of free public education as an aid to "the social and political efficiency of the State. . . ." As in the 1890s, though, he argued that state appropriations should focus on primary and secondary education, rather than pouring money into state universities that served "less than five per cent of the population" even in 1912.[6] Throughout his administration Poteat and other Baptists worked, as the occasion arose, against major bond issues for state higher education on the grounds that such funding favored the small minority of youth who actually attended college and neglected public primary and secondary schools serving all young North Carolinians.[7]

Poteat conceived of the relationship between the state and the cultural and religious training of denominational colleges as a mutually beneficial one. If the state would avoid creating unfair competition through overly generous appropriations for public higher education, Poteat believed, the church colleges could help social stability. The strengthening of denominational education represented the only hope for social improvement in a time that he perceived as growing more secular and materialistic yet also more democratic (for whites at least) and individualistic. Institutions such as the agricultural and mechanical college in Raleigh could aid the state's economic progress. However, they could offer nothing to counter the "social emergency" that had developed in part because "material prosperity" had caused "the elevation of sense over soul and the materialization of life." The denominational colleges in contrast stood "for the supremacy of the world of ideas and ideals as against the dominion of selfish and material aims," and as such they would "join hands" with state schools "in the common struggle against ignorance and inefficiency and in the common endeavor to serve the brightening future of North Carolina." The "right education for the New South" as a whole included economic progress and cultural development, as well as religious training. For Poteat, Wake Forest College had much to offer.[8]

Throughout the 1890s Poteat continued to speak out against purely technical or vocational training, even for black students and educators. In 1895 Booker T. Washington of the Tuskegee Institute made his influential appeal to fellow blacks to stress industrial training and to concentrate on economic progress rather than pursuing political equality. White New South boosters in turn could envision little beyond practical training for blacks in their idealized region; the place of blacks in the burgeoning order could only be as subordinate laborers in agriculture and industry.[9] Though Poteat never questioned the rigid segregation that also marked New South "progress," he urgently encouraged blacks to seek full intellectual development within their own institutions rather than simply asking for job training. To the teachers and students of Shaw University in Raleigh in 1896 Poteat powerfully reiterated that education does not "consist in the knowledge of how to make a living." It should instead produce "the man of liberal culture" marked by such characteristics as self-control and devotion to the truth.[10] The encouragement of broad intellectual strivings among blacks represented Poteat's ultimate assessment of the bankruptcy of New South educational ideas, while stretching to somewhat broader limits the dominant southern prejudices about education and race.

Beginning in 1895 Poteat began to construct his own philosophy of education in place of the regional orthodoxy he rejected, and the liberal culture he recommended at Shaw lay at the heart of his ideas. He recorded with pleasure that at Wake Forest "little heed . . . has been paid to the current cry of 'the practical,' and the idea of culture retains its supremacy." He lamented the inflexibility of education: it "ought never to have been systematized" because, like theology, its "formal organization" could not adapt to the fast-moving times, instead becoming "a burden and hindrance to the new life with whose development it has not kept pace."[11] The pursuit of culture as the goal of education would equip students with a more flexible, vigorous capacity to cope with changing times, and the development of mental discipline would aid in every profession and situation.

To explain the role of culture, he turned to an old favorite for him as for many other intellectuals in the region, Matthew Arnold. "Culture is hard to define," Poteat complained. Nonetheless, he endeavored at length to do so:

> Mr. Matthew Arnold . . . will probably be of most service to us here. He has given several definitions. For example, culture is 'knowledge of the best that has been thought and said in the world.' Again, 'The ability to see things as they really are.' The last is better, for it recognizes the truth that culture is not so much acquirement as power; and this is more clearly said by him in another place: 'It implies not only knowledge but right tact and delicacy of judgment forming themselves by knowledge.' . . . Culture is not mass of information so much as a state of mind; not quantity of learning, but quality of spirit and taste which has ripened on the use of it. For our present purpose we may say that it is the sum of the factors of the intellectual life,—a mental tone and quality, point of view, attitude.

From the beginning, Poteat conceived of culture as the province of the intellectual elite, stating "that the culture of a given period is to be sought in the leaders of its thought." Others "merely serve to show which way the leaders have gone."[12]

Most of these definitions are in a single work by Arnold. His superlative statement on the theme, *Culture and Anarchy*, was published in 1869 at a time when conservative English intellectuals felt under siege. They had witnessed with some fear the extension of the vote in 1867 to many working-class men and identified the time as one of moral disintegration and cheap sensationalism in literature and journalism. *Culture and Anarchy*, Arnold's major foray into social criticism, labeled and bitingly censured aristocratic "Barbarians," materialistic middle-class "Philistines," and the rough and illogical "Populace" for all failing to seek reason and perfection, the pursuit that characterizes men of culture. Instead, the only arbiters of conduct in his time were either individual desire or narrow religious constraints, and general intelligence dissolved in the mediocrity of momentary passions. Only the adoption of culture, or "sweetness and light," as the general goal could restore a lasting and disinterested center of authority and guard against the "anarchy" that Arnold perceived threatening England. Then, according to Arnold, the English would draw from the best intellectual ideas of the world to critique and correct the shortcomings of their own society.[13] Though some objected to Arnold's fulminations against religion, his work received great praise from intellectuals in the American South in the late nineteenth and early twentieth centuries, both for its sanctioning of critical investigation and its conservative defense of social order.[14]

Poteat turned to Arnold at a time of unrest in the South that bore many suggestive resemblances to Arnold's England of the 1860s. Fear of the masses aroused by the Populist party inspired many Progressives to action, and Poteat, like many others, perceived the decade as one of sensationalism and moral decay. Poteat continued to draw on Arnold's ideas the rest of his life as inspiration for his educational program. Over the decades, he returned frequently to *Culture and Anarchy* for definitions of culture, but he did not accept all that the English critic expounded. For Poteat, culture was no panacea alone: "Mere collegiate training . . . cannot of itself purify politics and right our social wrongs. It may, indeed, but equip the forces of evil with a sharper intelligence and a higher efficiency. Culture is no safe-guard against anarchy, for it does not touch the root out of which anarchy springs."[15] Arnold had condemned "Hebraism" as the tendency of religions to emphasize narrow moral conduct above devotion to intellectual development and contrasted that tendency with "Hellenism," or open pursuit of knowledge and intellectual insight.[16] In seeking to root out the foundations of the social disharmony that delineated anarchy, Poteat rejected Arnold's Hellenism as an adequate solution. Rather, "anarchy and all social distresses" were "expressions of *moral evil*" and required moral training for their solution. He explained, "It is 'Hebraism'—not 'Hellenism'—which can in any way modify and restrain" anarchic social tensions.[17] To be an intellectual in the evangelical South meant that one virtually had to confront religion in evaluating any intellectual pronouncement. In Poteat's case, he read widely and was willing to examine and consider even the most heretical of authors; however, he adopted only those thoughts to which he could imaginatively reattach religion.

The constant tension between Poteat's rejection of Arnold's disdain for religion and his admiration of Arnold's social outlook with its fear of disorder in society permeates a remarkable series of talks that Poteat delivered as baccalaureate addresses during his presidency of Wake Forest. At each commencement, just before dismissing the new graduates, he spoke briefly to the students for a final time. Beginning in 1908, his third year in office, he titled each address "Culture and ———," filling the blank with whatever significant theme he felt appropriate to the year. Some were general, such as "happiness," while others confronted topics of more immediate interest—"crisis," "kultur," and "internationalism," for example. Arnold frequently and explicitly appeared as the reigning spirit, but Poteat always added the religious component. While still president, Poteat began to seek a publisher for the growing stack of speeches and continued to do so unsuccessfully after his retirement. They were published only posthumously, as *Youth and Culture,* in a collection that also included his 1905 inaugural speech. The maintenance of the theme through the turbulent years between 1905 and 1927 indicates the adaptability with which Poteat applied his unchanging moral concepts and demonstrates the robust protean capacity of southern Victorian thought. As he wrote of the talks in his preface, "They present the reaction of a fairly intelligent man to the changing intellectual interests of the two decades covered by them, and taken together they provide an authentic cross-section of this tumultuous and pregnant period."[18]

"The Christian College in the Modern World," his inaugural address on December 7, 1905, set the tone for Poteat's presidency. Outlining his rationale for the importance of denominational higher education, he closely linked the college to Christian Progressivism. He always professed that the reform of society that would bring the kingdom of God on earth had to operate through individuals, rather than through the involvement of the organized church in politics. In education he discerned the beginning point of "the regeneration of the social unit"—the individual—that would lead to "the salvation of organized humanity, the creation of a just society." He elaborated, "Christianity supplies motive, education supplies efficiency." As a result, "the Christian college stands side by side with the Christian ministry as an agency for the realization of all social good."[19] The college, "guardian of the culture of mankind," would motivate the students by the power of example. "Character is the teacher's crowning achievement," Poteat announced, and "the moulding, cultural agency is not the teaching, but the teacher, in whom the highest demand is manhood and inspirational power."[20] Manhood in this context involved self-control and reverence in a modern world distinguished by its "very knowing," "disillusioned," "self-seeking," and "crude" lack of restraint.[21]

Poteat's formal inauguration—the first such ceremony ever conducted by Wake Forest College—celebrated the school's coming of age under Taylor and looked forward to future improvement under Poteat. Held in conjunction with the Baptist State Convention, the event "witnessed the most notable assemblage of Baptists ever held in this State," according to one reporter. The crowd included Poteat's mother; his brother Edwin, the president of Furman University, gave the invocation; and son Hubert played the organ. After Governor Robert B. Glenn heralded the importance of denominational education, Henry Louis Smith, president of Davidson College, spoke as the representative of the denominational colleges of the state, and George H. Denny, president of Washington and Lee University, expressed the congratulations of higher education in general. Their vision of education made clear that Poteat did not stand alone in his aversion to the New South Creed's emphasis on practicality. Smith lamented that a "rushing flood of mammon-worship has sprung up a new cult in the South—the worship of Success," with the result that "the old cultural education . . . is giving place to technical training" dominated by public institutions. The "Christian colleges of liberal culture are the hope of the South," he concluded, "against this muddy tide of luxury, frivolity, and shallow money-worship. . . ." Denny also looked to denominational colleges for "the education that subordinates material gain to the integrity of moral character that the country most needs at this hour."[22] From his illustrious audience and fellow educators in classical and denominational colleges, Poteat could expect agreement with his belief in liberal learning.

The disinterestedness that Poteat praised as the motive for Progressive reform also marked the person of culture in his definition. He elaborated in various baccalaureate orations that culture brought "freedom from prejudice and provincialism, a wide expansiveness of sympathies." It imposed "a lofty, unselfish life ideal," and its adherents could never be "exclusive, sectarian, or partisan" because broad understanding would lead to tolerance of other viewpoints.[23] Poteat especially emphasized these notions during the patriotic fervor of World War I and the immediate postwar years and during conservative anti-evolutionists' attacks on himself and Wake Forest during the 1920s. Speaking on patriotism in 1916, he urged that the reaction of college graduates to "the new world of jostling sovereignties" should be "a tolerance and sympathy which are the fruit of knowledge of men and things." The war strengthened a fear of "barbarism," in Poteat's language, a word often used by nineteenth-century Victorians, as he condemned the intolerance of barbarians, presumably in Germany. Culture would work to chasten nationalism and prevent its decay into hatred.[24] Poteat particularly criticized German education, contrasting culture with *kultur*. Germany and its atrocities offered him an example of what could happen when the state completely harnessed education toward self-serving ends and removed the Christian element from it. Vocational training reflected "the German ideal of economic efficiency," Poteat argued, turning the European war to his advantage in his continuing battle with the New South spokesmen. He applied similar concepts in 1923, in the midst of discord among Baptists regarding the teaching of evolution: "Culture recognizes not only the fact and legitimacy of other views, but also the limitations which beset its own." Even under attack, though, he remained the uplifter, noting that "the responsibility of tolerance lies with those who have the wider vision."[25]

Poteat's idea of higher education was distinctly meritocratic, in line with the Progressive emphasis on efficiency and accomplishment, and the beneficiaries of college training faced the obligation of leading a hierarchical but supposedly unified society. Poteat considered the Progressive Era to be a time of rising democracy, which he defined as "the spirit of fraternity and justice." Democracy was too dear "to sacrifice . . . on the altar of culture," but that was not necessary, in Poteat's view, because "the modern college is the most democratic of social institutions." Especially at a small college like Wake Forest, "recognition on other grounds than those of merit of personal worth" was not possible. Further, culture, like democracy, aimed at the perfection of virtue and character. Reflecting his concern that public opinion guided democracy, Poteat sought to position college graduates as a breakwater against the tides of bad decision-making: "The responsibility to guide and correct this king of the new democracy falls heavily upon you and those who share with you the privilege of college education." The direction of public affairs was a "natural" path for those trained in the liberal arts: "Culture is the call to leadership; Christian culture to the leadership of the forces of righteousness." However, leadership was "not a prize, but a burden, not so much a distinction as an opportunity."[26] To the graduates Poteat dictated a form of noblesse oblige with a Christian twist—a prime motive for the uplift associated with Progressive social initiatives. The fulfilling of these obligations would constitute a Christian manhood.

The "sweetness and light" of Arnold's culture fused seamlessly with the Christian imagery of Christ and light in the college seal as well as the goals of Wake Forest College. In 1908 Poteat and his predecessor as president, Charles E. Taylor, designed the seal at the request of the board of trustees. They asked Poteat's sister Ida, professor of art at the Baptist University for Women, to draw their ideas in final form, and the insignia was adopted enthusiastically. Poteat felt the emblem accurately depicted the mission of the school: "The symbolism of its seal represents correctly its ideal and aim. In the center of [the] seal is the Greek monogram of *Christ* from which issue rays of light. The words *pro humanitate* are inscribed below. The meaning is apparent. Christ is the light of [the] world and Wake Forest College is an agency in its dissemination for the benefit of mankind." Poteat was fond of quoting a newspaper report from 1834, just weeks after the opening of Wake Forest Institute, that noted with anticipation, "They have kindled a light in the Wake Forest Institute that I trust will soon shed its beams over the whole State." He liked "to think of the founding of Wake Forest College under that figure" and rejoiced that in its early years the institution had "knitted inextricably its culture in with the Divine purpose, so that no diversity of interests and no multiplicity of external contacts of after time might cloud its loyalty to [Christ] or divert it from its primary mission of service in His Kingdom." As his presidency of the college closed in 1927, Poteat felt sure that "its early purpose is unspent, undiverted, altho[ugh] we are come into a new world."[27] In his theory Arnold's Hebraism and Hellenism worked in harmony to spread illumination, and the changing currents of the New South had flowed past the Wake Forest lighthouse without undermining its mission of Christian culture. The reality was somewhat more complicated.

The Presidency of Wake Forest

The Wake Forest College that Poteat headed beginning in 1905 was a very different place than when he had arrived there in the 1870s. The single building of his student years was just one of six by the end of Poteat's first session as president, with a seventh under contruction.[28] The five professors and one tutor with six "schools" in 1872 had become in 1905–6 a faculty of twenty-seven men—sixteen professors (plus the director of physical education) working in sixteen "schools," with the aid of one associate professor and nine student assistants.[29] On taking the office of president, Poteat inherited a college that, in his assessment, had been "modernized" by his predecessor. Taylor remained at Wake Forest as a close friend of Poteat and a fellow member of the faculty, but Poteat rapidly assumed full leadership of the changing institution. Despite opposition, Charles E. Taylor had created schools of law and medicine, and in 1900 he had added a school of pedagogy that would become increasingly important as the state's system of public education expanded.[30] Before stepping down, Taylor had laid the groundwork for the college to prosper in the twentieth century and had been rewarded by a record enrollment of 328 in 1903–4.[31] New South ideals of progress had already begun to creep into Wake Forest.

In Poteat's twenty-two years as president, Wake Forest reaped the benefits of Taylor's foresight and of the system of public high schools that New South boosters formed in North Carolina. Secondary schools and relative prosperity for some in the region created a rising pool of young men seeking college education, and Wake Forest provided opportunities for the growing middle class to acquire professional skills in law, medicine, and teaching as well as to pursue a more traditional education for careers as ministers or journalists. Attendance boomed. A record 345 students enrolled in Poteat's first year, and with the exception of the disruption of World War I, records were approached or set virtually every year thereafter. Enrollment topped 500 in 1915–16 and 1916–17 and resumed a rapid rise after the war, reaching an unprecedented total of more than 740 students in 1926–27, in Poteat's last regular session as president.[32] The number of graduates increased more than proportionately, from 41 in Taylor's last year to 131 in the final graduating class of Poteat's administration.[33]

The rapid growth of Wake Forest forced Poteat to surrender part of his devotion to the careful nurture of Christian culture. He failed to raise enough new endowment funding to keep pace with the need for income. As the number of students climbed, the college could not expand the faculty fast enough to maintain the same level of close individual attention and moral guidance for students. Poteat had to create the beginning of an impersonal administrative bureaucracy to handle the mounting management and business requirements. Also, the demand for professional education in teaching, law, and medicine expanded specialized training at Wake Forest, and Poteat pragmatically conceded part of the curriculum to career preparation. Student life evolved away from cultural edification; the literary societies gave ground to a distinctly nonintellectual emphasis on athletics and fraternities. Chapel services concomitantly declined in importance. Though Wake Forest remained staunchly Baptist, the gap between the theory and practice of Christian culture only widened over the two decades of Poteat's presidency.

The arrangement of the curriculum changed little over Poteat's twenty-two years in office, but demands placed on teaching personnel heightened.

The college's sixteen schools of instruction in 1905 fell to fifteen departments and professional schools by 1927. Over the years moral philosophy became the department of psychology and philosophy; political science broadened to social science with the addition of sociology and the division of political economy into government and economics; and "applied" mathematics with its pre-engineering emphasis joined "pure" mathematics in a single department.[34] The offerings in virtually every subject expanded and diversified, however, and a more rationalized system of faculty rank became necessary as more departments began to require multiple professors. The school of medicine went from two teachers to five between 1904–5 and 1926–27, while in the same period the school of law expanded from one to three. The increasing popularity of medicine also necessitated in part more faculty to teach the prerequisites in the science departments. Nonetheless, the expansion of the faculty did not keep pace with the enlarged enrollment. The total number of professors in 1926–27 was thirty-one, aided by nine instructors and student assistants. The ratio of students to professors grew worse, from eighteen students per professor (full, associate, or assistant) in 1904–5 to twenty-four students each in 1926–27. More teaching duties became the responsibility of poorly qualified instructors and student assistants.[35]

The degree programs also evolved relatively slowly during most of Poteat's administration, but one major alteration early in his leadership reveals Poteat's coming to terms with so-called practical training in colleges. In a revision of degree requirements in 1910, he compromised his belief that all four years of college should be directed toward liberal learning. In doing so he curtailed "the chaos of the elective system" that for more than a decade had given Wake Forest students almost complete freedom in choosing their last two years of coursework. Like colleges throughout the nation, Wake Forest had turned to the elective system as a way of making the transition from a classical curriculum to one that included many new subjects in the sciences and social sciences. In the first decade of the twentieth century, however, many schools were seeking to return order to the new and broader curriculum by creating systematic requirements for core courses and arranging elective courses into loose groups. Some leading colleges took the next step and created a system of majors and minors, but Poteat was not prepared for that level of specialization. In March 1909 he proposed to the faculty a "scheme for the reorganization of higher education" that would adjust the degrees "more vitally to the new complexion and content" needed for modern life. Two years of liberal arts classes remained mandatory, and Poteat tried to bring order to the second two years by creating eight groups of electives that would begin training the students for a career, with the expectation that students would then enter a professional school or otherwise seek additional career training. He proposed groupings for medicine, engineering, letters, education, ministry, law, business, and government and diplomacy, but the faculty modified part of his plan. The scheme ultimately published in 1910 left law as a separate three-year course; guided B.S. candidates toward general science, engineering, or medicine; and required B.A. students to select letters, civics, ministry, or education.[36]

If the diversity and specialization of the times meant that students could not pursue the traditional curriculum, Poteat felt that guidance toward career goals at least was superior to unlimited choice by immature youth. He explained to the trustees that often in the past a graduate had "passed out of college into life to discover that he had been occupied with intellectual pursuits more or less remote from the interests to which he must henceforward devote himself." The elective system had only relaxed "the severity of the old standards" while "dissipating in numerous superficialties [sic] the solid attainments" that the B.A. represented. His proposal, Poteat contended, would allow for choices to "be controlled and directed into channels" that would lead into a career, and he added hopefully that the vocational groupings did not represent any "loss of culture value" despite being clustered toward a practical end.[37] This compromise solution endured until 1929–30 with only minor variations, such as the addition of commerce as an option in 1920–21 and the temporary elimination of the B.S. from the catalog from 1916–17 until 1922–23 (in favor of awarding all the career paths except law as B.A. degrees). Well after Poteat stepped down, the scheme was replaced by an even more utilitarian system of majors and minors.[38] The flow of New South notions seeped into Wake Forest's curriculum, but only gradually.

Poteat had initially opposed the medical school on the grounds "that the sphere of Wake Forest was the sphere of liberal culture, the making of men, not specialists."[39] However, he quickly softened his opposition to professional training at Wake Forest. In 1907 he informed the trustees in regard to the schools of law and medicine, "While the original introduction of these subjects appeared to be an invasion of the College ideal by the professionalism of the university, they have found a place—not forced it—in the strictly college degrees, and have amply justified themselves by their fruits." The law courses were open to all the undergraduates, and the faculty allowed some credit in law to count as electives toward other undergraduate programs. The classwork for medicine, Poteat convinced himself early in his administration, was "only semi-professional" and "was strictly an extension of the pure science work already offered." As such, medical courses were allowed as elective credit toward B.S. degrees in medicine.[40] In 1914 he congratulated the law school on its twentieth anniversary, noting that it had "given the College the opportunity to impress its moral and intellectual standards upon the State in a way quite impossible otherwise."[41] In his own evolving vision, professional training became in some ways a slightly more specialized sort of Christian culture in service of humanity and was incorporated into Poteat's compromised overall understanding of education at Wake Forest.

Equally directly, the creation of a summer school represented, like the professional schools, a recognition of the need for practical skills in the New South. The faculty briefly and unsuccessfully tried a summer school in the 1890s, and the law school had from its inception offered summer study. Not until 1921, however, did the college again offer a full-scale summer session, and the rebirth resulted directly from the triumph of the public education crusade launched by New South reformers. In 1919 the state superintendent of public instruction implemented a plan to improve the quality of teaching in public schools. Tarheel teachers thereafter needed certification from state officials, and the requirements included a minimum of college credit. The attendance at the summer school exploded from 195 (excluding law students) in the opening session to 637 in 1926 (excluding law students but including the students at a branch school operated by Wake Forest in New Bern beginning in 1925). Though general college courses were offered, teachers and their needs dominated the curriculum and the student body during the summer.[42]

As far as possible, Poteat diverted the invasion of another form of professional secular instruction at the college—military training—but during World War I he had no choice but to compromise for the sake of the college's survival. Militarism was a value antithetical to Poteat's mission for the creation of Christian culture, but he nonetheless welcomed a contingent of the Student Army Training Corps (SATC) at the campus in the fall of 1918, when enlistment and the draft swept away much of the regular student body. Poteat praised President Woodrow Wilson's call for all students not drafted to remain in college by echoing that acquiring a college education was patriotic preparation to serve the country. In 1917–18, even though enrollment fell by a quarter to 384, the faculty resisted the influence of "the propaganda of hate and militarism" on the minds of students. Nonetheless the faculty allowed drilling in military tactics to replace physical education classes. During the summer of 1918, as in many other colleges around the country, Wake Forest officials accepted the war department's plan of using colleges to train young soldiers, with the military controlling most of the curriculum. In return the government agreed to prevent "any financial loss attendant upon this patriotic service." Poteat tried initially to maintain the usual admission standards, but with the college's capacity still not full, the standards were lowered by order of the war department. Of 386 students registered in the fall, 246 belonged to the military units, with only 140 regular students, mostly ministerial hopefuls or below draft age.[43]

The SATC unit demobilized in mid-December 1918, and Poteat indicated that the faculty "rejoiced when the military regime was ended." He concluded, "The instruction of these soldiers was far from satisfactory, both in the conditions under which it was done and in the results which were achieved." Thus, when government officials inquired if the college wished to continue military training for students by establishing a unit of the Reserve Officers' Training Corps, Poteat sent "an unequivocal and emphatic 'No' . . . in reply." Enrollment fell slightly in the spring of 1919 as many of the military trainees left and some regular students returned, but in the next session the college renewed its growth. Poteat summarized, "For the time Wake Forest was military, but not militarized." As the trustees had decreed upon accepting the SATC unit, it was abolished as soon as the war ended with Poteat's enthusiastic support.[44] One professor remembered about military training, "President Poteat thought it out of place in a Christian college except in time of war. . . ."[45]

Poteat's newfound acceptance of the more traditional professional schools may have been quickened by the improvement under his watch of the liberal arts foundation prerequisite for entering the study of law or medicine. The bachelor of laws degree required only two years of work, with only a few courses outside law, when Poteat was inaugurated, but after his first year the degree required three years of study or two years and some summer classes. In the 1921–22 catalog a year of general liberal education was prescribed before beginning the three-year law course, and the requirement in the 1924–25 catalog extended that general study to two years.[46] In medicine, general requirements likewise became stricter under Poteat's guidance. Though students initially were allowed to take just the two years of medical study and then transfer without a degree to a four-year medical school, from the beginning of Poteat's term the students were encouraged to take two years of general preparation and treat the two years of medical courses as electives toward the B.S. By 1909–10 the medical school began requiring two years of study before starting medical classes and mandating the completion of a degree at the college before the professors of medicine would recommend the student for advanced standing at four-year medical schools. In the 1923–24 catalog the faculty extended from two years to three the requirement for most students for general classwork (in addition to the two years of medical tutelage) in order to earn the B.S. in medicine.[47]

The strengthening of undergraduate admissions requirements was a marked accomplishment of the Poteat years as well, and better high school preparation of the students may have allowed him to make peace with a more specialized orientation of part of the college course. In Poteat's first year, entering students had only to be fifteen years of age and to take examinations in various subjects to determine their ability. Any "conditions" upon their entrance—substandard knowledge of a particular subject—had to be removed by the end of their first year by taking sub-collegiate classes offered for that purpose.[48] At the beginning of Poteat's second year, he and the faculty rejected two applicants, sending them back to high school for further preparation. The entering students of that year had better overall preparation, and Poteat rejoiced that there were half as many in the preparatory Latin classes as the year before. This gave the faculty enough courage to raise the entrance requirements and to codify the minimum as fourteen units of high school work. Poteat recounted that "we find that we can insist upon our high entrance requirements without seriously limiting the work of the College for its larger constituency."[49] By May 1908 the college had eliminated two of the classes taught for unprepared students, and Poteat expressed pleasure that "some real progress has been recorded."[50] Educational opportunity had reached enough Baptist children through denominational academies and public high schools that Poteat felt at ease with the stronger requirements beginning to take hold at Wake Forest and many other southern schools. In 1916–17 the requirement was raised to fifteen units. However, not until the 1922–23 session did the college rigidly enforce the entrance requirements; until then some students entered with deficiencies that could be removed through sub-collegiate classes in their first year.[51] The observance of requirements, at first rhetorical and then in practice, represented the substantial recognition that in the New South, as well as the rest of the country, clear and rational guidelines were necessary in modern higher education.

As the demands on his office grew, Poteat found it necessary to create a more complex bureaucratic structure within his own administration. At the end of his second year, he verified that "the business of the College grows from year to year with the increase in its patronage." He asked the trustees to place the financial affairs of the college under the control of a full-time official, rather than having the professor of mathematics perform the duties with the help of a student. Accordingly, the trustees created the position of secretary and bursar.[52] One concrete result was the request by the bursar, approved by the trustees, to pay professors regular monthly checks, rather than irregular payments of varying amounts, even if it meant temporarily borrowing money to smooth cash flow.[53] The multiplying number of students also necessitated the creation of the position of dean in 1912. Poteat conceded that "certain of the duties of the President are incompatible with promptness of attention to the requirements of individual students." He believed it would "enhance the efficiency of the College throughout" to give a dean the responsibilities of discipline and solving the personal problems of students. The trustees obliged with the appointment of a part-time dean, one of the faculty who received slight extra compensation.[54]

Poteat's continuing need to carry a sometimes heavy teaching load necessitated the delegation of some administrative tasks to the dean. In his first year, despite an absence from college of nearly a month, Poteat continued as the only biology professor, probably leaning heavily on a recent graduate who served as his assistant while pursuing the master's degree. At the close of his first session Poteat asked the trustees to appoint an associate professor of biology, but they economized by appointing the assistant, with his new M.A., to be an instructor of biology.[55] (While it is amazing to the modern observer that a school with such limited resources offered graduate degrees, Wake Forest began to offer master's degrees shortly after the Civil War.) Over the next eight years the instructor "during much of that period conduct[ed] entirely all the courses except one" each year. In 1914 he requested a promotion. However, the trustees seem to have refused, and the overworked and underpaid young teacher left the department.[56] His successor as instructor was apparently a student, probably seeking the M.A. and compensated with college fees and a very small salary. To keep the department functioning with so little qualified help, Poteat taught two courses in 1915–16.[57]

Only gradually did his situation improve. In 1917–18 his teaching load in the understaffed department included three year-long classes, a situation he found "incompatible with so much of outside public work as it seemed wise to accept, incompatible also to a degree with the best discharge of administrative duties."[58] The appointment of an associate professor fell through, however, and Poteat had "nine hours of actual class work" the next spring term, rendering it "impossible to teach or to administer efficiently. . . ." The wartime uncertainty and financial stringency again prevented the appointment of an associate, and in 1919–20 Poteat "carried fifteen hours of scheduled class work in Biology throughout the session," probably an introductory course and advanced classes in botany and zoology with the instructor handling laboratory supervision. He asserted a bit more aggressively to the trustees, "This teaching load has restricted [my] public representation of the College and compromised the internal administration."[59] They obliged with the appointment of a young Ph.D. graduate from Princeton, who reduced Poteat's teaching load to one course at most. In Poteat's final three years, at least, he had no teaching duties; the trustees had finally acknowledged that the presidency was a full-time job.[60]

Poteat's constant travel, for both official purposes and social reform, hampered his teaching and also contributed to the need for subordinate administrators. Only his endless energy enabled Poteat to succeed as president. He maintained a very visible presence among everyone connected with the college—students, faculty, trustees, and the Baptists of North Carolina and the South. A typical period of his presidency in 1913 involved the following:

> The President of the College made an address before the Laymen's Missionary Convention at Chattanooga, Tenn., . . . February 6th . . . . He made an address before the North Carolina Conference for Social Service on . . . February 11th; at Chapel Hill, two addresses February 23d; at the Baptist Tabernacle, Raleigh, March 2d; before the Philosophers' Club, Danville, Va., on Heredity, March 4th; before Wilson Woman's Christian Temperance Union on Prohibition, March 9th; before the Bible Conference, First Baptist Church, Elizabeth City, two addresses, March 29th and 30th; before the Wake Forest Young Men's Christian Association on . . . April 7th; at the Warren County Educational Rally, April 12th; before the Young Men's Christian Association at Durham April 13th; at the banquet of the Young Men's Christian Association State Convention at Lynchburg, Va., April 18th; before the Southern Sociological Congress, Atlanta, on . . . April 26th, with an address at the Second Baptist Church of that city, April 27th; the Commencement address at the Liberty-Piedmont High School, May 2d; at the Baraca Union, Hartsville, S.C., and at Coker College, May 4th; the Commencement address at Mississippi College, Clinton, Miss., May 27th; the Commencement address at Carson and Newman College, Jefferson City, Tenn., May 29th; the Commencement address at Catawba College, Newton, N.C.,

June 4th. He attended the meeting of the Board of Trustees of the Southern Baptist Theological Seminary, May 14th, and of the Southern Baptist Convention at St. Louis, May 14–17. He is announced for three lectures at the Virginia Baptist Encampment, July 11–20, and for the Alabama Baptist Assembly, August 3–8.[61]

As Poteat wrote in 1906, "I go so far and see so much in a day, the day looks [like] a week." He reassured his wife in 1922, "Remember my love even if I seem so constantly away from yours."[62] One professor of the period, who later wrote the school's history, hinted that there was opposition to Poteat's frequent absences, but Poteat's deep religious need to evangelize through social reform activities, in addition to increasing the awareness of the school via more routine addresses, meant that he refused to cut back on any facet of his myriad interests.[63]

The college's financial well-being also required that Poteat be gone frequently and that a full-time and increasingly impersonal bureaucracy be present on campus. Poteat felt that wherever he was known, the reputation of the college spread as well and enhanced the likelihood of wider support for the college. The major challenges of his administration were to develop an endowment, campus facilities, and a faculty to match the explosive expansion of the student body. The school's annual budget swelled from $35,000 in 1904–5 to $220,000 in Poteat's last year.[64] To keep up with the ever-increasing need for income, Poteat worked from virtually the moment he entered office to raise endowment funds, a goal at least partially underlying his speeches within the state and many trips to court northern philanthropic organizations. Upon hearing from the Wake Forest trustees about the need for more money for the college, the Baptist State Convention resolved in December 1905 that the state's churches should raise $150,000 for the endowment, and by the following summer Poteat had negotiated a deal with the General Education Board, John D. Rockefeller's important philanthropy, to supply a fourth of the total if the other $112,500 was pledged from elsewhere by the end of 1907 (with payment due by the end of 1910).[65] A statewide canvass by Latin professor J.B. Carlyle resulted in the desired total in pledges, but a nationwide economic slowdown hindered collections. Even with an extension of the General Education Board's deadline to the end of 1911, the campaign netted only $117,798.56 for the endowment.[66]

For the remainder of Poteat's administration the college concentrated on raising funds from denominational sources, with supplements from the General Education Board. By 1915 the endowment had grown to $508,139.23 from $286,932.87 in 1905; however, another campaign was already in the planning stages.[67] In December 1913 the trustees recommended that the state's Baptist churches make education one of the objects of regular contributions, and they asked Poteat to contact the General Education Board about providing matching funds for a joint campaign to benefit all the denomination's colleges and high schools in the state. The convention agreed to recommend that churches place more emphasis on giving to education on a regular, budgeted basis. The new campaign took shape slowly. In May 1916 the trustees approved a fund-raising canvass to begin "at the earliest possible date," but apparently little was accomplished in the next year. In May 1917, though, the board endorsed the convention's plan for the Baptist schools and colleges of the state to raise a million dollars over four years, $300,000 of which would go to Wake Forest, and in December 1917 they again sent Poteat to ask the General Education Board to match donations from the canvass.[68] The proceeds of the movement were to go not only to endowment but also "for the adequate equipment and enlargement" of the schools.[69]

The state convention's education board launched the fund-raising in the midst of wartime uncertainty, and Poteat noted he had "put himself at the disposal of the management of the Million-Dollar Campaign for such service as he was able to render."[70] Under the direction of a Wake Forest professor, the campaign began in January 1918 with the cooperation of managers in each Baptist association across the state and the use of speakers, including Poteat, and conferences to publicize the cause—strategies long familiar to the denomination's educational fund-raisers. By November 1919, nearly $600,000 had been promised and over $248,000 in cash, bonds, and stamps from the government's wartime borrowing had been collected for the campaign. In May 1919 the state canvass was absorbed into a larger regional drive by the Southern Baptist Convention to raise $75 million over five years for all its objectives, $20 million of the total to go to Baptist educational institutions.[71]

Poteat followed the regional push closely and argued that North Carolina should perhaps retain the proceeds from the statewide canvass (or receive more than its initially budgeted amount in the larger campaign for education) because the statewide solicitation had already been underway. His participation in the Southern Baptist Educational Association, and beginning in January 1920 his presidency of the group, gave him wide acquaintance that aided in pressing the claim, and he helped to secure a favorable allotment for the state.[72] Poteat had optimistically projected that the $75 million crusade would add $600,000 to Wake Forest's endowment. However, the college's historian concluded that Wake Forest received $458,398.18 from the $75 million campaign and that only $143,280.63 of that (plus a supplement of $100,000 from the General Education Board) ever went into the endowment. The rest went to relieve a crisis that had been growing since the beginning of Poteat's administration.[73]

The spiraling numbers of students combined with the slow growth of the endowment created tremendous pressure on the facilities of the college and forced Poteat for a time to choose between an adequate faculty and decent physical accommodations for classes and students. The experience of his own understaffed department of biology exemplified the potential for decline in the quality of teaching. Through most of his presidency, Poteat insisted on devoting any newly found resources to enhancing faculty salaries or numbers, but he recognized the increasing pressure on buildings. Ultimately both facets of the college faced decline. The college provided no food services, and most of the students had to rent rooms in town because the college had only one dormitory in Poteat's early years as president. In the summer of 1907 the trustees began consideration of building a second, larger dormitory, but the delay of a major donation forced postponement. In the meantime the need of new accommodations for the growing law school became "more and more pressing." Finances simply were not there. Even with the growth in endowment from Poteat's first campaign, he reported in 1910 that "the financial situation of the College requires the further postponement of the appointment of a Professor of Mathematics" to aid the overworked instructor in that department. Not until 1909 did the college even invest the money necessary to procure electric lights.[74] By 1912, with 435 students registered and room for only 88 men on campus, the price of lodging in the village reached an "almost prohibitive" level, but it was the summer of 1913 before the construction of a new building, to be built by borrowed funds, began.[75]

With the completion of the new dormitory, the inadequate faculty and their low salaries took the forefront. Poteat pleaded in 1913 that the low salaries were "embarrassing in the extreme" and that too few professors already meant that "the classes in several of the departments are now too large for the best results in teaching." He recommended that an increase in salary take precedence over new hires, however, and the trustees followed his advice. The next year Poteat again called for higher salaries and more faculty, but the financial predicament worsened to the point that the college ran a deficit in 1914–15 for the first time in many years. In 1916 he recorded that "some classes have been too large for any of our lecture rooms, and the teaching force has been too small for the needed sectioning of classes." He warned the trustees that "the situation presents a clear alternative: more money, or no more students." The trustees responded by asking that, in the interest of economy in the face of deficits, professors teach more hours. The trustees recommended a total of from twenty to twenty-four in some humanities and mathematics classes and from fifteen to twenty in other disciplines, an increase from the twelve to twenty hours that most professors already taught.[76]

The decline in enrollment during the war temporarily relieved some of the overcrowding, but Poteat announced in 1918 that a major goal of the endowment campaign underway was to increase salaries. By 1919 the crisis atmosphere returned. Inflation had further eroded salaries, and both faculty and students had difficulty finding accommodations. The decision to increase salaries by 25 percent in 1919 and 20 percent in 1920 left little opportunity to meet the need for an addition to the chemistry laboratory or the building of homes for professors and a dormitory. As a result, for 1921–22 efforts at new construction were eliminated, several faculty vacancies went unfilled, and some professors found it necessary to teach subjects outside their departments. The continuing deficit even forced the rescinding of a portion of salaries.[77]

Even though inadequate dormitories and classrooms "seriously embarrassed" the college when the enrollment continued to increase, Poteat tried continually to keep the trustees focused on the faculty. He lectured them in 1920, "The main matter in all our schools is not buildings, important as buildings are, but men. Our primary need is not fine buildings, but fine men, and enough of them so that each student may come every day into vital contact with some inspiring personality, and paid enough to retain them against university raids and to get from them the full measure of their capacity."[78] These pronouncements fully accorded with Poteat's unwavering belief that personal cultivation of a student's character—the building of culture—took priority over any classroom attainments. Nonetheless, the physical plant could not be neglected forever, and the quality of education had slipped as the waves of students threatened to submerge the beleaguered faculty.

The number of students attending Wake Forest without paying tuition contributed to the lack of income. One direct response to the presence of state universities, the embodiment of New South ideals, was the creation of scholarships, with Poteat's support, for many Baptist academies and the extension of those to some state high schools. In order for Wake Forest to compete with the low cost of state-supported higher education, in Poteat's first year the trustees had already established scholarships for a top graduate of twenty-five high schools across the state, and thirteen of those students had taken advantage of the free education. Poteat approved of the scholarships for attracting the most able students and advocated that more be created. As the number of the state's high schools mushroomed so did requests for scholarships. In 1910 Poteat presented a number of such pleas with the comment that "the usual argument urged in support of these requests is that the other leading colleges of the State" had allowed them. By 1915 the trustees had approved seventy-four scholarships, more than any other college in the state, and decided not to approve any more for financial reasons. In Poteat's final year, the number had crept up only slightly, to eighty-one, though not all were used every year.[79] Further, ministers and the sons of ministers attended Wake Forest without paying tuition. Scholarships and tuition remission for clergymen and their sons meant that throughout Poteat's administration a substantial portion of the student body paid only fees. For example, tuition was waived for 46.8 percent of students registered in the spring of 1907 and 39.3 percent in the spring of 1920.[80] Maintaining the affordability of Christian culture was a costly drain on the college's finances.

Though the pressures of growth were not relieved before his retirement, several factors allowed Poteat to resolve the worst of the crisis during his last few years in office. In 1923 Poteat announced grandiose building plans for the next five years.[81] Despite the failure of this huge expansion of the college's facilities, significant progress occurred on enlarging the campus. First, portions of the money from the $75 million campaign went to repay an accumulated debt of over $82,000, to expand the chemistry laboratory, to build several homes for professors, to erect an expensive and much-needed heating plant, and to supplement current operating expenses, a temporary expedient. Clearing the debt allowed Wake Forest to meet the General Education Board's requirements and receive additional funding from them.[82] Poteat's second saviour in meeting the crisis appeared like a deus ex machina in 1923. Jabez A. Bostwick, the New York Baptist who at President Taylor's behest gave generously to the college in the 1880s and 1890s, died in 1921 and unexpectedly left a trust fund to the college. After two years of litigation, the college finally received a bequest with a market value of about $1.2 million. The college used the accrued interest of over $100,000 to build another dormitory, and the principal went into the endowment.[83] A third and smaller lifeline for the college came from Tarheel native and tobacco magnate Benjamin N. Duke. At the request of his friend J.W. Lynch (the Wake Forest pastor) and Poteat, in 1925 Duke gave shares valued at $150,000 for the endowment, which were supplemented by $75,000 from the General Education Board.[84] At the close of his administration, Poteat proudly reported an endowment of about $3 million.[85]

Poteat already saw in the near future an enrollment of a thousand students, and he cautioned the trustees that, even with the new funds, the school's income would not suffice. In 1924 he argued that despite the new dormitory the school was already stretched beyond capacity. Many departments faced "overcrowded conditions in laboratory and classroom equipment, and some seem to be suffering acutely, almost to the point of actual sacrifice in quality of the work accomplished." The following year he recommended that the trustees authorize the faculty to limit the size of the entering class and allow the college to "recover from the relative neglect into which certain features of our physical equipment have been allowed to fall in the interest of course and personnel." The trustees probably sought both income and size limitation when they raised tuition in March 1925.[86] Students sat on windowsills, and one class met in a hallway, Poteat reported to a potential donor that same year. He explained, "At Wake Forest the emphasis has long, perhaps too long, been placed on courses and personnel, so that educational standards have been maintained under the handicap of unfavorable conditions now hardly longer endurable."[87] In Poteat's last year, the college expanded the library, formerly a fire hazard, with the aid of alumni donations, but in his final communication to the trustees, he cautioned that "the primary need of the College is more income" and recommended that another $500,000 be sought for the endowment. The college required at the least a student center, more dormitory space, and an adequate gymnasium in order to keep up "with the current standards of educational equipment and efficiency and a constantly enlarging opportunity."[88] He left those problems to a younger successor.

Despite the difficulties of teaching, administering, traveling, and raising money, Poteat sought to keep in close touch with the students in order to contribute to the formation of their broader views beyond biology. He kept office hours to give students easy access, from 9:30 a.m. to 12:30 p.m. (apparently daily) in 1913–14, for example. When he was at the college, his duties included leading the daily chapel service, an occasion he used to exhort the students to cultivate moral character, reverence, moderation and self-control, and fidelity to duty and service. Though for a time he gave up teaching Sunday school "because my duties called me away from home so frequently," he taught a class for much of his time as president. Further, he "always welcomed the opportunity of speaking to a Y.M.C.A. audience" and was "an enthusiastic supporter" of the group on campus.[89]

Despite his efforts, student life at Wake Forest College inevitably changed with institutional growth. Personal guidance possible with a hundred men in Poteat's student days became less and less feasible. The intensive Christian cultivation and intellectual exchange required in Poteat's vision of culture became more difficult to achieve, even though he tried hard to maintain old standards of reverence. In his first year as president, the student body outgrew the small room in which morning chapel had been held for decades and moved into the larger hall used for church services. Throughout Poteat's administration, students were required to attend the morning services, lasting about twenty minutes each day except Sunday. As the student body grew, however, enforcement became more difficult. Poteat's own frequent absences often left the chapel service in the hands of the dean, and many faculty did not bother to attend. Further, in 1914 the faculty lifted the long-term requirement that students attend Sunday church service.[90]

The decline of the literary societies represented another instance in which the institution's growth and the changing expectations of students forced Poteat to modify his cherished ideas about the college and culture. During Poteat's administration, the Euzelian and Philomathesian societies—which had dominated the campus's social life almost from its formation—dramatically declined in significance. They were victims of the college's expansion. The faculty required that every student belong to one of the societies, and the students spent Friday nights and Saturday mornings in the obligatory meetings in their elaborate halls, debating, declaiming, or conducting business. The societies sponsored the student magazine and celebrated their creation with Anniversary Day ceremonies that were the highlight of each spring term. Poteat fondly recalled his days in the Euzelian society, and he considered the groups to be vital to the intellectual life of the campus. They were "at once the means and the center of culture" for the students, developing the "enthusiasm for the things of [the] mind which is the sign of our citizenship in the kingdom of culture."[91]

Their decline from the height of importance was gradual. Interest dampened as the growth in the number of students meant that more and more men were forced to become idle spectators in the debates and formal transaction of business that characterized society training. Senior speaking was the first event to be abandoned. In the late 1800s the requirement of public speeches by seniors had been dropped, with a short essay being an acceptable alternative and only selected speakers given the rostrum. In 1914 senior speaking was dropped altogether as a separate event and incorporated into Society Day, a fall occasion for a debate by selected underclassmen. Society Day soon became obsolete itself, however, because students with increasing transportation options took advantage of the cancellation of classes on that Friday or Monday to leave campus for an extended weekend. The increasing number of members had already forced the societies in 1896 to divide into two groups for debate, one debating on Friday as usual and the other on a different evening. However, this expedient failed to forestall the problem for long because each hall could only accommodate about a hundred persons. Enthusiasm waned during Poteat's term, especially during and after World War I, as lack of room made full participation impossible for many members despite their payment of the required fee for the support of the societies. In February 1922 the faculty made membership in the societies voluntary, and participation plummeted.[92]

In the campus social life, literary societies lost their preeminence to an institution that Poteat had fought for many years—fraternities. In 1882 the faculty and trustees had responded to an attempt by rebellious students to organize a chapter of the Kappa Alpha order by banning fraternities, but the issue periodically plagued the campus thereafter. In May 1903 Poteat and two other faculty members composed an investigating committee that ferreted out three groups, but the illegal organizations returned again the next year, possibly with the encouragement of one faculty member. For the year 1904–5 the trustees voted to give local fraternities a trial period, but in May 1905 they voted to outlaw them altogether. In his opening year as president, Poteat entered the continuing controversy. Fraternity members continued to "fight for supremacy on the Campus" and "were menacing the integrity and proper functioning of the Literary Societies," according to the college's historian. The battles continued in the 1906–7 session as well. Poteat complained that the *Raleigh News and Observer* had reported wrongly "that secret fraternities and hazing are rife in the College with the connivance of the Faculty." He acknowledged to a concerned Baptist "that these evils distress us from time to time," but he assured the college's constituency that the article was quite wrong. Nonetheless, the board of trustees in May 1907 called for the resignation of the faculty member involved and expressed thanks to the literary societies "for their active co-operation with the Trustees in suppressing fraternities."[93] Poteat's son Hubert, an instructor in the college and future national leader of the Masons, contributed to his father's problems by supporting the fraternities. Hubert avoided the trustees' censure that ended the employment of his friend and fellow faculty member, but Poteat let his son know that it was the first time Hubert had "disappointed" him.[94]

Despite strong proscriptions, fraternities returned as a problem in 1914 and again during and following World War I. Writing in the student newspaper in 1918, Poteat argued that fraternities violated "the Wake Forest spirit" in their tendency to "disintegrate the unity of the student body." On another occasion, he lashed out at fraternities in a speech before the Southern Baptist Education Association in January 1920. He opposed them on several grounds: they were "often unfavorable to scholarship," expensive, "unfavorable to the spirit and work of the literary societies," and undemocratic. Despite these objections, fraternities replaced literary societies as the focal point of student life. In May 1922, only months after membership in the literary societies became elective, the trustees authorized fraternities in the college as a way to provide an alternative social outlet for students and to help return order to a campus that had been troubled by discipline problems.[95]

In addition to fraternities, Poteat perceived undue interest in intercollegiate athletics as a second major enemy of the literary societies—and of culture—and once again culture lost ground. The appointment of a full-time athletic director in Taylor's final year had given athletics new momentum when Poteat took office. Basketball came to campus in 1905, and in 1908 students who had learned to love football in the new high schools pressured the trustees into allowing the return of the sport, prohibited since 1895. Intercollegiate teams were initially funded by athletic associations of students and alumni, but by 1914 a faculty committee assumed control because of increasing deficits. A mandatory athletic fee funded the teams beginning in 1915–16, and in 1921 the faculty and trustees took both full control and financial responsibility for the program.[96]

By 1912 Poteat decried the waxing importance of athletics. He contrasted the lagging expression of college spirit through literary societies and their "intellectual contests" with the vociferous support of athletics. In 1917 he spoke out not only against the "outrageous" cost of athletics but also the "excessive and disproportionate interest" in sports that actively involved very few of the students. He protested that "rivalry between competing colleges is so keen and the passion to win burns so hot that subterfuges, concealments, and positive misrepresentations sometimes form part of the staples of the athletic program of committees and coaches." This emphasis on winning, a moral problem to Poteat, sometimes became a discipline problem, as in 1916 when six of the college's students defaced walls and fences on Trinity College's campus with paint. Poteat disavowed to Trinity's president their "shameful and inexcusable" behavior and placed the athletic program on probation the remainder of the year. Poteat's dislike of the athletic distraction to learning is apparent even in his speech at the dedication in 1922 of an expensive athletic field built by a generous donor. He noted that some students considered "a college to be an athletic club with certain irritating appurtenances."[97]

Despite accepting the evolution of Wake Forest away from his stated vision of Christian culture, Poteat assured alumni and friends that the college maintained a close relationship with the Baptist denomination that gave it life. Throughout his presidency he worked on behalf of education at every level of Baptist organization. He had a leading role in the Wake Forest Baptist Church and believed that "no congregation can be quite so important as one composed largely of college students, who themselves extend and reproduce the preacher's thought and life as no other set of hearers can." He helped select pastors and supported the raising of an impressive church building on the campus border in 1913 and 1914. Poteat also served on the executive committee of the Central Baptist Association for nearly two decades, and at the state level he represented Wake Forest at virtually all state conventions. He continued to serve on Meredith College's board of trustees as well. In 1910 he addressed the Southern Baptist Convention with a significant report on non-theological education, and, further, he sat on the board of trustees of the Southern Baptist Theological Seminary from 1910 until the early 1930s.[98] He never wavered in the belief that education and Christianity belonged together.

The age of standardization in higher education made it more difficult for an institution to retain a unique and distinctive mission in the way that Poteat believed denominational colleges should represent liberal culture. Nonetheless he sought to maintain such a balance. He believed that "the strong college ought to be protected against the drag of the low standard of a weak college" through a process of accreditation. But he cautioned that "the responsibility of the college to its particular constituency is displaced by conformity to a common standard" if taken to extremes.[99] Typically, Poteat sought a compromise. Soon after Wake Forest entered the Association of Colleges and Secondary Schools of the Southern States, the region's foremost accrediting agency, in December 1921, Poteat began helping to articulate precepts for specifically Baptist accreditation. As a member of the executive committee of the Southern Baptist Convention's Commission on Promotion and Standardization, selected in June 1922, he helped to study Baptist colleges across the South and to recommend guidelines for a curriculum "unquestionably superior to those institutions which are not under Christian control." The commission created standards encouraging resources and quality equal to the mandates of the accepted accrediting agencies but stipulated further that teachers be Christian and that Christianity be encouraged among the students.[100]

Though Poteat never questioned Wake Forest's Baptist affiliation, the trustees guarded the relationship even more closely. They consistently refused to hire new faculty, even at Poteat's recommendation, unless the professor was a Baptist.[101] That devotion was not enough to satisfy the Baptist State Convention. Before the Civil War the convention had nominated and approved new members of the board of trustees, but after the war the board began selecting its own members except for one occasion in the 1880s. However, in 1912 W.C. Barrett, a minister from Gastonia, began arguing that the convention should elect the trustees of Wake Forest and Meredith Colleges in order to assure that the institutions did not adopt policies opposed by Baptists. Further, trustees should be required to be Baptist, elected for a limited term, and removable by the convention at any time. Poteat advanced several objections to the proposal. He asserted, "It is unwise to turn over to a popular assembly, all whose actions and discussions are public, the purely personal problem of determining the fitness of a man to be Trustee." He feared that nomination, possibly of an unfit man by "partial friends," would be tantamount to election because no one would feel free to offer criticism. Besides, "business men know that a limited number of men will act more prudently than a mass-meeting," and they might thus stop making contributions to the college. Proponents of the new plan pointed to the Baptists' slipping control of Brown, Rochester, Colgate, and Stetson Colleges. Undoubtedly, the example of Vanderbilt University also loomed large in everyone's minds in North Carolina. It was then engaged in a long war to free itself from the Methodist church, a skirmish begun when some conservative Methodists perceived that the chancellor and sympathetic trustees were seeking to loosen ties to the denomination in order to create a great nondenominational university.[102]

The convention passed a version of Barrett's plan "without a word of discussion and to the absolute satisfaction" of the delegates in a "singular and glorious tribute to the effectiveness of our Baptist democracy. . . ." Trustees were to be Baptist and elected by the board for a term of six years subject to the confirmation of the convention. The state General Assembly approved the changes to the college charter.[103] Poteat served his first fifteen years with little hint of public opposition to his administration, but the ease with which democratic Baptists swept aside his pleas for unfettered management of the college presaged a major conflict that dominated Poteat's final years as president.[104] Tarheel Baptists demanded greater control of an institution that they had been asked to fund for nearly a century. Strife among the president, the board, and state Baptists was only a matter of time and a confluence of issues.

5

Christianity, Enlightenment, and Baptist Democracy

✟

Between 1920 and 1927, conservative Baptists in North Carolina subjected William Poteat and Wake Forest College to a searching critical examination. Fearing that the college and Poteat in particular had fallen under the influence of modern liberal ideas, Tarheel Baptists demanded to know if Wake Forest was failing to guide their sons toward proper Christian conduct and understanding. In 1920, amid contrasting assumptions about who should direct Baptist colleges and worries about worldliness and slipping discipline at Wake Forest, fiery criticism began of Poteat's theological views. In the beginning, the issue was his interpretation of the atonement, but focus soon shifted to the teaching of evolution. For the next five years, Poteat had to fight to retain his position as head of the denomination's flagship college in North Carolina. His outspoken combination of Christian belief and scientific learning helped to pave the way for successful opposition to a state law that would have prohibited the teaching of evolution in the state-supported schools of North Carolina. Poteat became a symbol of academic freedom for surviving as an evolutionist in the South.[1]

In the 1920s the principle of academic freedom for college professors was in its infancy, and its very birth had depended upon assumptions that were not widespread among Baptists in the South. The discussion of Darwinism in the Northeast in the late nineteenth century resulted in the acceptance of new ideas about science, and this first bout of contention between evolution and traditional ideas had far-reaching results. As historians Richard Hofstadter and Walter P. Metzger conclude, "A 'new' rationale of academic freedom grew out of the Darwinian debate." Though pressure for the freedom of inquiry for teachers has a long history, the idea in its modern form required a recognition that an understanding of truth, like the idea of evolution, rested on a changing foundation, that "all beliefs are tentatively true or tentatively false, and only verifiable through a continuous process." As a result, to a certain extent differing viewpoints contained the potential for truth and had to be tolerated. This new ethic prescribed that ideas had to be open to the criticism of those most competent to evaluate their truthfulness: an academic's professionally trained, expert peers. Lack of expertise and "scientific competence" thus constituted the reason that untrained administrators, trustees, and the public should not limit the freedom of academic discussion. Aided by the formation of the American Association of University Professors in 1915, academic freedom slowly gained support in the 1920s in some parts of the country.[2]

Many North Carolinians accepted neither the modern view of science with its lack of absolute truth nor the claims that only experts could evaluate ideas such as educational policies and content. Therefore, even the proponents of free discussion of evolution in the colleges seldom advocated academic freedom, instead relying on appeals for a more general liberty of thought in pursuit of truth. Conservative Baptists framed the evolution controversy and other matters of college governance in republican terms.[3] They asserted their right to control the institution in which the denomination had a proprietary interest, both by appointing the trustees of Wake Forest and also by pressuring those trustees to implement the beliefs of the majority of the state's Baptists. Against that understanding, Poteat argued that the majority had no right to limit the pursuit of truth. In his own career Poteat did not emphasize professional research, and he had always cautioned against overspecialization and undue emphasis on professional training. Nonetheless, when under attack he revealed the extent to which his scientific knowledge and agitation for Progressive bureaucratic expansion had led him to a modern reliance on the authority of professionals. He expected Tarheel Baptists to respect academic freedom as encouraging the search for truth. Ultimately, Poteat retained his position not only because the trustees (though never most of the Baptist constituency) grudgingly began to accept the competence of scientific experts and the freedom of intellectual inquiry, but also, and more importantly, because his personal charm, his open Christian faith, and testimonies by alumni left no room for the criticism that he was undermining students' religious faith.

Initial Conservative Attacks, 1920–1922

In the late nineteenth century, liberal theologians in the North gradually developed an understanding of the Bible that incorporated higher criticism and scientific knowledge. Higher criticism was the application of German methods of historical investigation and literary criticism to the stories of the Bible. Critics questioned the dating, authorship, and literal authenticity of various books of the Bible and began to view it as a human document reflecting not timeless truth but the teachings of men embedded in the prejudices and challenges of particular times and places. Therefore, one could not take literally the portions of the Bible that conflicted with modern scientific knowledge unknown to the ancient writers. One result of this new perception of the Bible was the social gospel. Religious leaders concerned with the social problems of urban, industrial America discovered through the historical reading of the Bible, in the words of Walter Rauschenbusch, that originally "the essential purpose of Christianity was to transform human society into the kingdom of God by regenerating all human relations and reconstituting them in accordance with the will of God." Poteat closely followed all these developments, accepting a historical and nonliteral comprehension of the Bible and rhetorically at least partially following Rauschenbusch on the social role of Christianity.[4]

The introduction of evolution and higher criticism into theological debates initially caused little stir, but, as liberal theologians increasingly incorporated natural processes into explanations of events that the orthodox regarded as supernatural, conservatives rallied to the defense of older ideas. The flowering of social gospel notions among some clerics spurred conservative belief that the new theological viewpoint had introduced into spiritual matters an unacceptable level of human knowledge and control. Many conservatives rejected the idea that the kingdom of God could come on earth, a staple of the social gospel, adopting instead the premillennial belief that Jesus must return before the kingdom could arrive. Fundamentalism was a fragmented coalition of conservative Christians who opposed the liberal theological changes. The Fundamentalist movement began in the North, and its adherents organized their viewpoints in a series of twelve pamphlets issued between 1910 and 1915. Funded by two wealthy Californians, *The Fundamentals* were given direction by Amzi Clarence Dixon (1854–1925), who edited the first five of the dozen collections of articles. The elder brother of Thomas Dixon Jr., Dixon was a graduate of Wake Forest who had belonged to the Euzelian literary society during Poteat's first year as a member. Dixon had declined the presidency of Wake Forest in 1882 at age twenty-eight and had gone on to fame as a Baptist minister in New York, Boston, Chicago, and London.[5] In the unsettled intellectual atmosphere of the postbellum South, Poteat and Dixon chose quite different paths, and their viewpoints clashed in the twenties.

The Fundamentals concentrated largely on theological issues and addressed evolution only in a moderate way, indicating that some forms of evolution could be reconciled with the Bible. World War I then dramatically changed the tone of the debate between modernist theologians and Fundamentalists. The sense of instability, uncertainty, and social crisis that accompanied the years during and immediately after the war blended with theological concerns to add a new urgency and stridency to old battles. Many blamed materialistic thought, including higher criticism and evolution, for Germany's brutal willingness to wage war, and the optimism that characterized social gospel reform attempts seemed delusory. Conservatives sought to counter these teachings. In May 1919 premillennial Fundamentalists organized the World's Christian Fundamentals Association to bring together the uncoordinated followings of a number of prominent Fundamentalists. By 1920 an offensive of Bible conferences and speeches, including many by Dixon, had begun as a way of spreading the Fundamentalist message.[6]

In the South Fundamentalism initially gained few adherents because the targets of its attacks—higher criticism, evolution, and the social gospel—had relatively few followers in the region. A small but significant number of educated urban intellectuals accepted or flirted with the new ideas, but these liberal doctrines remained virtually devoid of influence among the vast majority of southern faithful. Poteat was among the few who adopted this unholy trinity to any appreciable extent. Conservative Christianity ruled so strongly in the South that the new aggressiveness, interdenominationalism, and central organization of the Fundamentalists were largely superfluous. However, many southern evangelicals, Baptists prominent among the number, agreed strongly that liberal ideas had no place in their denominations and were quite willing to investigate charges that heretical teachings had entered their schools. National Fundamentalist spokesmen toured the region enhancing awareness of the threat that liberal theology posed to traditional religion, and J. Frank Norris of Fort Worth, Texas, the only major southern leader of Fundamentalism in the twenties, generated a stream of invective that flooded across the region.[7]

Baptists in North Carolina faced the same challenges that troubled members of the Southern Baptist Convention throughout the region. In the unsettled days following the war, Baptists had reaffirmed their commitment to eschew ecumenical movements and by the end of 1919 had found affirmation in the successful pledge drive for their $75 million campaign. The denomination expected to combat the irreverence and materialism of the time by spreading Christianity to the world. Dissension shattered this optimism, however. Antagonism toward modernism, defined as liberal theological acceptance of evolution and higher criticism, caused controversy among Southern Baptists in various states, despite the fact that relatively few members of the denomination questioned narrow orthodoxy.[8]

The conservative fight against evolution and liberal heterodoxy erupted at a crucial moment, when the South was moving from a society characterized by local control and direct democracy to one guided by the authority of experts heading impersonal bureaucracies. The Progressive movement, with Poteat as one of its major figures in North Carolina, had scored many successes between 1880 and 1920. But as state bureaucracies attempted to implement such reforms as compulsory school attendance, Prohibition, and public health legislation, they discovered that the objects of reform, the masses of poor or rural residents, objected to any infringement of local control by outside experts.[9] In their activity in denominational affairs, many North Carolina Baptists revealed a similar animosity toward professional, expert guidance, and their endorsement of direct democracy resonated with traditional Baptist doctrines of local control and the primacy of the individual's understanding. Attempts to squelch the teaching of evolution blended antipathy to theological liberalism with a rejection of Progressive bureaucratic control of both church and state. Poteat received one of the opening blows of the attack on liberalism in the South and remained a central figure throughout the controversy. The assault occurred at a time when many Tarheel Baptists were refusing to acknowledge the right of professional educators or even appointed trustees to govern Wake Forest and were reacting against the imposition of bureaucratic standards in denominational education.

In North Carolina, committed members of all denominations fought against the teaching of evolution. Baptist attacks on Poteat opened the public conflict, but Methodists and most prominently Presbyterians fought the theory in public and denominational education for much of the 1920s. In regard to outlawing evolution in public education and requiring Bible study in the schools (another major issue in the early twenties), Baptists showed more restraint at times than the other major denominations because of the strength of their traditional reverence for the separation of church and state. Some Baptists consequently wavered in their support of proposed laws against teaching evolution in public schools when the bills came before the legislature in 1925 and 1927. However, most Baptists held their belief in direct democracy and local control to be equally sacred. Because the separation of church and state was not a factor in regard to their own institutions, their longtime beliefs prompted them to aggressively assert their control over their college and its head.

Poteat was "the most thoroughgoing Southern Baptist evolutionist in the 1920s," and the censure of his liberalism was among the "earliest charges" that conservatives leveled in breaking the denomination's solidarity after the war.[10] The initial criticisms, however, focused largely on theological questions other than evolution. Apparently in early 1920, D.F. King of Leaksville, North Carolina, reprinted in pamphlet form the address on behalf of the moral influence theory of the atonement that Poteat had made to the Baptist Congress two decades earlier. King widely distributed copies of the speech, taken without permission from the published proceedings of the meeting, to Baptists in North Carolina and other southern states.

The stir caused by King's action brought to the surface a layer of suspicion about Poteat's orthodoxy that had troubled some in the denomination since before Poteat's election as president of Wake Forest. Once King raised the issue, Livingston Johnson, editor of the *Biblical Recorder* and a longtime trustee of the college, admitted that the trustees had had similar questions before choosing Poteat as president. They had selected him only after Poteat presented a statement to the board members that satisfied their questions about his views on the atonement and other religious matters. As Johnson remarked, "Does any one . . . believe they would have voted to elect a man as president of Wake Forest whose soundness of faith was questionable, especially since the question had been raised and an investigation made?"[11] Not everyone was satisfied with Poteat, though. One writer noted in 1920 that he had entered the state around 1900 and had "heard the rumblings of discontent in the camp ever since" about Poteat's religious views.[12] King had privately voiced his displeasure during the endowment campaign in 1907, and in 1920 his anger apparently stemmed from a similar source of inspiration, the million dollar campaign launched the year before. King said that he "told the brethren I would not give anything while a Higher Critic was President of Wake Forest College" and had sent the trustees a copy of Poteat's address from 1900 in hope of inciting an investigation. Failing that, he distributed the pamphlets that brought the matter to the public attention.[13]

Thomas T. Martin, dean of the school of evangelism at Union University in Tennessee, received one of King's reprints. In January and February 1920 in the Baptists' *Louisville Western Recorder* and other denominational papers, he wrote three widely read articles assailing the "three fatal teachings" of Poteat. He launched the series with a blistering description of Poteat's published musings on the atonement as "but the Southern echoes from . . . Chicago University"—the academic center of much critical scholarship on the Bible and conservative shorthand for liberal heresy. Poteat's error, in Martin's argument, lay in seeing the death of Jesus as changing a man's attitude and convincing him to reject sin and to accept a welcoming God. Martin and other conservatives taught instead that the crucifixion served as a substitute payment to appease a stern God angered by the sins of man (the so-called substitutionary theory of the atonement). He worried that Poteat's influence would "contaminate the young men of Wake Forest and especially the young Baptist preachers who are educated there."[14] Martin continued to dissect the address from 1900 in his second article, contending that Poteat incorrectly portrayed God as the father of "unredeemed" sinners as well as of Christians. "This means the utter repudiation of the teaching of the Scriptures along this line," Martin contended, "and it is a fearful responsibility for North Carolina Baptists to keep President Poteat as president of Wake Forest, to thus poison the sons of those who support the college with their hard-earned money. . . ."[15]

Martin concluded the series with an early example of the conservative offensive on the teaching of evolution; the final piece focused on the theory's alleged German connections and blamed it for causing Germany to welcome the horror of war as an exercise in the survival of the fittest. He expanded his evidence beyond the single address by Poteat. In May 1915 Poteat delivered a series of talks at the Southwestern Baptist Theological Seminary in Fort Worth at which even he admitted at the time that he "talked pretty frankly about evolution" to the seminary students and faculty. Martin brought Poteat's visit to Texas to the attention of his readers and claimed that "so positive was he with his teachings of evolution that President [Lee Rutland] Scarborough of the seminary publicly repudiated the address."[16] In his final commentary Martin also featured a second tactic of conservative attempts to discredit liberalism, particularly evolution. Fully aware that the authority of science carried great weight in society, conservatives attempted to find and array in their support scientific objections to evolution. Martin quoted from "twenty-one really great scientists of the world" who had rejected the theory.[17]

In conclusion Martin penetratingly summarized the fears that animated conservative opposition to Poteat throughout the early twenties: "Every honest man knows that accepting evolution means the giving up of the inspiration of Genesis; and if the inspiration of Genesis is given up, the testimony of Jesus to the inspiration of the Scriptures goes with it; and if his testimony to the inspiration of the Scriptures is given up, his deity goes with it, and with that goes his being a real Redeemer and we are left without a Savior and in the darkness and in our sins." He went on to suggest the anti-bureaucratic solution that fiercely democratic and localistic conservatives repeatedly turned to during the controversy. He raised "a question of honor with President Poteat and men like him." The Tennessee evangelist explained, "They are supported by the hard-earned money of Baptists who gave the money for the purpose of propagating Baptist doctrines, Baptist teachings. The teachings of Baptists are well known. The money would never have been given to propagate the teachings of President Poteat. . . ." Therefore, Poteat was guilty of "a breach of trust, a misappropriation of funds," and "obtaining money under false pretenses."[18]

Perhaps because Martin's first two articles probing the talk from 1900 brought a counterattack from North Carolina's *Biblical Recorder,* the ensuing debate centered almost exclusively on the theory of the atonement rather than evolution, the issue that would later take the spotlight. Livingston Johnson, editor of that Baptist weekly, agreed from the outset with Martin that "Dr. Poteat made a great mistake in delivering that address," but he defended Poteat by arguing that the president's views had since changed. "His brethren should remember that he had not reached the mature conclusions on the great doctrine of the Atonement to which his subsequent study has led him," Johnson asserted. He quoted a comment by Poteat from the fall of 1919 that he was seeking to have a series of sermons at the college to "put under the feet of our boys at Wake Forest the fundamentals of the Christian faith—the Scriptures as the infallible rule of faith and practice, the deity, atoning work, and lordship of Christ, [and] personal regeneration which makes men new creatures in Christ Jesus." The editor concluded, "One can almost hear the crackling of the fagots as he reads the words by which [Martin] consigns to outer darkness Dr. Poteat and all who have ever sat at his feet and accepted his teachings."[19]

Poteat replied appreciatively in print the following week: "I am indebted to you . . . for your sympathetic representation of my attitude toward the fundamentals of our Christian faith. Of course, I accept the New Testament as the law of my life and the standard of my thinking. To find its meaning and to extend its power have been the business and joy of these forty years." With careful, evasive wording he sought to assure readers of his orthodoxy, indicating that "the mystery of His compassion and His redemption I do not understand, but to his sacrificial life and atoning death I look for the forgiveness of sin and the life eternal." He closed, "My savage critic doesn't know me, and that, I think, is why he raves. I think he has the same reliance I have, and I hope it sheds in him, when he is calm, the same great peace."[20] His calm, tolerant demeanor and unabashed faith were typical of Poteat's outlook. Privately, though, he saw some danger to his job, assuring his wife in late January, after the release of Martin's first article, that "we can make a living if they turn me out of my stewardship!"[21] His confidence returned only after he was "overwhelmed" by letters of support.[22]

Poteat's critics, King and Martin, pushed Poteat specifically to adopt the substitutionary theory of the atonement and to repudiate his early views, both of which his reply to them had studiously avoided. Martin demanded a level of logical rigor that Poteat had concluded decades before was not possible or desirable in matters of faith. He refused to state publicly, as he had found unnecessary to determine privately, a closely reasoned justification of his faith. He explained to his brother, "Things seem to be pressing me to adopt somebody's theory of the atonement, a thing which I do not feel disposed to do, for I don't think the New Testament has one. I prefer to leave the matter where Jesus left it,—the birth by the Spirit is like the mystery of the wind."[23] The *Biblical Recorder* stood by its belief that Poteat's statement that he looked to Jesus for atonement was a repudiation of his earlier views, and Poteat left it at that. Martin had no choice but to declare victory and move on, though he had the whole exchange printed as a pamphlet for free distribution.[24]

Many a lay reader wrote to the *Biblical Recorder* in the next several weeks. Using arguments that would reappear throughout the early twenties, nearly all asserted their right to control the school they had created and to demand that its employees teach Baptist doctrine. Though he urged restraint in the matter of Poteat, W.C. Barrett, leader of the move in 1912 to tighten the state convention's hold on Wake Forest, noted, "I believe that any man who holds a position in a denomination where his influence might affect the belief of the people ought to be ready at any time to make a clear statement of his belief on any point when questioned by persons who have a right to raise such questions."[25] In addition to debating issues that would continue to plague the denomination, this initial clash also revealed that Poteat had significant support. Though no one seconded his view of the atonement, several friends and alumni declared that their confidence in his character and Christian faith were enough to win him their backing, themes that reappeared in Poteat's defense until his retirement. One minister gushed typically, "All Wake Forest men, and all who know him, respect and love President Poteat for his sound Biblical views and his great life."[26]

Poteat's declaration of faith, despite its evasiveness, satisfied the moderate editor of the *Biblical Recorder* and apparently eased the worries of some of the more tolerant leaders within the denomination (some of whom were educated at Wake Forest). The controversy quieted by April 1920. Perhaps as a gesture of respect for conservative convictions, A.C. Dixon was selected as commencement speaker for June 1920. Dixon helped make rejection of evolution a primary test of orthodoxy among Fundamentalists.[27] Johnson praised his commencement address as "a great exposition of the most fundamental things of the Gospel" and "worth far more than the ornate essays on Social Service which are often palmed off on commencement occasions as Gospel sermons." Dixon spoke on "the menace of evolution," linking it to Nietzsche, Germany, and the World War. Further, he rejected evolution as a scientific "absurdity." His comprehension of science insisted on direct observation, a caricature of the scientific method that was problematic when applied to evolution and much of modern science. Dixon could not see a species evolve, thus he and other conservatives rejected it, confident that the believers in evolution were the ones practicing bad science. He elucidated, "Though I confess a repugnance to the idea that an ape or an ourangotang [*sic*] was my ancestor, I have been willing to accept the humiliating fact, if proved, but the more I have investigated, the more thoroughly I have been convinced that, if I am to be an evolutionist and thus keep up with the modern academic drift, I must refuse to let the gray matter of my brain work, while I permit others to do my thinking for me and accept their authority, not because of the reasons they give for their theory, but solely because of their eminence in the literary and educational world." At a banquet during commencement one trustee welcomed Dixon's viewpoint, indicating that it was the duty of the board of trustees "to see that the College is true to the doctrines of the New Testament, and that no German rationalism is taught within the College walls."[28] Though assured for the moment that the college was orthodox, that conception of the responsibility of Baptists toward the college did not disappear.

Despite the relative quiet by mid-1920 on the issue of religious unorthodoxy, assertions of popular control of educational policy continued on other topics. At the annual gathering of the Southern Baptist Convention in the summer of 1921, John E. White, a Wake Forest graduate and president of Anderson College in South Carolina, guided to adoption a resolution urging that Baptist colleges "should be kept executively independent and administratively free under the sole control of the Baptist bodies to which they belong. . . ." White crafted his resolution in opposition to Baptist schools becoming members of a regional accrediting body, the Association of Colleges and Secondary Schools of the Southern States. The previous fall the education board of the Baptist State Convention in North Carolina, under the direction of secretary Richard T. Vann, had recommended that Wake Forest and Meredith Colleges apply to join the association. White argued that the convention had approved the policy "without a word of discussion" and committed Baptist institutions to "a situation of helpless submission to the academic sovereignty of the Southern Association." White objected to placing "an outside power" in "an inside position between the denomination and its institution."[29]

In White's view, boards of trustees and college administrations should have no authority to decide whether their college joined a standardizing group. He contended, "In reaching such a decision . . . the conventions and the associations are to be trusted. . . . They are more likely to arrive at sound and inspiring policies of education than any small group of educational experts." He verified, "I am opposed to the absorption of the academic program of denominational colleges in any standardizing organization which has no place for the consideration of Christian ideals." Vann defended his board's recommendation against White's charges on the grounds of improving academic quality but took pains to assure Baptists that the Southern Association would not have control of their institutions. Poteat led Wake Forest into the Southern Association in December 1921. However, the agitation for more discussion and debate convinced him as president of the Southern Baptist Educational Association to organize the group's meeting that same month around the topic of standardization. At that conference, Rufus Weaver of Mercer University, also a Wake Forest graduate, introduced a resolution that led to the formation of a parallel Baptist accrediting body that he and Poteat helped to lead during the 1920s.[30]

In a spirit of watchfulness about the denomination's democracy, D.F. King briefly tried another direction of attack. He denounced Wake Forest for accepting money from the General Education Board despite the board's requirement that the funds not go to theological education. This too meant allowing outsiders and skeptics to "dictate to us how to run" the college.[31] White's and King's demands for more participation by Baptists in educational matters came at a time when many perceived their state convention becoming more bureaucratic and less open to democratic debate. The president of the group admitted in November 1921 that "the Convention has practically ceased to be a deliberative body and has become a mass meeting through which we must, from the nature of the case, rush many things about which we cannot stop to take time to consider so as to form a mature judgment as a result of the thinking of many of those present. We must, and do, trust many things to the wise judgment of our leaders."[32] In opposition to such a surrender to bureaucratization, moves to intervene in college administration represented in part an attempt to reinvigorate the democratic localism within the denomination that was slipping in favor of professional educators.

In the fall of 1921 an incident at Wake Forest led Baptists to perceive a need of further oversight of the school. Hazing of new students by upperclassmen had intermittently troubled the college, but it took a more serious turn that semester when the subject of an attempted hazing shot and wounded one of his assailants. At the court trial the college's part-time dean, a professor of law, pleaded for clemency for all involved. Soon thereafter, the same young man was again attacked, bound, his head shaved, and "nitrate of silver" placed on his bald pate. The incident made sensational headlines in a Raleigh paper, and the *Biblical Recorder* concluded, "Wake Forest has been disgraced, the denomination humiliated, and the State insulted!" Poteat scrambled to assure the denomination that the faculty actively opposed hazing and had worked closely with the students to suppress the evil, but editor Johnson did not back down from the inquisitiveness of the *Biblical Recorder.* He leveled a warning to the college, "If faculties cannot cope with the situation trustees may be forced to take a hand, as denominations hold the trustees ultimately responsible for the management of the colleges committed to their care." Another trustee also published letters of criticism, to which Hubert Poteat felt compelled to reply that the professors "do feel that we have the right to ask the friends of the institution to reserve judgment until all the evidence is in." Others censured the request for leniency for the attackers. After the end of the spring 1922 semester the board took steps to remedy the problem by approving the hiring of a dean to work full-time handling such problems as discipline and by accepting a new system of student government and rules of conduct that the faculty had initiated. The new rules included controversial provisions limiting the freedom of first-year students and requiring them to wear distinctive caps. Further, in hope of ending hazing and coopting disorder into a formal system capable of regulation, the trustees legalized fraternities.[33]

Not everyone in the state approved, and as in all the cases of college governance they exercised what they saw as their democratic right as Baptists to enter the issue. Throughout the summer of 1922 the deluge of letters to the denominational newspaper almost unanimously opposed the legalization of fraternities. One noted accusingly, "We have surrendered to the forces that have long been in rebellion against an established policy of the college, and against the principles for which Baptist churches and institutions have stood through all these years." The principles most often cited as in peril included democracy and unity, and critics felt that elitism, competition, debauchery, poor grades, increased expenses for poor students, the demise of the literary societies, and even dancing would surely follow. There were rumblings that Wake Forest was losing touch with "the common people." Livingston Johnson countered that the trustees by about a two-to-one margin "thought it better to have legalized fraternities rather than the outlaw affairs which have existed at the college for years." Other Baptists expressed outrage that trustees would surrender to the disorderly element rather than repress it, comparing the argument for fraternities to the pressure to repeal prohibition because of its imperfect enforcement. The new restrictions on entering students meant endorsing "the undemocratic discrimination between the old and new students by forcing the freshmen to wear distinctive garb, with other restrictions as a bribe to the sophomores not to haze them."[34]

Some called for a vote by the alumni or the denomination to decide the issue, and at least two churches and one association responded to a call that churches should express their will on the subject because they constituted "the final court of appeals for Baptist matters in the State." By the end of the summer, public pressure on the trustees forced them at a special meeting to rescind the limitations on freshmen and to state publicly their reasons for legalizing fraternities, though they refused to bow to the pressure to outlaw the groups again. They gave as their rationale the widespread national acceptance of fraternities and the need to have them in order to compete for students, motives of expediency that would hardly satisfy a constituency vigorously expressing its will and commitment to popular control. Antagonists continued to express opposition, and the topic was expected to be a contentious one at the Baptist State Convention in December 1922.[35] Conservatives had growing reason to doubt the responsiveness of the appointed trustees.

Even as critics expressed their belief in democratic control of the college on relatively local issues, the unrest between liberals and conservatives within the denomination increasingly crystallized around the teaching of evolution. On this subject some Baptists would later express most vociferously their dissatisfaction with Wake Forest. Though specific censure of Poteat ceased relatively quickly following Martin's articles, across North Carolina and the South antagonism toward evolution grew. Several nationally known evangelists, including Baxter F. McLendon, Mordecai F. Ham, and Billy Sunday, toured the state in the early twenties, and William Jennings Bryan's nationwide crusade against evolution influenced Tarheels. Further, the World's Christian Fundamentals Association held conferences in Raleigh in 1920, 1921, and 1922 that attracted national Fundamentalist figures. In May 1922 an exchange on the matter of science and religion between Fundamentalist speakers and scientists at the state college in Raleigh led to a widely discussed debate between eminent Fundamentalist William B. Riley and entomologist Zeno P. Metcalf of the college on the topic of evolution.[36]

In February 1922 Poteat looked around the South and saw the anti-evolution movement "rising to the volume of a flood." He and Rufus Weaver of Mercer University worried about "a procession of college presidents marching steadily to martyrdom" over evolution. Weaver suggested Poteat respond to the anti-evolution outcry "with a constructive statement of beliefs," but Poteat was "disinclined" to write such a declaration. He explained, "It looks too much like a concession of ignorance. I am afraid I am too proud to make it."[37] Poteat instead tossed a catalyst into this saturated atmosphere of sensitivity toward the college and evolution and precipitated a whole new deluge of criticism. The tempest began when in early 1922, at his brother's urging, he put into print his thoughts on a parallel between the theory of evolution and a passage in the writings of Paul. A northern religious journal first published the short piece, "Was Paul an Evolutionist?," and the *Biblical Recorder* immediately reprinted it in early March for North Carolinians. Quoting Acts 17:26 that God created man "from a common origin," Poteat attested, "I am quite unable to frame a neater statement of the doctrine of the descent of existing organisms from earlier organisms under the divine impulsion and guidance."[38]

Tarheel Baptists quickly called for Poteat to answer the question that his article posed and to give a clear account of his views. A prominent adversary maintained that Poteat "ought . . . to explain what he means by theistic evolution, and tell how and where God operates in such a scheme." He wondered, "Can he afford to assume the Vanderbilt attitude toward the Christian public?"—a reference to Vanderbilt University's successful suit to free itself from the control of the Methodist denomination. Baptists were determined that they would retain a hold on their college. No one denied Poteat's right to believe as he wished and be damned; however, his opponents disavowed his right to do so as an employee of the Baptist denomination. This same assailant noted, "It is not a question of liberty in teaching. . . . Evolutionists and their supporters also have their rights, and they are at liberty to establish and maintain schools that promulgate their views." Throughout March and April the pressure rose for Poteat to justify that article and also a statement published in February in which he indicated that "the doctrine of evolution as the divine method of creation has been taught here frankly for many years, and that proclaims God and supports the fundamental tenets of our holy religion." Critics assailed Darwinism as an unscientific guess contrary to the Bible. Poteat's defenders occasionally supported evolution but for the most part concentrated on his character and the religious soundness of those who studied at Wake Forest. Prominent minister and convention official Walt N. Johnson proclaimed him "a Christian gentleman" who was "one of God's demonstrations that Jesus Christ saves and keeps safe even an evolutionist who trusts him."[39]

The clamor for clarification led Poteat to write two articles for the *Biblical Recorder* in late April. In the first he defined evolution, explained the difference between evolution and the still debatable question of how species originated, and made clear that evolution itself was accepted as fact by scientists. Poteat perceived that conservatives were mistaken in their rejection of evolution as unscientific. His opponents held the practice of science to be only the collection of facts and not their analysis. Thus, to religious conservatives, calling evolution a theory demoted it from valid science to wild guess, while Poteat recognized that the practice of science depended upon interpretative hypotheses. He returned to the list of supposedly great scientists who rejected evolution, one aspect of Martin's denunciation of the teaching of the theory in 1920 and apparently still cited by some critics, and concluded, "two do not appear in the biographical dictionaries, five are misrepresented, seven won reputation in other than biological fields, and six have been in their graves more than forty years, two of these having died long before Darwin's great book was published." That left one scientist, who was seen as "peculiar" among "biologists of responsible position." Quoting "authoritative" sources, Poteat demonstrated evolution's acceptance. He inquired if the attack on evolution could sincerely be in earnest since the controversy "was settled amicably, certainly in professional circles, thirty years ago. . . ."[40]

The second article likewise referred to "a few authoritative theologians" for evidence that evolution and religion were compatible. Because the two could co-exist, "the inspiration of the Scriptures sanely interpreted, the Deity of Christ, His incarnation, atonement, and resurrection are ours, evolution or no evolution." He concluded with a ringing challenge: "That being so, it is manifestly unjust for men who have had no opportunity of training in the biological sciences to seek to discredit Christian men who hold evolution as God's method of creation by charging them with disloyalty to Christian truth, with toadying to rationalistic high-brows, and with a venal and clandestine effort to undermine our religion. It is not right. It is not fair. It is not Christian. It ought to stop."[41] Ironically, even though Poteat often rhetorically rejected the specialization and professionalization that was at the foundation of claims of professional scientific veracity (and of experts' right to rule Progressive bureaucracies), he expected the public to accept as valid and authoritative the claims of scientists, just as he expected them to give him the autonomy due a professional educator in managing Wake Forest's curriculum. The worldviews of democratic localism and specialized professionalism clashed repeatedly as the fight to end liberal heresy among Baptist educators continued.

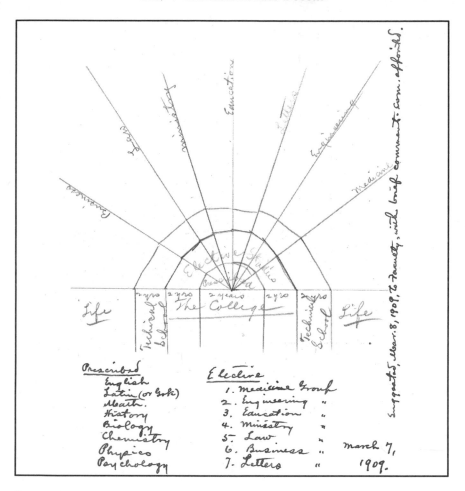

Poteat presided over Wake Forest during a tumultuous time for southern colleges. In 1910, he responded to the broadened curriculum and the decline of the classics by implementing a plan of study, diagrammed here in a proposal to the faculty in 1909, that preserved a core curriculum while encouraging students to look toward specialized training in the various professions.

Poteat's declaration of faith did not satisfy everyone. Years later Poteat appraised his articles on evolution, "I never argued the issue which was raised. . . . They were both statements of fact, not arguments."[42] The most persistent adversary of evolution rightly discerned that Poteat's articles failed "to meet the issue involved" by not responding to specific theological questions of how God operates through evolution, and he was not impressed with citations to "opinions of men." But some influential Baptists agreed that Poteat's forthright statement of religious faith "ought to satisfy every honest Baptist in North Carolina who wants to see right prevail."[43] In May 1922, at the same time they were dealing with the hazing and fraternity issues, the trustees appointed a committee of three, including the perennial Richard T. Vann, "to have an interview with Dr. Poteat and secure from him a statement in regard to the fundamentals of our faith." The committee reported that regarding "the great fundamental doctrines of our faith" Poteat was "in hearty accord" on "God, as the Creator of all things; Jesus of Nazareth as His Son incarnate; Redemption from sin through His atoning death; His resurrection from the dead; Regeneration through the Holy Spirit; The distinctive principles generally held by Baptists; The divine inspiration and final authority of the Bible, in matters of faith and practice." The trustees then unanimously "expressed their confidence in President Poteat as a Christian and a teacher." Concluding that all should now be convinced, Johnson closed the pages of the *Biblical Recorder* to further discussion of evolution.[44]

The controversy was far from over. Many Tarheels continued simply to reject claims of autonomy for the professionally skilled in such areas as education, and their egalitarian sense meant that no deference was due the board of trustees or Poteat. In May 1922 the Southern Baptist Convention condemned the teaching of evolution as a fact, and tensions grew in other southern states as well as North Carolina. With the principal Baptist paper having bowed out of the dispute, the controversy in North Carolina continued in the meetings of the Baptist associations in the summer and fall of 1922. For example, the Cape Fear–Columbus and the Alexander Asociations formally objected to the teaching of evolution, as did the Gaston County Association and the First Broad Baptist Church. A conference of Baptist pastors in Asheville also called for Poteat to explain to the convention his idea of evolution.[45]

Vann, head of the state convention's board of education, spoke in favor of moderation at a number of associations, and at Vann's request Poteat traveled to several of the regional gatherings in order that the "brethren might discover that I was just a plain man without horns and cloven feet." He reported a cordial reception in most areas, and after his talk the Tar River Association formally approved of Wake Forest. At the Flat River meeting he "made a speech that literally swept the association," a preview of the convention to come. The Gaston County assembly hinted at the uncertainty of many as the convention approached. Though the association's anti-evolution resolution passed by a twenty-three–to–four margin, almost three-quarters of the hundred or so delegates present reserved judgment and abstained.[46] The state convention, set to occur in Winston-Salem in early December, would decide the matter.

Both sides prepared for an altercation. Poteat was confident of victory, and he and his supporters planned to "propose a resolution of endorsement of the College, and so put the opposition on the defensive." He defined the stakes much differently than the conservatives. He would "not allow myself to be made an issue," Poteat wrote; "The real issue is whether a man can accept scientific truth as he sees and yet be a Christian." On the other side, W.C. Barrett maintained, "The people who support the colleges have a right to a voice and . . . whatever the majority want should be done" in the matters of evolution and fraternities, noting that both would be topics of contention.[47]

The convention opened on a Tuesday with nearly five hundred messengers (delegates) present by the first afternoon. B.W. Spilman—who had boarded in Poteat's home while a student at Wake Forest—presided over the sessions. He wielded a gavel made from wood that was taken from the birthplace of F.M. Jordan, who was the minister, ninety-four years old in 1922, who had preached the service in the 1870s at which Poteat dedicated his life to religion. Not until Wednesday night did the long-awaited moment arrive, Poteat's address to the convention on education. After a brief introduction by his old Euzelian mate Vann, Poteat faced the denomination that had enveloped him and given his life meaning for five decades. The moment was "tense," and "the Convention was on the tip-toe of expectancy."[48]

At this crucial instant, Poteat's oratory, honed for fifty years since he first entered the hall of the Euzelian society, rescued him. He was a symbol for the importance of the freedom of intellectual thought, but he turned instead to exhortation and evangelism and fired up the audience with an address titled "Christianity and Enlightenment." His eloquence and skill guided the emotions of the convention messengers through an hour-long oration that did not even mention evolution. He met the audience with scriptures in hand: "Permit me to read to you a little passage out of a little book. I love the little book and accept all it says. It has been the light and joy of my life. I commend it to you. It is our final authority for faith and practice. It is our most precious possession." He read from the book of John for evidence "that the revelation of Christ, according to His own declaration, is an expanding revelation," sanctioning Poteat's own liberal interpretation. Christian education—defined as "Christianity operating in the field of enlightenment"—offered the best hope to redeem a world that he depicted in a state of chaotic moral decline. Socialism, Prussianism, secular education, and "the scientific temper" had all failed to avert crisis because of "the same fatal absence of the moral dynamic." "No, no. None of these," Poteat cried, "It is Anarchy or Christ."[49]

Poteat movingly testified to his own conversion at Jordan's revival and reiterated his understanding of Christian Progressive reform—that social change would come with the conversion of individuals. "The cross is the central fact toward which all previous history converges, from which all subsequent history diverges with a crimson tinge forever," he proclaimed, "Redemption is there, or it is nowhere, individual redemption and social redemption." Poteat decried those who feared "lest the truth be bad"; with Christ as a guide, no form of truth could be antagonistic to faith. The jeremiad closed with a call for unity: "We are on a campaign to recover to our Lord a rebel world, and we talk of division. . . . Yonder gleams His banner above the battle line. Have done with these debates in the rear. Up and after Him through blood and tears, after Him to victory!"[50]

The sermon overwhelmed the convention. Livingston Johnson reported that it "was more nearly like a revival than anything we have seen in the Convention in years." Poteat escaped with his pride intact, feeling he had not lowered his standards to compete with ignorance. His persuasiveness left his conservative opponents no opening for combat that did not look petty. One of the strongest critics of evolution, who sat directly in front of Poteat as he spoke, introduced a resolution the next morning "that this Convention commend Wake Forest College in its present policy expressed in the above address by President Poteat endorsing the Bible truth as a basis of faith." Fraternities and evolution did not come before the meeting despite the resolutions adopted beforehand by at least ten associations. Some delegates had come specifically to defend Wake Forest against attack, and many of them did not even remain for the final two days of the convention following Poteat's speech. The rest was anticlimactic.[51]

Throughout the early twenties most North Carolina newspapers praised Poteat's stand for the freedom of teaching. However, even one of his supporters questioned the speech at Winston-Salem by declaring that Poteat "won a great victory by chloroforming his enemies" with rhetoric, while leaving the conservative movement "as strong and bigoted and ignorant as it ever was."[52] In praising Poteat's masterful speech, his brother also struck a foreboding note about conservative Baptists: "When they have forgotten your superb eloquence, they will come home to their own house of life and see again Evolution mocking their faith in the uniqueness of their Lord. And President Poteat will be more a puzzle to them than ever." Edwin went on to urge that "pity for such ignorance" as some of Wake Forest's opponents displayed should inspire Poteat "to make a plain statement in answer to the questions which in your great hour at Winston-Salem you left unanswered." Edwin could think of no one better "to mediate the transition for Southern Baptists from uncritical conservatism to conservative progressivism."[53] At the end of 1922, intellectual freedom and professional autonomy were safe for the moment, and liberal thought in North Carolina had established a strong precedent. Edwin's warnings soon proved correct, however, and Poteat would again be forced to justify his teachings. Rather than regarding Wake Forest as a beacon lighting troubled waters, many of the state's Baptists remained eager to kindle a blaze beneath Poteat to encourage him to relinquish his post in deference to popular religious sentiment.

The Second Round and an Uneasy Peace

Though some minor displays of discontent over Poteat's beliefs continued, the focus of the anti-evolution agitation in North Carolina shifted away from the Baptist denomination for a time beginning in 1923. In April of that year William Jennings Bryan, a Presbyterian with broad appeal, gave an inspiring address in Raleigh urging, according to one historian, "the Christian taxpayers of North Carolina to drive the evolutionists from their public schools in order to preserve true Christianity and public morality." This majoritarian justification of anti-evolution legislation, similar to the arguments Baptists used within their denomination, was the rationale for efforts to restrict the teaching of evolution in the state's public schools and universities. Conservative religious leaders tried first to arrange for biblical instruction for academic credit in public schools and colleges as a counter to unorthodox teaching, but the proposal failed to gain adequate support, particularly among Baptists who worried about the separation of church and state. Most in the denomination had no such hesitation about proscribing the teaching of evolution, however, because they regarded the makeup of the science curriculum as similar to other policy decisions open to democratic influence. The conservative cause got a substantial boost in January 1924 when Governor Cameron Morrison, another Presbyterian and ex-officio chairman of the State Board of Education, removed two biology textbooks from a list of those recommended for use in public schools, citing their approval of evolution.[54]

Poteat kept a fairly low profile on the evolution issue during 1923 and 1924, though the debate continued within other denominations in the state. In the summer of 1923 he accepted the offer of a wealthy alumnus to pay for him and Emma to attend the Baptist World Alliance meeting in Stockholm. From late June until mid-August they enjoyed traveling in western Europe. In the summer of 1924 they took an extended trip through the western United States as well, relaxing from presidential duties and denominational controversy.[55] Also in the summer of 1924 Poteat attended a liberal conference on theological matters arranged by the Reynolda Presbyterian Church in Winston-Salem, but he gave "no formal talk, only answered questions and made suggestions."[56] Nonetheless, he made no effort in this period to hide his liberal views. Appearing before the Baptist church in Chapel Hill in March 1924, he lectured that the Bible "partakes in general of the qualities of the Oriental mind. It presents practical morals, not metaphysics."[57]

Poteat's patient and tolerant stance toward anti-evolutionists dissipated somewhat as the controversy persisted. In early 1924 in Memphis he lashed out against religious conservatives while speaking to the Council of Church Schools of the South (a group formed the year before when the Southern Baptist Education Association agreed to cooperate with similar bodies from the Methodist and Presbyterian denominations). Poteat proclaimed that theology had incorporated evolution forty years previously and castigated the "few gentlemen, sincere and devout and capable," who were spreading "excitement and alarm" about evolution. "For the most part trained in pre-scientific days, they could not be expected to have the scientific habit or attitude," he explained. Still, he had no sympathy for their failure to keep up with modern thought, worrying that by their attacks on science "these ardent propagandists are in reality producing no effect whatsoever on scientific opinion, but only scattering thorns in the path of young Greeks of our day who would see Jesus." Such men invoked "a crass theory of inspiration most unfair to the precious documents of our faith" and threatened "by legislative enactment and executive order, by inquisition and torture, to disentangle the hated doctrine from the web of contemporary thought, which it undoubtedly controls." He denounced "the religious faddist" with only slightly less vigor closer to home in May 1924 in an address at Wingate College near Charlotte.[58]

The assaults on Poteat did not entirely cease, either. Shortly before the Baptist State Convention in December 1923, flyers unfavorably comparing Poteat's statements on evolution with quotations from Genesis had been anonymously mailed to various Baptists. The convention ignored the matter, but similar papers were sent out in February 1924.[59] Also in the spring of 1924, Fundamentalist leader J. Frank Norris announced in his newspaper that Poteat's right to a seat in the upcoming Southern Baptist Convention gathering in Atlanta as a messenger from Wake Forest Baptist Church would be challenged on the basis of his teaching of evolution. Despite Baptist policies of local control that made such a challenge unfeasible, Norris's aggression continued to keep Poteat's views spotlighted before Tarheel Baptists. Poteat wrote his brother, "Nothing happened at Atlanta in the direction of the fulfillment of threats about the seating of a certain delegate from North Carolina." Norris was not even present. However, at their commencement meeting, the college's board of trustees "had what they called a heart to heart meeting in executive session, talking frankly as I learned afterwards about the College, the President and the recent agitation." Apparently the board reaffirmed its confidence in Poteat, and two members reported to Poteat that "they had never known the Board so melted in cordiality and unity in all their experience."[60] Poteat's many years of close cooperation with the board paid dividends in the loyalty of a majority who accepted his faith as legitimate.

Religious conservatives elsewhere scored a number of victories in the twenties. Several Baptist schools gave in to popular pressure. For example, Norris consistently accused Baylor University, controlled by Texas Baptists, of harboring evolutionists, and his criticism and that of Thomas Martin led to the resignation of sociology professor Grove S. Dow in late 1921. Mercer University fired biology professor Henry Fox in the fall of 1924 for liberal religious views, and in 1926 Andrew Lee Pickens was driven from Furman University for his belief in evolution. Across the nation, opponents of evolution also worked to bar the doctrine from public schools, justifying the campaign by citing their rights as taxpayers. In the South, the Kentucky legislature defeated an anti-evolution measure early in 1922 only after the president of the University of Kentucky led a battle against it. In the spring of 1923, legislators in the Texas house of representatives passed such a bill, but it was defeated in the state senate. In Oklahoma, however, an anti-evolution bill passed in early 1923. Of course, the most famous triumph for anti-evolutionists occurred in Tennessee when the legislature prohibited the teaching of evolution early in 1925. The trial in July of that year of John T. Scopes, a high school teacher, for teaching the theory in violation of the statute is the most renowned event of the anti-evolution movement. Though the spectacle of the trial shamed many southern intellectuals and helped inspire them to advance the region's cultural standing, the death of Bryan following the trial gave anti-evolutionists a martyr and their movement further strength. In 1926 the teaching of evolution was outlawed in Mississippi public schools, and in November 1928 the voters of Arkansas banned the teaching of evolution by passing a referendum on the matter.[61]

In North Carolina, the antipathy toward evolution in state-supported schools and universities erupted with especial fervor in early 1925. Howard W. Odum, a controversial sociologist at the University of North Carolina, had launched the *Journal of Social Forces* in 1922 to provide a forum for critical examination of southern problems. In the January 1925 issue two articles that questioned religious orthodoxy brought condemnation on Odum and his journal. The scholarly articles treated religion in terms of the development of myth and of Hebrew folkways, and they furthered in Tarheel minds an equation of Chapel Hill with secularism and heterodoxy. A second major statewide uproar involved evolution more directly. Before an extension class in Charlotte, Albert S. Keister of the North Carolina College for Women briefly discussed evolution and said it required one to see parts of the Bible as mythology.[62] With these incidents to exhibit, Raeford's state representative, David Scott Poole, had good evidence for the heresy that he saw rampant in tax-supported schools. Elected principally on the issue of evolution, Poole introduced in the state legislature on January 8, 1925, a resolution condemning as "injurious" the teaching of evolution in state institutions.[63] He found support among members of all denominations, with conservative Presbyterians most vocal.

As Poteat recalled later, he "took no part in the public discussion of the 'monkey bill,'" but he cheered as it went to its defeat. He believed that leaders of state-supported institutions should head the opposition to the resolution, and Harry W. Chase, president of the University of North Carolina, assumed that role with great effectiveness. "You have fought our battles long enough, and now we are going to do some fighting ourselves," Chase informed Poteat. Along with science faculty from North Carolina State College, Chase made an important speech at a committee hearing on the resolution. He cast the issue in terms of human liberty and the freedom of speech, rather than a narrow academic freedom. Poteat attended the hearing to symbolize his opposition to the bill, but both he and Richard T. Vann declined to speak despite calls by the audience to do so. Poteat may have believed the divisiveness that his name might arouse would harm the opposition to the Poole bill, or he may have not wanted to risk another outbreak of antipathy by Baptists toward Wake Forest. Anti-evolutionists made their characteristic arguments that evolution was scientifically unreliable as well as a moral danger. The committee issued a negative report by one vote, but a week later a minority report brought the Poole bill before the full house of representatives. As with Poteat's views about evolution, the state's newspapers generally endorsed Chase's arguments, and he rallied sufficient support. The resolution failed by a vote of sixty-seven to forty-six, but it got substantial backing from those legislators without a college education. Of the legislators educated at Wake Forest and the University of North Carolina, a majority opposed the restrictions. Eighteen of the twenty-one who had attended Wake Forest voted against Poole's resolution, an indication of the liberalizing influence of Poteat among the college's alumni.[64]

An additional bit of fuel for the anti-evolution blaze in early 1925 was the naming in January of Poteat to deliver the McNair lectures at the University of North Carolina in May of that year. The purpose of the series was to explore the relationship between science and theology, and it had aroused controversy in 1922 when a professor from Yale had offended anti-evolutionists with his support for evolution and higher criticism of the Bible. Though Poteat at least was not open to charges of being an outsider, his three speeches sparked even more opposition.[65] They were delivered beginning May 1 to successively larger crowds that Poteat estimated at fifteen hundred persons by the third night. The lectures capture his growing impatience as he recognized that intelligence had still not widely prevailed over ignorance on the matter of evolution. He presented his ideas with unusual aggressiveness, perhaps feeling confident after the Poole bill's defeat and the consistent backing of his own board of trustees. A front-page headline announced accurately, "Dr. W.L. Poteat Takes Sharp Fling at Fundamentalists." A reporter heralded, "He has taken the warpath against his former tormentors."[66]

In introducing his topic, he targeted the Chapel Hill students and sought "to inquire whether your culture is going to be at home with your religion." He took as his topic "Can a Man Be a Christian To-day?" The first lecture, "To-day," summarized the scientific discoveries of the nineteenth century and sketched the resulting changes in social and intellectual arrangements.[67] He noted that "the prophets of the new knowledge have always been crucified by the scribes of old" and pointedly criticized anti-evolutionists. "About the principle and fact of evolution," he explained, "there is no question in the minds of responsible biologists. . . . This great conception is embedded in the texture of the intellectual life of to-day." He continued, "One wonders whether the proposal to disentangle and expunge it by ecclesiastical or legislative enactment can by any possibility be really serious." Fundamentalists sought the impossible—"by executive order, by organized propaganda, by inquisition and the refinements of modern torture, to crowd the eagle back into the shell and then, in Voltaire's famous phrase, crush the infamous thing."[68]

The other two talks in the series were equally blunt. The second lecture, "Baggage," presented conclusions that Poteat had reached in the 1880s. He counseled the students to look beyond the theorizing of theology to find inspiration in the direct teachings of Jesus. With this formula Poteat could avoid resolving the theological ambiguities in his own position. By asserting the validity of Christian experience as springing from a more direct relationship with the divine, he could ignore many of the dilemmas that conservatives faced as they feared historicizing the Bible would destroy its transcendent authority. The absoluteness of Christian morality and the inward experience of responding to Christ's call "to the soul of man" were unchanging, he asserted, but theological interpretations of Christian writings and teachings were mutable. Theology resulted from "the rationalizing habit of the West," but "a man may be a Christian and not understand the phrases of your theology and be wholly unable to subscribe to its main propositions." Under the influence of theology, Christianity had moved from its original emphasis on conduct and a new way of life toward requiring belief in specific logical interpretations of doctrine. One result was the Fundamentalist tenet that God had dictated the Bible, and now "a few unimportant men" had revived that conception and were leading Christians into a "morass" because their theology conflicted with scientific findings. Poteat repeated that evolution instead was God at work in nature. He urged his young listeners, "You may revise your conception of the origin and purpose of the Bible and so retain your reverence before its Divine authority without embarrassment before the assured results of science."[69] In the final speech, "Peace," Poteat reinforced his ideas that "faith is independent and is as reliable in its sphere as reason is in its sphere."[70] For Poteat, reconciling science and religion meant holding rational theology and religious experience rigidly separate.

Even as Poteat was delivering the McNair lectures, talk circulated that he planned to retire at the commencement the following month. The *Greensboro Daily News* reported the rumors and noted that Poteat "is now at the peak of his popularity. He has routed utterly the bigots and the blackguards who have been sowing the state . . . with anonymous propaganda." A prominent trustee posited that, if anything, Poteat might announce at commencement his plans to retire at a specific date in the future, but the president of the alumni association encouraged him to remain. At the beginning of May, Poteat said only, "There is nothing to discuss and cannot be until after the meeting of the board of trustees on June 3 as I have no definite plans and will have none prior to that meeting."[71] If he did intend to step down, he probably regarded the McNair lectures as a summary statement of his brand of religious liberalism, a final opportunity to cement his victory over "his former tormentors." As he quickly discovered, however, those tormentors were far from vanquished.

In the month following the McNair lectures, Poteat trumpeted his understanding of evolution to at least two additional audiences. Reporter Nell Battle Lewis publicized a speech he gave to Raleigh's Fortnightly Review Club meeting at the home of Delia Dixon Carroll, sister of A.C. and Thomas Dixon. Also, to an audience of about five hundred at the invitation of the Greensboro Open Forum, he explained that science and religion did not conflict. He pleaded for people to let scientists freely investigate the theory, "I think we'd better leave the technical questions for those equipped to handle them."[72] The McNair lectures and these additional speeches reignited the opposition of Baptists across the state, feeding the "flame of resentment," one headline declared. In late May at a joint meeting of the education and mission boards of the Baptist State Convention, ministers and laymen from across the state reported that the denomination's membership resented Poteat to an extent that could no longer be ignored. As a result, the meeting adopted a resolution that recommended that the trustees of Wake Forest—who had long refused to oust Poteat despite opposition—be elected directly by the state convention. The *Raleigh News and Observer* rightly worried that the new outcry would complicate the "generally anticipated" retirement of Poteat at the upcoming commencement.[73]

The *Greensboro Daily News* polemically set the stage for commencement: "It will determine whether President W. L. Poteat voluntarily retires as he has had it in mind two whole years to do, or whether he will give his tormentors another good beating and while they are quiet and subdued, he will set a new time for resignation." The majority of the faculty of Wake Forest responded by signing a letter asking Poteat to remain; the alumni meeting applauded him; and the trustees met in closed session and reportedly almost unanimously expressed confidence in Poteat. Poteat gave no public acknowledgement of the uproar, but "he was represented by friends as taking the position that he was unwilling to take any step that would appear as a surrender in whole or in part of the traditions which have been built up at the college. . . ."[74] With no action taken at the June graduation, the agitation was left to build until the state convention in November.

Throughout the summer and fall of 1925, the question of evolution bedeviled the state. The Scopes trial in neighboring Tennessee captured the nation's attention in July, and the *Biblical Recorder* under pressure again allowed debate on the issue during July and August, for the first time since mid-1922. Further, the bequest that established the McNair lectures stipulated that they be published. The University of North Carolina Press, formed only three years before and the single important nonreligious press in the region, had agreed to print the lectures. Despite Poteat's controversial content, the press fulfilled its commitment. The little volume, *Can a Man Be a Christian To-day?*, gave assistant director of the press, William T. Couch, his first limited opportunity to release a book critical of regional mores, and its very publication was a significant step for liberals in the state. The book was out in June, and Couch personally devoted much effort to promoting it throughout the state, even in small towns. It sold rapidly, well over a thousand copies by the end of August and nearly two thousand by December. Due to fear of conservative opposition in the 1927 legislative session, his university later interfered with Couch's exertions to push sales of a second edition of the book, but its widespread distribution in 1925 broke new ground. Reviewed widely in the state and even in some national publications, the work generally received praise from southern secular publications, just as newspapers had typically sided with Poteat on protecting the freedom of inquiry.[75] For his conservative Baptist opposition, however, *Can a Man Be a Christian To-day?* was just another red flag; even the title was a heretical question.

Poteat's critics tore apart the book page by page. Most prominently, S.J. Betts, a Baptist minister in Raleigh, completed a pamphlet of burning criticism by early August in which he analyzed quotations from the book to determine that Poteat wanted "to discredit and tear asunder our Bible." He gave the typical evidence that evolution was not scientifically sound and called for religous Tarheels to help elect representatives to banish the doctrine from state schools and also to stop tolerating it in the denomination's college. In a longer and more detailed criticism released somewhat later, James R. Pentuff, a minister in Concord, likewise examined "Poteat's utterances" in great detail, reaching conclusions similar to those of Betts. The religious fear, antiquated views of science, and rejection of expert authority remained the same as in the earlier rounds of the fight against Poteat.[76] However, the strategy changed somewhat. Recognizing that Poteat had gradually gained an unyielding shield composed of sympathetic trustees and vocal alumni, conservatives emphasized the idea premiered at the May meeting of the education and mission boards—securing direct election of the trustees by the convention. They apparently believed that if such a measure were passed by the convention, Poteat and the trustees would acknowledge their repudiation by resigning at once, thereby allowing the convention to elect a whole new group who would select a more sympathetic head for Wake Forest.[77]

Poteat was by no means quiet during the summer and fall months. He maintained his "characteristic willingness . . . to express himself boldly upon any and all occasions" by repeating the McNair lectures to five hundred southern college students at the Blue Ridge, North Carolina, facilities of the YMCA; by lecturing on evolution to ministers and teachers in Asheville; and by giving a variety of talks at a week-long Christian meeting in Northfield, Massachusetts. To the Raleigh Rotary Club he denounced the Scopes trial: "I look on this thing happening in Dayton with the deepest humiliation. Apart from the trifling and ludicrous incidents associated with it, the idea that any group of men should undertake to settle a scientific fact by ma[j]ority vote in any assembly is a travesty on the intelligence of our race and we ought not to stand for it."[78] Despite his incredulity, Poteat recognized the threat that the turmoil posed to him and his ideals in the college. In August he acknowledged, "The issue here appears to be acute again, I mean the issue of extreme fundamentalism. . . . The prospect is there will be a warm time at the Baptist State Convention. We have contemplated a conference with a view to forestalling if possible radical action by that body."[79] As he explained to one supporter, a Wake Forest alumnus at the Southwestern Baptist Theological Seminary, "I have known all along of your sympathy with the attitude Wake Forest has maintained these years past, and you will agree with me that it is very difficult even to appear to surrender it under the heavy pressure now exerted."[80]

Battle lines formed by late summer. A conference including the executive committees of the trustees and the board of missions, leaders of the alumni association, and other prominent Baptists convened for five hours in Raleigh in late August to discuss the evolution matter and the consequent drop in donations to the denomination. The meeting produced no action, however. Meanwhile, several of the associations meeting around the state heatedly debated evolution and Poteat's role as president.[81] Poteat worked to rally the alumni, and at their annual meeting in September they endorsed Poteat once again.[82] The sides were soon clear. By the end of September W.C. Barrett had announced that he would introduce a resolution proposing the change in trustee selection procedures at the convention, and the anticipation had begun once again to build as everyone knew a showdown was inevitable at the Charlotte convention. Citing the Methodists' loss of control of Vanderbilt University as a dangerous precedent to be avoided, Barrett claimed his resolution would not only assure that Wake Forest could never "get out of the hands of the Baptists of North Carolina" but would also "tend to bring the institutions closer to the people."[83] Probably trying to keep out of the spotlight and leave the defense of the college to trustworthy alumni, Poteat told an alumni meeting in Charlotte "that he would take the attitude of a bystander" at the convention.[84]

The convention convened on November 17, and a record of over a thousand delegates enrolled. Not until the second day did the issue of education surface. R.J. Bateman of Asheville, an outspoken opponent of Poteat since the previous May, introduced in the afternoon session a convoluted resolution that was adopted with no discussion. It resolved "that we interpret the record in Genesis not as myth, but as God's inspired revelation. We believe that it is literal and unassailable as to the fact of creation by God; . . . that it is supernatural in its method of revealing the truth that God by special act, created man in His own image apart from the rest of the animal creation. . . ." The proclamation went on to recommend that Baptists influence "so far as we can" denominational colleges to adhere to "God's word" and to teach only "the attested facts of Science." Yet the decree also claimed that its supporters had no desire to hinder "investigation of all discoverable facts" by teachers.[85]

Barrett's resolution on the election of trustees was reserved for the evening session, allowing time in the afternoon, shortly after Bateman's success, for Poteat to address an alumni meeting. He moved many of the crowd of 250 to tears with a wry but passionate statement intended to prepare them for possible battle against Barrett on behalf of Wake Forest:

> I am not averse to withdrawing. I had thought of doing so before these good men gently suggested it to me. But they have made it impossible. I decline to be whipped out on a false issue which involves the respectability and the opportunity of my Alma Mater. For I am merely the point of contact which the College establishes with the public, the expression of the attitude of the College maintained through all the years of my service in it,—the attitude of hospitality to Truth, no matter through what little window of our life she may shine in on us. That is the issue. I have loved the College too dearly and too long . . . to consent now by surrender or silence to her sacrifice. . . .

Perhaps recognizing the strong support Poteat had amassed, especially in the form of alumni, the conservatives at the convention compromised. In the evening, Barrett introduced a resolution that "the trustees shall be elected by the Baptist State Convention of North Carolina, and hold office at the will of the Convention." B.W. Spilman, a supporter of Poteat, immediately seconded the motion, and after its adoption offered a motion of his own that Barrett seconded. Spilman's motion dictated that the convention would exercise its powers of election by having the trustees themselves nominate candidates. The convention would then elect the proposed slate or make substitutes. Both proposals were quickly adopted with no debate, and the convention dispatched the topic by singing "Blest Be the Tie That Binds."[86]

Both sides emerged claiming victory. The conservatives had their statement of faith in Genesis, but it was worded such that Poteat and other liberal interpreters of the Bible could still believe the facts of evolution. Further, Bateman's resolution made no call for resignations, did not actually mention evolution, and criticized no one personally. The conservatives could claim a triumph in passing the Barrett resolution, but in actuality it changed little once Spilman's motion gave the trustees the right of nomination. As the dust cleared, Poteat, the trustees, and their supporters remained unshaken. One observer commented, "The fundamentalists gained everything they asked the convention for, but they asked for exceedingly little." The leaders of the denomination apparently wanted to avoid the divisions and bitterness of an open battle. On the third day of the meeting the college's supporters did not press for a resolution of endorsement for the institution, and rumors that conservatives would attack Ora C. Bradbury—newly hired as professor of biology at Wake Forest and formerly under assault at Baylor University by J. Frank Norris—did not materialize.[87] A reporter represented Poteat as "entirely satisfied" with the outcome, as were the professors and students of the college. Poteat wrote a few weeks later, "I think the atmosphere is distinctly clearing, and if we can be patient with good but misguided men, I think the controversy will quiet down into silence before very much longer."[88]

The furor over evolution gradually expired in North Carolina. Conservatives in the state organized in 1926 to push again for a law in the 1927 legislative session, but internal disarray and a split between the major state group and lobbyists (including Thomas Martin) from national organizations contributed to their campaign's distinct lack of success. Though evolution was an issue in a few of the primary races for state legislators in 1926, anti-evolution activists decisively failed even to get a new measure out of committee in early 1927. The Committee of One Hundred, organized in Charlotte in mid-1926, was the center of the anti-evolution lobby, but its leaders strenuously denied any desire to single out Poteat.[89] His position at Wake Forest was secure as his foes awaited the retirement of their aging nemesis. Nonetheless, Poteat recognized that he had not convinced his opposition. In May 1926 the Southern Baptist Convention formally declared against evolution. Despite Poteat's protest that the resolution was "inappropriate, ineffective, and injurious," the board of trustees of the Southern Baptist Theological Seminary later endorsed the statement by a wide margin in January 1927. In a speech at

Vassar College in Poughkeepsie, New York, in March 1927, Poteat expressed pessimistically, "The untrained masses have had no defenses against misinformed enthusiasm, and their response to the appeal of the Christian faith harried by science has demonstrated at once their docility and devotion."[90]

Such an understanding of the limitations of his success left Poteat to celebrate his preservation of Wake Forest's freedom even while lamenting a broader failure of liberal thought. If he had any doubt about the continuing strength of anti-evolution sentiment, an incident in the spring of 1931 would have dispelled it. Poteat accepted an invitation to speak about the report of the education commission at the Southern Baptist Convention's meeting in Birmingham that year. However, a member of the commission informed its head, according to Poteat, "that if it is announced in the papers that an evolutionist is to appear on the Convention platform, there will be public protest, which I understand to mean that he himself will make the protest." Poteat withdrew his name "to save the Commission from any possible embarrassment. . . ." Still, he chafed at the lack of respect given expert knowledge. He told his brother, "my first reaction was to speak, protest or not protest; it might do the protesters good, and I have a deep seated resentment against Paul's weaker brother determining policy for the whole bunch." He was "chagrined that the old silly controversy, which I had though dead and deeply buried, has arisen to say the report was greatly exaggerated."[91] The issue would last even beyond Poteat's lifetime.

In addition to his skilled oratory, Poteat survived the criticism of the twenties—unlike Baptist liberals at Baylor, Mercer, and other southern colleges—due to his extreme visibility within the state, unimpeachable personal faith and reputation, the strength of the loyal network of college alumni, and the moderate nature of his liberalism.[92] The evolution fight secured for Poteat his lasting reputation as a southern intellectual leader. The early students of southern liberalism, Edwin Mims and Virginius Dabney, considered Poteat a pioneer of tolerant and progressive thought in the region. In his *Advancing South* released in 1926, Mims devoted several pages to praising Poteat's McNair lectures, hailing him for striking a middle ground between modernism and orthodoxy while being "the chief protagonist of the liberal forces" among Baptists. Dabney considered Poteat "a commanding figure among Southern liberals" and in *Liberalism in the South* in 1932 praised him as "a dauntless spirit, liberal in his religious, educational and social attitudes, ever valiant in the search for truth."[93] Commentators since have likewise acclaimed Poteat's role in the evolution battle.

Poteat understood the limited achievements of southern liberalism perhaps more clearly than the somewhat polemical Mims and Dabney. In assessing Mims's book for the *Yale Review,* Poteat discerned, "An intellectual renascence is on the horizon. But, heavens! what a distance we have yet to compass." He analyzed Mims's examples of liberals, "What we see here is a progressive leadership shown up against the general population's indifference and backward look. Even the leaders are not quite independent in their liberalism." In religious circles, Poteat later explained to Dabney, "the situation would perhaps be more accurately described as showing men of liberal attitude sifted all about in the churches, the majority of whose membership are quite orthodox with opinions not yet in contact with the new knowledge, much less revised by it."[94] The gap between leaders and membership continued to plague southern churches throughout the overwhelmingly conservative South. Liberals such as Poteat were vital in introducing new ideas, but the extent to which those ideas were adopted was limited.

Further, national reviewers of *Can a Man Be a Christian To-day?* made clear that even liberal thought in the South was conservative in a broader context. H.L. Mencken guardedly praised the work, but he noted about Poteat's interpretation of the Bible, "Unfortunately, there is a hole in his argument." Mencken explained, "What he asks us to do, in brief, is to give full faith and credit, on the ground that we are yet unable to show their falsity, to passages that are inextricably linked to passages that every schoolboy now knows to be nonsense." A *New Republic* reviewer similarly contended, "The individual consciousness is the product of social tradition. While Mr. Poteat seems to be independent of the authority of tradition he is not." The reviewer argued that Poteat's adherence to "dreamland" religion grew out of tradition in the sense that "intelligence or reason" were "not the ultimate test of validity in case of religious conviction." Writing from Baltimore, Gerald Johnson summed up, "As regards the body of his teaching, this chief of the vanguard of southern modernism would be regarded north of the Potomac as extremely old fashioned, if not downright fundamentalist." Even some within North Carolina acknowledged the moderation of their liberal trailblazer: "The strength of W. L. Poteat that so puzzles visitors from outside the state, is due to the fact that, although he leans toward modernism, he is a moderate man."[95] This moderation typified southern liberals. The South allowed them voice, if not effectiveness, because they never promoted radicalism.

As the contentions about evolution drifted to a close after 1925, Poteat was finally beyond the dissension and controversy that had clouded his past several years, and he perhaps longed for the harmony and efficient leadership that he felt should characterize a proper society. It was not to be. He had at least partially won in the controversy over evolution, but the assertive, organized rejection of expert guidance that characterized the evolution dispute soon spread to other topics of importance to Poteat. As the subtle encounter over evolution in 1931 hinted, Poteat's final decade was not one of triumph for many of the causes that he had long held dear. Despite the inevitable continuing triumphs of the juggernaut of bureaucratization, many southerners fought for local control. During the late 1920s and the 1930s, they continued to vigorously show disdain for the Progressive values of harmony, efficiency, paternalism, and educated leadership that Poteat embodied.

6

Spokesman for Another Lost Cause

✝

When William Louis Poteat stepped down from the presidency of Wake Forest College in June 1927, a perceptive editorialist prophesied that "the retirement of Dr. Poteat from the presidency doesn't mean that he will drop out of the public eye, for a man of his recognized ability as a leader in education and religion cannot disappear, even if he should desire." Another observer agreed, "So long as he retains his health, no matter what position he occupies his leadership in the realm of culture and intellect in North Carolina is inevitable."[1] These predictions proved true, for in the decade following his presidency Poteat remained exceptionally active.

To a large extent, Poteat's final decade was notable for the failure of many of the values and causes that he had advocated for a lifetime. His Progressive vision since the 1890s was that modernization would result in a liberal, interdependent community led harmoniously by cultured elites. He anticipated a moral society that would bring the kingdom of God on earth. By the early 1920s the internal contradictions of his social philosophy were becoming visible. Poteat retained an emphasis on individual acceptance of the Christian morals at the foundation of his imagined community, yet he sought to exclude more and more of the recalcitrant immoral from society by proposing eugenic programs, and to forcibly include other objectors in the kingdom through conservative moral legislation such as Prohibition. The hoped-for harmony naturally did not result. The conservative religious backlash of the anti-evolution controversy represented a substantial number of Tarheels who refused to acquiesce to elite guidance within a seemingly liberal framework of social Christianity. The late twenties and the thirties brought many additional instances of full-scale rejection of the Progressive idea of a united, organic community.

Social conflict—antithetical to Progressive values—became more routine. Even within Wake Forest College, the veneer of unity that sustained the school through the evolution battle splintered on internal issues. Further, the religious conservatives remained alert and ready to attack any sign of liberalism or worldliness at the college. More broadly, the moral forces, as Christian

Progressives sometimes styled themselves, were unable to sustain support for Prohibition as competing social groups refused to acknowledge the legitimacy of a moral standard enforced from above. Poteat also spoke for peace, tolerance, and an international alliance for moral diplomacy, but national trends again moved in opposite directions. He worked for racial peace in a segregated but interlinked society, but fearful whites and black activists assaulted his middle ground from all sides. Big business ignored appeals for social cooperation and moral management, and the objects of Poteat's proposed eugenic reforms likewise questioned vigorously the idea of a society united behind a moral quest for a southern kingdom of God. The search for an orderly, unified society to replace the cohesive, self-contained communities of the nineteenth century ended in the 1930s with the normalization and spread of competition among interest groups within society.

Retirement and an Evolving Wake Forest

The Fundamentalist attack on the teaching of evolution was not the only controversy stirring Tarheel Baptists in the period just before Poteat's retirement. Though he publicly credited his retirement solely to advancing age, in the months leading up to the announcement Poteat faced a storm of criticism and factional controversy from within the college. A series of articles in the spring of 1926 in the student newspaper, *Old Gold and Black,* accused the Poteat administration of dragging Wake Forest into "a state of dry rot, decay, and stagnation" by missing fundraising opportunities with the wealthy Duke family, failing on two much-needed building campaigns, lowering the quality of the instruction by hiring fewer professors with doctorates, and poorly investing the endowment.[2] Another accusation alleged that a small cadre of the faculty kept a tight control of the college and maintained a false facade of unity. Further, "it was charged that the management of the college was in the hands of a few members of the board of trustees whose interests were centered in other denominational schools in the state and that the administration was unprogressive and not what the Baptists of the state expected and demanded of it." The students accused the board of trustees of putting the interests of Meredith College ahead of those of Wake Forest because of a variety of personal ties to the Baptists' college for women.[3] The dozen or so students signing the articles claimed only to want to bring the matter before the Baptists of the state "in order that something may be done to restore Wake Forest to that position of prestige and leadership which is her rightful heritage."[4] Most students remained supportive of the administration, however.

At a faculty meeting an angered Hubert Poteat, William's son and a professor of Latin at the college, recommended that a student partially responsible for the editorials not be allowed the honor of speaking at commencement. In response, Thurman D. Kitchin, dean of the medical school, protested that the students should be allowed to express themselves and that he in fact agreed with certain of the charges leveled at the Poteat administration. The situation worsened when Fountain W. Carroll, a professor in the medical department, decided he could "not remain in a department whose head was against the administration" of the college. Kitchin resigned on May 15, 1926, followed in the next few days by Carroll and Walter F. Taylor, a Poteat supporter and another member of the medical faculty.[5] Poteat sought desperately to restore peace to the medical department by indicating to Kitchin that Carroll had withdrawn his statement. He asked Kitchin in turn "to withdraw your resignation and so relieve the crisis in the department of Medicine which you have done so much to standardize."[6] With the college in disarray, the board of trustees formed a fact-finding committee to investigate the allegations of poor administration and the ensuing problems.[7]

Poteat was quite displeased by the attitude and actions of the special committee. At their meeting in June 1926 the trustees expressed disapproval of Hubert, tried to improve internal administration by selecting a new registrar over Poteat's recommendation, and criticized certain faculty members for perhaps encouraging the student editorials by talking too frankly with the young men. Regarding the attempt to punish the critical students, "the Com. had objected to . . . the penalizing [of] a student for free speec[h,] a thing for wh[ich] the College had been standing against its critics." Poteat, revealing his views of students' need for a guiding hand, "objected that there was no analogy," but to no effect. In the end, Kitchin returned to his post, and as Poteat summarized, "the only criticism of me by the Com[mittee] was that discipline had become lax in my administration, tho[ugh] the Dean was mainly responsible." In addition, the trustees "felt the ideal situation w[oul]d be for me to continue in my present relation with an able full-time dean to look after the details of the internal administration,—continue as long as my health and vigor lasted." In a summary of a conversation with an influential trustee, Poteat noted, "If I wished to be relieved of administrative duties, he thought the B[oa]rd to a man w[oul]d retain me as President Emeritus and Professor of Biology. When I reported that Judge T had said that if I remained as President now . . ., it w[oul]d be remaining under a cloud, S. protested that there was no fo[u]ndation for such a remark."[8]

The whole situation apparently grew out of an internal attack on Poteat's presidency. Becoming penitent, Taylor, one of the professors who resigned, explained the motives in a letter to Poteat:

> It is very generally known that each and every one of those articles which appeared in the Old Gold and Black . . . were planned in series, and actually outlined by certain members of the faculty of Dr. Kitchin's political machine, the program having its sole inception in a desire to drive President Poteat and his Administration from control, leaving Dr. Kitchin the supreme dictatorship of the College. . . . I personally read drafts of most of these articles before they were ever turned over to a selected group of students to sign and publish as "student articles." Finally, when the thing got

so rotten that I could stand it no longer, I had enough manhood left to come out in the open and say so. Yet [the] Fact Finding Committee accepted my resignation without allowing me before them, although I asked for this privilege, and they found, after a thorough investigation that "The articles . . . were published without faculty supervision and without the faculty expressing [an] opinion as to the accuracy of the statements contained in them."[9]

The attacks on Poteat may have reflected a sense that Poteat's reputation among some Baptists over evolution was interfering with obtaining adequate resources for the college, and they may also have resulted from the desire of younger faculty such as Kitchin to have a modernizing voice as the college faced the challenges of its rapid expansion. Feeling triumphant from the previous year's evolution battle, yet under a cloud and facing a divided Wake Forest, in November 1926 the seventy-year-old Poteat announced to the trustees, "In the sole consideration of my age and no other, and in conformity with a long settled purpose, I now request you to relieve me when the present session ends of the administrative responsibility to which you called me on June 22, 1905."[10] He carefully publicized his resignation only when "it could be made without the appearance of surrender or flight before opposition."[11] Though the trustees as a group had always backed Poteat, some individual members had long disliked his stands on matters internal and external to the college. His opponents on the board breathed a sigh of satisfaction that Poteat was at last stepping down: "You can't know how some of us have worked to get this result," one wrote, "and the relief we felt when he read the announcement."[12]

Poteat approved quite strongly of his successor in the presidency, Francis Pendleton Gaines, a scholar of southern plantation literature. Gaines took the reins in June 1927 to the applause of all North Carolina. One journalist described him as "a man after Dr. Poteat's own heart. . . . He has the qualities that are needed for the place—ability, scholarship, vision, character, personality."[13] Poteat soon noted that "President Gaines is fitting in here admirably. He is a delightful man, personally, and is going to make us a great president."[14]

Poteat celebrated his retirement with a visit of two and a half months to Europe and the Near East, including Egypt, Palestine, Syria, and Constantinople. Donations from Wake Forest alumni, principally his former students, covered the expenses, and Poteat, though his wife was too weak to accompany him, concluded that it was the "best trip" of his four voyages abroad.[15] Then, at the promised invitation of the college's trustees, he resumed his professorship in the department of biology and assumed the title of president emeritus, a position carrying a separate salary that kept his total income equal to that of his active presidency. "I have again risen to the dignity of teaching," he rejoiced to a friend, "and my two Biology classes must have some of my time."[16] Poteat generally taught in the mornings, Tuesday through Friday, and his classes soon topped 250 total students, more "than ever before." His time for other interests was "severely" limited by his teaching, which included biology and a class for freshmen on health and hygiene.[17] He continued to devote special attention in his lectures to alleviating any concern among students that science conflicted with religion, even reading parts of Genesis with the biology classes. A sympathetic grader, Poteat gave almost half his students a final mark of A or B.[18]

With the years "flying round ever faster," Poteat also worked hard to keep his knowledge of biology up-to-date. He made plans during his first session of teaching to attend the meeting of the American Association for the Advancement of Science. "You see," he noted to a scientist friend, "I must get in again on my science of Biology, find out who the boys are and what they are thinking about." Like most teachers, he lamented that "I don't get time to read one-tenth of what I'd like to read. My science, biology, is so on the move, so expansive, that I can't keep up with that." Nonetheless, he ordered stacks of scientific monographs and in 1933 was elected a fellow of the AAAS. He continued to correspond with other scientists, presented a paper with a Wake Forest graduate student to the 1928 meeting of the North Carolina Academy of Science, served on various committees for the academy, and continued to present papers and collect botanical and zoological specimens. In addition to perusing his scientific literature, he found time to be a close reader of the *New Republic* and *Harper's* magazines, as well as continuing his lifetime love of poetry.[19]

The Poteats' family life was also exceptionally rewarding to the aging couple during this period. William and Emma remained close, and their old friend, author Thomas Dixon Jr., found the pair to be "young and vital and forward looking" despite their advancing age. Emma wrote William almost daily when he traveled to meetings or speaking engagements. She was sensitive and often sick and relied heavily on her husband's love. "The 12:20 bell is ringing now," she wrote longingly to her absent husband, "and I'd like to take my seat at the front window to watch for your grey hat to appear over the hedge." He often responded from the road and affectionately signed once as "the same Old Timer." Within the close confines of the town of Wake Forest, they also spent a lot of time with Hubert and his wife and two children. Poteat's sister Ida often visited from Raleigh, and their daughter Louie lived in nearby Williamston with her husband and son. Time with their daughter Helen was a special treat once she and her writer/journalist husband, Laurence Stallings, moved to the New York area. Visits to this dashing, intellectual couple helped to keep Poteat in touch with the changing social mores of the younger generation. Through this connection Poteat also came to know such prominent critics as Walter Lippmann. Helen's daughter Sylvia was a favorite among their five grandchildren and a special guest in Poteat's laboratory. Her picture occupied a special spot on Emma's bookshelf, and Poteat wrote poems in praise of Sylvia and soon of her younger sister Diana.[20] The presence of their children and grandchildren and their accomplishments were sources of great satisfaction; Poteat celebrated "the overflow of the happiness of children, then of the grandchildren" in his life.[21]

William and Emma Poteat spent fifty-seven years together in a marriage that produced three children. They enjoyed a serene and supportive family life in the little town of Wake Forest, socializing predominantly with other members of the college community.

William and Emma often visited Lake Junaluska, the state's Methodist retreat, and Blue Ridge, the YMCA retreat, both in the beautiful mountains of western North Carolina. Poteat particularly enjoyed his trips to Blue Ridge, having been a regular visitor since around 1910.[22] They also frequently traveled back to Poteat's childhood mansion "Forest Home," once he and his siblings sold the dilapidated home, long used by tenants, to Helen and Laurence. The Stallings restored and extended the old showplace, creating a haven for themselves from their busy life that shifted dizzyingly from New York to California.[23] Amid his own travel, Poteat also found time for reflection. He and Emma spent much of the summer of 1928 in Westport, Connecticut, with Helen, and Poteat took advantage of the distance and relaxation to jot down some reflections on his early life. He also devoted some time to genealogy, hoping "to put the pedigree in proper shape."[24] Musings about his early life appeared in a more formal form a few years later when he wrote an article for the *American Scholar* at the request of his old Chapel Hill friend Harry W. Chase, who had become chancellor of New York University.[25]

Poteat's spare time after his retirement went predominantly to speaking and lecturing to groups including high school and college commencements, chambers of commerce and civic clubs, garden clubs, and even the sixth grade class of Wake Forest Public School. Not too unusual was his realization in

February 1928 that he had "four engagements in as many days." He made a good deal of money from his speeches because his "usual honorarium for . . . special addresses" varied from $50 to $150, though for local groups he charged less. Speaking for extra income was both "necessity and choice" for him; he often spoke for free on behalf of causes of interest to him but turned down other events that offered no money. Poteat felt he had much to offer an audience; he prodded an administrator for a late payment by noting "you certainly could not have expected me, with an extensive and varied experience, to pay for the privilege of speaking" at the commencement in question. The Poteats lived quite comfortably on his dual income, but when the onset of the Great Depression brought pleas for financial assistance from old acquaintances, he admonished, "The little I have been able to save from my monthly salary—sometimes that little is nothing—goes into a savings account against the time of my incapacity."[26]

A signal event of the early thirties was the Poteats' golden wedding anniversary. In July and August 1931 they celebrated with a fifty-day trip to Europe, hitting the high points from London to Rome as part of a group. Poteat enjoyed the trip, his fifth abroad, noting "the best way for an average man to travel, under limitations of time and money, is with a conducted party without worry." On the way from Venice to Milan, Poteat composed a touching tribute to his wife: "I have loved you, / These fifty golden days of thirty-one,— / These fifty golden years since eighty-one,— / And, please God, at length we'll take together / The same street in the golden city of our dreams."[27]

In addition to each other, the Wake Forest Baptist Church was a constant in the Poteats' later lives. Emma was active with the missionary circle, sometimes taking leadership roles there. Poteat chaired the board of deacons for the church and performed such duties as searching for a new pastor and acting as delegate to the state convention. Especially noteworthy was the couple's choice in 1933 to leave the choir after fifty-two years of singing there.[28] William Poteat also remained influential in Baptist educational circles. He continued to serve on the board of trustees of Meredith College, though he did not always attend the meetings, and he often appeared on the campus there.[29]

In a more time-consuming duty soon after his retirement, he was drawn into the Baptist Centennial Campaign that the state convention organized to mark its hundredth anniversary. Planning began by early 1927 for the celebration to occur in 1930, and the denominational leaders sought to use the occasion and the campaign to raise $1.5 million to free the state's six smaller Baptist colleges from debt and to add $250,000 to Wake Forest's assets. The canvass was launched in October 1927, and Poteat was from the first "under obligation" to meet "numerous engagements in North Carolina on the Centennial program." Demands on him were "pretty heavy" in 1928 as well, but he found the work "exciting." Poteat's assignment in his frequent appearances was to inspire the church audiences with a speech of twenty to thirty minutes, and he offered a talk that traced the history of Baptists in the state and lauded the early proponents of education, such as Samuel Wait, who over-came "indifference and opposition." He asked the faithful to carry out those pioneers' commitments by funding the Christian colleges in the interest of the kingdom of God. In 1929 Poteat was named to a special committee to plan the celebration, and as part of the daylong commemoration in March 1930 he delivered a speech on the "Growth of Education, 1830–1930." Appropriate to his own long service there, he concluded correctly, "The Wake Forest which we know and love today is rooted with a continuous life in the past."[30]

Poteat also played a variety of more mundane roles at Wake Forest and within the denomination following his retirement. He often taught at the chapel service for students. At the college, he worked hard to raise funds from alumni for building projects, chaired a building committee, again sought Carnegie Foundation funds for library development, and begged old friends to solicit new students for Wake Forest. In 1932–33, depression-era stringency caused a salary cut of 30 percent for faculty, in the wake of smaller cuts the year before. Poteat circumspectly brought before the board of trustees the faculty's concern about their priority in the budget in relation to funding activities such as athletics. In 1935 he urged the administration to rebel against the American Medical Association's attempt to close Wake Forest's two-year medical school. Poteat also represented Wake Forest at official functions such as inaugurations and anniversaries at other colleges. In these and a myriad other ways in addition to teaching, he continued to contribute to the college.

Within the denomination he served uneventfully on the board of trustees of the Southern Baptist Theological Seminary, and under the auspices of the Southern Baptist Convention Poteat remained a member of a committee on the promotion and standardization of denominational colleges. The committee, with Poteat's frequent input, sought to assure that colleges endorsed by the convention not only had solid academic resources but also continued the emphasis on religion that justified their separate existence. Poteat also served a more general administrative duty during the 1930s, first as a member then as chairman of the board of trustees for the state convention, dealing with such matters as the debt load during the depression. In 1933 he was honored as the first layman ever to preach the state convention's introductory sermon.[31]

In a battle that erupted closer to home in 1930, Poteat was forced to defend his belief that Wake Forest existed to combine religion with academics and that the college should remain rooted in its past. Poteat's successor as president, Francis P. Gaines, departed to head Washington and Lee University, and in the ensuing scramble for the presidency some old animosities resurfaced.[32] Thurman Kitchin, the center of much ill will in 1926, seized the new opportunity to further satisfy his ambition. A medical school professor recalled, "After Dr. Poteat had retired, Dr. Kitchin's disappointment at not getting the presidency led him to start a campaign to discredit President Gaines." Kitchin also "continued his campaign by attacking Dr. Poteat's friends on the campus. . . ."[33] In 1930 Kitchin saw his chance. He had a subordinate "arrange to have a petition circulated among the students asking for Kitchin's election." Further, as one historian summarized Kitchin's tactics, the assistant "also lobbied the faculty, while Dr. Wingate M. Johnson and Kitchin's brother, Leland Kitchin, both trustees, were Kitchin's campaign managers in the board of trustees."[34]

Poteat was bitterly disappointed. He had felt that Kitchin would not continue the disruptions after 1926, but by 1929 he admitted to a friend that "it appears you were right and I wrong when we spoke of such a possibility."[35] In 1930 Poteat leaped forward to correct "the impression which the campaigners for Dr. Kitchin have made in the public prints and by a recent letter in the minds of the trustees that the faculty of the College is practically united in support of Dr. Kitchin. . . ."[36] On the contrary, Poteat demonstrated, the faculty was deeply divided, and "the men who have been longest connected with the College are, for the most part, the men who find themselves unable to support Dr. Kitchin."[37] In a sense, this struggle represented a group of young, politically able professors attacking the older, established leaders of the college.

In his protests against Kitchin, Poteat revealed the vision of Wake Forest that he and his senior colleagues cherished. Though Kitchin was capable within his specialty, Poteat asserted, "to general scholarship he lays no claim." In other words, he lacked the encompassing literary understanding of the genteel, classical tradition. "A more serious defect," Poteat noted, "is that he is not by training or habit active in church work." For instance, "it would embarrass him to be called on to lead in prayer." Further, "it is difficult to imagine him representing the spiritual emphasis of our intellectual life in the pulpit of a church or before an association or State Convention, or at college in private relations and at the chapel hour. That emphasis is, of course, precisely what justifies our place in the educational scheme." Kitchin's leadership style also gravely offended Poteat. "Now we need a vigorous religious leadership which will unite all our forces and institutions in harmonious co-operation on our grave denominational task." However, "Dr. Kitchin and his leading campaigners have shown themselves incapable of such leadership, for they are now for the second time in five years leading a divisive movement in the College community and in the denomination at large."[38]

Poteat's opposition to the narrow specialized attainments of Kitchin reflects the aging professor's broader dislike of the trend toward specialization and secularization. As he boasted in an interview in the thirties, "I decline to be a specialist. And that accounts for my general interest in public matters, I suppose. I have a definition of a specialist. He is a man who has one interest and no horizon." Poteat especially disliked the specialist in science: "What they call scientific research is . . . 75% bunk. Here is a man who gets his Ph.D. degree in some university on the 'Bacterial Content of Cotton Undershirts.' . . . I understand, of course, that this little item of observation may contribute something to human knowledge, but they have no relation to culture at all." Scientists furthermore do not "know how to talk," Poteat worried. Two presenters whom he saw at a conference "did not open their mouths. They pointed out figures on the board, addressing the wall instead of the audience."[39]

Just as Poteat ultimately lost the broader battle against specialization, he also failed to secure his view on the future of Wake Forest. On July 2, 1930, at a meeting of the trustees, the nominating committee's only strong candidate refused to be considered; Kitchin "was nominated from the floor"; and in Poteat's unbelieving words, "the impossible has again happened."[40] Ever the genteel peacemaker, Poteat wrote Kitchin the same day that, although he had actively and publicly opposed his selection, "now that the Board has decided the matter and you are our President, I offer you any service I am able to render to make your administration successful."[41] Though Poteat also wrote a number of other upset partisans in the interest of cooperation, privately he could not "feel very hopeful."[42] True to his words, though, Poteat was able to work effectively if not affectionately with Kitchin, and Wake Forest did not significantly change direction under Kitchin until soon after Poteat's death, when agreement was made for first the medical school and then the whole college to move to Winston-Salem.

In the summer of 1936 another controversy tore across the Wake Forest campus, and again Poteat unsuccessfully advocated denominational harmony and a genteel approach to solving the problem. The board of trustees, at the request of the student body, agreed to allow supervised dancing to occur on campus. The denomination's *Biblical Recorder* publicized the action, and a flood of criticism poured in from associations and individual Baptists across the state. Soon, the inaction of the faculty, along with "the unbecoming conduct of the fraternities," was included in the attack against "worldliness at Wake Forest. . . ." Demand grew among the state's Baptists for a meeting of the trustees to be called to rescind the action, but President Kitchin "felt it would be unfortunate for the college to be dominated by this element," which comprised "for the most part those who were outnumbered in the last attack on the liberal policies of the college. . . ." Despite Kitchin's request, Poteat refused to support the trustees with a public statement, probably recognizing that his name would only cause conservatives to redouble their attacks. However, he tried to calm the situation with personal letters.[43]

Poteat addressed "a friendly private word to the editor" of the *Biblical Recorder,* accusing him of "conducting a propaganda of misrepresentation." Baptists were "whipped up to a radical division" on an issue that had been dead for forty years because the churches "have grown intelligent." Demonstrating his lack of understanding of popular belief, Poteat claimed that it was "an erroneous assumption . . . that the Baptist churches of North Carolina think dancing is sin per se." He believed it to be "outrageous" that Baptists would consider ending their support of the college and would accuse it of having "betrayed their trust."[44] Poteat circulated the letter among various trustees and convention leaders. Several agreed with his "liberal and young point of view," but popular pressure nonetheless forced a compromise. The students agreed to present the executive committee of the trustees with a withdrawal of their plea for dancing. "This way out is on the face of it a compromise and humiliating aspects of it make it difficult to swallow," Poteat reported, "but I guess we shall have to consent."[45] For perhaps the first time, conservatives had defeated the liberal leadership of the college in one of the many hotly contested battles about college governance. Community harmony was slipping in the arena most dear to Poteat.

An Old Ideology in a New Time

The genteel Christian community led by a liberal elite that Poteat envisioned began to encounter strong popular resistance in the 1930s. Within Baptist circles, believers in conservative Christianity continued to chafe under the leadership of religious liberals. The vestiges of a conservative religious movement defeated on the evolution issue in the twenties, returned to demand a voice on such matters as dancing, just as political elites during the Great Depression were forced to acknowledge popular sentiment.[46] A broader challenge to Poteat's values was the national trend away from the morality and intellectual pursuits of the Victorian era and toward the new period's emphasis on individualism and specialization. Kitchin's ambition, political savvy, and success despite a lack of religious leadership and literary achievement foreshadowed changes in the world Poteat knew. The failure of Poteat's brand of liberal uplift and general evangelical guidance spread to circles beyond Wake Forest and the Baptist denomination. Poteat continued to be active in the late 1920s and the 1930s on behalf of numerous causes that directly continued reform efforts from North Carolina's Progressive Era. On state and national issues—as in local struggles—Poteat's solutions, anchored in religion and unchanged for many years, began to lose their appeal and efficacy in the decade following his retirement. The Progressive community that he imagined would bring the kingdom of God on earth instead splintered even further in a new political atmosphere.

Poteat constantly became involved in symbolic and minor issues in support of a number of campaigns, but the bulk of his speaking and activism was on behalf of a handful of causes. In 1927 Poteat had a reputation as "North Carolina's leading liberal," and he used the resulting recognition to continue, with less and less effectiveness, the Progressive crusades of an earlier era.[47] He recognized in the late twenties that times had changed, but even at his death he still tried to apply old remedies to society's problems. Poteat had identified a deep moral and social crisis following the World War, and he continued to argue that the solution lay in the application of Christian tenets. He persevered in using scientific language in morally charged recommendations for eugenics planning and stricter marriage and divorce legislation. Likewise, to Poteat the industrial unrest and economic antipathies of the depression era required only the calming hand of Christian brotherhood, as did the international arena of war and arms buildups. The fight for repeal and the end of Prohibition represented to him immoral attacks on social righteousness and welfare, while the South's ever-present racial tension also demanded a religious solution. In each of these cases, Poteat was building on interests held during the Progressive Era from the turn of the century to the early twenties. At that earlier time, the recommendations of Poteat and his fellow reformers were in many cases implemented, but on certain issues the same ideology encountered increasingly effective resistance in the new era, as political and social relations in the South began to resemble the rest of modern America. Progressives had pioneered modern pressure politics in the South, but by the 1930s they had lost their monopoly and faced well-organized resistance on issues such as Prohibition, race relations, and industrial unrest.[48]

Poteat lent the prestige of his endorsement to several minor causes in the late twenties and early thirties, frequently serving only in a symbolic capacity. He was part of a committee to encourage commemoration of the 400th anniversary of the printed Bible; he joined a list of supporters for a proposed children's magazine; and along with the governor and some senators he allowed the use of his name "to give added prestige to the work being done by the North Carolina State Art Society." Because of his "sympathy with the aims of the Federal Writers' Project," he accepted appointment to its State Advisory Council, and at the request of the 1927 General Assembly he was part of the Andrew Johnson Memorial Commission to preserve the presidential birthplace. Poteat even declined to serve for other causes for he preferred "not to hold a merely formal position" if he did not have time to be active. The governor likewise honored Poteat and asked him to serve on a committee of arrangements to organize a celebration of the 150th anniversary of the Battle of Guilford Courthouse. Only scheduling conflicts forced Poteat to turn down other honorary gubernatorial appointments. The widespread desire to use his name underscores Poteat's success in being a liberal without going against traditional southern mores.[49]

Even Poteat's minor activities were often on behalf of causes in tune with the ideology of the Progressives. He was a member of the national committee of the Clean Amusement Association that advocated "clean" movies, entertainment, and literature. His interest in children made him a natural to serve on the advisory committee for the Lee School for Boys near Blue Ridge, North Carolina. Likewise in a Progressive vein, Poteat—ever eager to establish appropriate boundaries—lauded the State Highway Commission for expanding the use of the center line on paved highways.[50] On similar assumptions about morality and social control, Poteat devoted a bit of time to fighting legalized gambling. In 1931 he wired his state senator not to "sell the conscience of N.C." by voting for a gambling bill, and in 1933 he asked his old friend and now U.S. Senator Josiah W. Bailey not to appoint a particular state politician "to any post of public duty." Poteat explained, "I deeply resent his smuggling the gambling bill through the late General Assembly." His objection was to attempts in 1933 to pass the measure, which allowed a particular county to hold a referendum about a race track, by suspending the rules and avoiding a reading of the bill.[51] While minor, these associations and activities reveal the consistency and unity of Poteat's Progressive intellectual views.

Of somewhat more consequence was Poteat's service on the central committee of the Citizens' Library Movement, a campaign in 1928 led by perennial Tarheel liberal Frank Graham to agitate for "a county-wide library service" in every one of the state's forty-six counties that lacked one. In the now familiar Progressive method, the state was divided into districts, a speakers bureau was organized, and local advocacy began in cooperation with other interested groups. "Heaven knows our State is very backward in its reading habits," Poteat ruminated to Graham, "and something ought to be done for the general enlightenment." Apparently relatively little was accomplished, however, for the movement soon faded and had to be revived in 1934.[52]

Poteat had a strong working relationship with Graham when Graham headed the North Carolina Conference for Social Service (NCCSS) from 1928 to 1930. By virtue of his 1919–20 term as president of that body, Poteat remained on its board of directors, and Graham sought to keep him active. The conference met in Raleigh during each legislative session and lobbied, in 1929 for example, on behalf of the members' belief "in the Australian ballot, in workmen's compensation, in adequate guarantees for the education of children, in progress in the care of the wards of the state: orphans, juvenile delinquents, prisoners, the mentally defective, and the physically ill." Poteat, in cooperation with the women's clubs of the state, pushed especially for the secret ballot, perhaps reflecting the same interest in improving the voting process that landed him on the advisory committee of the North Carolina League of Women Voters. During the late twenties and early thirties, the emphasis of the NCCSS shifted to include industrial problems, and Poteat advocated harmony for that troubled area as well. As chairman of the conference's legislative committee, Poteat pushed, in cooperation with the League of Women Voters, to strengthen somewhat the eight-hour law regulating the labor of children. The NCCSS's overall work was in "attempting to embody the spirit" found in "the Social Principles of Jesus." Poteat continued his work with the NCCSS even after Graham cut back on his involvement after 1930 when he was elevated from professor of history to president of the University of North Carolina.[53] As sociologist E.C. Branson noted to Poteat, "You and Frank Graham make an unbeatable team."[54]

Poteat and Graham remained in close contact, with the Wake Forest–North Carolina football game being an annual ritual. In 1936 Poteat enthusiastically accepted Graham's invitation "to attend an informal regional conference here of representatives of the Catholic, Jewish, and Protestant religions in the Southeastern states." Sponsored by the University of North Carolina and the Duke University School of Religion, the conference brought together Tarheel liberals to address evidence that "inter-racial and inter-religious tensions in the United States [are] multiplying." The group's makeup underscored the longtime prevalence of religious motives for Progressive social measures in North Carolina, and their methods reflected the experience of many of the same people in the state's Commission on Interracial Cooperation. Graham explained the gathering, "The sessions are not to be meetings for speech making, but genuine conferences for the exchange of experiences, ideas, points of view, with a view to planning for our Southern area in these fundamental matters of inter-group relations for a more deeply spiritual life and faith in our three religious communions."[55] At its meeting, the group recommended several ways to ease the crisis, again reminiscent of earlier methods. "A round table in every community" and teams of visiting clergymen in urban areas, along with observance of Brotherhood Day and seminars in teachers' colleges, were sponsored in this top-down, uplifting liberal method.[56] The old approach of spreading recognition of the interdependence of social groups remained the Progressive option, but in changing times its Protestant proponents reached out to include additional religious circles.

Poteat's endorsement of these goals was consistent with the view of government, arrived at decades previously, that he continued to hold late in life. On the level of the individual, happiness required "harmony in all concentric circles of our relationships," and he applied this belief to higher forms of organization.[57] The nation to him was an "aggregation of states," which were in turn composed of communities. Poteat tellingly defined a community as a "group of people in a single locality united by common interests and subject to common laws."[58] "Members of the community" should "act together" in a "spirit of unity and of practical cooperation. . . ." With developments in communication and transportation, "the opportunities for community action through government are enormously multiplied. . . ." Operations such as building roads needed "the general consent of the people," in Poteat's view, and should not involve political antagonism among competing interests. The acceptance of self-interested activity risked falling victim to the "shallow theory of democracy and personal liberty" that was one of the "most dangerous enemies" of "social order." Instead, "we must maintain without wavering [the] policy of expert superintendence" that would remove such decisions as road-building from the political arena.[59] Outdated local loyalties represented another danger to good government. He explained, "our internal development in the gigantic machinery of communication, in industry, and in agriculture has welded all sections into a close interdependence, and in spite of laments over the vanishing rights of the States we are now accustomed to writing Nation with a capital N."[60]

Democracy continued to have many problems in Poteat's opinion, even at a time when democratic participation was a combative rallying cry for many of a new generation of reformers. For him, "equal participation in government, universal suffrage, and majority rule are not democracy itself so much as the mechanism of democracy." Instead, "the essence of democracy is the spirit of fraternity and justice, which recognizes corporate responsibility as well as individual rights, and renders mass action possible in unprecedented volume and variety." This "democratic spirit," however, was as yet in the twenties "gravely backward in development."[61] His organic view of government was an ideal of the Progressive Era that became increasingly anachronistic and fell under attack, rather than developing further toward fulfillment.

North Carolina faced something of a predicament in the twenties, Poteat believed, yet many in the state failed to notice because they were too busy congratulating themselves on progress already made. Poteat urged that the Tarheel state move beyond its jingoistic boosterism and recognize that problems remained despite the obvious progress. The state, he wrote, "needs to sober her pride by recognizing her sins, to drop tail feathers for a cool minute to glance at ugly feet." Her education, for instance, remained "inferior" in comparison to the rest of the country, with heavy dropout rates, illiteracy, and "too much emphasis on method at the expense of subject matter." A second major challenge for the state was "law and order" because North Carolina led the nation in the illegal production of alcohol. "The intelligence and conscience of the state," Poteat urged, "need to be organized and made practically effective" in order to stop the violations. "Men of character and better equipment" were needed to overcome the problem that "our native independence is lapsing into license," while "ever and anon the mob digs into the foundations of our ordered life" (through the lynching of blacks).[62]

Poteat recognized that southern states other than North Carolina were similarly sensitive to criticism, but within limits he welcomed a constructive analysis of the problems. He could understand southern resentment "about the Cash and Mencken attitude toward the South" but advised that "any reply to them would only lay us open probably to the charge of the hypersensitiveness of an inferiority complex."[63] Poteat admitted that he was "unfamiliar with the so-called literature of the South" that had begun to blossom by the late twenties. He could not "feel any great sweep of enthusiasm about a body of literature that may be described as distinctively southern. . . ." Unlike the southern intellectuals of the twenties and thirties described by historian Michael O'Brien, Poteat did not seek solace from the South's problems by working to recreate a completely romantic southern identity of the nineteenth century. Instead, he tried to modify tradition by creating an updated form of community that at least partially acknowledged regional shortcomings.[64]

For him the discussions of the South had to do more than dwell in the past or expose the states' dark side. One difficulty, Poteat believed, was that "our people do not read," except perhaps newspapers that were not helpful in solving any problems. He still found journalism to be offensive: "What urge or enrichment for ambitious minds is there in the sporting page—pages, in the execrable funny paper, in the selfish scheming of many politicians and their low trading in the public welfare, in the sordid details of crime in remote places, in nauseating stories of social scandals." In the ultimate statement against the Modernist view then entering the South, he concluded, "Why nose around in garbage?" Jesus, after all, "understood life without exploring its dregs."[65]

Typically, Poteat did not limit his vision to his home region; his ideas about the problems of the twenties and thirties encompassed the nation, even the Western hemisphere. The situation began with "the new individualism and freedom since the World War" that was a "reaction and recoil from the earlier repressive discipline. . . ."[66] The root of the problem lay in the revival since the war "of old antipathies, as between the English and the French, white and black, labor and capital." He recognized that his envisioned Progressive community had not materialized. The "new individualism" at fault "passes easily into license and the denial of the rights of others and all forms of authority." Poteat elaborated, "Indeed, there seems to be a sort of frenzy of insubordination and crime. The unity of civilization itself is menaced by the forces of disunion and anarchy."[67]

Poteat felt no need to restore a fragmented worldview through a regional construct, nor to dwell on the negative potential of human nature, because he had never lost the comfortable hold of centering his life around religion. This intellectual and teacher of science, summarized his views in one urgent paragraph: "Religion is universal. Some science speakers have told us of finding a race of men so low they are destitute of religion but I contend that no race of men is destitute of religious belief and sentiment. Every man has a trace of religion in him. Why, it's the organizing force of human life. Things would fly apart but for the centralizing force and power of religion. . . . The very bond of union in society is religion. What holds our people together is religion and certainly not our politics."[68] He felt strongly that the rest of society needed to regain that "organizing force" to counter the uncertainties of the late twenties and the thirties.

He detailed his timeworn response to resolving the moral and social crisis in a series of speeches in 1928. In June he accepted an invitation to deliver three lectures the following October to the School of Religion at Chapel Hill, a religious organization intended to educate students regarding religion but independent of the secular university there. He retreated that summer to Westport, Connecticut, to spend time with his daughter, and began preparations that lasted until he was "furiously driven" to complete the talks in the three weeks prior to delivering them at the Methodist church in the active college town of Chapel Hill. Poteat received a tidy $250 for his efforts, and W.T. Couch and the University of North Carolina Press published the series in 1929 as *The Way of Victory*.[69] For his acquaintance Walter Lippmann, the eminent New York journalist and social critic, Poteat elaborated on his intentions in the book: "It starts out with the moral confusion and relaxation which your *Preface to Morals* describes with such terrific clearness, and proceeds to discover in Jesus at once the standard of the good life and the efficient incentive of conformity. Even if, as you say, Modernism does cast doubt upon the truth of the New Testament story, we still have him, for it is fair to distinguish between essentials and incidentals or glosses, between picture and features."[70] The book illuminates Poteat's view of society's unprecedented problems in the late twenties but underscores his belief that there was no need to develop new solutions.

Always careful not "to inquire how Christianity theorizes, but how it works," Poteat found that the inspiration of Jesus' example "gives stability, order, elevation, and aim to the individual life, and practically applied in our social life it will subordinate personal interest to the common good, compose our personal, class, and national antagonisms, and bring all the features and activities of our organized life into conformity with the will of God."[71] Society requires, he argued, "an inward, inviolable loyalty to goodness" to avoid "anarchy in the realm of morals. . . ." In a time marked by the "slackening of moral restraints," intellectuals especially seemed "hardly less free of restraint on elemental impulses than the Bambala of Africa." For the chaos, Poteat prescribed his longtime answer, the kingdom of God—defined as a "social spirit" that would "transfigure" family, state, and industrial and political organizations. Once individuals began to follow Christ, Poteat still believed—despite much evidence to the contrary in his long life—they would naturally transform whatever social, political, or business groups to which they belonged in accord with the ideals of Christ.[72] As Poteat confirmed elsewhere, "evangelism is first in time and first in importance."[73] He announced with some optimism in 1928 that "there are not wanting signs of a changing attitude of capital toward labor and the public, and this new attitude of conciliation and interest is met by less suspicion and resentment." In the economy, at least, Poteat felt that the kingdom of God showed signs of arrival as employers and employees discovered themselves to be "brothers in Christ."[74]

The onset of the Great Depression and the international militarization of the 1930s heightened Poteat's sense of alarm. In 1931 he lamented that "the situation now is radically different from that of a century ago." Then, he explained, "religion and its moral sanctions" were "practical forces controlling democracies"; and in politics, principles were recognized over expediency. A century later, legislators ruled by expediency, and "sharp practice, graft, extortion in business," and "wealth flashing vulgar extravagance in [the] face of starvation" characterized America.[75] Perhaps his earlier optimism led him to feel particularly betrayed when businessmen failed to respond to the depression in accord with religious principles. "Economic values appear to be the only values," he concluded. "It would seem, as one phrases it, that the day of prophets is gone and the day of profits is come." The "new industrialism" joined individualism on his list of contributors to social chaos.[76] "Unfettered competition," he fretted, "would shatter society to atoms."[77] Business corporations had clearly failed to recognize their obligations within a moral, interdependent community, and he condemned them to an extent that he would never have considered in the more optimistic early years of the Progressive Era.

As America's outlook bottomed out in 1931, Poteat went on the offensive against the sense of helplessness and bewilderment of the times. He asserted that despite "the economic revolution" that science had brought, "the fundamental interests and needs of human life are the same as they have ever been. It is only the conditions under which they assert themselves that are new." He refused to be cowed by the age of machines:

I decline to adjust myself to the new order. I adjust it to my needs. I decline to be embarrassed by its complexities. I unify them in a common subjection. I decline to be frightened out of my inner securities and commitments by the clatter of apparatus. Our scientific civilization is not an end, but a means to an end. It provides a condition of social life in which men have leisure for noble aims. And we are lost if . . . we do not insist on the eternal supremacy of mind over things and hold those guardians of our precious inheritance, the home, the school, and the pulpit, severely to their proper functions of affirming and promoting the spiritual values of life in our time, as in all times.[78]

That same year he also attacked, in a widely noticed address, "the sorry plight and extremity to which we are reduced by the genius and enterprise of American business." Noting that debutante balls occurred side by side with starvation, he asked for the "emancipation" of education and government from business interests. He concluded, "We must substitute guidance for drift, planning for this riot of disorder, co-operation for competition, service for profit, social justice for organized greed, political and economic."[79]

Overcoming the challenge of business hegemony and poor education was a difficult one. By 1935 Poteat had "to admit that the kingdom of the world does not present now any impressive prospect of soon becoming the Kingdom of our Lord." The power of "the economic motive" remained unchecked; family and education were threatened; "and what of racial discriminations, from the stupid cruelty of the Hitler regime to the passion of the Southern tradition."[80] In 1937 he sighed that the continuing presence of such immorality showed "our great business of evangelism is unfinished, possibly poorly done."[81]

Battling for Lost Causes

Poteat did more than simply lament the growth of greed and social conflict. He worked to shore up the decaying possibilities for a unified society that could be governed by Christian morality. Labor unrest—the implicit refusal of the mass of workers to accept that cooperation would bring a moral outcome—tore through some parts of North Carolina in the late 1920s. Poteat and others urged peace and cooperation by both labor and business, but to no avail. Force won the day. Big business in the shape of the alcohol industry triumphed as well—despite virtually a door-to-door defense by Poteat and other Prohibitionists who feared alcohol's immoral repercussions. Peace advocates such as Poteat also berated the weapons industry for pushing aside morality in a quest for profits. With the Great Depression intensifying Poteat's sense of postwar crisis, industry in these various forms had become, in his reformist rhetoric and direct advocacy, possibly the major obstruction to a peaceful, moral community. Nonetheless, Poteat could not entirely surrender his earlier trust of businessmen and his bias against aggressive organization by the lower classes. With industry unyielding, Poteat continued to try other routes to reform by maintaining a constant barrage of declarations on the front of eugenics, expanding his list of immoral people to be eliminated in the interest of future progress. On this topic, however, he finally pushed too far and found public and private rejection of his views. The strained Progressive search for community had finally snapped, but this adamant and faithful old reformer continued to pursue the futile quest.

The most important manifestation of Poteat's opposition to unfettered industrialism came with the violence surrounding the strikes against cotton mills in Gastonia and elsewhere in 1929. Through the North Carolina Conference for Social Service (NCCSS), at the request of Frank Graham, Poteat had already pressured the 1929 legislature to tighten regulation of child labor and to pass a workmen's compensation bill, using the NCCSS strategy that included cooperation with textile industrialists such as Robert Hanes and Kemp Battle.[82] In March and April 1929, in the wake of layoffs and lowered wages, a series of strikes began in the North Carolina textile industry, centering around the Loray Mill in Gastonia. The owners eventually defeated the strike with a combination of violence, red-baiting, and the use of the North Carolina National Guard. A mill worker named Ella May Wiggins, the strike's "balladeer and martyr," was killed, as was Gastonia police chief Orville Aderholt. In a travesty of justice, no one was convicted for the death of Wiggins, but seven strikers were questionably convicted in the death of Aderholt.[83]

Nell Battle Lewis, a noted liberal columnist for the *Raleigh News and Observer,* spoke out quickly against the lack of protection afforded the strikers by police. She solicited a guardedly liberal statement from Poteat for her column about the trial of the strikers accused of killing Aderholt: "The gentlemen who bear the responsibility of the Gastonia case will need to exercise especial care against any possible compromise of our State's honor and fair name. I very much hope the course of justice will not be clouded or diverted by local feeling."[84] Such mild statements did not prevent conviction, and a few months later protest against the acquittal of Wiggins's killers was similarly ineffective. Poteat cautiously stated to the *News and Observer* in October 1929 that "there is on the face of reports from Gastonia the appearance of partiality in administering the criminal law." He continued, "If such partiality is the real explanation of the failure of justice in Wiggins case then the Gaston grand jury has outraged the moral sense of North Carolina and deeply wounded the law itself and put in jeopardy the public order. The intelligence and conscience of the State expect the Governor to go to the limit of his authority and resources to secure conviction of perpetrators of this horrible murder."[85] The statement was hardly a ringing endorsement of the rights of labor, but it was a cautious call for impartial justice in a state where there was strong bias against the concept of labor unions.

The American Civil Liberties Union entered the case with a more active strategy of supplying counsel to strikers and of filing civil suits for damages "on behalf of those who have been kidnapped and beaten and maliciously prosecuted." The New York–based organization also offered a reward for information leading to the conviction of Wiggins's murderer. The group's leaders proposed "that the time is ripe for the organization of a group of citizens of North Carolina who will stand for the civil liberties of these workers. . . ."[86] Poteat responded unequivocally to this appeal, "I incline to think that the organization of a Civil Liberties group in N.C. at this time is unnecessary for the purpose contemplated, and it might quite possibly stir some resentment and so compromise such service as it might render." He answered similarly to a second request that he join a meeting in Raleigh held by the ACLU.[87] The ACLU's aggressive approach and legalistic antagonism conflicted strongly with Poteat's desire, typical of Progressive thought, for social problems to be settled in an orderly, efficient manner without overt conflict.

Poteat also expressed his dismay at the industrial unrest through a report to the Baptist State Convention on "Public Morals." He attested, "Recent industrial strife, stained with tragedy and the partial failure of justice, within the bounds of this Convention calls for rebuke and a fresh assertion of [the] inescapable authority of Christ's law of brotherhood in the world of business." Citing a fair wage as a prerequisite to peace, Poteat argued that it could only be determined "by a survey of the economic condition of industry by a State commission which represents the management, the workers, and the public. A survey of women and children in industry . . . is likewise advisable." The report was endorsed by the convention and even brought a rare comment of approval from the *Charlotte News*, located in the heart of the textile industry.[88]

Though Poteat and his brand of southern liberalism could not support direct action for the benefit of labor along the lines of the ACLU, he did welcome Frank Graham's subsequent suggestion, perhaps made to counter such outside agitation, that North Carolina citizens "make some sort of a declaration with regard to the issues raised by our industrial conflict." Poteat was "glad of the opportunity to unite in a North Carolina statement in relation to the industrial situation in our State" and noted the similarity between Graham's ideas and his own as expressed in the state convention report.[89] Graham and the NCCSS had decided soon after the strikes to take the industrial problem as its theme for 1930. Initially working informally through his NCCSS connections, Graham garnered over four hundred signatures for the petition, most from prominent Tarheel citizens. Graham, too, spurned the ACLU's offer of cooperation. "We are acting as a group of North Carolinians in our North Carolina way," he wrote to an ACLU official.[90] This attitude reflected Graham and Poteat's realization that sentiment against outsiders was so strong in the state that a connection with the ACLU would cost them local support. However, it also revealed the limits of their liberalism, which did not consider direct action a necessary step, despite the ineffectiveness of liberal declarations of principle.

The statement embodied moderate liberal-Progressive principles. Graham boasted, "Mr. Kemp Battle of Rocky Mount, who belongs to the family that has been in the cotton manufacturing business for 112 years, gladly signed the statement and suggested that the Board of Directors of the Conference sponsor its issuance in order that it may have a local habitation and a name." Graham anchored the proclamation in tradition: "It is in keeping with our North Carolina traditions that interested citizens try to look through the confusion and antagonisms of the hour to a few simple working principles born of our democratic experiment and experience." He argued that constitutional rights such as the freedoms of speech and assembly should be guaranteed regardless of unionism and that holding to the bill of rights would defeat the "fanaticism" of communism and fascism. Further, Graham noted that liberty allowed both capitalists and labor to organize and bargain collectively, "and, despite abuses on both sides, this equal right, when fairly recognized and cooperatively promoted, becomes economically productive, democratically stabilizing and humanly valuable." Third, the statement asked that "a nation-wide non-partisan economic and social survey and analysis of the textile industry be made at once." Finally, the petition asked for specific measures, drawn from conference goals, such as reduction of the sixty-hour week, "the gradual abolition of night work for women and young people," and a strengthening of the child labor law.[91] In its gradualism, urge for cooperation rather than confrontation, lack of partisanship, and longing for stability, the statement revealed a liberalism, anchored in Progressive ideals, that had little effect in the violent industrial South of the late twenties.

Beginning in 1929, Poteat also expressed his belief that industry was taking unfair advantage of the country by speaking out against any increase in tariff protection for American manufacturing. He wrote to an approving Senator Furnifold M. Simmons, "Why in the name of good sense and justice does not the great mass of the citizenship of our country protest . . . against any further levy upon their poverty to enrich a few men whose coffers already burst with unearned wealth?" The liberal Santford Martin, editor of the *Winston-Salem Journal,* reprinted Poteat's letter with a ringing endorsement. Poteat wrote as well to the *New York World* with a parable that reveals both his economic liberalism and his patronizing attitude toward portions of the very citizenry he wanted to uplift: "A friend tells me he was driving through a remote mountain district and saw a woman dash around the corner of the house and a four-year-old boy close on her heels. Later he asked the boy why he chased the women. 'She's my mother,' he said, 'and she's tryin' to wean me, dern her!'"[92] To Poteat, so-called infant industries similarly needed to be weaned from dependence on tariffs, and their protest could be expected.

Poteat's assumption that the relationship between industry and society should theoretically be a cooperative one found expression during the New Deal. He was unable to turn loose of his old tendency to believe (originally about child labor and railroads) that economic interest need not cloud moral issues. In January 1934 Governor John C.B. Ehringhaus appointed Poteat as one of two assistants to the Commissioner of Public Utilities, with responsibility for regulating the booming power industry of North Carolina. "We in North Carolina are not corporation baiters or corporation haters," the governor explained. He found Poteat to be qualified for the job because he was among the "best informed men in" the Old North State and was "known over the entire State as a man of honor, foresight and integrity." Poteat's appointment would assure "that the actions of the commission will be beyond the suggestion of unfairness either to the public or the utilities." The oath of office, however, contained the stipulation that the regulator have no interest in a public utility. In 1928 Poteat and his wife had invested much of their savings in shares of the Carolina Power and Light Company, money upon which they relied heavily, especially after the failure of a cotton mill early in the depression destroyed some other funds. It had not occurred to Poteat that owning stock in a utility company should in any way interfere with his ability to be impartial as a commissioner. When he discovered the stipulation at a gubernatorial ceremony, he was forced to withdraw in an embarrassing episode, understandably refusing to sell his stock at a depressed period in the market. Politics, to him, still represented a paternalistic duty, not a tightly controlled arena for competing groups. He could not envision the need to legislate against the bias of a man of integrity.[93]

Nonetheless, Poteat had for decades been a part of the first modern organized interest group in southern politics—the Prohibition lobby.[94] The Progressives had pioneered such political methods late in the nineteenth century, but by the 1930s their opponents had learned to use the same tactics successfully. In the case of Prohibition in North Carolina, dry advocates maintained the state Anti-Saloon League even after the Eighteenth Amendment was ratified. This "organization largely of church-going people" pressed for effective enforcement of Prohibition by using churches as a forum for field days advocating stronger laws. In 1923 a strong state law, the Turlington Act, passed with league support.[95] The league, however, faced destruction after 1928 when superintendent C.A. Upchurch, a Baptist minister, led the league in support of Herbert Hoover against the Democratic (and wet) Al Smith. Hoover took the state, but the group was left virtually nonexistent for three years afterward because even though the league was officially nonpartisan it was dominated by Democrats who resented Upchurch's decision to back a candidate of the Republican party. Upchurch tried to revive the organization by calling a statewide convention in January 1932, but the opposition and lingering resentment of some Democratic drys prevented effective action.[96] Poteat encouraged superintendent Upchurch in his thankless task of holding together "the fragments" of the organization.[97]

In 1928 Poteat worked against the nomination of Al Smith, informing a senator that it was Smith's "avowed opposition to the Eighteenth Amendment which is so universally offensive in the South and West."[98] Poteat specified that he was "entirely out of sympathy with the raising of the religious issue" and went so far as to declare later that "if I had felt that the religious issue was sharply drawn and dominant in the campaign, I should have voted for Smith by way of protest, in spite of my objection to him on other grounds."[99] Poteat did not accept the action of the Southern Baptist Convention (SBC) pledging its members to vote against Smith; though the SBC's opinion would carry much weight, he argued, it "cannot pledge its constituency to any definite policy, religious or political, or impose its view upon any Baptist in affiliation with it."[100] He had no difficulty with his own departure from the Democrats, though, for he had been "several times unable to vote for" the candidate of his usual party, the Democrats.[101]

By 1930 Poteat acknowledged the need for more effective work in defense of Prohibition. Despite the Eighteenth Amendment's overwhelming success, Poteat noted, its advocates "have allowed the defeated minority aggressive propaganda all but unobstructed and unanswered, and it has developed a situation too serious to be ignored." At the behest of the league he observed the tenth anniversary of the date that Prohibition became effective by speaking to two crowds the same Sunday. He defended the policy against claims that it encouraged lawlessness, that it was an unjustified invasion of liberty, and that alcohol was a needed stimulant. In his opinion, only a "unified plan of enforcement" was needed to overcome the "caricatures" and "sophistry" of advocates of repeal.[102] On another occasion he despaired that "one of the most discouraging things in American public life is the success which designing men secure in putting over on our people specious logic and wholesale misrepresentation." He was most perturbed by the opposition's influential claim that Prohibition was the result of a group of fanatics who caught the country napping.[103] In 1931 Poteat was part of a special committee of ten set up by the league's board of trustees (of which he was a member) to reinvigorate the cause.[104] Despite their efforts, the group, he observed that year, "appears to have hard going in North Carolina. . . . Perhaps the most important factor is the activity of the League . . . for Mr. Hoover in a democratic state." Its finances were in deficit due also to the depression and the "complacency" of victory.[105]

Poteat supported the 1932 reorganization of the league. He was elected president at its January 1932 convention and soon joined the board of directors alongside a number of the state's most influential ministers, as well as Frank P. Graham. The new board replaced Upchurch with George J. Burnett, also a Baptist minister, and launched a weak and unsuccessful offensive on behalf of the senate candidacy of dry incumbent (and former anti-evolutionist governor) Cameron Morrison. Poteat praised Morrison's defense of "a wise and good law against the attack of many self-seeking politicians and misguided private citizens, and against its indifferent and loose administration."[106] Morrison's defeat left the situation "quite clear. We must fight. We are advised to go back to teaching temperance in the Sunday School, but we must fight now to preserve what generations of such teaching have won for us." He sought to overcome the challenge of both "the drinkers of coarser fibre . . . whose pay checks and sorrows dissolve in liquor" and "the elegant tipplers . . . together with the intellectuals who want release for the full flowering of their art" but who "command the organs of opinion, in which they have been very free with caricature and offensive epithets for the ignorant unwashed who dare to differ with them."[107] Relying on the "authoritative announcements by the Federal Government," Poteat argued that Prohibition had cut liquor consumption by 60 percent despite never having had an administration committed to enforcement.[108] He introduced a resolution at the 1932 Baptist State Convention to protest anticipated attempts to loosen the Volstead Law by legalizing beer, and headed the committee that transmitted the protest to President Hoover, Franklin Roosevelt, and all of North Carolina's senators and representatives.[109]

As the drys had feared, the 1933 state legislature authorized the sale of beverages of up to 3.2 percent alcohol and provided for an election in November 1933 to decide whether North Carolina should call a convention to ratify the Twenty-first Amendment, with its repeal of Prohibition. Recognizing the incapacity of the Anti-Saloon League to handle the challenge, thirty dry leaders from the league, the WCTU, the YMCA, and various other dry organizations gathered in Raleigh and formed the United Dry Forces of North Carolina, a nonpartisan, interdenominational group that chose Poteat as president. He brought before a state house committee an impressive array of speakers, including Josephus Daniels, to oppose both pieces of legislation, but to no avail. The group organized permanently after the legislature ended and decided to contest the November election on the repeal issue using a central committee of three hundred members from across the state. Poteat continued as president, and Raleigh attorney Cale K. Burgess was chosen to lead the campaign.[110]

The drys attacked on the grounds that if North Carolina voted for national repeal, it would mean the end of state Prohibition, even though North Carolina would revert to its old state law. As Poteat voiced it, "the liquor forces, which were so successful in bamboozling the politicians . . . , will be satisfied with nothing short of the destruction of Prohibition root and branch and the return of the licensed liquor traffic."[111] The United Dry Forces utilized a well-organized and bipartisan lineup of speakers, coordinated by an eastern and a western headquarters and rallying around branch organizations formed in each of the Tarheel state's one hundred counties. Mass meetings planned for every county on September 3 launched an offensive that lasted until the repeal election on November 7. Even a junior phalanx was involved in some counties. Poteat argued that the vote was not even needed "because our people. . . . have not asked that the issue be re-opened." The whole outcry was "by a small number who are financially interested in the restoration of the liquor traffic."[112] The drys raised their successful counterattack by using prominent speakers such as Clyde R. Hoey, setting aside a day of prayer before the election, and keeping their cause before the people through weekly press releases.[113] The result on election day was what the campaign director Burgess termed a "glorious victory" for "the forces of righteousness. . . ." North Carolina voters rejected a repeal convention by a margin of over 170,000 votes.[114] Poteat had made "about twenty addresses, including one radio address, a number of them printed in full," during the 1933 campaign. He rejoiced that the "Dry sentiment unwavering since 1908 found its voice."[115]

The victory was short-lived, however, and though Poteat fought against it at every step, alcohol returned to North Carolina following the national passage of repeal. The old Progressive ideas and methods could not withstand the onslaught of organized wet sentiment that gradually overwhelmed dry opposition. The United Dry Forces retained a permanent organization with Poteat as president even after their victory to continue "a constructive program of education in favor of temperance and against the evils of alcohol."[116] He lamented in early 1934 that "we lost the battle, but we have not lost the war." Nonetheless, beginning with the 1935 legislative session, victories began for the wets.[117]

Bills were introduced to raise the alcoholic content of beers to 5 percent and to hold a state referendum on repealing state Prohibition laws in favor of county option. Though troubled by illness during the session, Poteat appeared before a legislative hearing and personally lobbied his representative. He opposed the referendum supporters' appeal to democracy by arguing that the issue had only recently been decided with the 1933 vote; "to ask them again so soon is to be disrespectful, not to say contemptuous."[118] Perhaps learning from 1928, Poteat attempted to keep the appeal nonpartisan as well in order "to resist the intrusion of politics into our great and victorious cause. . . ."[119] Despite these efforts, not only was the legal alcohol content raised, but also on the day of the legislature's adjournment the General Assembly passed a bill providing for local option elections in nearly twenty counties in eastern North Carolina that would allow the complete return of liquor under the regulation of an Alcoholic Beverage Control Board. Despite the continuing opposition of the dry forces, virtually every eligible county voted for repeal.[120]

In 1933 Poteat had begun planning a little book "on the physiological and social effects of beverage alcohol," and after determinedly but futilely offering it to northern publishers, he concluded reluctantly that "they don't like the doctrine in that region" and allowed Broadman Press of the Baptist Sunday School Board to publish the book in 1935. It sold quickly, over a thousand copies by May 1936, and a second printing was necessary by late 1935. The ninety-one-page book, titled *Stop-light*, was widely and positively received in the South, with reviewers noting Poteat's authority as a scientist, but the *Journal of the American Medical Association* scathingly evaluated it as propaganda.[121]

He sought to erect a stoplight on "the highway of gaiety and indulgence" that threatened to mislead rebellious and individualistic youth and to direct attention "upon the elementary and undisputed facts of beverage alcohol as they are presented in the cold science of the time." From those facts, however, would come "suggestions for corporate action to safeguard at once the individual and social life." Poteat cited what one reviewer called "ancient literature" in laying out the history of alcohol, discussing its physiological function as a depressant and its effect on the central nervous system, and countering arguments that alcohol was medically useful. An example of his discussion of alcohol's effects on youth reveals the book's tone: "It narcotizes their centers of control, and they themselves lapse into creatures of impulse likely to do or to say anything,—*anything*—which the instinct of the moment suggests." As a result, "self-control, caution, respect for the proprieties and decencies of our ordered life, are lost."[122] The crux of his argument was moral; law existed "to prevent that which is evil." Alcohol ranked high on that list; to Poteat it represented "the greatest single enemy of mankind, and some means of limiting its devastation mankind must discover, or suffer a progressive deterioration which will land us once again in the gulf of barbarism."[123]

Throughout 1936 Poteat and the dry forces remained active, but the strategy shifted farther toward a reliance on evangelical morality. As campaign director Burgess noted, "The longer I work in this fight against strong drink, the more I realize that our salvation can come only through a great Christian crusade, led aggressively by our Ministers and backed up strongly by our Church members." This strategy was embodied in the organization's use of field days, in which each Sunday a particular county would be targeted and twenty to twenty-five churches would be opened to Prohibition speakers. Poteat contributed to the Forsyth County field day with two addresses, and he argued elsewhere that "we must protect our people against the sophistries of men who are interested in misleading them. . . ." This religious approach did not excite enough enthusiasm, however, for donations remained scant and the financial situation of the dry forces grew desperate. Poteat's answer was to "appeal to our stronger churches, Methodist and Baptist, some of whose members could give $500 and not miss it."[124]

The under-funded organization faced another major challenge when the 1937 legislature sought to extend the county option measure to the entire state. In contrast to 1933, Poteat protested that a referendum *should* be held before changing the status quo, perhaps fearing county voters would more easily be swayed by the "millions of money supplied by the fat liquor lords" but revealing the dry forces' ambiguous relationship with majority rule. Poteat had no political solution when the majority opposed the judgment of the so-called better classes, the middle-class reformers. Arguing that the legislature should not overrule the 1933 victory, he protested "against the contemplated invasion of the sacred principle of democracy. . . ." He again addressed two relevant legislative committees, but despite a strong dry showing, the legislature voted in favor of a county option law across the state. Poteat was incensed that the legislators were "ignoring and flouting the intelligence and morality of the State," and in appealing to influential ministers to fund a continuing battle, he noted that "if this fight against liquor is not a fight for the Kingdom of Christ, I don't know what it is."[125] Poteat optimistically claimed that despite the defeat "the campaign against liquor goes on," and he worked especially hard in the election in his home county of Wake.[126] As late as October 1937 he proclaimed "that only a year or two more" of increasing consumption of alcohol would convince areas with alcohol "of their blunder."[127] Nonetheless, the greatest of Progressive crusades, Poteat's interest since the 1870s, had ground to a halt in the assertive political world of the 1930s.

Just as Poteat detested the whiskey companies for making money from immoral exploitation, businessmen profiting from the military industry particularly rankled him, and he spoke often on behalf of peace and international cooperation. He had not given up on the idea that the moral modern community should be international in scope. The interest was an old one for him; as one editorialist noted in 1928, "Dr. Poteat is re-affirming a position he has held all his life. He was speaking against furious jingoism as many years ago as some of its leaders are years old."[128] Poteat seldom skipped an opportunity to advocate his views; in 1924 he gave a series of chapel service addresses about "Internationalism," praising Woodrow Wilson's "application of the moral law to state action," discussing self-determination, and advocating "the outlawry of war." In 1927 he reaffirmed his opinion before a capacity crowd at the Baptist church in Chapel Hill as part of a Human Relations Institute sponsored by the YMCA. Referring to American failure to join the League of Nations, he declared, "We have lapsed shamefully from the high mind of 1917 into the absolutism and selfish isolation which we sought to destroy." He opposed possible U.S. intervention in Mexico, Nicaragua, and China, noting, "The old diplomacy of selfish, exclusive nationalism is again in the saddle. Unless we break the tradition which dominates that diplomacy, it will land us in another war which will end by being the end of the nations that resort to it."[129]

At the invitation of the Durham post of the American Legion, Poteat gave an Armistice Day address before five hundred people in 1927. He courageously called attention to "the effort to militarize us under the guise of patriotism," citing the failure of recent disarmament efforts and "demands for the biggest army, the biggest navy, the biggest air force in the world" as a way of guaranteeing "the peace of the world." To the post commander Poteat acknowledged, "Of course, resistance to aggression or oppression is legitimate." He continued, though, "In this period of social progress and national interdependence, those who are responsible for the precipitation of war are both stupid and criminal." Further, he was "unable to sympathize with propaganda for heavier armaments for defense, when nobody is able to name the enemy of whom we are afraid."[130] Poteat's address did not fail to name the source of militarism: "Remember concessionaries, whose investments in foreign lands must be protected; munition manufacturers who must have a market for enlarged output; swashbuckling officers, and then there are the wise ones, the guardians of the status quo, who know of a surety that man is a fighting animal. . . ."[131] Poteat's solution was his usual. He wrote and guided a resolution through the Baptist State Convention that declared, "War may be on occasion a terrible necessity, but it is high time that the war tradition inherited from a barbaric past be broken and the Christian standard everywhere applied to personal relations be applied also to national relations." The resolution, a liberal statement that passed despite some opposition, asked that war be outlawed and military training be blocked from colleges and high schools.[132]

Poteat's stand was particularly courageous because, in the twenties and thirties, opinion in North Carolina was strong against pacifism. He had reason to oppose the popular militaristic attitude that condemned "pacifism with the sinister connotation of disloyalty."[133] In January 1928 Sherwood Eddy, an avowed pacifist, was verbally attacked by the American Legion and by military officials at Fort Bragg when he scheduled a series of speeches in North Carolina. Of Eddy's six engagements, three were canceled.[134] In a subsequent speech condemning increased spending on naval armaments, Poteat came out boldly in defense of free speech, "No peril on all our national horizon is so loaded with disaster as the limitation of free discussion of public questions. . . ." The American Legion responded in its publication by naming Poteat as "preaching wild and radical doctrines, conjuring up remedies that are impossible of application." Poteat was one of "these gifted peddlers of platitudes that were old when Moses was paddling around in the bulrushes."[135] After this surge of controversy, Poteat was in demand as a speaker on behalf of peace and internationalism.

Poteat scoffed at opponents of the League of Nations who feared a loss of sovereignty in a world already marked by interdependence, and he used similar, futile arguments to back U.S. endorsement of the World Court. "Now that war has been universally renounced as an instrument of national policy," he suggested, "there remains the judicial method of settling disputes, and the World Court supplies the needed apparatus." In 1928 he urged Senator Furnifold Simmons to promote a resolution "suggesting to the President the reopening of discussion on the World Court" to overcome the "unaccountable hesitation" that the U.S. showed in joining. Perhaps encouraged by Simmons's positive response, Poteat informed Calvin Coolidge, "The co-operation of independent nationalities to promote common ends is, in reality, an assertion of their sovereignty." He fumed further, "Here is the United States Senate, aloof from the organised conscience and intelligence of mankind, insisting that international barriers long ago transformed by science into means of communication are barriers still ordained by God and George Washington. . . ." He carried the same torch before the Baptist State Convention in 1929, and in 1935 was still futilely backing the cause to Senator J.W. Bailey.[136]

In the 1930s Poteat reiterated his opposition to combat, and as the Great Depression deepened, he more and more singled out corporations as the source of war. "Big business is proposing to fool us again, as it did in 1916 and 1917, into boosting its venal profits under the guise of patriotism," he complained in 1936. In a prescient comment, he concluded, "The favorite expedient . . . is to cry 'Moscow!' whenever international peace is mentioned."[137] He vigorously continued to support the right to opposition, "I decline to be set down kerplunk as un-American because I am not a hundred per-center. I resent being tagged traitor because I recognize international relations and obligations."[138] At the request of Bishop Paul Kern and Dean Elbert Russell of the Duke School of Religion, Poteat enlisted as a sponsor for "a nation-wide series of peace meetings" in the spring of 1936 amid controversy over American levels of preparedness for war. The gatherings were held under the auspices of the Emergency Peace Campaign, "a cooperative endeavor on the part of peace workers from many religious centers interested in world peace."[139]

In May, Poteat delivered his salvo in the campaign at the Methodist church in Asheville, one of three hundred cities targeted across the country. He opened, "We are here to think as clearly and calmly as we may on the major problem of civilization, the threat of war, and possible means of pre-venting it." He deplored that national leaders, in a time of tension and rising nationalism, were seeking to militarize, again "under the guise of patriotism." He suggested that a first step toward avoiding a war was to wean industry from "the wickedness and economic stupidity of the high protective tariff, an important factor in the strife of nations." Further, voting for advocates of joining the League of Nations and the World Court would advance the cause and help avoid "the grossest and most tragic of national sins. . . ." Poteat continued to aid the campaign until illness forced him to resign in 1937.[140]

One reason that Poteat so vigorously opposed war was its destruction of "our best blood, which is our most precious possession. . . ." He mourned, "It has been spilt by the hogshead to fertilize crops in silly and criminal wars." In the late twenties and early thirties, Poteat continued to translate his knowl-edge as a biologist into strong support for preserving and even enhancing society's supply of the "best blood" through eugenics. Poteat was familiar with the ideas of John Watson and the behaviorists, who stressed the effects of the individual's training and environment, but he did not accept their argu-ments. "Environment, training, heredity,—these three," he intoned, "but the greatest of these is heredity."[141] The predicament only grew worse over time in his imagination. He identified an "increasing percentage of defect" that constituted "a social emergency. . . ." Insanity and feeble-mindedness put nearly two million people in institutions, Poteat complained, and "five mil-lion of us are unable to master the primary grades of the public school. Twenty million are capable only of superintended labor."[142] For one solution, Poteat turned to science in a new way, "Recent biological opinion appears to favor general birth control as the only effective corrective of this menacing differ-ential birth rate."[143]

Eugenics "has no program," Poteat assured in the best nonpartisan Pro-gressive style. "It is merely the study and guidance of the agencies within human control which will improve or impair the inborn qualities of future generations." However, he continued to recommend restrictions on the re-production of the chronically diseased and mentally handicapped.[144] Further, at times his accounting also specified "deformed people and the congenitally blind and deaf." Speaking before the NCCSS in 1929, Poteat went to his furthest extreme in desiring to impose his social ideology through the denial of parenthood: "I should add to this list of dangerous parents to be rejected, the self-centered, the cynical, the critical, the coarse-fibered, the discourteous. For though the children may be well-born, their plastic natures, like good clay in the hands of an unskilled potter, may be moulded by such parents into distortion, weakness, and deformity." On the other hand, if children could choose their parents, they should "go in for character, good sense, and vigor, counting position, possessions, and callings secondary."[145] On occasion Poteat's fervid desire to avoid social catastrophe led him to be unclear about the relative effects of environment versus heredity, but at all times he was clear about an ever-growing list of traits he wanted to eliminate. In that listing his typical blending of social with scientific arguments appeared most clearly, and the implications of overemphasis on the role of heredity became obvious to many North Carolinians.

Poteat's views, once quietly tolerated if not widely accepted, now excited opposition, expressed both in the press and in personal letters. The *Raleigh Times* complained, "No doubt a Doctor Poteat as a boss of a human stock farm might produce physical and moral blood strains of distinction— but there would be lost the dearest privilege of man in general, the right independently to love where and how he chooses." Drawing on his own understanding of evolution, the editorialist argued, "man could not conceivably have become even what he is had he not reserved the right to attend to this matter of fundamental instinct for himself."[146] Noting that Poteat identified 10 percent of the population as degenerate, the same paper asked the crucial question, "But who is to decide? . . . Is some spectacled young college professor to act as a director of the budget of vital statistics? Who, after all, is a moron?"[147] The *Greensboro Daily News* also opposed Poteat's view, asking "What has happened to estop the operation of Darwin's law of the survival of the fittest? . . . Indeed, there is visible all about us a steady improvement in the physical appearance of the race. . . ."[148] A hearing daughter of deaf parents wondered if Poteat "would condemn quite so severely the marriage of congenitally deaf people if you knew them as well as I do," but Poteat retreated behind numbers. He stated, "Of course, the statistical method is the only one available for the study of the forms of human defects" and defended himself with a study showing that a fourth of the time the mating of deaf parents produced some deaf children.[149] Poteat's beliefs not only drew from scientific study but were also social biases supported by the language of science.

Because he so clearly perceived all people as linked in an organic society, Poteat could not conceive of the right of those he considered inferior to exist independent of control. The family explicitly equaled "society in miniature" for Poteat.[150] Because the objects of his proposed reforms affected him, as part of an organic civilization under threat after World War I, he had the right to guide and control their lives. He knew that others might look upon his believers in the NCCSS as "idealists, well-wishers, would-be reformers and re-fashioners"[151] and ask "by what authority do they interfere with personal rights and intrude into the intimacies of family life?" However, he disregarded such critics, congratulating his fellow NCCSS reformers, "Instead of acquiescing in the drift of things, you propose to study that drift and change it by enlightened corporate action, if it needs to be changed; to impose intelligence upon the course of nature and modify it for the advantage of man."[152] The result was a very traditional social program supported by modern methods. As Poteat asked, "What value [is] modern knowledge if it does not save us from personal defeat and social catastrophe[?]" Since "social progress" was dictated by the "limitation of inferiors," eugenics was a matter of "civilization versus barbarism."[153] Ultimately "the future of the race" was at stake, and there could be no "taint of defect in the ancestry of the men who are to be our leaders."[154]

Poteat believed that one "cannot hope to correct mental defects fixed in a faulty heredity, except to forestall them by building up public opinion and sentiment against improper matings." Accordingly, most of his work on behalf of eugenics took the form of speeches vainly advocating the idea. Through the NCCSS, however, he did make some concrete efforts to strengthen restrictions on mating in the Tarheel state.[155] The "peril" of poor breeding was "exaggerated by the industrial revolution and the relaxation of moral standards following the World War," Poteat found.[156] As a result of the moral lapse, the home was threatened, and "the home," Poteat argued, "sends out into society the defective, the delinquent, the incorrigible, the diseased, the insane, the anti-social. When will parents recognize their responsibility and tremble before it, and trembling clutch at every guiding hand, count parenthood the chief business of life, and get ready to discharge it with a grave happiness and intelligent efficiency." As his contribution toward forcing parents to produce better children, Poteat was asked to report on marriage and divorce to the 1932 meeting of the NCCSS.[157]

Poteat first surveyed the registrar of deeds in various counties, the official responsible for administering the marriage laws; consulted the State Board of Health; and even checked precedents with historian Guion Griffis Johnson. He discovered that North Carolina's marriage rate was falling because the license cost ten dollars and required a medical test. Couples simply went to neighboring states where laws were more lax and the ceremony less expensive.[158] Both the prospective groom and bride, by virtue of a 1927 North Carolina law, had to present medical proof of having a sound mind and no infectious tuberculosis. Men, in addition, had to prove that they had no venereal disease. Poteat also lamented that divorce had grown more frequent, thanks in part to liberalized laws in Nevada, causing "a notable loss in family stability. . . ." He admitted that little research had been done but recommended as a start that marriage and divorce laws be standardized by federal legislation, that applicants of both sexes be subject to the same strict medical requirements, that sexes be more severely segregated in homes for defectives and paupers, and that marriage prohibitions be extended to include epileptics and those for whom either parent was "mentally defective" or "unsound." Despite identifying these issues as major social problems, Poteat optimistically closed his report by citing a biologist from Johns Hopkins University "that the monogamous family with its life-long union of mates is the final term of a long evolutionary series." Poteat, as always, found what he sought and was at peace: "So science confirms the teaching of religion, which regards marriage as a sacrament and the permanent association of one man and one woman as the only foundation of family life and the only promise and security of the noblest type of society."[159]

Poteat continued to work with the NCCSS on the eugenics issue by serving on its health committee and advocating eugenics measures as late as 1936, including the legalization of "family restriction advice" given by doctors. In 1937 he also joined the recently revived North Carolina Society for Mental Hygiene.[160] Further, he brought the topic of "human sterilization" into his classroom via a pamphlet on "the actual results of eugenic sterilization in practice."[161] Naturally, eugenics also entered his religious activities as he cooperated on the Southern Baptist Convention's Commission on Social Service in 1932 with longtime commission chairman A.J. Barton on "a strong statement" on marriage and divorce for the convention.[162] These efforts produced few results in the democratizing political atmosphere of the thirties.

Final Campaigns

For historians, a tolerant stand on race relations is a litmus test in identifying a southern white liberal. Since his childhood days with Nat, his slave companion, race had been a subject of importance to Poteat, and during the Progressive Era he had come to realize that tensions between whites and blacks might doom the peace and unity he envisaged for the South. By the late 1920s and the early 1930s, however, the limits of that conception of social relations were becoming ever more clear. Black activists began demanding more than peace in a segregated society, and the Progressive-Era plan for unequal negotiations for peace, conducted only between elite members of the two races, looked ever more anachronistic in the national picture. Poteat recognized in his last months of life that the topic would be incredibly important in future years, but his suggestions just before he died retained fully the hierarchy and racism typical of even the most liberal of southern white reformers during most of Poteat's life.

Race relations, like eugenics and alcohol consumption, was another issue for which Poteat applied "scientific" evidence to back his social agenda in a futile quest for certainty and automatic acceptance of what he saw as obvious. For example, Santford Martin, editor of the *Winston-Salem Journal,* wrote Poteat in 1930 for advice about a presentation Martin was preparing as "a defense of the Southern position, namely, that the negroes should have their own churches, Y.M.C.A.'s, Y.W.C.A.'s, etc." His goal was "to oppose amalgamation and favor segregation." That desire to defend segregation led immediately to the issue of sex. He wanted from Poteat "a letter I could use showing the biological effects of amalgamation, inter-marriage, etc., of the white and black races." He concluded, "I want you, in short, to give me the reason why you, as a biologist, oppose amalgamation and inter-marriage of the white and negro races."[163]

Poteat readily responded and did not challenge the view that segregation and sex were automatically linked. He reiterated axioms of scientific racism that he had long held. Appealing to professional authority, he began, "From the biological point of view the white and black races are too remote in relationship for a certainly advantageous crossing. . . . When a backward race crosses with an advanced race, the backward usually has little or nothing to contribute physically or mentally to the advanced." He continued, "The mulatto will exhibit marked hybrid vigor in the first generation, but it declines in the later generations." He feared undesirable genetic combinations affecting "resistance to disease and social inadequacy" and concluded that "the results of the intermixture of white and black races are on the average unfavorable." Also in the spring of 1930 Poteat revealed his support of segregation by supporting the nomination of John J. Parker to be a U.S. Supreme Court justice despite Parker's avowed opposition to black political rights.[164]

Poteat was nonetheless, as he phrased it to one black correspondent, "interested in all the progress which your race is making in our State." Near the end of his life, the governor appointed him to the board of trustees of the North Carolina Agricultural and Technical College, a black institution in Greensboro. In 1929 he gave a commencement sermon at Tuskegee and garnered praise for a "wonderful" address.[165] In 1931 he was also appointed as one of about two dozen members around the globe of the Baptist World Congress's Commission on Racialism. In a draft report he requested changes in a sentence arguing that racial antagonism could be eased "by Christian teaching of the young concerning racial self-respect. . . ." He asked that it be revised to read "racial integrity and self-respect," a crucial addition. He could conceive only that "millenniums hence" the interaction of racial groups "may come to swamp racial divergence into the original uniformity."[166]

As long as racial "integrity" remained secure behind segregation, Poteat was a spokesman for racial peace. He lamented that "the barbarity of lynching still stains American annals" and that "equality of opportunity for ability and merit from any quarter waits below the horizon." Tweaking an audience's conscience, he admonished, "Remember the word of Christ, 'You are all brothers,' and that in spite of social status, theological opinions, color of skin, latitude and longitude." However, the appeal was inevitably filtered through liberal condescension, "Let society take note and be just and generous to all its handicapped members," such as blacks.[167] On lynching, he was "not opposed" to a federal law, a controversial issue throughout the twenties, provided that it was a "reenforcement not usurpation of local law," a qualification that left him in essence aiding the violent status quo.[168] Poteat took some pride in his Progressive views. In submitting a speech manuscript to a religious periodical in Chicago, he declared, "As you see, a Southern man undertakes to present the New Testament teaching on Race and challenges the Christian South to apply it to our treatment of the Negro."[169]

Poteat's most significant work toward easing racial tension was in his continuing involvement with the Commission on Interracial Cooperation during the late twenties and early thirties. Poteat remained a member of the South-wide commission based in Atlanta, actively followed its work, and served on a national committee in 1929 and 1930 that mounted an unsuccessful fund-raising campaign intended to stabilize the commission's financial future despite the depression. The commission chairman illustrated Poteat's reputation as a racial liberal by assuring him "that the committee will be greatly pleased that the great weight of your name will be behind this movement." He explained, "As is usual with most such Committees, there is no work for its members. . . . We simply want the approval and interest of a number of people whose word means something to the country." The regional esteem for Poteat was reaffirmed when the commission voted him an honorary membership in 1936, during his nephew Edwin McNeill Poteat Jr.'s term as president.[170]

Poteat's activity with the autonomous but closely linked state Commission on Interracial Cooperation was much more substantial. Though no longer state chairman, he continued in the late twenties and early thirties to serve on the state executive committee, first under his successor as chairman, Walter C. Jackson, a professor in Greensboro, and then with the encouragement of chairman Howard W. Odum, the prominent sociologist at the University of North Carolina. Like the larger commission, the North Carolina group faced a crisis in this period, and the Tarheel liberals responded with the strategy of somewhat broadening their selected elite group. A careful reorganization in 1928 was inadequate once the depression struck. The 1931 annual meeting then authorized the invitation of 500 new members, selected by Governor Max O. Gardner from a list prepared by the commission. Of those invited, 450 accepted within a week. His successors as governor also invited as members "people who count for much in the affairs of the state," and by 1934 the total membership had grown to between 1,150 and 1,200 with the help of Governor Ehringhaus. In 1933 the strapped Atlanta-based commission ended its field work due to lack of funds and transferred its emphasis "to educational efforts calculated to change general public opinion." In cooperation with its Virginia counterpart, the strengthened Tarheel group hired their own field worker and continued operations. For its first ten years, through 1929, the state Commission on Interracial Cooperation was "able largely to depend for its financial support upon certain foundations and church boards," but after 1929 its direct appeal for money from members and the public served it well.[171] To a limited extent, Progressives had to broaden their idea of leadership of an ideal community, but it was still seen as a carefully selected group. The masses of people, white or black, had no business making decisions for society.

Poteat recognized that the commission had evolved since its formation; he summarized in 1931:

The original purpose of the Inter-racial Commission to facilitate the reception of Negro soldiers returning from the World War into American life without friction has been expanded into a general program of applying the spirit and teaching of Jesus to the relations of the races. Its method has been a frank survey of conditions with conference of men and women of both races. I believe in the purpose and the method. The work of the Commission is of high social value, all the more important now, when a large group of Negroes mainly in the North is dominated by a radical and dangerous leadership.[172]

Poteat did his part to forestall such so-called radicalism by strengthening the already powerful links between the commission and Tarheel evangelicals.

In 1928, with the support of the state chairman and the church relations committee of the North Carolina Commission on Interracial Cooperation, Poteat helped write and secure the passage of a resolution in the Baptist State Convention that created a North Carolina Baptist Commission on Inter-racial Cooperation and authorized it to cooperate with its state and regional counterparts. The action was welcomed by regional commission director Will W. Alexander as "very significant." Poteat was named to the denominational committee of fifteen and in 1929 authored its first report. Giving a brief history to introduce the movement, he assured the Baptists that at its formation after World War I "there was a clear understanding that neither amalgamation nor social equality was contemplated. The Negro participants in these general conferences insisted themselves on the preservation of their racial integrity." He listed achievements in improved race relations and noted with foresight that among the needs outstanding was "the transportation of Negro school children from distant points" (an issue that later took center stage in the Civil Rights movement).[173]

This intermingling of race, religion, and reform was nowhere better demonstrated than in the person of Poteat's close colleague, educator W.C. Jackson. In 1930 he succeeded Poteat as head of the Baptist Interracial Commission, and in that year Jackson headed interracial commissions at the denominational, state, and regional levels. He called a meeting in March 1930 for representatives of all Tarheel denominations to discuss interracial work. The suggestions produced were "based mainly upon those given by the group from the Baptist State Convention, headed by Dr. W. L. Poteat, of Wake Forest." The strategy offered included encouragement of denominational action; inviting speakers to churches, schools, and civic groups; being "a friend to whom the Negroes may come to iron out differences they may have with any White people"; encouraging interracial meetings of clergy; and being "most careful in discussing any matter relating to the Negroes where the maid or man of all work may hear, as many times the most kindly remarks even might be taken in the wrong light."[174] This cautious tactic hints that liberals such as Poteat recognized that their approach was not always welcome among either race, and the concluding remark presaged the strengthening divisions among whites and blacks about the future of race relations.

When the issue of Prohibition gained renewed importance in the early thirties, Poteat devoted less time to race relations, and age began to be a factor in his busy life. His health declined gradually only in the final three years of his life, and he finally gave up golf, a favorite hobby for several years.[175] An injured leg, "not at all serious," and a general checkup confined him for the first time ever to the hospital at Duke University for twelve days in February and March 1935, yet even there he found the humor to essay about "the hospital nightshirt" ("I am for it and I am against it"). He was soon "doing my usual stint of work,—two lectures in succession five days in the week."[176] In July 1935, however, he reported to President Kitchin that "my physicians insist that my own teaching load be reduced from ten hours to six at most." Even with a lightened load, he battled illness in 1936.[177] In June of that year he also narrowly escaped serious injury when a car in which he was a passenger was struck at an intersection and toppled over. The accident occurred at nine o'clock in the morning, and Poteat, unhurt and relatively unruffled, proceeded on in a separate vehicle to his temperance address at Winston-Salem's First Baptist Church.[178] The close call did inspire him to reflect in verse about his "Rendezvous with Death," who "appeared and then withdrew / . . . Thought he of tasks but just begun, / Of services still incomplete. . . ."[179] Poteat replaced the car with a new frosty green Chevrolet sedan, and with chauffeurs (frequently students) to compensate for vision narrowed by glaucoma, he maintained his ever active schedule.[180]

The principal incomplete task that his good fortune allowed Poteat to complete was the presidency of the Baptist State Convention. Meeting in Durham in November 1936, the state's Baptists elected the eighty-year-old Poteat to their highest post on the first ballot. Poteat, and various liberal journalists, saw the occasion as one of reconciliation within the denomination. "At Winston-Salem in 1922," Poteat reminisced, "it was thought that my head would be cut off by that body (the convention.) And my election as president is interesting to me as showing the changing attitude of the people." He continued with unrealistic optimism, "I just went along, maintaining that Christianity and science are not incompatible, and people generally seem to believe it now."[181] Liberal newsmen hailed the election as well. "In all the deliberations of their great convention this year," editorialized the *Winston-Salem Journal,* "the mighty hosts of Baptists of North Carolina did nothing bigger or better than [his election] for the cause which they espouse."[182] The *News and Observer* succinctly agreed that the election "showed how completely his stand [on evolution] was vindicated."[183]

His brother's death in June 1937 following a long illness did not deter Poteat from his duties but instead affirmed for him in his memories of Edwin the value of an unorthodox but deep faith. As state president Poteat worked to develop the program for the annual convention. He advocated the inclusion of such trademark topics as "Christianity Securing the Intellectual Life" and "Christ and the Emerging World Culture" and, always the mediator, carefully allotted time to professors from the denominational seminary at Louisville as well as to the state's ministers.[184] Poteat was "looking forward to [the meeting] with enthusiasm and exhilaration." He returned to his interest in race relations and carefully polished an old speech idea into proper form for his presidential address.[185]

"Christ and Race" was Poteat's "last great utterance," but it had to be read to the convention on his behalf by the Reverend John Allen Easley of the Wake Forest Baptist Church.[186] On October 28, shortly before the 1937 convention, Poteat had a stroke that left him partially paralyzed, only a week after the *News and Observer* commemorated his eighty-first birthday with a front-page spread of photographs. At the beginning of October, he had been "at my college work in my usual health." Nonetheless, age was beginning to show. "This," he had mused, "will be my last session of teaching. It is fifty-nine years since I started."[187] He never taught again after the stroke, but fortunately "Christ and Race" was ready. At the convention, vice-president Robert N. Simms, Poteat's laboratory assistant in 1895–96, presided. Easley read Poteat's address "splendidly and it was recognized as the outstanding deliverance of the Convention."[188]

Poteat had written the speech in 1927 and 1928 and presented it in only slightly revised form several times. The national turmoil and changing racial situation in the intervening decade did not lead him to change his ideas about race, only to keep its importance at the forefront.[189] To the new social puzzles Poteat offered only the solution that he had advocated since the unrest of the late 1800s—"Christian brotherhood," which for example makes it "possible for peoples who are so diverse as whites and Negroes to live together successfully. . . ." In short, "the obligation of Christians to love one another as brothers and to cooperate in making the will of God prevail" extends "across racial barriers." Poteat prefaced the religious prescription with his typical important caveat. "Holding racial integrity to be inviolable," he wrote, "we shall be respectful to racial endowments and racial achievements" and be "willing to judge the race by its best specimens."[190] "Christ and Race" defined the limits of Poteat's racial liberalism, and like many other white intellectuals of his generation, he could not imagine a world beyond segregation, a world where blacks demanded rather than supplicated. That "racial integrity" was "inviolable" needed so little justification to his audience that Poteat mentioned it only in a passing participial phrase before offering his usual paternalistic solution to create a cooperative but segregated community.

Following his stroke and absence from the convention session, Poteat recovered somewhat. His "six weeks of relative helplessness" eased enough by mid-December that he stopped employing a special servant, and on December 4 he wrote "a first labored letter with my lame right hand. . . ." He rejoiced soon after the New Year "that it pays to be ill because you find out how many good people there are in the world and how many friends you have." Poteat recorded a Victrola rendering of part of "Christ and Race" but was able to answer only a few of the dozens of messages of encouragement that poured in from former students, fellow educators, and other reformers—

many of the correspondents fitting all three categories.[191] In early March, however, Poteat "suffered a relapse," and, according to a news report, on March 12 as he awaited his son to drop by and read to him after supper, "death came gently. . . ." Perhaps his final thoughts were similar to comments drawn from Browning that he made at a funeral ten years before: "To have faith in immortality is to live in the eternal world while our feet walk the earthly pathways."[192]

The statewide outpouring of tribute upon Poteat's death underscored his status as one of North Carolina's leading liberal intellectuals. More than a thousand people attended his funeral at Wake Forest Baptist Church, including Governor Clyde Hoey.[193] The *News and Observer* hailed him as "a leader for culture and freedom in North Carolina and the South, an unrelenting advocate of personal and public morality." The *Winston-Salem Journal* termed him "a Christian statesman" who "dared to champion the cause of intellectual liberty long before it ceased to be dangerous to do so in North Carolina," while the *Asheville Times* optimistically asserted that Poteat fought "a winning fight for larger understanding and more tolerance in science and religion."[194] The many condolences offered to the family confirm Poteat's state and regional influence. Senator Josiah Bailey, Josephus Daniels, and George W. Truett were among the most prominent, but scores of others from several states joined them. Nell Battle Lewis and Samuel Chiles Mitchell published tributes, and the United Dry Forces, the North Carolina Academy of Science, and the NCCSS all honored him.[195] Both inside and outside the state, commentators highlighted the anti-evolution battles as Poteat's most significant moment, and several journalists noted that Clarence Darrow died the day after Poteat's death, at age eighty. "Both were great liberals," concluded one, but all singled out Darrow's agnosticm as a critical point of contrast with Poteat.[196]

To be an influential liberal in the South meant blending into established traditions, and his publicly expressed faith enabled Poteat to tread where secular reformers could never have ventured. Poteat's view of an organic, moral society had long defied the modern political system that originated in the North and crept into the South beginning with the Prohibition campaign around the turn of the century. However, his protests against a politics of antagonism centered around organized interest groups began to fall on deaf ears in the late 1920s and the 1930s, accounting for the failures of the Progressive initiatives of his later years. His efforts against repeal of Prohibition lost ground gradually, his battle for stronger marriage laws and eugenics failed, preparedness advocates in the militant South ignored his pleas for peace, business boosters continued to court greedy industries, and conservatives grew in denominational power. Progressivism had ended; the modern South was on the way.

Conclusion

✠

A thinker in the South is regarded quite logically as an enemy of the people, who, for the common weal, ought to be put down summarily—for, to think at all, it is necessary to repudiate the whole Southern scheme of things, to go outside God's ordered drama and contrive with Satan for the overthrow of Heaven.

W.J. Cash, "The Mind of the South"

William Louis Poteat's 81 years of life in North Carolina covered fully half of the 162 years since the birth of the nation in 1776, and the year of his death coincided with the beginning of the South's full entry into modern America. The year he died, 1938, marked a divide for the region.[1] Civil rights, the great political and social battle that would cleave the South for years to come, gained strength and direction in that year. The legal strategy of black activists began to pay off when the Supreme Court ruled in their favor for the first time in the case of Lloyd L. Gaines, a black man who sought admission to the previously all-white law school of the University of Missouri. One analyst has written that this ruling marked "the first milestone on the road to desegregation."[2] In the same landmark year, white southern liberals began to split on the issue of race when a small number finally questioned the savage ideal and considered engaging in more direct political advocacy. The Southern Conference for Human Welfare met in Birmingham and managed two integrated sessions before Eugene "Bull" Connor enforced the city's segregation law.[3]

The South's economic system also changed course toward full modernity in the year of Poteat's death. Scholars acknowledge 1938 as a crucial moment because the Fair Labor Standards Act (FLSA), which reformers passed despite southern opposition, helped to change economic incentives that had been in place since the end of the Civil War. Various New Deal initiatives, capped by the FLSA, blocked "the low-wage expansion path for regional industry" that had been in place since Reconstruction, and by the beginning of World War II conditions were ripe "for a rapid transformation."[4] With economic change comes political change, and 1938 was likewise a watershed year in the South's relationship with national political structures. President Roosevelt's *Report on Economic Conditions of the South* proclaimed the region to be "the Nation's No. 1 economic problem. . . ." For the first time, a nationally oriented group of southern politicians began to actively funnel national investment into the South and to pursue northern industry with greedy eyes that the religious Poteat would have found wanting. This shift of regional leadership found validation when Roosevelt failed in his attempt to unseat conservative southern senators in the 1938 elections.[5]

Anticommunist hysteria, later to devastate the ranks of critical intellectuals, was also a component in the political upsurge of conservatism. For example, an elderly Thomas Dixon wrote his old friend shortly before Poteat's death. He singled out Poteat's contention that whites should judge blacks by their elite—such as W.E.B. Du Bois—rather than by the average person. Dixon raged that Du Bois "is now a red Communist" and "an uncompromising Atheist." He cautioned Poteat, "You can not believe in making America mulatto," considering that development to be the logical end of Du Bois's path.[6] Militarism, corporate values, and political and social conflict blossomed as Poteat's genteel, Progressive sentiments died away.

In Poteat's final years he delivered numerous jeremiads against the modernizing social, political, and economic changes that gained permanent influence in the year of his death. He had endured the chaotic transformations without having succumbed to the fragmented world view and emphasis on critical thought that are characteristic of modernism. Chronicling the struggles of Poteat's mental life lifts the shadows from the liberal southern Victorian who translated into the language of the South the intellectual and theological challenges of modernity. The strength and dynamic potential of organic southern Victorianism is demonstrated by its durability in this single life. His belief system incorporated modern problems and offered modifications of old truths as solutions for emerging conflicts. In the southern context this continuity was made possible by the underlying lack of economic and social development marking the bleak period from the Civil War until the 1930s.[7] Radical new ideas were not required or welcomed in a rural, agricultural society evolving only incrementally.

Religion has been one of the South's great continuities, and underlying Poteat's intellectual steadfastness was a southern evangelical understanding that changed relatively little in the century and a half after its triumph in the Great Revival. The mainstream southern churches had not moved beyond the stewardship doctrine apparent as early as the dawn of the nineteenth century. The theology that swept through the South between 1801 and 1805 presumed that "private perfection would produce social improvement."[8] Indeed, the same limits of southern religious liberalism continued to define the boundaries of the dominant religious tradition in the South long after Poteat's death. Evangelist Billy Graham, remarking on later and more severe southern racial conflict during the Civil Rights movement, indicated that "the one great an-

swer to our racial problem is for men and women to be converted to Christ."
Graham too believed "social sins . . . are merely a large-scale projection of
individual sins. . . ."[9] While Poteat's longtime exhortations in favor of southern stewardship do not separate him in kind from the more otherworldly of
Southern Baptists, his greater degree of activism within traditional doctrine
marked the vanguard of liberalism within the church and foreshadowed a
small, later group of more radical southern churchmen.[10]

Poteat was a man riven by unresolved tensions once his encounter with
evolution forced him to entertain new ideas. He wrongly assumed that those
coming of age in a scientific world could attain an emotional religious experience without relying on the conservative Biblical beliefs that had originally
been a vital part of his own formative religious experience. He expected twentieth-century youth to accept Christ's morality as absolute without requiring
a logical system of biblical interpretation. In that sense his inability to com-
prehend others' need to apply logic to their understanding of the Bible—
whether through liberal theology or in fundamentalists' rejection of
symbolism—left Poteat out of touch with the troubling religious struggles of
many fellow Christians in his own time. To some Poteat's simple call for an
untroubled, nonrational faith must have seemed glib.

Poteat's denigration of rational theology left him comfortable with the
irresolution of many other intellectual contradictions. He was not a systematic thinker and had no compulsion to analyze himself or the world in a rigor-
ously logical way. As a result he could agitate fiercely for both eugenics and
social reform without deciding the relative importance of environment and
heredity. He could recognize the interdependence of society without giving
up his reliance on individualism. He could support the professionalization of
science and education yet decry the specialization that threatened to undermine liberal culture. Amid his frantic schedule of activities as an educator,
reformer, and speaker, he had no time to be torn by his own internal struggles
between modern and traditional thought or to overcome his own weakness as
an intellectual. The unrest of the 1890s, the social upheaval following World
War I, and the onset of the Great Depression successively created and intensified Poteat's perception of social crisis, his conviction that society was falling
from harmony into anarchic conflict. His work in education, religion, and
reform was calculated to counter the crisis and restore order. Ironically, he
helped to set the stage for the modern South.

Poteat belonged to the generation of intellectuals described by historian
Bruce Clayton, men who in the 1890s created the South's first "full-fledged
intellectual community" and "who criticized the entire life of the South. . . ."
Though he could see the problems of the region and sought to alleviate them,
like his contemporaries Poteat remained a captive of what Richard King has
called "the southern family romance," a tangled web of belief in social harmony, gentility, moderation, longing for the supposed cultural achievement
of the antebellum period, and the displaying of a profound reluctance for
fundamental change. He did not revolt against nearly all tradition, as did the

Shown here in 1937 reminiscing over photographs of his early years, Poteat was similar to many other southern intellectuals of his time in maintaining some romantic attachment to the Old South and southern tradition despite his many attempts at Progressive social reform.

younger founders of the so-called southern renaissance, nor did his intellectual center crumble, as it did for so many of the southern writers of the 1920s and 1930s. Poteat instead fits easily into Daniel Singal's characterization of the southern Victorian, but unlike typical Victorians, for whom the barrier "between the cultured and the uncultured" was "virtually uncrossable," Poteat was an evangelical Victorian. Denominational education—the focus of his life's work—could carry both culture and religion to all intelligent people willing (and genetically qualified) to accept a little uplift and a guiding hand.[11]

 Late in life Poteat characterized himself as a man who "loves little children and the great poets. . . ."[12] It was an apt description. He is remembered as a loving husband, father, and grandfather and as a strong paternal figure for the young Baptist men who filled his college classes for decades. His sense of humor and personal charm became legendary in the minds of followers such as Gerald W. Johnson, and he exuded such an air of learning that a stranger on a train once guessed that Poteat was a professor.[13] Nonetheless, when human character changed on or about December 1910, as Virginia Woolf memorably proposed, Poteat was preoccupied at his presidential desk, on the podium, or reading Browning in his study. But he at least looked out from his magnolia-studded campus and selected from the menu of new ideas those that he could adapt to his region. That practice made him the leading southern liberal that he was.

For Poteat the Old South and a happy childhood coincided, and his memories of the antebellum past were lightly colored through the rosy lens of a child. At the age of seventy-two, Poteat revealed in a moment of quiet reflection the gentle and genteel spirit that animated a life of conflict but ultimate unity—extending from the South's antebellum peak to the verge of its jarring admission to modern America. He ever maintained a delicate balance between past and present:

> It is June 24 in the home of my infancy and childhood, and the anniversary of my marriage 48 years ago. I greeted the bride at breakfast in the presence of Sister, of our two daughters Louie and Helen, and of our granddaughter, Sylvia, Helen's three-year old. Forest Home is restored and extended and modernized. The autos whisk by on the highway at the bottom of the front lawn, and two airplanes, one close on the tail of the other, roar faintly under the far gray clouds southward. Indoors the wizard electricity, caught and fettered at the old spring under the hill, is giving me on the Knabe Ampico tender passages of Madame Butterfly precisely in the interpretation of Howard Brockway. The Frigidaire is humming its chilling monotone not a hundred yards from the great deep pit in which the ice harvest of the mill pond a half mile away was stored winter by winter in the years long gone by.
>
> But there can be no new world apart from the old. Forever the present is the child of the past, just as this new marvel of alertness and vigor and beauty named Sylvia is bound by indissoluble hereditary bonds to that midsummer happiness of 1881. The Bob Whites whistle as of old in the sedge and stubble, and immemorial oaks and hickories drop me down even yet the old time morning melody of wood thrush, cardinal, warbler, summer red bird, and robin, and wrens and fly-catchers continue their unbroken domesticities about the house. And I seem to hear the voice of my Father ringing clear, now rollicking and jovial, now commanding, and to see the form of my Mother moving about the place like a serene radiance and ruling all its atmosphere with sweetness and gentility.[14]

Ultimately, Poteat's deep attachment to southern tradition and the past exacted a high price. It consigned him to mediocre status as an intellectual in the national context, and it assured that he would remain insensitive to many of the most important problems facing the South. His love of hierarchy and a narrow morality blinded him to not only deep structural inequalities but also visibly blatant exploitation in his home region, and he and other Progressives offered no real solutions in their stunted liberal proposals. However, to expect much more from southern liberalism between the Civil War and World War II is to be quite ahistorical. Few people are ever willing to abandon work and home for the sake of intellectual consistency, as was often necessary if a native outrightly condemned the South during this period. Poteat's equilibrium between adherence to tradition and advocacy of change not only allowed him to maintain peace in his own temperate mind, but it also gave him the opportunity to endure in and serve the South while standing haltingly for social awareness and the freedom of intellectual inquiry. A thinker residing in the Progressive-Era South could hardly hope to do more.

Notes

Introduction

1. H.L. Mencken, *Prejudices: Sixth Series* (New York, 1927), 140.

2. Fred Hobson, "Introduction," Hobson, ed., *South-Watching: Selected Essays by Gerald W. Johnson* (Chapel Hill and London, 1983), xvii.

3. Gerald W. Johnson, "Billy with the Red Necktie," in Hobson, ed., *South-Watching*, 193 and 199.

4. W.J. Cash, *The Mind of the South* (New York, 1941), 329.

5. Ibid., 349.

6. *Shelby (N.C.) Cleveland Press*, October 23, 1928, quoted in Bruce Clayton, "W.J. Cash: A Mind of the South," in Paul D. Escott, ed., *W.J. Cash and the Minds of the South* (Baton Rouge and London, 1992), 18–19.

7. Clayton, "W.J. Cash," 21.

8. Suzanne Cameron Linder, *William Louis Poteat: Prophet of Progress* (Chapel Hill, 1966), 62. Linder's book has been criticized for being "thoroughly admiring and sympathetic with its subject. The narration and description of the life of this famous Baptist educator, who spoke so firmly for academic freedom, make for fascinating reading, but Mrs. Linder has not estimated Poteat's lasting place in the state's history except in a sentimental way" (Sarah McCulloh Lemmon, "North Carolina in the Twentieth Century, 1913–1945," in Jeffrey J. Crow and Larry E. Tise, eds., *Writing North Carolina History* [Chapel Hill, 1979], 176).

9. Linder, *William Louis Poteat*, 103 and 77.

10. Ibid., 199.

11. Willard B. Gatewood Jr., *Preachers, Pedagogues, and Politicians: The Evolution Controversy in North Carolina, 1920–1927* (Chapel Hill, 1966), 231 and 232.

12. Ibid., 230 and 232.

13. Linder and Gatewood's books are the only extended treatments of Poteat's activities that have been published. A much earlier, unpublished study is George McLeod Bryan, "The Educational, Religious, and Social Thought of William Louis Poteat as Expressed in His Writings, Including Unpublished Notes and Addresses" (Masters thesis, Wake Forest College, 1944). Bryan is at times more evenhanded in his outlines of Poteat's ideas, but he fails to grapple adequately with their sources and implications. His limited work does not attempt to be a biography or to provide significant context. Poteat is mentioned briefly in various other works of southern history, always in the role of a liberal ahead of his time. Rufus B. Spain identifies Poteat "among the prominent Baptists who seemed to lean toward social Christianity . . ." (*At Ease in Zion: Social History of Southern Baptists, 1865–1900* [Nashville, 1961], 211 n). John Lee Eighmy examines Poteat's denominational activity in a bit more detail in *Churches in Cultural Captivity: A History of the Social Attitudes of Southern Baptists*, rev. ed. (Knoxville, 1987). Poteat was "one of

the earliest and foremost advocates of social Christianity" and played "a key role in introducing the new ideas to the denomination" (84). Eighmy hints that the Southern Baptist Convention's Social Service Commission, of which Poteat was the first chair, would have been more meaningful had Poteat not quickly been replaced by Arthur J. Barton, who "lacked the broad social sympathies, the intellectual depth, and the liberal spirit of William Poteat" (86). Dewey W. Grantham also lists Poteat among "a remarkable cast of leaders [who] contributed to progress in the second decade of the century" in North Carolina (*Southern Progressivism: The Reconciliation of Progress and Tradition* [Knoxville, 1983], 384). John Egerton numbers Poteat among those who "took a progressive stance on the issue" of the treatment of strikers during the 1929 textile labor unrest in North Carolina (*Speak Now against the Day: The Generation before the Civil Rights Movement in the South* [New York, 1994], 72). More generally, he singles out Poteat as "perhaps the most noted of a number of Southern Baptists who took a liberal or progressive view on most theological and social questions" (121–22). This brief survey of historians' references to Poteat reveals the lack of in-depth analysis of the sources of Poteat's ideas, the limitations of his liberalism, or the implications of his Progressive plans. All ignore the traditional underpinnings of his thought and goals.

14. Clipping from *Charlotte News,* November 8, 1925, folder 554, William L. Poteat Papers, Special Collections, Z. Smith Reynolds Library, Wake Forest University, Winston-Salem, N.C.

15. This study endeavors to be in historiographical "conversation" with a number of historical works. Prominent among them are Gatewood, *Preachers, Pedagogues, and Politicians;* James L. Leloudis, *Schooling the New South: Pedagogy, Self, and Society in North Carolina, 1880–1920* (Chapel Hill and London, 1996); William A. Link, *The Paradox of Southern Progressivism, 1880–1930* (Chapel Hill and London, 1992); George Brown Tindall, *The Emergence of the New South, 1913–1945* (Baton Rouge, 1967); Grantham, *Southern Progressivism;* and several other works that address southerners' understandings of the social role of religion.

1. Genesis of a Southern Reformer

1. *Poteat Newsletter (Also Allied Families)* 1 (July 1988). A copy of this first issue of the family genealogical newsletter was used at the public library in Yanceyville, N.C.

2. William S. Powell, *When the Past Refused to Die: A History of Caswell County, North Carolina, 1777–1977* (Durham, 1977), 1–22, 33–53, and 110–16 (quote and population statistics on 110).

3. Ibid., 468–72.

4. *Raleigh Biblical Recorder* (hereafter cited as *BR*), December 20, 1871 (quote); and Nannie May Tilley, *The Bright-Tobacco Industry, 1860–1929* (Chapel Hill, 1948), 24–36.

5. "A List of Taxable Property in Caswell County for the Year 1838 . . ." (microfilm at public library, Yanceyville, N.C.); Katharine Kerr Kendall, *Caswell County, 1777–1877: Historical Abstracts of Minutes of Caswell County, North Carolina* (Raleigh, 1976), 61 and 70; and Kendall, *Caswell County, North Carolina, Deed Books, 1817–1840* (Franklin, N.C., 1992), 256, 264, and 273. The duty of the standard keeper was probably to hold the county's set of standard weights and measures that was purchased in the 1780s. See Powell, *When the Past Refused to Die,* 94–95 and 101. The author thanks Robert Anthony of the North Carolina Collection at the University of North Carolina at Chapel Hill for this citation.

6. Kendall, *Historical Abstracts,* 75 and 80.

7. Ibid., 82, 84, 85, and 86.

8. William Louis Poteat (hereafter cited as WLP) to Lewis Hoffman Kemper, February 17, 1936, folder 208, Poteat Papers.

9. Katharine Kerr Kendall, *Caswell County, North Carolina, Marriage Bonds, 1778–1868* (Raleigh, 1981), 119; and Kendall, *Caswell County, North Carolina, Will Books, 1843–1868* (Raleigh, 1986), 56.

10. Kendall, *Caswell County, North Carolina, Will Books, 1814–1843 . . .* (Raleigh, 1983), 156.

11. Manuscript Census Returns, Seventh Census of the United States, 1850, Caswell

County, North Carolina, White and Free Colored Population, National Archives Microfilm Series M-432, roll 623; and handwritten notes by WLP, folder 995, Poteat Papers. The children, and their ages in 1850, were Felix Lindsay [or Lindsey], age 12; John Miles, age 10; Sarah Elizabeth, age 8; and James Preston, age 2. The daughter who died in infancy was named Virginia. See also Ben L. Rose, *Thomas McNeill of Caswell County, North Carolina: His Forebears and Descendants* (Richmond, 1984), 50; and the 1850 census cited above.

12. Certified copy of will of John Poteat, folder 1175, Poteat Papers; and Kendall, *Will Books, 1843–1868,* 59 and 69.

13. Kendall, *Historical Abstracts,* 78.

14. Ibid., 69.

15. Ruth Little-Stokes, comp., *An Inventory of Historic Architecture, Caswell County, North Carolina: The Built Environment of a Burley and Bright-leaf Tobacco Economy* ([Raleigh], 1979), 110.

16. Kendall, *Marriage Bonds, 1778–1868,* 119.

17. On Julia Poteat's attendance at the Oxford seminary see Charles F. Hudson, "The Authorized Personal Interview of Dr. W.L. Poteat," folder 532, Poteat Papers; *BR,* April 7, 1859, February 22, 1855 (quotes), and July 5, 1855; Rose, *Thomas McNeill,* 8, 38, and 50; Jeannine D. Whitlow, ed., *The Heritage of Caswell County, North Carolina, 1985* (Winston-Salem, 1985), 380; and WLP to P.W. Hidin, March 8, 1934, folder 143, Poteat Papers. On Julia's father Hosea McNeill's local leadership roles see references throughout Kendall, *Historical Abstracts.*

18. Manuscript Census Returns, Eighth Census of the United States, 1860, Caswell County, North Carolina, Schedule 1, National Archives Microfilm Series M-653, roll 891. James Poteat is listed as owner of one group of ten slaves, perhaps hands rented out, then his principal listing includes eighty-four more (Schedule 2, Slave Population, National Archives Microfilm Series M-653, roll 921). See Powell, *When the Past Refused to Die,* 113, for ranking. Age is from the 1860 census.

19. Powell, *When the Past Refused to Die,* 114.

20. Little-Stokes, comp., *Historic Architecture,* 194.

21. On the prominence of her father Hosea McNeill among state Baptists see *BR,* August 27, 1857. On James Poteat and the church see *BR,* February 27, 1867, and June 1, 1910. Quote from report of Yanceyville revival in *BR,* September 25, 1856. See also Hudson, "Interview."

22. Kendall, *Will Books, 1843–1868,* 116.

23. Poteat, "Memoirs," folder 479, Poteat Papers.

24. *BR,* August 16, 1860, and August 29, 1866, on executive committee and August 21, 1867, August 19, 1868, August 11, 1869, and August 23, 1871, for his service as moderator. No association meeting was held in 1870, despite the encouragement of the embattled Governor Holden, because it was scheduled for Yanceyville and Caswell County was involved in the Kirk-Holden unrest of the time. *BR,* July 5, 1871, and August 10, 1870.

25. *BR,* March 1, 1871 (for number of churches), July 9, 1873, June 9, 1869, and October 9, 1867.

26. *BR,* June 5, 1867, October 30, 1867, November 16, 1870, and August 19, 1874. On appointment as trustee see C.E. Taylor, [comp.], *General Catalogue of Wake Forest College, North Carolina, 1834–5—1891–2* (Raleigh, 1892), 16.

27. *BR,* August 21, 1872 (first quote), and July 31, 1867 (second quote).

28. James Poteat, "Systematic Benevolence," handwritten speech manuscript, folder 55, McNeill-Poteat Family Papers, Special Collections, Reynolds Library.

29. The argument that the reform tradition that produced the southern Progressive movement originated in evangelical missionary ideas is strengthened by the fact that missions and benevolence and also later Progressive activities provoked opposition from the same quarters—the more isolated, rural, and lower-class southerners who were the objects of uplift. See Bertram Wyatt-Brown, "The Antimission Movement in the Jacksonian South: A Study in Regional Folk Culture," *Journal of Southern History* 36 (November 1970): 501–29; and Link, *Paradox of Southern Progressivism.* Anne C. Loveland claims that "the involvement of southern evangelicals in be-

nevolent activities increased steadily throughout the antebellum period" and that "they continued to support many of the national benevolent societies headquartered in the North" even as
sectional tensions appeared. (*Southern Evangelicals and the Social Order, 1800–1860* [Baton Rouge
and London, 1980], 173 and 174). Loveland lists a number of antebellum causes, such as helping the poor and physically challenged, that were consistent with later Progressive crusades.
Further, the antebellum ethic allowed for the continuation of "existing social and economic
differences among men" yet "fostered brotherhood among men of different classes and conditions" (169). This accords perfectly with Progressivism. Further, temperance advocates and guardians of morality on such issues as dueling were already resorting to political involvement before
the Civil War. The resumption of that strategy in the 1880s, once the southern evangelicals had
regained security and sought to regain hegemony, constituted the emergence of Progressivism.
Opposition to alcohol was a strong continuity. On southern benevolence see also John W.
Kuykendall, *Southern Enterprize: The Work of National Evangelical Societies in the Antebellum
South* (Westport, Conn., and London, 1982); John W. Quist, "Slaveholding Operatives of the
Benevolent Empire: Bible, Tract, and Sunday School Societies in Antebellum Tuscaloosa County,
Alabama," *Journal of Southern History* 62 (August 1996): 481–526; and Quist, *Restless Visionar-
ies: The Social Roots of Antebellum Reform in Alabama and Michigan* (Baton Rouge and London,
1997).

30. Hudson, "Interview" (quote); and Poteat, "Memoirs"; *BR*, June 1, 1910; and minutes of Yanceyville First Baptist Church, microfilm, Special Collections, Reynolds Library. On
biracialism in southern churches see John B. Boles, *Religion in Antebellum Kentucky* (Lexington,
Ky., 1976); and Boles, ed., *Masters and Slaves in the House of the Lord: Race and Religion in the
American South, 1740–1870* (Lexington, Ky., 1988).

31. Poteat, draft of "An Intellectual Adventure" (quote); Poteat, "Memoirs"; and *BR*,
June 1, 1910. Also see outline of "The Text-Book of the Sunday School" in notebook in folder
999, Poteat Papers.

32. *BR*, July 27, 1870 (quote), August 18 and November 24, 1869; and Hudson, "Interview."

33. *BR*, April 20, 1870.

34. Manuscript Census Returns, Ninth Census of the United States, 1870, Caswell County,
North Carolina, Population Schedule, National Archives Microfilm Series M-593, roll 1128.

35. On James Poteat's giving see *BR*, February 12, 1868. He gave $60 in cash to the
causes at that meeting and was one of the few for whom the pledges were immediately paid. On
giving within his local church see minutes of Yanceyville First Baptist Church.

36. *BR*, February 27, 1867; and handwritten notes, folder 995, Poteat Papers.

37. Whitlow, ed., *Heritage of Caswell County,* 436; Poteat, "Memoirs"; and Oath of
Amnesty, August 17, 1865, folder 65, McNeill-Poteat Family Papers. William Poteat recalled in
1898 that the move occurred when he was fourteen (Poteat diary, August 9, 1898, in possession
of family).

38. L. Ruby Reid, "Forest Home," folder 1238; and Poteat, "Memoirs."

39. WLP to Fate Murray, September 2, 1928, folder 252; and Poteat, "Memoirs."

40. Poteat, "Memoirs."

41. Draft of "The Role of the South in the 20th Century," April 1895, in notebook in
folder 1126, Poteat Papers.

42. Poteat, "Memoirs." For a study that addresses the role of women in household production and their embrace of plantation life see Elizabeth Fox-Genovese, *Within the Plantation
Household: Black and White Women of the Old South* (Chapel Hill and London, 1988).

43. Poteat, "Memoirs."

44. Draft of "The Role of the South in the 20th Century."

45. Poteat, "Memoirs" (first quote); and WLP to Emma Poteat (hereafter cited as EP),
August 5, 1915, folder 1166 (second quote), Poteat Papers.

46. Helen Poteat Stallings, "Ida Isabella Poteat, 1859–1940," *Meredith College Bulletin*
34 (November 1940): 6–7; clipping on Edwin McNeill Poteat Sr. from *Southern Baptist Encyclopedia,* folder 1, Poteat Papers; and *BR*, June 1, 1910.

47. Hudson, "Interview"; Poteat, "Memoirs"; handwritten notes, folder 995, Poteat Papers; and Powell, *When the Past Refused to Die,* 395.

48. Hudson, "Interview" (first quote); Little-Stokes, *Historic Architecture,* 38; Poteat, "Memoirs"; James Poteat Hotel Register, Special Collections, Perkins Library, Duke University, Durham, N.C. (second quote); and Manuscript Census Returns, Ninth Census of the United States, 1870, Caswell County, North Carolina, Population Schedule.

49. Minutes of Yanceyville First Baptist Church; and *BR,* June 5, 1867. On the postwar separation of blacks from formerly biracial churches see Spain, *At Ease in Zion,* chap. 2; and Paul Harvey, *Redeeming the South: Religious Cultures and Racial Identities among Southern Baptists, 1865–1925* (Chapel Hill and London, 1997), chaps. 1 and 2. Both emphasize black initiative in this overall process.

50. Minutes of Yanceyville First Baptist Church.

51. [Report of the Select Committee of the Senate to Investigate Alleged Outrages in the Southern States], 42 Cong., 1st sess., 1871, S. Rept. 1, serial 1468, 1 (first quote); Otto H. Olsen, "The Ku Klux Klan: A Study in Reconstruction Politics and Propaganda," *North Carolina Historical Review* 39 (summer 1962): 340–62 (341 for second quote); and Jeffrey J. Crow, "Thomas Settle Jr., Reconstruction, and the Memory of the Civil War," *Journal of Southern History* 62 (November 1996): 689–726. On state politics during this period see Paul D. Escott, *Many Excellent People: Power and Privilege in North Carolina, 1850–1900* (Chapel Hill and London, 1985).

52. *Greensboro Daily News,* October 2, 1935.

53. Olsen, "Ku Klux Klan," 345 and 354; and Allen W. Trelease, *White Terror: The Ku Klux Klan and Southern Reconstruction* (1971; reprint, Baton Rouge and London, 1995), 198–99.

54. Hudson, "Interview."

55. Poteat, draft of "An Intellectual Adventure" (quotes); and minutes of Yanceyville First Baptist Church.

56. *BR,* August 18, 1869 (quotes); and minutes of Yanceyville First Baptist Church.

57. Poteat's conversion mirrors Loveland's summary of the conversion experiences of nineteenth-century evangelicals: "It frequently came at a time of unsettlement for the youth—not merely the emotional unsettlement accompanying puberty or young adulthood, but unsettlement in the conditions of life which also produced emotional upheaval and sensitiveness . . . For a number of young men, the change in the conditions of life occurred as a result of attending college" (*Southern Evangelicals,* 6). Poteat's rededication to religion upon reaching college strengthens the link between religion and order in his life.

58. Confession of John G. Lea, *Greensboro Daily News,* October 2, 1935 (first quote); W.W. Holden, *Answer to the Articles of Impeachment . . .* ([Raleigh], 1870), 36 (second quote); and Trelease, *White Terror,* 215–16.

59. Trelease, *White Terror,* 216–25.

60. Minutes of Yanceyville First Baptist Church.

61. Entry for Saturday before the 4th Lord's day in August 1870, minutes of Yanceyville First Baptist Church.

62. Poteat, "Memoirs" (first quote); Report of the Select Committee, 401 (second quote), 406 (third quote), and 407 (last quote); and Holden, *Answer to the Articles of Impeachment,* 26, for list of detained.

63. *BR,* August 21, 1867.

64. On the continuing sense of paternalism by white Baptists see Harvey, *Redeeming the South,* esp. 49–53.

65. George Washington Paschal, *History of Wake Forest College,* 3 vols. (Wake Forest, N.C., 1935–43), 1:297; minutes of Yanceyville First Baptist Church, March 1870, for J.P. Poteat transferring his membership from Wake Forest Baptist Church; Poteat, "Memoirs"; and Hudson, "Interview" (quote).

66. *BR,* December 3 and 24, 1873, and March 4, 1874; and Paschal, *Wake Forest,* 1:53–71 and 171–73.

67. Paschal, *Wake Forest,* 1:302, 341, and 360.

68. Ibid., 2:11–13 and 64 (quote).

69. Ibid., 2:113–30.

70. Hudson, "Interview"; and Julia Poteat to WLP, [June 1903], folder 1180, Poteat Papers.

71. James P. Barefield, "The Wake Forest Curriculum: A Brief History" (unpublished paper in author's possession), [6] (first quote); Hudson, "Interview" (second and third quotes); Poteat, draft of "An Intellectual Adventure" (fourth quote); and *BR,* June 16, 1875 (last quote).

72. WLP to R.T. Vann, November 23, 1931, folder 433 (first quote); Poteat, draft of "An Intellectual Adventure" (second quote); Hudson, "Interview" (third quote); notes in folder 944 (last two quotes); and press release dated May 8, 1933, folder 981, all in Poteat Papers.

73. *BR,* March 2, 1870 (first and second quotes), and July 21, 1875 (third and fourth quotes).

74. Paschal, *Wake Forest,* 2:157–59; *BR,* May 28, 1873; Poteat, "My Approach to Religion," folder 961 (first two quotes); Poteat, "Christianity and Enlightenment," December 13, 1922 (pamphlet published by Baptist State Convention), folder 811, Poteat Papers (last quote); and WLP to Rev. F.M. Jordan, November 10, 1917, folder 23, F.M. Jordan Papers, Special Collections, Reynolds Library.

75. Paschal, *Wake Forest,* 1:146–59.

76. Paschal, *Wake Forest,* 1:489–502 and 534–59 (first quote on 490); and Hudson, "Interview" (second quote).

77. Paschal, *Wake Forest,* 2:367.

78. Minutes of the Euzelian Society, Euzelian Society Records, Special Collections, Reynolds Library.

79. Paschal, *Wake Forest,* 2:365–84 (quote on 384); and *BR,* February 17, 1875, and February 2, 1876. The emphasis on oral ability in education was being challenged beginning in the 1870s by educators who were part of the New South movement. The University of North Carolina adopted "a radically new vision of education and society" when it reopened in 1875, moving from its antebellum role of classically educating local leaders to a competitive, scientific curriculum utilizing lectures rather than recitations, and including electives. Rather than acquiring genteel polish, students sought to enter the professional, middle-class world. Leloudis, *Schooling the New South,* chap. 2 (quote on p. 55). On the so-called New South see C. Vann Woodward, *The Origins of the New South, 1877–1913* (Baton Rouge, 1951); and Paul M. Gaston, *The New South Creed: A Study in Southern Mythmaking* (Baton Rouge, 1970).

80. *BR,* February 28 (first quote), May 23, and June 20 (speech title), 1877.

81. Description from Poteat's U.S. passport in folder 708, Poteat Papers.

82. "Ripples on the Sea of Life," folder 1048, Poteat Papers. On self-control as manliness for southern evangelicals see Harvey, *Redeeming the South,* 165. See also Ted Ownby, *Subduing Satan: Religion, Recreation, and Manhood in the Rural South, 1865–1920* (Chapel Hill and London, 1990).

83. Poteat, "Life's a Battle—Man a Soldier in It," in *BR,* August 1, 1877.

84. *BR,* May 8, 1878 (temperance quotes). On reading law see Hudson, "Interview"; and WLP to M.S. Revell, November 4, 1933, folder 348, Poteat Papers. For Poteat's advertisement for Yanceyville Male Academy see clipping in notebook in folder 701, Poteat Papers. In a letter from 1923, Poteat writes, "I can report that I was defeated in my effort at discipline in a primary school many years ago." This indicates that his proposed school may have been operated for a time during the year following graduation. See WLP to Margarette Gladys Freeman, February 23, 1923, folder 113, Poteat Papers.

2. Separate Spheres—Personal, Professional, Religious

1. There is relatively little work on the history of higher education in the South. Parts of Leloudis's *Schooling the New South* present the most important interpretation of the topic. See also Joseph M. Stetar, "In Search of a Direction: Southern Higher Education after the Civil

War," *History of Education Quarterly* 25 (fall 1985): 341–67. In this chapter Wake Forest College will be compared with a number of similar southern schools, using the institutional histories that represent the only significant source of secondary information on southern colleges and universities. See Earl W. Porter, *Trinity and Duke, 1892–1924: Foundations of Duke University* (Durham, N.C., 1964); George R. Fairbanks, *History of the University of the South* . . . (Jacksonville, Fla., 1905); Mary D. Beaty, *A History of Davidson College* (Davidson, N.C., 1988); Alfred Sandlin Reid, *Furman University: Toward a New Identity, 1925–1975* (Durham, N.C., 1976); Paul K. Conkin, *Gone with the Ivy: A Biography of Vanderbilt University* (Knoxville, 1985); and Hugh Hawkins, *Pioneer: A History of the Johns Hopkins University, 1874–1889* (Ithaca, N.Y., 1960). On national trends in the professionalization of education see Bruce A. Kimball, *The "True Professional Ideal" in America: A History* (Cambridge, Mass., and Oxford, 1992), chap. 4; and on the Victorian middle class see Burton J. Bledstein, *The Culture of Professionalism: The Middle Class and the Development of Higher Education in America* (New York, 1976); and Daniel Joseph Singal, *The War Within: From Victorian to Modernist Thought in the South, 1919–1945* (Chapel Hill, 1982), chap. 1. On the national trends in higher education see Frederick Rudolph, *Curriculum: A History of the American Undergraduate Course of Study Since 1636* (San Francisco, 1977).

2. Historians of science have in recent years acknowledged that, contrary to the assertion of Clement Eaton in *The Mind of the Old South* (Baton Rouge, 1964), science in the Old South was not squelched by intellectual orthodoxy, but flourished within the limits of its demographic and environmental resources. See Ronald L. Numbers and Janet S. Numbers, "Science in the Old South: A Reappraisal," *Journal of Southern History* 48 (May 1982): 163–84. As evidenced by, among many other works, Ronald L. Numbers and Todd L. Savitt, eds., *Science and Medicine in the Old South* (Baton Rouge and London, 1989), study of science in the Old South has thrived. In contrast, the study of science in the New South remains undeveloped. The major work is Nancy Smith Midgette, *To Foster the Spirit of Professionalism: Southern Scientists and State Academies of Science* (Tuscaloosa and London, 1991), along with her related articles, "In Search of Professional Identity: Southern Scientists, 1883–1940," *Journal of Southern History* 54 (November 1988): 596–622; and "The Alabama Academy of Science and the Maturing of a Profession," *Alabama Review* 37 (April 1984): 98–123. Other significant works include Thomas R. Williams, "The Development of Astronomy in the Southern United States, 1840–1914," *Journal for the History of Astronomy* 27 (February 1996): 13–44; Lester D. Stephens, "Darwin's Disciple in Georgia: Henry Clay White, 1875–1927," *Georgia Historical Quarterly* 78 (spring 1994): 66–91; James A. Ramage, "Thomas Hunt Morgan: Family Influences in the Making of a Great Scientist," *Filson Club History Quarterly* 53 (January 1979): 5–25; James Summerville, "Science in the New South: The Meeting of the AAAS at Nashville, 1877," *Tennessee Historical Quarterly* 45 (winter 1986): 316–28; Clement Eaton, "Professor James Woodrow and the Freedom of Teaching in the South," *Journal of Southern History* 28 (February 1962): 3–17; James E. Brittain and Robert C. McMath Jr., "Engineers and the New South Creed: The Formation and Early Development of Georgia Tech," *Technology and Culture* 18 (April 1977): 175–201; and Charlotte A. Ford, "Eliza Frances Andrews, Practical Botanist, 1840–1931," *Georgia Historical Quarterly* 70 (spring 1986): 63–80. Some information on science in the New South can also be garnered from works that focus predominantly on the period before the Civil War but extend somewhat into the postbellum period. See Tamara Miner Haygood, *Henry William Ravenel, 1814–1887: South Carolina Scientist in the Civil War Era* (Tuscaloosa and London, 1987); Haygood, "Henry Ravenel (1814–1887): Views on Evolution in Social Context," *Journal of the History of Biology* 21 (fall 1988): 457–72; Marcus B. Simpson Jr. and Sallie W. Simpson, "Moses Ashley Curtis (1808–1872): Contributions to Carolina Ornithology," *North Carolina Historical Review* 60 (April 1983): 137–70; and Lester D. Stephens, *Joseph LeConte: Gentle Prophet of Evolution* (Baton Rouge and London, 1982).

3. Edward L. Ayers, *The Promise of the New South: Life after Reconstruction* (New York and Oxford, 1992), 420.

4. Bledstein, *Culture of Professionalism,* chap. 3.

5. Minutes of the board of trustees, June 13, 1878 (all minutes of the Wake Forest board

of trustees are in Special Collections, Reynolds Library); and *Wake Forest College Catalog, 1878–79*, 6, 12, and 19. A full run of the college's annual catalog is in Special Collections, Reynolds Library. See Porter, *Trinity and Duke,* 9 and 11; Fairbanks, *University of the South,* 361; Beaty, *Davidson College,* 177–78 n. 20; Reid, *Furman University,* 24; Conkin, *Gone with the Ivy,* 87; and Brittain and McMath, "Engineers," 189.

6. Minutes of the board of trustees, June 10, 1879 (quote); June 11, 1879, and June 8 and [10?], 1880.

7. *Catalog, 1880–81,* 17 (quote); Conkin, *Gone with the Ivy,* 44–45; Hawkins, *Pioneer,* 45–49 and 135–49; Reid, *Furman University,* 22 and 26; Beaty, *Davidson College,* 179–80; Porter, *Trinity and Duke,* 74–75; Jessica Harland-Jacobs, *Balancing Tradition and Innovation: The History of Botany at Duke University, 1849–1996* ([Durham, N.C.], 1996), 3; and Midgette, "In Search of Professional Identity," 608–9.

8. Minutes of the board of trustees, March 1 and June 10, 1879, and June 6, 1882 (quote); minutes of the faculty meetings, December 22, 1879, and March 19, April 2, and October 1, 1880 (all minutes of the Wake Forest faculty meetings are in Special Collections, Reynolds Library). This method of founding a library was also used by Wake Forest's peer among Tarheel Presbyterians, Davidson College, in 1887. Beaty, *Davidson College,* 157.

9. Minutes of the faculty meetings, May 30 and November 14, 1879, March 26, 1880, March 18, 1881, February 24, March 17, April 21, August 31, and September 8 and 29, 1882.

10. Minutes of the board of trustees, June 12, 1883.

11. Minutes of the board of trustees, November 15, 1883, and June 10, 1884; Porter, *Trinity and Duke,* 12–13 and 89; Beaty, *Davidson College,* 177–80 and 206; and Reid, *Furman University,* 22.

12. *Wake Forest Student* (hereafter cited as *WFS*) 3 (September 1883): 33; Edward S. Burgess to WLP, August 20, 1898, folder 44, Poteat Papers; and "Burgess, Edward Sandford" q.v. *National Cyclopaedia of American Biography* . . . (New York, 1931), 21:124–25. This institute operated between 1878 and 1905 in the village of Oak Bluffs, and in its Agassiz Hall, built in 1882, hundreds of teachers received "special instruction in advanced studies, scientific and literary" for five weeks each July and August. "Annals of Oak Bluffs," in Charles Edward Banks, *The History of Martha's Vineyard, Duke's County, Massachusetts,* 3 vols. (1911; reprint, Edgartown, Mass., 1966), 2:67–68 (quote on 67).

13. *Catalog, 1883–84,* 24–25 (quote on 25). See also notebook, folder 884, Poteat Papers; Hawkins, *Pioneer,* 223–24; Jane Maienschein, *Transforming Traditions in American Biology, 1880–1915* (Baltimore and London, 1991), 115–17; and Keith R. Benson, "From Museum Research to Laboratory: The Transformation of Natural History into Academic Biology," in Ronald Rainger, Keith R. Benson, and Jane Maienschein, eds., *The American Development of Biology* (Philadelphia, 1988), 62–67.

14. *Catalog, 1884–85,* 22 (first quote); and *Catalog, 1886–87,* 31 (other quotes).

15. *WFS* 3 (November 1883): 123 (first quote); 6 (May 1887): 377 (second quote) and 388; and 7 (October 1887): 38; and Benson, "Museum Research," 66–71.

16. Poteat, "The Laboratory as a Means of Culture," *WFS* 12 (July 1893): 519.

17. Clipping from *Raleigh News and Observer* (hereafter cited as *N&O*), dated September 16, 1885, in scrapbook in folder 701, Poteat Papers; and *Catalog, 1896–97,* 6.

18. Clipping from *N&O,* dated October 2, [1885] (quote), and various other clippings in scrapbook in folder 701, Poteat Papers.

19. Paschal, *Wake Forest,* 2:233–34, 236, 251–52, 258, and 260; Porter, *Trinity and Duke,* 18, 22, and 37; Conkin, *Gone with the Ivy,* 112–14; Beaty, *Davidson College,* 193–94; and Reid, *Furman University,* 22–24.

20. Minutes of the board of trustees, June 8, 1892 (first quote), June 12, 1894 (second quote), September 8, 1894, May 27, 1896, May 29, 1900, and July 31, 1902; Paschal, *Wake Forest,* 2:281; Reid, *Furman University,* 22 and 26; Fairbanks, *University of the South,* 291 and 302; and Porter, *Trinity and Duke,* 92.

21. *Catalog, 1894–95,* 46–48; *1896–97,* 47–48; *1902–3,* 62; and *1904–5,* 10–11, 15–16, and 84.

22. Minutes of faculty meetings, September 10, 1885, February 18, 1887, September 2, 1887, September 15, 1893, December 3, 1886, and March 8, 1888; *Catalog, 1893–94*, 9; *WFS* 10 (December 1890): 142; and Fairbanks, *University of the South*, 327.

23. *WFS* 8 (December 1888): 137 (first quote); minutes of the board of trustees, June 9, 1891 (second quote), June 8, 1892 (third quote), June 11, 1895 (fourth quote), and May 26, 1896; minutes of faculty meetings, November 5, 1888, December 14, 1888, November 15, 1895, September 6, 1890, September 16, 1892, and September 13, 1895; and Porter, *Trinity and Duke*, 52.

24. *Catalog, 1892–93*, 10 and 36–37; Philip J. Pauly, "The Appearance of Academic Biology in Late Nineteenth-Century America," *Journal of the History of Biology* 17 (fall 1984): 369–97; Benson, "Museum Research," 71–76; Toby A. Appel, "Organizing Biology: The American Society of Naturalists and Its 'Affiliated Societies,' 1883–1923," in Rainger, Benson, and Maienschein, eds., *Development of Biology*, 87–120; and Philip J. Pauly, "Summer Resort and Scientific Discipline: Woods Hole and the Structure of American Biology, 1882–1925," in *Development of Biology*, 121–50.

25. *Catalog, 1890–91*, 46; *1892–93*, 10, 22, 23, and 36–37; *1894–95*, 11 and 36–39; *1901-2*, 35–39; *1902-3*, 57–58; and *1903-4*, 10 and 30–33; minutes of the board of trustees, June 8, 1892 (quote); Porter, *Trinity and Duke*, 10 and 72–73; Conkin, *Gone with the Ivy*, 87–88; Reid, *Furman University*, 20; and Beaty, *Davidson College*, 220–21.

26. Karen Crowe, [ed.], *Southern Horizons: The Autobiography of Thomas Dixon* (Alexandria, Va., 1984), 153. See also Dixon to WLP, January 14, 1934, folder 288, Poteat Papers.

27. Rufus Weaver to WLP, August 12, 1931, folder 21, Poteat Papers; Paschal, *Wake Forest*, 2:343; *WFS* 4 (November 1884): 121; 6 (July 1887): 463; 6 (November 1886): 83; 10 (November 1890): 92; and 13 (May 1894): 397; and on the importance of college museums see Sally Gregory Kohlstedt, "Museums on Campus: A Tradition of Inquiry and Teaching," in Rainger, Benson, and Maienschein, eds., *Development of Biology*, 15–47. On evangelical moral objections to circuses in the South see Ownby, *Subduing Satan*, 56–65.

28. Poteat diary, February 16, 1896, in possession of family.

29. Poteat diary, April 18, 1896, in possession of family; J.P. Gulley to WLP, December 17, 1930, folder 125; William E. Hatcher to WLP, April 17, 1897, folder 153; and G.W. Greene to WLP, June 22, 1903, folder 140, Poteat Papers.

30. *WFS* 5 (December 1885); 5 (April 1886): 313; 5 (May 1886): 359; 13 (November 1893): 83; 20 (October 1900): 48; and 19 (February 1900): 349; and Paschal, *Wake Forest*, 3:83.

31. Paschal, *Wake Forest*, 3:3, 73, 82, and 83; minutes of the board of trustees, June 9, 1892, and June 11, 1895; and *Catalog, 1894–95*, 52.

32. Central Baptist Association, *Minutes . . . 1885*, 4; *1886*, 2–4; *1887*, 4; *1888*, 13; *1889*, 10–11; *1896*, 7–10; *1900*, 8–9; *1901*, 7; *1902*, 8–9; and *1904*, 11. All minutes of the Central Baptist Association that are cited are in Special Collections, Reynolds Library.

33. WLP to R.T. Vann, August 8, 1889, folder 713, Poteat Papers.

34. Paschal, *Wake Forest*, 2:455, 474, and 479; Baptist State Convention, *Minutes . . . 1878*, 28; *1885*, 51; *1892*, 11; *1893*, 47; *1895*, 62; and *1898*, 14; and Harvey, *Redeeming the South*, 137–44. All minutes of the Baptist State Convention that are cited are in Special Collections, Reynolds Library.

35. Mary Lynch Johnson, *A History of Meredith College*, 2nd ed. (Raleigh, 1972), chap. 2; Hawkins, *Pioneer*, chap. 14; Conkin, *Gone with the Ivy*, 90–91; Porter, *Trinity and Duke*, 63–64; Fairbanks, *University of the South*, 333; Beaty, *Davidson College*, 152 and 198–99; and Reid, *Furman University*, 21.

36. Poteat diary, April 14, 1897, in possession of family (quotes); Johnson, *Meredith College*, 46–47; "Statement of the Trustees . . . January 1894" (pamphlet); Charles J. Parker to WLP, April 5, 1899; and WLP to John B. Brewer, January 18, 1894, all in folder 543, Poteat Papers.

37. Poteat diary, March 18, 1899, in possession of family (quote); WLP to Blasingame, March 9, 1899, folder 543, Poteat Papers; and Johnson, *Meredith College*, 53.

38. Poteat diary, October 10 (quote) and 14, 1899, in possession of family; and Johnson, *Meredith College,* 83–84. The college enrolled 220 students in its first year, far beyond expectations. The catalog, released even before the school opened, listed a faculty of sixteen (including two assistants). Johnson, *Meredith College,* 53–54 and 57.

39. Poteat diary, November 27, 1899 (quotes), and February 2, 1900, in possession of family; Johnson, *Meredith College,* 84; Susie to Roy, June 7, 1900, Letters (copies), 1897–1900 folder, William C. Powell Papers, Special Collections, Perkins Library, Duke University; and WLP to William C. Tyree, May 21, 1900, William C. Tyree Papers, Special Collections, Perkins Library.

40. Johnson, *Meredith College,* 37 (quote) and 106–7.

41. Stetar, "In Search of a Direction," 341–67 (quotes on 344 and 358).

42. Midgette, *Spirit of Professionalism,* chaps. 1 and 3; and Robert V. Bruce, *The Launching of Modern American Science, 1846–1876* (New York, 1987).

43. For representative examples see *WFS* 1 (January 1882): 39–40; 1 (February 1882): 86–87; 1 (April 1882): 184–85; 2 (April 1883): 359–63; and 3 (September 1883): 30–31.

44. *WFS* 3 (November 1883): 117; F.P. Venable, "President's Report for 1884," *Journal of the Elisha Mitchell Scientific Society* (hereafter cited as *JEMSS*) 1 (1883–84): 3 (quote); Venable, "Report of the Secretary," *JEMSS* 3 (1885–86): 6; Venable, "Report of the Secretary," *JEMSS* 4 (January–June 1887): 9; "Public Lectures," *JEMSS* 4 (July–December 1887): 108; Poteat, "North Carolina Desmids—A Preliminary List," *JEMSS* 5 (January–June 1888): 1–4; and Benson, "Museum Research," 49–83.

45. *WFS* 7 (June 1888): 378; Edwin McNeill Poteat Jr., "Edwin McNeill Poteat Sr.," copy of entry in *Southern Baptist Encyclopedia,* folder 1, Poteat Papers; notebook containing notes from June 21 to June 28, 1888, folder 937, Poteat Papers; Hudson, "Interview" (quotes); and Paschal, *Wake Forest,* 3:456.

46. Minutes of the board of trustees, June 11, 1889; and minutes of the faculty meeting, May 27, 1889.

47. "Report on Progress in Microscopical Botany," folder 1012, Poteat Papers; "Thirty-Ninth Meeting," *JEMSS* 5 (July–December 1888): 132; and Poteat, "A Tube-Building Spider: Notes on the Architectural and Feeding Habits of Atypus Niger Hentz (?)," *JEMSS* 6 (July–December 1889): 132–47.

48. Poteat, "Notes on the Fertility of Physa Heterostropha Say," *JEMSS* 8 (July–December 1891): 70–73 and 130; *JEMSS* 9 (January–June 1892): list of officers facing contents page; and *WFS* 10 (April 1891): 364–65; 11 (November 1891): 87; 11 (December 1891): 127; 11 (February 1892): 213–14; 11 (March 1892): 255–56; 11 (June 1892): 387; 12 (November 1892): 100–101; 13 (April 1894): 349; 18 (February 1899): 338–39; 20 (February 1901): 342–43; 21 (December 1901): 176; and 27 (January 1908): 385.

49. Midgette, *Spirit of Professionalism,* 29.

50. Jane Maienschein, introduction to Maienschein, ed., *Defining Biology: Lectures from the 1890s* (Cambridge, Mass., and London, 1986), 3–50 (quote on 9); and Poteat, "The Effect on the College Curriculum of the Introduction of the Natural Sciences," *Science* 21 (March 31, 1893): 170–72.

51. WLP to EP, August 9, 1893, folder 1166, (quote); and notes in notebook in folder 937, Poteat Papers; Frank R. Lillie, *The Woods Hole Marine Biological Laboratory* (Chicago, 1944), p. 90 and chap. 6; "The Marine Biological Laboratory at Woods Hall [*sic*], Mass.," *American Naturalist* 27 (June 1893): 594–98; W.D. Russell-Hunter, "An Evolutionary Century at Woods Hole: Instruction in Invertebrate Zoology," *Biological Bulletin* 168 (supplement, June 1985): 88–98; Jane Maienschein, "Shifting Assumptions in American Biology: Embryology, 1890–1910," *Journal of the History of Biology* 14 (spring 1981): 89–113; Pauly, "Academic Biology," 369–97; and Paul R. Gross, "Laying the Ghost: Embryonic Development, in Plain Words," *Biological Bulletin* 168 (supplement, June 1985): 62–79.

52. Poteat, "Penikese," *WFS* 13 (October 1893): 4 (quote); *WFS* 13 (October 1893): 36; Poteat, "Effect on the College Curriculum," 170–72; and WLP to EP, August 9, 1893, folder 1166; and notes in notebook in folder 937, Poteat Papers.

53. Poteat diary, September 6, 1898, in possession of family; *Nature* 50 (May 24, 1894), 79; "The Zoological Section (F) of the American Association for the Advancement of Science," *Science*, n.s., 8 (September 23, 1898); and Poteat, "Leidy's Genus Ouramoeba," *Science*, n.s., 8 (December 2, 1898): 778–82.

54. Poteat's notes in notebook, folder 937, Poteat Papers; Maienschein, *Transforming Traditions*, 120–22; Maienschein, introduction to Maienschein, ed., *Defining Biology*, 21–24; Edmund B. Wilson, "The Mosaic Theory of Development," in *Defining Biology*, 66–80; "List of Biological Lectures," in *Defining Biology*, 51–56; and Maienschein, "Agassiz, Hyatt, Whitman, and the Birth of the Marine Biological Laboratory," *Biological Bulletin* 168 (supplement, June 1985): 31–33. The lecturers included Edmund Beecher Wilson, Edwin Grant Conklin, Jacques Loeb, John Ryder, and Shosaburo Watase.

55. "Proceedings of the North Carolina Academy of Science," *JEMSS* 20 (1904): 9–11.

56. Poteat's membership certificates from the AAAS for 1891 and 1898, folder 541, Poteat Papers.

57. H.H. Brimley to WLP, March 8, 1902, box 203, Herbert Hutchinson Brimley Papers, North Carolina Division of Archives and History, Raleigh, N.C. (quote); H.H. Brimley, "The Founding of the N.C. Academy of Science," undated typescript in North Carolina Academy of Science Records, Joyner Library, East Carolina University, Greenville, N.C.; F.P. Venable to WLP, November 22, 1902, folder 434, Poteat Papers; and Midgette, *Spirit of Professionalism*, 41–56.

58. Midgette, *Spirit of Professionalism*, 41–56; and Poteat, "Science and Life," handwritten speech manuscript in notebook in folder 1058, Poteat Papers (quotes).

59. WLP to EP, August 5, 1896, folder 1166 (first quote); and Poteat diary, November 21, 1896, folder 475 (second quote), Poteat Papers.

60. Poteat diary, January 15, 1898, in possession of family.

61. Hudson, "Interview."

62. Kimball, *"True Professional Ideal,"* chap. 4; and Bledstein, *Culture of Professionalism*. On the ideal home life of evangelical southerners of the time see Ownby, *Subduing Satan*, chap. 6.

63. Notebook in folder 883, Poteat Papers.

64. Minutes of the Euzelian Society, September 3, 1875, Euzelian Society Records; EP to WLP, January 13, 1881 (quoted), October 24, 1878, January 14, 1880, and April 12, 1880, folder 338, Poteat Papers; and *Wake Forest Old Gold and Black* (hereafter cited as *OGB*), October 28, 1939.

65. Notebook in folder 883 (poem); EP to A.V. Purefoy, July 29, 1881, folder 1166 ("Mr. Poteat"); WLP to Dear Friend, February 26, 1903, folder 223 (last quote), all in Poteat Papers; and Paschal, *Wake Forest*, 3:4–5.

66. Clipping of real estate listing, folder 1239; and WLP to James Poteat, October 14, 1888, folder 1173, Poteat Papers; *Babyhood* 4 (December 1887 to November 1888), in possession of family; Poteat diary, December 12, 1895, in possession of family; and Rose, *Thomas McNeill*, 50–51.

67. Poteat diary, March 2, 1896 (first quote), and April 6, 1897, in possession of family; and diary, January 28, 1897, folder 475, Poteat Papers.

68. EP to WLP, August 6, 1896, folder 1166 (quote); Poteat diary, June 8 and October 1, 1896, folder 475, Poteat Papers; and diary, July 17, 1897, and March 29, 1898, in possession of family.

69. EP to WLP, [1903], folder 1166, Poteat Papers.

70. WLP to EP, July 22, 1900, folder 963; and EP to WLP, [1906], folder 1166, Poteat Papers.

71. Poteat, "The Children's Hour," *WFS* 4 (November 1884): 108–9 (quotes on 109).

72. Poteat, "The Leadership of the Little Child," speech notes dated July 22, 1896, in notebook in folder 932, Poteat Papers.

73. *Babyhood* 4 (January 1888): 39; Poteat diary, August 3 and 18, and September 8, 1896, and January 24, 1897, folder 475; WLP to James Poteat, October 14, 1888, folder 1173, Poteat Papers; and Poteat diary, April 6, 1898, in possession of family.

74. Poteat diary, November 26, 1896, folder 475; and WLP to EP, August 6, 1896, folder 1166, Poteat Papers.

75. Poteat diary, October 1, 1897, in possession of family (first quote); and diary, August 24, 1896, folder 475, Poteat Papers (second quote).

76. Whitlow, ed., *Heritage of Caswell County*, 437; Poteat diary, August 26, 1896, folder 475, Poteat Papers; and Poteat diary, September 13, 1898, in possession of family.

77. Poteat diary, December 4, 1895 (first quote), April 10, 1896 (fourth quote), December 15, 1895, and February 2, 1896, in possession of family; and Poteat diary, June 8, 1896 (second quote), September 15, 1896 (third quote), July 17, 1896 (last quote), and September 8, 1896, folder 475, Poteat Papers.

78. Poteat diary, February 16, 1896, in possession of family.

79. Poteat diary, October 30, 1896 (first quote), February 15, 1897 (second quote), September 25 and October 1, 1896, folder 475, Poteat Papers; and Poteat diary, December 12, 1895, July 6, 1897 (third quote), September 19, 1897 (fourth quote), October 1, 1897 (fifth quote), November 11, 1897 (sixth quote), and June 21, 1898 (last quote), in possession of family.

80. Poteat diary, April 14 (quote) and 18, and October 6, 1898, in possession of family.

81. Poteat diary, February 23, 1896 (quote), September 6, 1897, and January 30, 1898, in possession of family.

82. Poteat diary, January 23, 1897, folder 475, Poteat Papers.

83. Poteat diary, September 24, 1898, September 30, 1899, January 2, 1900, September 4, 1900, and March 3, 1901, in possession of family.

84. W.I. Royster to WLP, August 22, 1903, folder 358; and Hubert's grade reports dated October 31, 1906, and May 24, 1907, folder 1171, Poteat Papers.

85. Paschal, *Wake Forest,* 3:37–38 and 74–75.

86. Poteat diary, September 16, 1902, in possession of family.

87. Rose, *Thomas McNeill,* 50–51; *WFS* 25 (October 1905): 89; Louie's grade reports from Baptist University for Women, folder 1180; Rosa Paschal to WLP, February 20 and March 13, 1906, folder 319; Louie Poteat to WLP, undated, folder 1180; and various letters from Louie to EP, 1906 to 1930, folder 1180, Poteat Papers.

88. Helen's grade reports from Meredith Academy and Meredith College; clipping labeled *N&O,* December 2, 1936; and clipping labeled *Portland (Maine) Press Herald,* August 10, 1926, all in folder 1179, Poteat Papers.

89. Poteat diary, April 30, 1896, in possession of family (quote); Johnson, *Meredith College,* 63; *BR,* June 1, 1910; and Ida Poteat to WLP, March 5, 1876, folder 1172, Poteat Papers.

90. Poteat diary, August 16, 1896, folder 475 (second quote); Edwin M. Poteat (hereafter cited as EMP) to WLP, March 9, 1897 (first quote); EMP to WLP, August 4, 1896 (third quote); EMP to WLP, August 30, 1896; EMP to Ernest Poteat, August 26, 1898; EMP to WLP, December 6, 1888; EMP to WLP, June 19, 1900; EMP to WLP, November [?], 1891; and EMP to WLP, December 1, 1897, all in folder 1162; Ernest Poteat to WLP, August 28, 1896, folder 1169; Edwin McNeill Poteat Jr., "Edwin McNeill Poteat Sr.," all in Poteat Papers; Poteat diary, January 4, 1899, in possession of family; and Whitlow, ed., *Heritage of Caswell County,* 14. In addition to editing a newspaper for a while, Preston also took an active part in the religious life of the Beulah Baptist Association, serving as a delegate and even the association's treasurer at the beginning of the 1890s. See *Minutes of the Sixty-Third Annual Session of the Beulah Baptist Association* . . . (Yanceyville, N.C., 1897), 3; and *Minutes of the Fifty-Seventh Annual Session of the Beulah Baptist Association* . . . (Winston, N.C., 1891), 1 and 3. Copies in Special Collections, Reynolds Library.

91. *WFS* 4 (February 1885): 261; and 13 (October 1893): 35.

92. Poteat diary, February 2, 1896, in possession of family (quote); R.W. Haywood to WLP, September 28, 1896, folder 143; and EP to WLP, [March 1906], folder 1166, Poteat Papers; and *WFS* 13 (October 1893): 33; 13 (February 1894): 242; 13 (June 1894): 452; and 20 (March 1901): 414–15.

93. Poteat diary, May 23, 1896, folder 475, Poteat Papers (first quote); and Poteat diary, August 7, 1897 (second quote), and May 17, 1898 (last quote), in possession of family.

94. Poteat diary, October 20 (quote) and December 16, 1895, in possession of family; and Poteat diary, May 6, 1896, folder 475, Poteat Papers.

95. Poteat diary, August 7, 1897, in possession of family.

96. Poteat diary, February 15, 1898 (first quote), and February 13, 1901 (second quote), in possession of family.

97. Poteat, "The Ideal Forces in Human History," *WFS* 1 (January 1882): 10.

98. Poteat, "In Winter-Quarters," *WFS* 3 (December 1883): 158.

99. Poteat, "The Lecture," *WFS* 3 (January 1884): 201–2.

100. Poteat diary, May 4, 1896, in possession of family.

101. *WFS* 20 (April 1901): 500; and *Christian Index* quoted in *WFS* 22 (April 1903): 473.

102. Notes and speech manuscript of "Dante and His World" in notebook in folder 842, Poteat Papers (first quote); and Poteat, "Lucretius and the Evolution Idea," *Popular Science Monthly* 60 (December 1901): 170.

103. EMP to WLP, February 20, 1891, folder 1162, Poteat Papers (first quote); and Poteat diary, October 20, 1895, in possession of family (other quotes).

104. Poteat diary, November 28, 1895, in possession of family.

105. Poteat diary, October 20 (quotes) and 22, 1896, folder 475, Poteat Papers; and Poteat diary, October 20, 1897, and October 20, 1898, in possession of family.

106. Stephens, *Joseph LeConte,* chap. 9; Haygood, "Henry Ravenel," 469; and Peter J. Bowler, *Evolution: The History of an Idea,* (1983; rev. ed., Berkeley, Los Angeles, and London, 1989), chap. 8. Ravenel had a more ambivalent belief in evolution than the other two.

107. Cash, *Mind of the South,* 142; Woodward, *Origins of the New South;* and Bruce Clayton, *The Savage Ideal: Intolerance and Intellectual Leadership in the South, 1890–1914* (Baltimore and London, 1972).

108. Eaton, "James Woodrow," 10–11. See also Stephens, "Darwin's Disciple," 66–91; and Oliver H. Orr Jr., *Saving American Birds: T. Gilbert Pearson and the Founding of the Audubon Movement* (Gainesville, Fla., 1992), 81.

109. Hudson, "Interview" (first quote); and Poteat, "An Intellectual Adventure: A Human Document," *American Scholar* 5 (summer 1936): 282 (last quote).

110. Poteat, "First Century of the Christian Era," clipping labeled *BR,* December 8, 1880, in scrapbook in folder 701, Poteat Papers.

111. *WFS* 1 (June 1882): 271–72.

112. *WFS* 2 (October 1882): 85.

113. Poteat, "No Conflict between Science and Revelation," *WFS* 2 (March 1883): 302

114. Poteat, "The Groundless Quarrel" [address given June 5, 1884], *WFS* 4 (October 1884): 40–41.

115. Poteat, "A Remarkable Book," *WFS* 4 (September 1884): 20.

116. Poteat, "On the Study of Natural History," *WFS* 6 (January 1887): 161.

117. *BR,* June 6, 1888.

118. *BR,* May 9, 1888.

119. Poteat, "The Physiological Basis of Morality," handwritten speech manuscript delivered November 14, 1895, in notebook in folder 1003 (quotes); notebook of notes for "The Physiological Basis of Morality," folder 1003; G. Stanley Hall to WLP, July 13, 1895, folder 181; and Walter Rauschenbusch to WLP, February 21, 1895, folder 345, Poteat Papers; Henry Drummond, *The Ascent of Man* (New York, 1894); and Benjamin Kidd, *Social Evolution* (London and New York, 1894). On religion, morality, and the social applications of evolution see Bowler, *Evolution,* chaps. 8 and 10. On Baptist Congress see Paul M. Minus, *Walter Rauschenbusch: American Reformer* (New York and London, 1988), 66.

120. Poteat, "Physiological Basis of Morality." See Bowler, *Evolution,* 233–36.

121. Poteat, "Physiological Basis of Morality."

122. Poteat diary, November 15, 1895, in possession of family.

123. Ibid., December 4, 1895.

124. Poteat, "Culture and Faith," June 11, 1895, handwritten speech manuscript in note-

book in folder 1113, Poteat Papers. For related looks by Poteat at the relation between science and literature see "Tennyson As an Evolutionist," *WFS* 13 (March 1894): 247–54; and "The Appeal to Nature," *WFS* 19 (October 1899): 2–14.

125. Poteat, "Culture and Faith."

126. Copy of John S. Hardaway to C. Durham, June 10, 1895, folder 104, Poteat Papers. See also copy of J.A. Stradley to Durham, June 7, 1895, folder 104, Poteat Papers. On Hardaway see *BR*, February 5, 1902.

127. C. Durham to WLP, June 17, 1895, and copy of WLP to Durham, June 18, 1895, folder 104, Poteat Papers.

128. *BR*, January 24, 1894.

129. *BR*, February 28, 1894.

130. *BR*, December 20, 1893.

131. Poteat, "Culture and Faith"; EMP to WLP, December 6, 1888, and November [?], 1891, folder 1162, Poteat Papers; and for later examples of referring to Renan see Poteat, *Youth and Culture* ([Wake Forest, N.C.], 1938), 38–39 and 137–38.

132. Poteat, "The Thirty Silent Years," handwritten manuscript from 1894 in folder 1097, Poteat Papers.

133. Poteat, "The Marks of the Educated Man," *WFS* 18 (October 1898): 43–44.

134. Poteat, "Wherein Lies the Efficacy of Jesus' Work in the Reconciliation," handwritten speech manuscript in notebook in folder 858, Poteat Papers. See also W.C. Tyree, "A Statement of the Orthodox View of the Atonement," *BR*, May 14, 1902. See *BR*, May 28 and June 4, 1902, for criticism of liberal theories of the atonement.

135. Poteat, "Efficacy of Jesus' Work."

136. Poteat diary, November 7, 1899, in possession of family. See also Poteat diary, November 28, 1895, in possession of family; and WLP to Edgar Y. Mullins, November 7, 1899, Mullins Papers, Archives and Special Collections, Southern Baptist Theological Seminary, Louisville, Ky.

137. As sources for these lectures see the works discussed above and also Poteat, "The People's Bible," *Eighty-Sixth Annual Report of the Bible Society of Virginia* . . . (Richmond, 1900), 7–15; along with the notes and manuscript for this address in folder 999; and "The Cell and What it Can Do," handwritten speech manuscript in folder 783, Poteat Papers.

138. Poteat, *Laboratory and Pulpit: The Relation of Biology to the Preacher and His Message* (Philadelphia, 1901), 12–13.

139. Ibid., 29–30.

140. Ibid., 32–40.

141. Rufus Weaver to WLP, February 2, 1898, folder 449, Poteat Papers.

142. Poteat, *Laboratory and Pulpit,* 44.

143. Ibid., 52 (first quote), 53 (second quote), 55 (third and fourth quotes), and 56 (last quote).

144. Ibid., p. 63 and chap. 3.

145. W.F. Powell to WLP, March 1900, with clippings from *Hendersonville Times,* folder 314, Poteat Papers. See also *Chapel Hill Tar Heel,* February 14, 1900, clipping in folder 538, Poteat Papers.

146. *BR*, April 4, 1900 (first quote); *Greenville (S.C.) Baptist Courier,* April 26, 1900; *Greenwood South Carolina Baptist,* May 9, 1900; *Louisville (Ky.) Courier-Journal,* March 24, 1900. For positive reviews of *Laboratory and Pulpit* see *BR*, May 15, 1901; and *Louisville Baptist Argus,* May 30, 1901, clipping in folder 879, Poteat Papers. For other reviews of the lectures and the book see folders 538 and 879, Poteat Papers.

147. Archibald Johnson to WLP, September 2, 1902, folder 202, Poteat Papers.

148. Notebook dated January 13, 1904, folder 1143, Poteat Papers; and Poteat, *The New Peace: Lectures on Science and Religion* (Boston and Toronto, 1915), 5.

149. Poteat, *New Peace,* 117 (first quote), 119 (fourth quote), and 120 (other quotes).

150. Ibid., 6.

151. For examples of much later use of virtually unchanged ideas, see the series of type-

written speech manuscripts from the early 1920s in folders 803, 804, 808, 814, 815, 839, and 840. See also "Christianity and Culture," May 9, 1917, typewritten speech manuscript in folder 810; Poteat, "The Natural History of Religion," January 1914, typewritten speech manuscript in folder 1224, Poteat Papers; Poteat, "The Supremacy of Christ in Human Culture," *Crozer Quarterly* 1 (July 1924): 251–57; and Poteat, *Can a Man Be a Christian To-day?* (Chapel Hill and London, 1925).

152. Minutes of the board of trustees, June 7 and 22, 1905; and Paschal, *Wake Forest,* 3:3–7. Poteat received honorary doctorates from Baylor in 1905, the University of North Carolina in 1906, Brown University in 1927, Duke University in 1933, and Mercer University in 1933. See biographical sketch, folder 1240, Poteat Papers.

153. *BR,* June 28, 1905.

154. Copy of letter to Josiah W. Bailey in Poteat diary, January 13, 1902, in possession of family.

3. Christian Progressivism in the South

1. The study of southern Progressivism began with Arthur S. Link, "The Progressive Movement in the South, 1870–1914," *North Carolina Historical Review* 23 (April 1946): 172–95.

2. Grantham, *Southern Progressivism,* 384; Morton Sosna, *In Search of the Silent South: Southern Liberals and the Race Issue* (New York, 1977), 23; Tindall, *Emergence of the New South,* 200; Egerton, *Speak Now,* 60, 72, and 121–22; Bruce Clayton, *W.J. Cash: A Life* (Baton Rouge and London, 1991), 27–28 and 39–40; Spain, *At Ease in Zion,* 211 n. 3; Jean Miller Schmidt, *Souls or the Social Order: The Two-Party System in American Protestantism* (New York, 1991), 256 n. 87; and Linder, *William Louis Poteat,* chap. 5.

3. Eighmy, *Churches in Cultural Captivity,* 84.

4. Grantham, *Southern Progressivism,* 17 (first quote) and 22 (other quotes).

5. On the importance of combining legislative enactments with crusades to change public opinion see Link, *Paradox of Southern Progressivism,* 94–95, 117, and 124 for example.

6. On island communities see Robert H. Wiebe, *The Search for Order, 1877–1920* (New York, 1967), esp. chaps. 2 and 3. Other good studies of the major changes occurring in America in the late nineteenth and early twentieth centuries include Samuel P. Hays, *The Response to Industrialism, 1885–1914* (Chicago, 1957); Alan Trachtenberg, *The Incorporation of America: Culture and Society in the Gilded Age* (New York, 1982); and Henry F. May, *The End of American Innocence: A Study of the First Years of Our Own Time, 1912–1917* (1959; reprint, Chicago, 1964).

7. On interdependence see Thomas L. Haskell, *The Emergence of Professional Social Science: The American Social Science Association and the Nineteenth-Century Crisis of Authority* (Urbana, Chicago, and London, 1977), esp. chaps. 1, 2, and 11 (quote on p. 254).

8. Poteat, "Freedom and Unity," *WFS* 20 (May 1901): 517; and Benedict Anderson, *Imagined Communities: Reflections on the Origin and Spread of Nationalism* (1983; rev. ed., London and New York, 1991).

9. Poteat diary, November 9 (first quote) and 11 (other quotes), 1895, in possession of family. In 1897 Poteat read the important social gospel work by George D. Herron, *The Christian State: A Political Vision of Christ . . .* (New York and Boston, 1895), but to him it took the wrong approach. He concluded that Herron "has certainly the Christian spirit and describes with a strong hand the social revolution which the life and teaching of Jesus must accomplish; but in his program of the union of vitalized Christianity with the regenerated State, he limits and materializes Christianity, which is larger than the State and has individual and social functions besides those that may be discharged by the State as one of its organs." Southern religious traditions and the social gospel had begun to clash in his thought (Poteat diary, April 14, 1897, in possession of family).

10. The classic study of the social gospel is Charles Howard Hopkins, *The Rise of the Social Gospel in American Protestantism, 1865–1915* (New Haven and London, 1940). More recent and subtle interpretations that demonstrate the sometimes conservative goals and unintended

results of the social gospel include Ruth Hutchinson Crocker, *Social Work and Social Order: The Settlement Movement in Two Industrial Cities, 1889–1930* (Urbana and Chicago, 1992); and Susan Curtis, *A Consuming Faith: The Social Gospel and Modern American Culture* (Baltimore and London, 1991). On the moderation of the movement see Robert T. Handy, "The Social Gospel in Historical Perspective," *Andover Newton Quarterly* 9 (January 1969): 170–80; Handy, *A Christian America: Protestant Hopes and Historical Realities* (New York, 1971), 156–70; John R. Aiken and James R. McDonnell, "Walter Rauschenbusch and Labor Reform: A Social Gospeller's Approach," *Labor History* 11 (spring 1970): 131–50; and Winthrop S. Hudson, "Walter Rauschenbusch and the New Evangelism," *Religion in Life* 30 (summer 1961), 412–30. See also Handy, introduction to Handy, ed., *The Social Gospel in America, 1870–1920* (New York, 1966), 3–16.

11. On the stirrings of social Christianity in the South and the predominance of traditional views among the major denominations in the region at the turn of the century see Woodward, *Origins of the New South*, 450–52 (first quote on 452); Kenneth K. Bailey, *Southern White Protestantism in the Twentieth Century* (New York, Evanston, and London, 1964), chap. 1; Spain, *At Ease in Zion*, 209–14; John B. Boles, *The Great Revival: Beginnings of the Bible Belt* (1972; reprint, Lexington, Ky., 1996), 196–203; Samuel S. Hill Jr., *Southern Churches in Crisis* (New York, 1966); and Schmidt, *Souls or the Social Order*, 193–96. See also Boles, *The South through Time: A History of an American Region* (Englewood Cliffs, N.J., 1995), 403 (second quote); Samuel S. Hill Jr., *The South and the North in American Religion* (Athens, Ga., 1980), 126–35; and Robert Moats Miller, "Fourteen Points on the Social Gospel in the South," *Southern Humanities Review* 1 (summer 1967), 126–40. Explorations of the social gospel or social Christianity that did develop in the South have been led by J. Wayne Flynt. See Flynt, "'Feeding the Hungry and Ministering to the Broken Hearted': The Presbyterian Church in the United States and the Social Gospel, 1900–1920," in Charles Reagan Wilson, ed., *Religion in the South* (Jackson, 1985), 83–137; and Flynt, *Alabama Baptists: Southern Baptists in the Heart of Dixie* (Tuscaloosa and London, 1998), chaps. 7–9. For other examples of work on southern social Christianity see Keith Harper, *The Quality of Mercy: Southern Baptists and Social Christianity, 1890–1920* (Tuscaloosa and London, 1996); and John Patrick McDowell, *The Social Gospel in the South: The Woman's Home Mission Movement in the Methodist Episcopal Church, South, 1886–1939* (Baton Rouge, 1982). On later, more radical movements see Anthony P. Dunbar, *Against the Grain: Southern Radicals and Prophets, 1929–1959* (Charlottesville, 1981); Robert F. Martin, *Howard Kester and the Struggle for Social Justice in the South, 1904–77* (Charlottesville and London, 1991); and David Stricklin, *A Genealogy of Dissent: Southern Baptist Protest in the Twentieth Century* (Lexington, Ky., 1999).

12. W.L. Poteat, "Christian Education and Civic Righteousness," in *Baptist Argus*, May 26, 1898 (quotation); Poteat, "The Civic Function of Christianity," *WFS* 17 (June 1898): 724–29; EMP to WLP, April [?], 1897, folder 1162; and notebook titled "Christian Education and Civic Righteousness," folder 798, Poteat Papers. On the origins of social Christianity in the 1880s and 1890s and its clash with evangelism in the 1890s see Schmidt, *Souls or the Social Order*, chaps. 3 and 4.

13. Notebook titled "Christian Education and Civic Righteousness."

14. Ibid.

15. Typed manuscript of "Christian Education and Civic Righteousness," folder 798, Poteat Papers.

16. Ibid.

17. The debate among scholars about the extent and nature of the relationship between southern denominations and social reform is summarized briefly in John B. Boles, "The Discovery of Southern Religious History," in Boles and Evelyn Thomas Nolen, eds., *Interpreting Southern History: Historiographical Essays in Honor of Sanford W. Higginbotham* (Baton Rouge and London, 1987), 540–44. See also Harvey, *Redeeming the South*, 197–226 and 301–9.

18. Typed manuscript of "Christian Education and Civic Righteousness."

19. Notebook titled "Christian Education and Civic Righteousness."

20. Poteat, "The Relation of Baptists to Social Questions," handwritten speech manu-

script delivered July 18, 1905, folder 1076, Poteat Papers. For a few samples of the many speeches and writings by Poteat on the theme of the kingdom of heaven and civic righteousness see "Christianity and the Social Order," handwritten notes from 1909, folder 816; untitled notes from 1912 speech at Greensboro Interchurch Association, folder 1077; "Anarchy or Christ," handwritten notes from 1920, folder 748; "Christ among the Doctors," *Blue Ridge Voice* 4 (November 1922): 1–5, in folder 793; "Roads to Peace," *Blue Ridge Voice* 7 (November 1925): 2–10, in folder 1050; "Young People in the Program of Jesus," typewritten notes dated June 23, 1926, folder 1157, Poteat Papers; and "Wake Forest College and the Kingdom," *WFS* 32 (March 1913): 475. On Lester Ward see Wiebe, *Search for Order,* 141.

21. Poteat, "Young People in the Program of Jesus."

22. Poteat, "Relation of Baptists to Social Questions."

23. Poteat, "The School as a Manufactory of Power," handwritten speech notes dated November 22, 1894, folder 1228, Poteat Papers.

24. Poteat, "Christian Education and the New North Carolina," handwritten speech notes dated Oct. 6, 1915, folder 1245, Poteat Papers.

25. Untitled and undated handwritten speech notes, folder 1246, Poteat Papers. On Progressives' almost unbounded belief in the power of education to aid the South see Jack Temple Kirby, *Darkness at the Dawning: Race and Reform in the Progressive South* (Philadelphia, New York, and Toronto, 1972), 100–107; Woodward, *Origins of the New South,* 396–406; Clayton, *Savage Ideal,* chap. 5; Grantham, *Southern Progressivism,* chap. 8; Link, *Paradox of Southern Progressivism,* 125–42; Louis R. Harlan, *Separate and Unequal: Public School Campaigns and Racism in the Southern Seaboard States, 1901–1915* (Chapel Hill, 1958); and most importantly Leloudis, *Schooling the New South.*

26. "The Public Wealth," handwritten speech notes dated April 5, 1910, folder 1244, Poteat Papers. See also "The Public Wealth," undated, handwritten speech notes, folder 1242, Poteat Papers.

27. "Abstract of Address to the Orange County School Commencement, Hillsboro, April 11, 1924," folder 986, Poteat Papers.

28. See "A North Carolina 'Chatauqua,'" *North Carolina Teacher* (hereafter cited as *NCT*) 1 (Aug. 1883): 104, for initial call to create "a splendid programme of lectures upon the methods of teaching and school discipline and every other department of schoolroom management. . . ." See "North Carolina Teacher's Assembly," *NCT* 2 (July 1884): 34–41, for discussion of first meeting. On Poteat's membership see "Members of the Assembly," *NCT* 2 (September 1884): 131.

29. "North Carolina Teachers' Assembly," *NCT* 2 (October 1884): 172.

30. "Organization for 1885–86," *NCT* 3 (September 1885): 27.

31. Program, "Fourth Annual Session of the North Carolina Teachers' Assembly to Be Held at the Atlantic Hotel, Morehead City, N.C., from June 14 to 29, 1887," (printed in Raleigh; all assembly programs cited are in Reynolds Library).

32. "The Assembly Reading Circle," *NCT* 5 (September 1887): 48–50.

33. *NCT* 5 (March 1888): 315.

34. On his service on executive committee see *NCT* 7 (March 1890): 385; 7 (October 1890): 85; 9 (September 1891): 36; and 9 (April 1892): 409.

35. "Programme Sixth Annual Session," *NCT* 6 (April 1889): 400; and "Seventh Annual Session," *NCT* 7 (April 1890): 431.

36. "Seventh Annual Session . . . ," *NCT* 7 (June 1890): 508. In 1895 he addressed the group on "Science in the Elementary Schools." See "Programme," *NCT* 12 (May 1895): 298.

37. *NCT* 8 (September 1890): 31; and program, "The North Carolina Teachers' Assembly: Fourteenth Annual Session, Morehead City, N.C., June 15 to 25, 1897," 9–10.

38. See "Officers and Meeting Places of the North Carolina Teachers' Assembly Since Its Organization," in "Program of the Thirty-Ninth Annual Session of the North Carolina Teachers' Assembly, Raleigh, . . . 1922." Poteat took the presidency at a time when internal wrangling over the future divided the assembly. See Charles J. Parker to WLP, June 5, 1896, folder 316, Poteat Papers. For much more on Alderman, McIver, and Joyner see Leloudis, *Schooling the New South.*

39. "Teachers' Assembly," newspaper clipping in folder 538, Poteat Papers.

40. Poteat, "The Child As Teacher," *North Carolina Journal of Education* 1 (November 1897): 13–17 ("practical" on 16; all other quotes on 17). For Poteat's handwritten speech notes of "The Child As Teacher," dated June 16, 1897, see folder 932, Poteat Papers.

41. Claxton to WLP, September 27, 1898, folder 58, Poteat Papers.

42. See "Officers, 1897," in the program "The North Carolina Teachers' Assembly: Fourteenth Annual Session, Morehead City, N.C., June 15 to 25, 1897"; and *Biennial Report of the Superintendent of Public Instruction, of North Carolina, for the Scholastic Years 1896–'97 and 1897–'98* (Raleigh, 1898), 169.

43. Ibid., 169.

44. Ibid., 198.

45. *Biennial Report of the Superintendent of Public Instruction,* 226; and Poteat diary, June 3, 1897, and February 25 and 26, 1898, in possession of family.

46. *Biennial Report,* 227.

47. Ibid., 229 (quote) and 230.

48. Ibid., 199.

49. *Proceedings of the First Annual Session of the Southern Educational Association . . . 1890* (Raleigh, 1890), 3 (quote) and 66; and *WFS* 9 (July 1890): 444.

50. Southern Educational Association, *Journal of Proceedings and Addresses of the Ninth Annual Meeting . . . 1899* (n.p., 1899).

51. "The North Carolina College Association," *NCT* 9 (December 1891): 184–85 (quote on 185). See also "The College Association of North Carolina," *NCT* 10 (May 1893): 356–84; and *WFS* 13 (April 1894): 350.

52. *North Carolina Journal of Education* 1 (May 1898): 8; and John Butler to WLP, June 4, 1898, folder 15, Poteat Papers.

53. *WFS* 20 (May 1901): 605 (quote), and 22 (May 1903): 560. See *Proceedings of the Ninth Conference for Education in the South . . .* (Richmond 1906), 185; *Proceedings of the Tenth Conference for Education in the South . . .* (Richmond, 1907), 257; *Bulletin of Wake Forest College* (hereafter cited as *BWFC*) 3 (July 1908): 134; *Proceedings of the Eleventh Conference for Education in the South . . . 1908* (Nashville, n.d.), 226; *BWFC* 4 (July 1909): 126; and *Proceedings of the Twelfth Conference for Education in the South . . . 1909* (Nashville, n.d.), 230. On the importance of the Winston-Salem meeting see Leloudis, *Schooling the New South,* 146–50.

54. "Education in the South," February 29, 1912, typewritten speech manuscript, folder 856, Poteat Papers. Robert Curtis Ogden was a New York merchant and philanthropist who played a crucial role in the Conference for Education in the South that brought together educators and philanthropists in annual meetings across the South beginning in 1898. John D. Rockefeller Jr. was also involved with this group and provided funding for the General Education Board, which sponsored a number of reforms in southern education. Leloudis, *Schooling the New South,* 146–51.

55. WLP to EP, March 1, 1912, folder 1166, Poteat Papers.

56. Poteat, "Specialism in Education," *North Carolina Journal of Education* 2 (February 1899): 25–26.

57. Poem dated January 14, 1903, in *BR,* January 31, 1906, clipping in folder 975, Poteat Papers.

58. Clipping of anonymous editorial from *Raleigh Times,* labeled June 16, 1904, and as by W.L.P., folder 924, Poteat Papers.

59. "The Liberty of the Press," handwritten manuscript from June 1911, folder 924, Poteat Papers.

60. Clipping dated November 24, 1912, folder 924, Poteat Papers.

61. "Liberty of the Press."

62. Poteat, "The Conservation of Resources," *BWFC* 11 (October 1916): 168.

63. WLP to the editor of the *Asheville Citizen,* October 29, 1927, folder 47, Poteat Papers.

64. Handwritten notes, "A Natural Despotism and Its Lessons," March 1907, folder 774, Poteat Papers. The Galveston plan of city government originated in 1901 in the wake of a disas-

trous hurricane that severely damaged the island. The plan provided for the elected officials to also be the administrators in charge of the departments of city government, and it eliminated the need for a mayor. Grantham, *Southern Progressivism*, 283–84.

65. "The Enrichment of Country Life," newspaper clipping from *N&O*, November 13, 1903 (first and third quotes); and handwritten manuscript of "The Enrichment of Country Life" (second quote), both in folder 837, Poteat Papers.

66. "The Enrichment of Country Life," newspaper clipping from *N&O*.

67. Ibid. On the role of the State Literary and Historical Association in procuring rural libraries see the information sheet, "Purposes and Work," put out by the association, dated February 23, 1903, folder 113, Poteat Papers. The creation of rural libraries was a cause dear to Poteat; he spoke to the Wake County Teachers Association on the subject in April 1898. Logan D. Howell to WLP, March 18, 1898, folder 186, Poteat Papers. "Something must be done to quicken and lead out the intellectual life of the country" (14), he urged in 1898, both to aid country dwellers and to enable the city to continue to draw sustenance from "the stream of humanity which is pouring out of the country into the city" (15). Urban areas depended on rural immigrants "for reinforcements of its jaded physique and languishing moral and mental vitality" (15). As "the best means of culture" (16), rural libraries would provide quality reading in place of newspapers. Poteat, "Rural Libraries," *North Carolina Journal of Education* 1 (May 1898): 14–17.

68. See for example "North Carolina's Highest Achievements," handwritten notes, folder 977; and "A Mountain Portrait," typewritten manuscript, folder 960, Poteat Papers.

69. Untitled, handwritten speech notes dated August 15, 1913, folder 1245, Poteat Papers.

70. "The Country School," handwritten and undated speech notes, folder 1242, Poteat Papers. He praises the results of corn clubs for boys in 1914, so likely a 1915 speech.

71. Poteat, "The Conservation of the Resources of North Carolina," 163–69 (quotes on 164 and 165).

72. Baptist State Convention, *Annual . . . 1911*, 49 (first and second quotes) and 50 (third quote). All annuals of the Baptist State Convention and the Southern Baptist Convention that are cited are in Special Collections, Reynolds Library.

73. Baptist State Convention, *Annual . . . 1912*, 75.

74. Baptist State Convention, *Annual . . . 1914*, 90 (quote); and Eighmy, *Churches in Cultural Captivity*, 86–87.

75. Eighmy, *Churches in Cultural Captivity*, 82–84; and Southern Baptist Convention, *Annual . . . 1913*, 76.

76. Southern Baptist Convention, *Annual . . . 1914*, 36–38.

77. Eighmy, *Churches in Cultural Captivity*, 85–86.

78. Ibid., 86 and 93.

79. Eighmy, *Churches in Cultural Captivity*, 94; and Southern Baptist Convention, *Annual . . . 1914*, 38.

80. Southern Baptist Convention, *Annual . . . 1919*, 7; and *Annual . . . 1935*, 5.

81. Baptist State Convention, *Annual . . . 1921*, 112–13 (quotes). Poteat chaired the state committee reporting on social service in 1915 (Baptist State Convention, *Annual . . . 1915*, 51–54). He returned to chair it and write the report in 1921, 1922, 1923, and 1924 (Baptist State Convention, *Annual . . . 1921*, 112–13; *1922*, 118–19; *1923*, 126–27; and *1924*, 107–9). Poteat approved the report of the Southern Baptist Convention's Committee on Temperance and Social Service (after 1920, the Commission on Social Service) in 1920, 1921, 1922, 1924, 1928, 1930, and 1937, indicating sporadic involvement despite his appointment to the commission throughout this period. See Southern Baptist Convention, *Annual . . . 1920*, 94–97 and 123–28; *1921*, 77–85; *1922*, 96–100; *1924*, 114–18; *1928*, 83–88; *1930*, 67–77; and *1937*, 69–78. For analysis of the Southern Baptist Convention's Commission on Social Service see Eighmy, *Churches in Cultural Captivity*, chap. 6.

82. *WFS* 31 (May 1912): 765; James E. McCulloch, ed., *The Call of the New South: Addresses Delivered at the Southern Sociological Congress, Nashville, Tennessee, May 7 to 10, 1912* (Nashville, 1912), 9 (quotes) and 369; Egerton, *Speak Now*, 45–46; Eighmy, *Churches in Cultural Captivity*, 65–67; and Sosna, *Silent South*, 17–18.

83. Walter Rauschenbusch, "The Social Program of the Church," in James E. McCulloch, ed., *The South Mobilizing for Social Service: Addresses Delivered at the Southern Sociological Congress, Atlanta, Georgia, April 25–29, 1913* (Nashville, 1913), 504–11 (first quote on 504, second and third quotes on 505, fourth quote on 508, fifth quote on 509, and last quote on 511). On the importance of this session see Woodward, *Origins of the New South*, 452.

84. Poteat, "The Social Task of the Modern Church," in McCulloch, ed., *South Mobilizing*, 534–40 (first quote on 535, second quote on 536, third, fourth, and fifth quotes on 537, sixth and seventh quotes on 538, and last two quotes on 539).

85. Section of handwritten speech notes titled "place of Southern Sociological Congress" and labeled "Southern Sociological Congress, Asheville, August 3, 1917, Central Methodist Church," folder 812, Poteat Papers (quotes); James E. McCulloch, ed., *Battling for Social Betterment: Southern Sociological Congress, Memphis, Tennessee, May 6–10, 1914* (Nashville, 1914), 197; McCulloch, ed., *The New Chivalry—Health: Southern Sociological Congress, Houston, Texas, May 8–11, 1915* (Nashville, 1915), 533; WLP to EP, May 10, 1915, folder 1166, Poteat Papers; and *BWFC* 12 (July 1917): 157.

86. See Grantham, *Southern Progressivism*, chap. 11. See also Curtis, *Consuming Faith*, chap. 4.

87. Virginia Wooten Gulledge, *The North Carolina Conference for Social Service: A Study of Its Development and Methods* (n.p., 1942), 12–15

88. See handwritten notes and speech outline in notebook, folder 774, Poteat Papers.

89. Poteat, "The Correlation of Social Forces," *Social Service Quarterly* 1 (April, May, June 1913): 30–32 (quote on 32).

90. "Baptists and Social Service," *Social Service Quarterly* 1 (October, November, December 1913): 76–77; and Baptist State Convention, *Annual . . . 1916*, 85–86.

91. WLP to EP, January 24, 1916, folder 1167, Poteat Papers.

92. *Social Service Quarterly* 4 (January–March 1916): 9.

93. "Program of the North Carolina Conference for Social Service . . . 1914," *Social Service Quarterly* 1 (January–March 1914): 88; Clarence Poe to WLP, December 10, 1915, folder 705, Poteat Papers; pamphlet, "Program of the Fourth Annual Session of the North Carolina Conference for Social Service . . . 1916," North Carolina Collection, Wilson Library, University of North Carolina at Chapel Hill; *N&O*, January 21, 1917; "Constitution and By-Laws," *Social Service Quarterly* 2 (January–March 1915): 100; and Alexander Worth McAlister to WLP, April 19, May 4, May 26, and July 21, 1916, and WLP to McAlister, July 19, 1916, all in folder 395, Alexander W. McAlister Papers, Southern Historical Collection, University of North Carolina at Chapel Hill.

94. Joseph Flake Steelman, "The Progressive Era in North Carolina, 1884–1917" (Ph.D. diss., University of North Carolina at Chapel Hill, 1955), 630–31. See Gulledge, *North Carolina Conference*, 18–29, on the importance of the bill and the role of the North Carolina Conference for Social Service (NCCSS). The *Raleigh News and Observer*, February 13, 1919, also credited the NCCSS with pressuring the legislature to make mandatory the employment of superintendents of public welfare at the county level, a step left optional for counties in the 1917 plan.

95. *N&O*, January 21, 23, and 24, 1917.

96. *N&O*, February 15, 1919.

97. Poteat, "The Old Method for the New World," *Bulletin of the North Carolina State Board of Charities and Public Welfare* 3 (April–June 1920): 6–11 (quotes on 10).

98. Gulledge, *North Carolina Conference*, 29–36; [Margaret Neal], "The North Carolina Conference for Social Service: The Record of Twenty-Five Years, 1912–1937" (bound carbon of typescript in North Carolina Collection), 59; "The North Carolina Conference for Social Service," and W.B. Sanders to Clarence Poe, January 15, 1923, both in box 1, NCCSS Papers, North Carolina Division of Archives and History, Raleigh. See also "Program: The Citizens' Committee of One Hundred on Prison Legislation, First Meeting of the Committee, Greensboro, Nov. 24, 1922," box 12, NCCSS Papers; and Wiley B. Sanders, "The North Carolina Prison Conference," *Journal of Social Forces* 1 (January 1923): 136–37.

99. Link, *Paradox of Southern Progressivism*, 176 and 177.

100. J.W. Bailey to WLP, February 12, 1907, folder 17, Poteat Papers; WLP to Charles L. Coon, January 25, 1911 (quote); Coon to WLP, January 30, 1911; and WLP to Coon, February 1, 1911, Charles L. Coon Papers, Southern Historical Collection. Poteat's attendance was so sporadic that Coon left his name off a list of the committee's members, though Poteat apparently remained a member. Coon to A. Rufus Morgan, October 19, 1911; and WLP to Coon, November 22, 1911, Coon Papers.

101. *BWFC* 7 (January 1913): 225–26; and Baptist State Convention, *Annual . . . 1914*, 92.

102. Poteat, "Guiding Principles in Child Labor Legislation," typed speech manuscript, folder 913, Poteat Papers.

103. *N&O*, February 15 and 18, 1919.

104. G.W. Manly to WLP, December 26, 1890, and February 20, 1891, folder 251; William L. Royall to WLP, September 15, 1910, folder 340; Locke Craig to WLP, November 21, 1913, with enclosure of Poteat's appointment to the commission, dated November 18, 1913, folder 655; typewritten "Report of the Special Freight Rate Commission," folder 655; J.W. Bailey to WLP, July 22, 1914, folder 655; notebook containing Poteat's notes from Asheville testimony and his handwritten draft of report, folder 1101; notes on railroads, folders 655 and 1247, Poteat Papers; *BWFC* 9 (October 1914): 201; *WFS* 33 (February 1914): 355; and *WFS* 34 (October 1914): 64.

105. Handwritten portion of a speech manuscript dated February 28, 1898, folder 1062; and Poteat, "The Peril of Our Prosperity," clipping from *Home and Foreign Fields* (June 1917) in folder 1000, Poteat Papers.

106. Handwritten notes dated January 1, 1915, in notebook in folder 1077, Poteat Papers.

107. "Tara! Tara! Boom!," editorial clipping by Poteat labeled *N&O*, August 12, 1903, in notebook in folder 909, Poteat Papers. On the Lost Cause see Gaines M. Foster, *Ghosts of the Confederacy: Defeat, the Lost Cause, and the Emergence of the New South, 1865 to 1913* (New York and Oxford, 1987); and Charles Reagan Wilson, *Baptized in Blood: The Religion of the Lost Cause, 1865–1920* (Athens, Ga., 1980). On violence see Edward L. Ayers, *Vengeance and Justice: Crime and Punishment in the 19th-Century American South* (New York and Oxford, 1984), 266–76.

108. Poteat, "Address before the North Carolina Peace Society, Greensboro, October 14, 1908," *BWFC* 3 (October 1908): 155–59.

109. "The Roots of Honor," February 22, 1912, typewritten speech notes, folder 1245; and "The Roots of Honor," handwritten speech notes in notebook in folder 909 (last quote), Poteat Papers. On one historian's argument for the predominance of the concept of southern honor see Bertram Wyatt-Brown, *Southern Honor: Ethics and Behavior in the Old South* (New York and Oxford, 1982). Poteat's revised definition is more in accord with the ideas expressed by Edward R. Crowther, "Holy Honor: Sacred and Secular in the Old South," *Journal of Southern History* 58 (November 1992): 619–36. On the importance to social gospel advocates of redefining manliness to fit a new age see Curtis, *Consuming Faith,* chap. 3.

110. "The New Patriotism," undated, typewritten speech notes, folder 1242, Poteat Papers.

111. *BWFC* 5 (January 1911): 251; and [H.C. Phillips, ed.], *Report of the Seventeenth Annual Lake Mohonk Conference on International Arbitration . . .* (Mohonk Lake, N.Y., 1911), 220.

112. "The Appeal of Heroic Belgium," November 22, 1914, handwritten speech manuscript in notebook in folder 909, Poteat Papers.

113. Handwritten in 1915 appointment calendar, folder 476, Poteat Papers.

114. "Wealth of N.C., 1916," handwritten speech manuscript, folder 1139, Poteat Papers.

115. Handwritten notes, folder 828, Poteat Papers. Most southern Progressives supported the war effort and worked for mobilization on the homefront. The war brought increased attention and resources to the South's social problems as well. Grantham, *Southern Progressivism,* chap. 12.

116. Handwritten, untitled speech notes labeled Third Liberty Loan Rally, Lenoir, N.C., April 6, 1918, folder 1230, Poteat Papers. Poteat spoke at the state fair in Raleigh on liberty bonds in October 1917. *BWFC* 12 (October 1917): 196; and "America in the War," handwritten speech notes, folder 747, Poteat Papers (contains last quote). See also *WFS* 37 (December 1917): 180, and 37 (May 1918): 441.

117. "The World Crisis and the Christian Opportunity," October 21, 1917, handwritten speech notes, folder 1153, Poteat Papers. Poteat thoroughly imbibed the wartime propaganda against the German people. See "The German Demonstration: Address . . . before the Southern Baptist Educational Association at Nashville, Tenn., January 24th, 1919," typewritten speech manuscript in folder 882, Poteat Papers. Poteat's reaction was typical for Baptists and other religious adherents across the nation. See Harvey, *Redeeming the South,* 222–23.

118. WLP to EP, April 25, 1919, folder 1167, Poteat Papers.

119. "Moral Gains of War," handwritten speech notes dated July 8, 1919, in notebook in folder 909, Poteat Papers.

120. "Strategic Place in the New World," March 16, 1919, handwritten speech notes in notebook in folder 909, Poteat Papers. Notes indicate speech was never delivered due to illness in Poteat's family.

121. WLP to the editor of the *New York Times,* December 17, 1918, folder 909, Poteat Papers.

122. "Armistice, not Peace," November 11, 1920, handwritten speech notes, folder 753, Poteat Papers.

123. Handwritten copy of telegraph to *New York World,* October 22, 1921, in notebook in folder 1077, Poteat Papers.

124. "League of Nations, Jan. 1924," handwritten speech notes, folder 1152, Poteat Papers.

125. *WFS* 41 (December 1921): 184; Baptist State Convention, *Annual . . . 1921,* 24; and handwritten copy of telegraph from WLP to *New York World,* October 22, 1921, in notebook in folder 1077, Poteat Papers. See also handwritten copy of WLP to Mr. President, September 14, 1921, in notebook in folder 1077, Poteat Papers.

126. Baptist State Convention, *Annual . . . 1924,* 108.

127. "Preliminary Statement of the State Reconstruction Commission," October 29, 1919, in R.B. House, ed., and Santford Martin, comp., *Public Letters and Papers of Thomas Walter Bickett, Governor of North Carolina, 1917–1921* (Raleigh, 1928), 294–96; Joseph Hyde Pratt to WLP, July 3, 1933, folder 314, Poteat Papers; and *WFS* 39 (December 1919): 148.

128. Poteat, "The Old Method for the New World," *Bulletin of the North Carolina State Board of Charities and Public Welfare* 3 (April–June 1920): 9.

129. "Christian Program in New World," July 26, 1919, handwritten speech notes in folder 1245, Poteat Papers.

130. Poteat diary, November 9, 1898, in possession of family.

131. WLP to EP, July 18, 1900, folder 963, Poteat Papers; and Glenda Elizabeth Gilmore, *Gender and Jim Crow: Women and the Politics of White Supremacy in North Carolina, 1896–1920* (Chapel Hill and London, 1996), 120.

132. See notebook titled "The Negro in the South" for Poteat's notes on various readings and his speech notes for the address, which he titled "The Negro of the South," folder 967, Poteat Papers; and *WFS* 31 (November 1911): 155.

133. Handwritten notes in notebook in folder 967, Poteat Papers.

134. "The Negro of the South," speech notes in notebook in folder 967, Poteat Papers. On the racist historical views of the Old South and Reconstruction prevalent at this time see Singal's discussion of historian Ulrich B. Phillips in *The War Within: From Victorian to Modernist Thought in the South, 1919–1945,* 37–57; Foster, *Ghosts of the Confederacy,* chap. 13; Clayton, *Savage Ideal,* chap. 8; and Peter Novick, *That Noble Dream: The "Objectivity Question" and the American Historical Profession* (Cambridge, 1988), 72–85.

135. "The Negro of the South," speech notes.

136. WLP to EP, January 28, 1916, folder 1167, Poteat Papers. On Dixon's writings and the film see Joel Williamson, *A Rage for Order: Black/White Relations in the American South Since Emancipation* (New York and Oxford, 1986), 98–115; Gilmore, *Gender and Jim Crow,* 66–70 and 136–38; Tindall, *Emergence of the New South,* 187; Kirby, *Darkness at the Dawning,* 98; and Joan L. Silverman, "Birth of a Nation," q.v. Charles Reagan Wilson and William Ferris, eds., *Encyclopedia of Southern Culture* (Chapel Hill and London, 1989), 947–48. Poteat first saw

the film in November 1915. See WLP to Willis G. Briggs, November 10, 1915, Willis G. Briggs Collection, North Carolina Division of Archives and History, Raleigh.

137. "The Negro in the South," March 27, 1911, handwritten speech notes in folder 967, Poteat Papers (distinct from speech notes in notebook for address in New York City); and *WFS* 30 (April 1911): 691.

138. WLP to Branson, December 20 and 27, 1916, folder 66, and January 6, 1917, folder 67, Eugene C. Branson Papers, Southern Historical Collection.

139. *WFS* 38 (February 1919): 33; and *OGB*, November 28, 1919.

140. On the origins of the Commission on Interracial Cooperation (CIC) see Ruth Gilliam Powell, "History of the Southern Commission on Inter-Racial Cooperation" (Masters thesis, University of South Carolina, 1935), 9–12; Edward Flud Burrows, "The Commission on Interracial Cooperation, 1919–1944: A Case Study in the History of the Interracial Movement in the South" (Ph.D. diss., University of Wisconsin, 1954), 49; Ann Wells Ellis, "The Commission on Interracial Cooperation, 1919–1944: Its Activities and Results" (Ph.D. diss., Georgia State University, 1975), 7–13; and Julia Anne McDonough, "Men and Women of Good Will: A History of the Commission on Interracial Cooperation and the Southern Regional Council, 1919–1954 (Ph.D. diss., University of Virginia, 1993), 37–43. On Weatherford see Wilma Dykeman, *Prophet of Plenty: The First Ninety Years of W.D. Weatherford* (Knoxville, 1966), and on Alexander see Dykeman and James Stokely, *Seeds of Southern Change: The Life of Will Alexander* (Chicago and London, 1962).

141. WLP to EP, April 10, 1919, folder 1167, Poteat Papers (quote); *OGB*, January 27, 1922; and *BWFC* 14 (July 1919): 135.

142. "Minutes of the Meeting of Inter-Racial Committee Held at Atlanta, July 24th, 1919," CIC Records, Atlanta University Library, Atlanta, Ga., microfilm, reel 20 (quote); Ellis, "Commission on Interracial Cooperation," 17; Burrows, "Commission on Interracial Cooperation," 51–54; and *BWFC* 14 (July 1919): 135.

143. Burrows, "Commission on Interracial Cooperation," 54–55; *BWFC* 15 (July 1920): 132; and minutes of meeting, February 17, 1920, CIC Records, reel 20.

144. Burrows, "Commission on Interracial Cooperation," 70 (first quote) and 141; "An Appeal to the Christian People of the South," *BR*, September 15, 1920 (other quotes); *OGB*, January 27, 1922; and Linder, *William Louis Poteat*, 100. See also Sosna, *Silent South*, 22–24.

145. Burrows, "Commission on Interracial Cooperation," 331–34; Ellis, "Commission on Interracial Cooperation," 235–36; Linder, *William Louis Poteat*, 102; *OGB*, November 12 and December 10, 1920; and WLP to EMP, December 6, 1920, folder 1163, Poteat Papers. Poteat also represented the commission in a speech titled "Christ and Social Justice" before the South Carolina Conference for Social Service in November 1920 in Columbia. *OGB*, November 12, 1920.

146. Minutes of meetings of CIC, Atlanta, March 29, 1921, and Blue Ridge, N.C., July 20–21, 1922, CIC Records, reel 20; *BWFC* 17 (October 1922): 26; and WLP to Edwin Mims, January 7, 1927, box 2, Edwin Mims Papers, Special Collections, Heard Library, Vanderbilt University, Nashville, Tenn.

147. N.C. Newbold, "Conference for Negro Education in Raleigh," *Journal of Social Forces* 1 (January 1923): 145–47; Powell, "Southern Commission on Inter-Racial Cooperation," 46; and the regional commission's letterhead with list of members in various collections.

148. C. Chilton Pearson, "Race Relations in North Carolina: A Field Study of Moderate Opinion," *South Atlantic Quarterly* 23 (January 1924): 1–9 (first and second quotes on 1, third quote on 2, and last two quotes on 4); WLP to E.C. Branson, March 17, 1921, folder 191, Branson Papers; and minutes from the early meetings, CIC Records, reel 20. On Pearson see Clayton, *W.J. Cash*, 25–27.

149. WLP to E.C. Branson, March 17, 1921, folder 191, Branson Papers. This letter is on YMCA stationery and is initialed GCH. Poteat's signature is not in his handwriting.

150. WLP to E.C. Branson, April 2 and 8, 1921; and Branson to WLP, April 5, 1921 (quotes), in folder 193, Branson Papers.

151. *BWFC* 16 (October 1921): 168; and "North Carolina Commission on Interracial

Cooperation—Source Book of Information, Feb. 6, 1928–April 30, '42," (quote) in folder 74, North Carolina Commission on Interracial Cooperation Papers, Southern Historical Collection. The collection has almost no information on the formation of the state group.

152. Will W. Alexander to WLP, July 15, 1921, copy in folder 9, Howard W. Odum Papers, Southern Historical Collection, University of North Carolina at Chapel Hill.

153. Burrows, "Commission on Interracial Cooperation," 94–96 and 186; and Ellis, "Commission on Interracial Cooperation," 41 and 48–49. Virginia and Texas were perhaps the other two most active state groups. Poteat and the state group helped to shape the racial attitude of a young college student named W.J. Cash. See Clayton, *W.J. Cash,* 38–39.

154. R.W. Miles, "The North Carolina Inter-Racial Committee," *Journal of Social Forces* 1 (January 1923): 154–55; and WLP to E.C. Branson, August 23, 1922, folder 237, Branson Papers.

155. Neal, "North Carolina Conference for Social Service," 54–55.

156. Joseph Hyde Pratt to members of the NCCSS executive committee, December 8, 1923, box 12; and "Minutes of the Meeting of the Executive Committee of the North Carolina Conference for Social Service Held in the Office of the State Commissioner of Public Welfare, Raleigh, Dec. 17, 1923," box 1, both in NCCSS Papers. In making this proposal Poteat likely recalled the regional commission's early efforts to cultivate a special relationship with the Southern Sociological Congress.

157. Neal, "North Carolina Conference for Social Service," 75.

158. Gulledge, *North Carolina Conference,* 51.

159. Ellis, "Commission on Interracial Cooperation," 115–17; and "Minutes: Meeting of the North Carolina Interracial Commission, Raleigh, N.C., Jan. 12, 1928," CIC Records, reel 53.

160. *OGB,* April 30, 1926; and W.C. Jackson to WLP, February 28, 1933, folder 199, Poteat Papers. The organization may have dwindled at some point because in this letter Jackson himself expressed confusion on exactly when Poteat withdrew from the chairmanship, even though Jackson succeeded him. As chairman at the 1928 meeting Jackson "spoke of the credit due Dr. Poteat for the success, materially and spiritually, of the State Commission." "Minutes: Meeting of the North Carolina Interracial Commission, Raleigh, N.C., Jan. 12, 1928."

161. See handwritten notes dated February 27, 1923, at end of notebook in folder 967, Poteat Papers.

162. "Final Exercises at Slater School Held Yesterday," newspaper clipping labeled June 11, 1921, folder 538, Poteat Papers.

163. Baptist State Convention, *Annual . . . 1922,* 118–19.

164. Poteat, "Attainable Standards of Individual Public Service: Abstract of Address . . . in the 'First National Regional Conference on County and Town Administration,' Chapel Hill, N.C., September 20, 1921," *BWFC* 16 (October 1921): 162 (first quote); and handwritten paragraph probably from 1922 or 1923 in notebook in folder 1077, Poteat Papers (other quotes).

165. Poteat, "Putting the Kingdom First," pamphlet printed in Raleigh in 1913, containing an address made February 6, 1913, copy in folder 1021, Poteat Papers; and *OGB,* March 23, 1923.

166. EP to "Papa," July 29, 1881, folder 1166, Poteat Papers; and Daniel Jay Whitener, *Prohibition in North Carolina, 1715–1945* (Chapel Hill, 1945), chap. 5. William Link identifies Prohibition as the crucial issue around which reformers developed the reform strategy of moral crusades and legislative lobbying. (*Paradox of Southern Progressivism,* 32–57 and 95–112). See also Richard M. Kissell, "Politics and Prohibition in North Carolina, 1880–1882 (Masters thesis, Wake Forest University, 1974).

167. Whitener, *Prohibition in North Carolina,* 142–43 n. 55. See also J.W. Bailey to WLP, May 21, 1903, folder 17, Poteat Papers.

168. "Unity and Faith," speaking notes jotted in book in folder 1212, Poteat Papers.

169. Baptist State Convention, *Annual . . . 1914,* 94; undated clipping titled "The Prohibition Lobbyists," folder 1077, Poteat Papers; and *WFS* 34 (February 1915): 408.

170. Baptist State Convention, *Annual . . . 1915,* 52.

171. *N&O,* January 17 and 21 (quotes), 1917.

172. Handwritten manuscript in notebook in folder 1077, Poteat Papers.

173. Baptist State Convention, *Annual . . . 1920,* 35; untitled, handwritten notes in note-

book in folder 1077; WLP to EP, January 30, 1921, folder 1167, Poteat Papers; *BWFC* 15 (October 1920): 149, and 16 (July 1921): 146–47; *WFS* 38 (February 1919): 34; *N&O,* January 18, 1919, and January 15, 1920; Whitener, *Prohibition in North Carolina,* 182; and Ernest Hurst Cherrington, ed., *The Anti-Saloon League Year Book, 1923* . . . (Westerville, Ohio, 1924), 288.

174. Cherrington, ed., *Anti-Saloon League Year Book, 1924,* 199; *1925,* 198; *1926,* 197–98; *1927,* 196; *1929,* 193–94; *1930,* 190–91; and *1931,* 189–90 (Westerville, Ohio, 1924–32).

175. "Democracy and Alcohol," handwritten speech notes in notebook in folder 1077 (first two quotes); untitled, typewritten speech manuscript, January 30, 1923, folder 912 (next two quotes); and "The Prohibition Issue," speech abstract, October 13, 1927, folder 685 (last quote), Poteat Papers.

176. Ethel M. Speas, *History of the Voluntary Mental Health Movement in North Carolina* (n.p., 1961), 1–3 (quotes on 3) (copy in North Carolina Mental Health Association [NCMHA] Papers [North Carolina Division of Archives and History, Raleigh]); *WFS* 33 (January 1914): 278; and Gulledge, *North Carolina Conference,* 12. Poteat's interest in mental health was longstanding. In 1887 he believed that the "darkest figures" from the census of 1880 were the statistics showing an increase in insanity. He noted that insanity was increasing in proportion to the growth "of civilization." Speech notes, "The Industrial and Religious Aspects of Education," May 6, 1887, folder 884, Poteat Papers. For an overview of the eugenics movement see Daniel J. Kevles, *In the Name of Eugenics: Genetics and the Uses of Human Heredity* (1985; reprint, with a new preface, Cambridge, Mass., and London, 1995). For "the menace of the feebleminded" in the early twentieth century see James W. Trent Jr., *Inventing the Feeble Mind: A History of Mental Retardation in the United States* (Berkeley, Los Angeles, and London, 1994), chap. 5. For discussion of the National Committee for Mental Hygiene and the North Carolina School for the Feeble-Minded see Steven Noll, *Feeble-Minded in Our Midst: Institutions for the Mentally Retarded in the South, 1900–1940* (Chapel Hill and London, 1995), 16–23. Relatively little has been written on the history of mental health in the South but see Peter McCandless, *Moonlight, Magnolias, and Madness: Insanity in South Carolina from the Colonial Period to the Progressive Era* (Chapel Hill and London, 1996). For the best work on the overall eugenics movement in the South (though unfortunately only the Deep South) see Edward J. Larson, *Sex, Race, and Science: Eugenics in the Deep South* (Baltimore and London, 1995).

177. Speas, *Voluntary Mental Health Movement,* 3.

178. Speas, *Voluntary Mental Health Movement,* 3–9; and minutes of the annual meetings in NCMHA Papers.

179. "Minutes of the First Annual Meeting of the North Carolina Society for Mental Hygiene, Held . . . on January 8th, 1915," NCMHA Papers; handwritten speech notes dated January 8, 1915, folder 1245; and handwritten speech manuscript in notebook, folder 774 (quotes), Poteat Papers.

180. Speas, *Voluntary Mental Health Movement,* 6–7; "Minutes of the Third Annual Meeting of the North Carolina Society for Mental Hygiene, Held in the House of Representatives on January 12, 1917," NCMHA Papers; and *N&O,* January 13, 1917.

181. Manuscript of "Address by William Louis Poteat on the Occasion of Accepting the Presidency of the North Carolina Society for Mental Hygiene, January 12, 1917," folder 949, Poteat Papers.

182. "Minutes of the Fourth Annual Meeting of the North Carolina Society for Mental Hygiene, Held in the Hall of the House of Representatives on January 18, 1921," NCMHA Papers; and Speas, *Voluntary Mental Health Movement,* 8–13.

183. Poteat, "Science and Life," November 28, 1902, handwritten speech manuscript in notebook in folder 1058, Poteat Papers.

184. *WFS* 34 (October 1914): 64, and 36 (October 1916): 46; and *BWFC* 14 (January 1920): 165, and 19 (November 1924): 37.

185. "The New Fates and the Web of Destiny," typed speech manuscript for a high school commencement, dated April 3, 1914, folder 969, Poteat Papers.

186. "The Standard Man: Presidential Address to the Southern Baptist Education Asso-

ciation, Birmingham, Ala., December 3–5, 1921," clipping from *Baptist Education Bulletin*, folder 1085, Poteat Papers.

187. Poteat, "The Social Significance of Heredity: . . . Presidential Address to the Southern Baptist Education Association, Memphis, February 21, 1923," clipping from *Baptist Education Bulletin*, folder 1078, Poteat Papers.

188. Link, *Paradox of Southern Progressivism*, xi–xii and 323–24.

4. Wrestling New South Education

1. Gaston, *New South Creed*; Gavin Wright, *Old South, New South: Revolutions in the Southern Economy Since the Civil War* (New York, 1986), chaps. 5 and 6; and Don H. Doyle, *New Men, New Cities, New South: Atlanta, Nashville, Charleston, Mobile, 1860–1910* (Chapel Hill and London, 1990).

2. Leloudis, *Schooling the New South*; Alice Elizabeth Reagan, *North Carolina State University: A Narrative History* (Ann Arbor, 1987), chaps. 2 and 3; Thomas G. Dyer, *The University of Georgia: A Bicentennial History, 1785–1985* (Athens, 1985), 136; Brittain and McMath, "Engineers," 175–201; Hal Bridges, "D.H. Hill and Higher Education in the New South," *Arkansas Historical Quarterly* 15 (summer 1956): 107–24; Michael Dennis, "Reforming the 'Academical Village': Edwin A. Alderman and the University of Virginia, 1904–1915," *Virginia Magazine of History and Biography* 105 (winter 1997): 53–86; Dennis, "Educating the 'Advancing' South: State Universities and Progressivism in the New South, 1887–1915" (Ph.D. diss., Queen's University, 1996); Dyer, "Higher Education in the South Since the Civil War: Historiographical Issues and Trends," in Walter J. Fraser Jr., R. Frank Saunders Jr., and Jon L. Wakelyn, eds., *The Web of Southern Social Relations: Women, Family, and Education* (Athens, Ga., 1985), 127–45; and Jennings L. Wagoner, "Higher Education and Transitions in Southern Culture: An Exploratory Apologia," *Journal of Thought* 18 (fall 1983): 104–18.

3. For others facing the conflict between utility and liberal Christian culture see Stetar, "In Search of a Direction," 341–67; and Mark K. Bauman, "Confronting the New South Creed: The Genteel Conservative as Higher Educator," in Ronald K. Goodenow and Arthur O. White, eds., *Education and the Rise of the New South* (Boston, 1981), 92–113.

4. Poteat, "Industrial Education," *WFS* 4 (March 1885): 293–94.

5. Poteat, "Industrial Training," clipping from the *Schoolteacher* labeled June 1887 in notebook in folder 701, Poteat Papers.

6. Poteat, "Report on Education," *BWFC* 7 (October 1912): 186–89 (quotes); Poteat, "Our Baptist System of Schools," *BWFC* 4 (January 1910): 176–77; David L. Smiley, "Educational Attitudes of North Carolina Baptists," *North Carolina Historical Review* 35 (July 1958): 316–27; and Paschal, *Wake Forest*, vol. 3, chap. 19.

7. WLP to Josephus Daniels, December 25, 1910, folder 87; WLP to editor of the *N&O*, December 25, 1910, folder 87; and WLP to EP, February 4, 1921, folder 1167, Poteat Papers; WLP to John Carlisle Kilgo, March 3, 1909, John Carlisle Kilgo Papers, Duke University Archives, Perkins Library; WLP to William Preston Few, January 28, 1911, and March 8, 1911, Few Papers, Duke University Archives; Poteat, "Wake Forest in the Present Educational Situation," *BWFC* 5 (January 1911): 233–42; and Baptist State Convention, *Annual . . . 1917*, 79.

8. Poteat, "Address on the Twenty-Fifth Anniversary of the College of Agriculture and Mechanic Arts, October 3, 1914," *BWFC* 9 (October 1914): 198–99 (first, fourth, fifth, and sixth quotes); Poteat, "The Denominational College," *BWFC* 3 (January 1909): 173–81 (second and third quotes on 173); and Poteat, "The Right Education for the New South," *BWFC* 1 (January 1907): 65–72.

9. See Leloudis, *Schooling the New South*, chap. 6; and Woodward, *Origins of the New South*, chap. 13.

10. "The Educated Person: Characteristics and Functions," delivered May 15, 1896, handwritten speech manuscript in notebook in folder 853, Poteat Papers.

11. Poteat diary, December 4, 1895, in possession of family. On efforts by others to maintain liberal culture in a materialistic time see Rudolph, *Curriculum*, chap. 6, esp. pp. 238–40.

12. Poteat, "Culture and Faith." On Arnold as an old favorite for Poteat see Poteat, "Poetry and Fact," *WFS* 6 (February 1887): 221–22. Matthew Arnold was a favorite of conservative "custodians of culture" in the Northeast as well in the late-nineteenth century. See May, *American Innocence*, 32–33.

13. Matthew Arnold, *Culture and Anarchy*, ed. J. Dover Wilson (1869; reprint, Cambridge, 1969).

14. On Arnold and southern intellectuals see Singal, *War Within*, 10 and 26–29; Clayton, *Savage Ideal*, 32–33 and 154; John Henry Raleigh, *Matthew Arnold and American Culture* (Berkeley and Los Angeles, 1957), 132–34; and Sidney Coulling, "Matthew Arnold and the American South," in Clinton Machann and Forrest D. Burt, eds., *Matthew Arnold in His Time and Ours: Centenary Essays* (Charlottesville, 1988), 40–56.

15. Poteat, "Christian Education and Civic Righteousness," typewritten manuscript. For examples of Poteat consulting Arnold see Poteat diary, April 27, 1898, in possession of family; notes summarizing chaps. 1 and 2 of *Culture and Anarchy*, [May 1909], in notebook in folder 821; and notes in preparation for baccalaureate address [1913] in notebook in folder 821, Poteat Papers.

16. Arnold, *Culture and Anarchy*, chap. 4.

17. Notes in notebook dated March 30, 1897, in folder 798, Poteat Papers.

18. Poteat, *Youth and Culture*, 8; WLP to Richard G. Badger, February 6, 1919, folder 690; Ruth Hill to WLP, March 3, 1919, folder 690; WLP to Henry Holt and Company, September 9, 1929, folder 144; Louis R. Wilson to WLP, January 18, 1928, folder 437; WLP to Shailer Mathews, September 7, 1935, folder 251; Mathews to WLP, September 13, 1935, folder 251; and WLP to J. Hardison, March 31, 1936, folder 149, Poteat Papers.

19. Poteat, *Youth and Culture*, 19–20.

20. Ibid., 12 (first quote), 13 (second quote), and 14–15 (third quote).

21. Ibid., 16.

22. Clippings in notebook titled "Wake Forest and Its New Head," folder 724, Poteat Papers.

23. Poteat, *Youth and Culture*, 45 (first two quotes) and 36 (last quote).

24. Ibid., 82.

25. Ibid., 86–90, 96 (first quote), 126 (second quote), and 127 (third quote).

26. Ibid., 33 (first and second quotes); 36 (third and fourth quotes); 46 (fifth quote); 59 (sixth quote); 58 (seventh quote); and 65 (last quote).

27. Untitled handwritten speech notes for 1921 Baptist State Convention in notebook in folder 823 (first three quotes); and "Culture and the Wake Forest Interpretation," baccalaureate sermon delivered June 1927, handwritten manuscript in notebook in folder 944 (last two quotes), Poteat Papers. See also 1912 comments in *Youth and Culture*, 43.

28. Minutes of the board of trustees, May 23, 1906; and *Catalog, 1905–6*, 6–7.

29. *Catalog, 1872–73*, 6 and 11; *Catalog, 1905–6*, 30–31; and minutes of the board of trustees, May 23, 1906.

30. Poteat, "The Educational Work of Dr. Charles E. Taylor," *BWFC* 10 (January 1916): 194; and undated, untitled notes by Poteat about Taylor [probably from 1915], folder 1246, Poteat Papers.

31. *Catalog, 1903–4*, 88; and minutes of the board of trustees, May 23, 1906.

32. *Catalog, 1905–6*, 99; *1915–16*, 37; *1916–17*, 41; and *1926–27*, 176. For comparison I am presenting figures for the number of instructors and the number of students, taken from *The World Almanac* editions for 1905, 1915, and 1927. The 1905 edition lists Wake Forest with 17 instructors and 328 students. Baylor University had 42 and 995; Davidson College had 23 and 248; Emory College had 16 and 258; Johns Hopkins University had 158 and 715; Mercer University had 23 and 273; Tulane University had 99 and 1,395; the University of North Carolina had 64 and 616; the University of Virginia had 47 and 664; and Vanderbilt University had 109 and 723 (*The World Almanac and Encyclopedia, 1905* [New York, 1905], 303–8). The 1915 edition lists Wake Forest with 41 instructors and 457 students. Baylor University had 49 and 1,500; Davidson College had 14 and 311; Emory College had 17 and 260; Johns Hopkins

University had 240 and 1,374; Mercer University had 23 and 357; Rice Institute had 35 and 255; Tulane University had 281 and 2,650; the University of North Carolina had 92 and 976; the University of Virginia had 103 and 919; and Vanderbilt University had 125 and 1,100 (*The World Almanac and Encyclopedia, 1915* [New York, 1914], 628–34). The 1927 edition lists Wake Forest with 45 teachers and 731 students. Baylor University had 76 and 2,433; Davidson College had 33 and 628; Emory University had 220 and 1,929; Johns Hopkins University had 430 and 1,802; Mercer University had 50 and 200; Rice Institute had 75 and 1,272; Tulane University had 409 and 2,763; the University of North Carolina had 189 and 2,306; the University of Virginia had 161 and 2,003; and Vanderbilt University had 250 and 1,400 (Robert Hunty Lyman, ed., *The World Almanac and Book of Facts for 1927* [New York, 1927], 385–91).

33. Report of the president, May 1927, 11–12. All presidential reports cited are printed pamphlets in Special Collections, Reynolds Library.

34. *Catalog, 1905–6*, 30–31; and *1926–27*, 67–115.

35. Paschal, *Wake Forest*, 3:137–40.

36. Notes and diagram dated March 7, 1909, in notebook in folder 821, Poteat Papers; *Catalog, 1909–10*, 86–91; and Rudolph, *Curriculum*, chap. 6, esp. pp. 227–30.

37. Minutes of the board of trustees, May 19, 1909.

38. Paschal, *Wake Forest*, 3:24.

39. Poteat diary, August 1, 1901, in possession of family.

40. Report of the president, May 1, 1907, 8 (first and third quotes); and Poteat, "The Wake Forest Plan of Medical Studies," *BWFC* 4 (October 1909): 150 (second quote).

41. Minutes of the board of trustees, May 20, 1914.

42. Paschal, *Wake Forest*, vol. 3, chap. 19; and report of the president, May 1927, 40–44.

43. Minutes of the board of trustees, May 22, 1918 (first quote), and June 11, 1919 (second quote); *BR*, September 18 and November 13, 1918; and Poteat, "College Training in War Time," *BWFC* 12 (July 1917): 135–38. On the Student Army Training Corps and its effect on higher education across the nation see Carol S. Gruber, *Mars and Minerva: World War I and the Uses of the Higher Learning in America* (Baton Rouge, 1975), chap. 6.

44. Minutes of the board of trustees, June 11, 1919.

45. Paschal, *Wake Forest*, vol. 3, chap. 8 (quote on p. 96).

46. Minutes of the board of trustees, May 23, 1906; and Paschal, *Wake Forest*, 3:312–14.

47. Paschal, *Wake Forest*, 3:338–40. The medical school remained a two-year school until it moved to Winston-Salem in the summer of 1941 and became a full four-year medical school. The Bowman Gray Fund of the Winston-Salem Foundation had agreed in 1939 to give the medical school resources of around a million dollars if it would move and become affiliated with the state Baptist hospital already there. See Paschal, *Wake Forest*, 3:433–35.

48. *Catalog, 1905–6*, 28–29.

49. Report of the president, May 1, 1907, 5–7 (quote on 7); and *Catalog, 1906–7*, 32.

50. Minutes of the board of trustees, May 20, 1908.

51. Paschal, *Wake Forest*, 3:18–19.

52. Report of the president, May 1, 1907, 10 (quote); minutes of the board of trustees, May 22, 1907; and Paschal, *Wake Forest*, 3:54–55.

53. Minutes of the board of trustees, June 30, 1908.

54. Minutes of the board of trustees, May 15, 1912 (quotes); and Paschal, *Wake Forest*, 3:56–57.

55. Minutes of the board of trustees, May 23, 1906, and July 30, 1906; and *Catalog, 1905–6*, 24–26; and *1906–7*, 18.

56. Minutes of the board of trustees, May 20, 1914.

57. Minutes of the board of trustees, May 19, 1915, and May 13, 1916.

58. Minutes of the board of trustees, May 22, 1918 (quote); and *Catalog, 1917–18*, 60–61.

59. Minutes of the board of trustees, June 11, 1919; and report of the president, April 20, 1920, 4.

60. *Catalog, 1920–21*, 12 and 73–74; report of the president, May 1925, 15; May 1926, 15–16; and May 1927, 23; and *OGB*, January 21, 1921.

61. *BWFC* 8 (July 1913): 147–48.

62. WLP to EP, August 3, 1906, folder 1166, and June 3, 1922, folder 1167, Poteat Papers.

63. Paschal, *Wake Forest*, 3:32–33 and 57.

64. Report of the president, May 1927, 11–12.

65. Minutes of the board of trustees, June 25, 1906, and July 30, 1906; and Baptist State Convention, *Annual . . . 1905*, 46.

66. Paschal, *Wake Forest*, 3:60–70; and minutes of the board of trustees, February 9, 1911, and May 15, 1912.

67. Minutes of the board of trustees, May 19, 1915.

68. Minutes of the board of trustees, December 10, 1913, May 20, 1914, May 19, 1915, March 10 and 18, and May 13, 1916, May 23 and December 5, 1917, and May 22, 1918; Baptist State Convention, *Annual . . . 1914*, 25–26; and *1917*, 77–78.

69. Baptist State Convention, *Annual . . . 1917*, 77.

70. Minutes of the board of trustees, June 11, 1919.

71. Baptist State Convention, *Annual . . . 1918*, 74–86; *1919*, 73–74; *1920*, 85–85; *1921*, 105 and 108; *1923*, 40–44; and *1924*, 35–38; and *BWFC* 13 (July 1918): 250.

72. *N&O*, January 19, 1919, and February 1, 1920; and Rufus W. Weaver to WLP, August 15, 1919; WLP to W.R. Cullom, July 25, 1919, and various other letters, all in folder 703, Poteat Papers.

73. Report of the president, May 1923, 5; and Paschal, *Wake Forest*, 3:136–37.

74. Minutes of the board of trustees, July 8 and September 12, 1907, May 20, 1908, May 19, 1909 (first quote), and May 18, 1910 (second quote).

75. Minutes of the board of trustees, May 15, 1912 (quote), and December 10, 1913.

76. Minutes of the board of trustees, May 15, 1912, May 21 (first quote) and May 22, 1913, May 20, 1914, May 19, 1915, and May 13, 1916 (other quotes).

77. Minutes of the board of trustees, May 23, 1917, May 22, 1918, November 10, 1919, May 26 and June 17, 1920, May 3, 25, and 26, 1921.

78. Report of the president, May 1920, 5.

79. Minutes of the board of trustees, May 23, 1906, May 18, 1910 (quote), and May 19 and 20, 1915; and *Catalog, 1926–27*, 36.

80. Report of the president, May 1, 1907, 5, and April 20, 1920, 8.

81. *OGB*, November 16, 1923.

82. Paschal, *Wake Forest*, 3:136–37; and minutes of the board of trustees, May 25, 1922.

83. Paschal, *Wake Forest*, 3:136–37; report of the president, May 1923, 6–8; and Baptist State Convention, *Annual . . . 1924*, 95.

84. Paschal, *Wake Forest*, 3:135; minutes of the board of trustees, October 30, 1925, November 19, 1925, and June 1, 1927; and WLP to Benjamin N. Duke, June 4, 1927, Benjamin N. Duke Papers, Special Collections, Perkins Library, Duke University.

85. Report of the president, May 1927, 12.

86. Report of the president, May 1924, 6–9 (quote on 9); and May 1925, 7; and minutes of the board of trustees, March 16 and 24, 1925.

87. Poteat, "Wake Forest College: A Statement," November 9, 1925, folder 715, Poteat Papers.

88. Report of the president, May 1927, 9–10. On Poteat raising funds for library see WLP to Mr. Chairman, September 20, 1926, folder 3; "Wake Forest Letter," typewritten article by Poteat, folder 726; and notes in folder 1091, Poteat Papers.

89. Sunday school notes in notebook dated September 1909 in folder 995 (first quote); chapel notes in book in folder 1212; handbook of the college YMCA from 1913–14 with Poteat's office hours on p. 20, folder 735, Poteat Papers; and *OGB*, September 23, 1916 (last two quotes).

90. Paschal, *Wake Forest*, 3:10–16.

91. Untitled, handwritten speech manuscript dated November 18, 1912, folder 1245, Poteat Papers.

92. Paschal, *Wake Forest*, 2:372–83.

93. Paschal, *Wake Forest,* 2:407–16 (first and second quotes on 412); WLP to Brother Pittman, January 2, 1907, folder 313, Poteat Papers (third and fourth quotes); and minutes of the board of trustees, May 23, 1907 (last quote).

94. Hubert Poteat to EP, June 5, 1907, folder 1171, Poteat Papers.

95. *OGB,* February 16, 1918; Poteat, "Fraternities in Baptist Colleges," *BWFC* 15 (October 1920): 146–47; and Paschal, *Wake Forest,* 2:413–15.

96. Paschal, *Wake Forest,* vol. 3, chap. 10.

97. Untitled, handwritten speech manuscript dated November 18, 1912, folder 1245, Poteat Papers; *OGB,* January 6, 1917; WLP to W.P. Few, February 2, 1916, Few Papers; and "Remarks of President Poteat in accepting the Gore Athletic Field," November 25, 1922, folder 885, Poteat Papers.

98. Paschal, *Wake Forest,* 3:77; WLP to W.C. Tyree, September 12, 1898, William C. Tyree Papers (quotation); for Poteat's involvement in building the new church building see various letters and notes in folder 713, Poteat Papers; his report on education to the Southern Baptist Convention was on May 14, 1910, and was published as a pamphlet, *Religion and Education;* on Poteat's election as a trustee of the Southern Baptist Theological Seminary see Southern Baptist Convention, *Annual . . . 1910,* 14, and see the various annuals for Poteat on list of members through 1932. See also yearly Central Baptist Association, *Minutes,* from 1904 through 1920 (in Special Collections, Reynolds Library) for Poteat on the executive committee and various routine committees. Poteat generally wrote, and delivered after receiving approval, the report of the Wake Forest board of trustees to the Baptist State Convention. See the various issues of the convention's *Annual* during Poteat's presidency.

99. Poteat, "The College and the Secondary School," in *OGB,* March 10, 1917. See also an editorial by Poteat in *New York Times,* August 9, 1915.

100. Southern Baptist Convention, *Annual . . . 1923,* 305 (quote), and *Annual . . . 1927,* 404–8; *OGB,* September 22, 1922; and Poteat, "Report of the President . . . On the Occasion of the Anniversary, February 3, 1925," folder 731, Poteat Papers. See also *BR,* August 23, 1922.

101. Minutes of the board of trustees, August 15, 1910, August 27, 1918, September 6, 1920, and January 22, 1924.

102. Paschal, *Wake Forest,* 3:237–40; and *BR,* October 16 and November 6, 13, and 20 (quotes), 1912. On the controversy at Vanderbilt University see Conkin, *Gone with the Ivy,* chap. 8. After a court case, the university separated fully from the Methodist denomination in 1914.

103. Paschal, *Wake Forest,* 3:240; *BR,* December 11, 1912 (quotes); and Baptist State Convention, *Annual . . . 1913,* 54–55.

104. WLP to EP, May 20, 1916 (folder 1167, Poteat Papers), mentions some open opposition to the college in Asheville, but that seems to have been an isolated instance.

5. Christianity, Enlightenment, and Baptist Democracy

1. Poteat's involvement in the evolution controversy is the only portion of his life that has been fully chronicled and narrated by other historians. Harriet Suzanne Cameron, "William Louis Poteat and the Evolution Controversy" (Masters thesis, Wake Forest College, 1962) traces the events of the 1920s in some detail, and her work in the thesis appears in slightly abbreviated form as Suzanne Cameron Linder, "William Louis Poteat and the Evolution Controversy," *North Carolina Historical Review* 40 (April 1963): 135–57; and Linder, *William Louis Poteat.* Poteat's role is also examined with some thoroughness in Gatewood, *Preachers, Pedagogues, and Politicians.* In addition, Poteat receives more than passing mention in James J. Thompson Jr., *Tried As by Fire: Southern Baptists and the Religious Controversies of the 1920s* (Macon, Ga., 1982); and Eighmy, *Churches in Cultural Captivity.* This chapter utilizes many of the same documents used by Linder and Gatewood and naturally follows a similar narrative. However, my interpretation differs strongly. Rather than regarding the religious conservatives opposing Poteat solely as irrational Fundamentalist zealots, I place the religious controversy more fully in intellectual and social perspective, including in my analysis the infant stage of academic freedom and the widespread opposition to bureaucratic governance by the Tarheel populace. Religious conservatives

who rejected modern science sought not only to suppress the teaching of evolution, but also to exercise a democratic right to govern an institution they owned, in lieu of surrendering it to bureaucratic control. Poteat, on the other hand, represented an encroaching worldview that included deference to expert knowledge and the right of intellectual authorities to guide society in the area of their expertise. The evolution controversy resulted from, but by no means resolved, this clash in North Carolina.

2. Richard Hofstadter and Walter P. Metzger, *The Development of Academic Freedom in the United States* (New York, 1955), chaps. 7–10 (first quote on p. 363; second quote on p. 364; and third quote on p. 365).

3. Thompson, *Tried As by Fire*, discusses local autonomy and denominational democracy in chap. 8 as among the several motivations for Fundamentalism.

4. Sydney E. Ahlstrom, *Theology in America: The Major Protestant Voices from Puritanism to Neo-Orthodoxy* (Indianapolis and New York, 1967), 536 (quote). On Fundamentalism's origin in nineteenth-century theological struggles in the North, its relative weakness in the South, and its development during and after World War I see George M. Marsden, *Fundamentalism and American Culture: The Shaping of Twentieth-Century Evangelicalism, 1870–1925* (New York and Oxford, 1980); Willard B. Gatewood Jr., introduction to Gatewood, ed., *Controversy in the Twenties: Fundamentalism, Modernism, and Evolution* (Nashville, 1969), 3–46, overemphasizes World War I at the expense of doctrinal concerns but is nonetheless useful; Ronald L. Numbers, *The Creationists* (New York, 1992), chap. 3; and George E. Webb, *The Evolution Controversy in America* (Lexington, Ky., 1994), chap. 3.

5. Marsden, *Fundamentalism*, esp. 118–23; Webb, *Evolution Controversy*, 54–55; Thompson, *Tried As by Fire*, 66–67; John R. Woodard, "Amzi Clarence Dixon," q.v. William S. Powell, ed., *Dictionary of North Carolina Biography*, 6 vols., (Chapel Hill and London, 1986), 2:71–72; and minutes of the Euzelian Society, February 1, 1873, April 5, 1873, and throughout the 1872–73 session, Euzelian Society Records.

6. Webb, *Evolution Controversy*, 54–57; and Marsden, *Fundamentalism*, 158.

7. Jeffrey Kirk Walters, "'Though the Heavens Fall': Liberal Theology and the Southern Baptist Theological Seminary, 1894–1925" (Masters thesis, Auburn University, 1992); Thompson, *Tried As by Fire*, esp. chaps. 4–6; Barry Hankins, *God's Rascal: J. Frank Norris and the Beginnings of Southern Fundamentalism* (Lexington, Ky., 1996); and Gatewood, *Preachers, Pedagogues, and Politicians*, 48–58.

8. Thompson, *Tried As by Fire*, chaps. 2–8.

9. Link, *Paradox of Southern Progressivism*.

10. Thompson, *Tried As by Fire*, 120 and 137.

11. *BR*, March 24, 1920; and T.T. Martin, *Three Fatal Teachings* (n.p., n.d.), 9.

12. *BR*, March 10, 1920.

13. *BR*, March 24, 1920.

14. Martin, *Three Fatal Teachings*, 18–22 (quote on 18). On Martin and the 1920 controversy see Gatewood, *Preachers, Pedagogues, and Politicians*, 30–37; and Cameron, "William Louis Poteat," 26–32.

15. Martin, *Three Fatal Teachings*, 22–26 (quotes on 24 and 26).

16. WLP to EP, May 7, 1915, folder 1166, Poteat Papers (first quote); and Martin, *Three Fatal Teachings*, 26–27 (second quote on 27).

17. Martin, *Three Fatal Teachings*, 29.

18. Ibid., 29–30.

19. *BR*, February 4, 1920.

20. *BR*, February 11, 1920.

21. WLP to EP, January 27, 1920, folder 1167, Poteat Papers.

22. WLP to EMP, March 8, 1920, folder 1163, Poteat Papers.

23. WLP to EMP, March 8, 1920, folder 1163, Poteat Papers; and *BR*, March 3 and 24, 1920.

24. *BR*, March 3 and 17, 1920.

25. *BR*, February 18, 1920.

26. *BR,* March 3, 1920.

27. Marsden, *Fundamentalism,* 160–61 and 170.

28. *BR,* June 16 (Dixon's address) and June 2 (other quotes), 1920. On "folk science" among Fundamentalists see Edward B. Davis, "Fundamentalism and Folk Science between the Wars," *Religion and American Culture* 5 (summer 1995): 217–48. The depiction of the battle over evolution in schools as a rejection of professional authority in science and education is enhanced in an ironic way by a comparison of Dixon's rejection of science with the following statement of historian Thomas L. Haskell, an expert on the history of professional authority. In outlining the stakes of contemporary historical debate about the authority of experts, Haskell (who would, of course, disagree entirely with Dixon's Fundamentalism and whose full discussion of trust in experts indicates that it is not a blind trust) declares: "Expert authority shapes our most fundamental assumptions. Consider, for example, my belief in Darwin's theory of evolution rather than the biblical story of creation. . . . I believe in evolution with nearly the same degree of confidence that I feel about the existence of the table I am writing on, or the accuracy of an account that I could give of some episode in my own life, based on personal experience and recollection. Yet my belief in evolution rests on no firmer basis than expert authority. Certainly I have not inspected the fossil record for myself, or worked my way through the intricate details of Darwin's argument in *The Origin of Species,* or followed the debates which led up to the present version of the theory. And although many imagine otherwise, I believe it is an illusion to think that the story of divine creation is *inherently* any less plausible than the idea of one-celled primeval slime gradually evolving into complex forms of life under the pressure of anything as abstract and directionless as natural selection. We non-fundamentalist laymen believe in evolution not because we have in mind the evidence and experience it would take to envision the process and grasp it in a fully rational way, but because we trust biologists." Haskell, introduction to Haskell, ed., *The Authority of Experts: Studies in History and Theory* (Bloomington, 1984), x–xi.

29. *BR,* June 8 (first quote) and October 5 (other two quotes), 1921; and Baptist State Convention, *Annual . . . 1920,* 85–86 and 88.

30. *BR,* June 29, August 31, October 5, October 26, November 16 (quotes) and 30, and December 14, 1921.

31. *BR,* September 7, 1921.

32. *BR,* November 9, 1921.

33. *BR,* December 21, 1921 (first two quotes), January 11 (third quote) and 25, February 1, 8 (last quote), 15, and 22, March 1, and May 31, 1922; Paschal, *Wake Forest,* 3:58–59; report of the president, May 1923, 4; and minutes of the board of trustees, May 25, August 3, and September 12, 1922. The move to a full-time dean did not occur immediately for lack of a suitable candidate.

34. *BR,* June 14 (first quote) and 21, July 12 (third and fourth quotes) and 19, August 2 (second quote), 16, 23, and 30, and September 6, 1922. One Baptist missionary wrote from China that legalizing fraternities was a "serious step toward Bolshevism . . ." *BR,* November 15, 1922. Freshmen were given the option of voting to wear a freshmen cap, and when "the suggestion was made that they could adopt a class cap if they saw fit to do so," the newcomers did in the fall of 1922. *BR,* October 4, 1922.

35. *BR,* June 14 (quote), August 9, and December 6, 1922; and minutes of the board of trustees, August 3, 1922.

36. Gatewood, *Preachers, Pedagogues, and Politicians,* 38–58.

37. WLP to EMP, February 9 (first quote) and 23 (other quotes), 1922, folder 1163, Poteat Papers.

38. Notes for "Was Paul an Evolutionist?" in notebook in folder 995, Poteat Papers; and *BR,* March 8, 1922.

39. *BR,* February 22 (fourth quote), March 22, April 5 (first three quotes), 12, 19, and 26, and May 3 and 31 (last two quotes), 1922.

40. *BR,* April 19, 1922 (quotes); WLP to William P. McCorkle, November 23, 1931, folder 282, Poteat Papers; Numbers, *Creationists,* 50–53; Marsden, *Fundamentalism,* 212–21; and Thompson, *Tried As by Fire,* 110–13.

41. *BR,* April 26, 1922.

42. WLP to William P. McCorkle, November 23, 1931, folder 282, Poteat Papers.

43. *BR,* May 3 (last quote) and 10 (first two quotes), 1922.

44. *BR,* May 31, 1922. See also minutes of the board of trustees, May 25, 1922.

45. *BR,* August 23 and October 25, 1922; Cameron, "William Louis Poteat," 43–45; Benjamin [Sorgee?] to WLP, December 5, 1922, with attached resolutions, folder 583; clipping from *Asheville Citizen,* December 11, 1922, folder 583; and Gaston County resolutions, folder 83, Poteat Papers.

46. *BR,* August 9, October 18 (second quote) and 25, and November 1, 1922; and WLP to EMP, October 28, 1922, folder 1163, Poteat Papers (first quote).

47. *BR,* December 6, 1922 (last quote); and WLP to EMP, October 28, 1922, folder 1163, Poteat Papers (other quotes).

48. *BR,* May 10 and December 20 (quotes), 1922; and clipping from *Thomasville Charity and Children,* December 21, 1922, in folder 586, Poteat Papers.

49. "Christianity and Enlightenment," December 13, 1922 (pamphlet published by Baptist State Convention), 1–7, copy in folder 811, Poteat Papers.

50. Poteat, "Christianity and Enlightenment," 8–13.

51. *BR,* December 20, 1922 (first quote); Baptist State Convention, *Annual . . . 1922,* 33 (second quote); and *N&O,* December 16, 1922.

52. Clipping from the *Elizabeth City Independent,* December 19, 1922, in folder 591, Poteat Papers.

53. EMP to WLP, March 4, 1923, folder 1163, Poteat Papers.

54. Gatewood, *Preachers, Pedagogues, and Politicians,* 94–109 (quote on 100).

55. *Wake Forest Bulletin* 18 (July 1923): 15; WLP to EMP, February 16, 1923, folder 1163; and notebook on trip to the West, folder 1102, Poteat Papers.

56. WLP to EP, June 18, 1924, folder 1167 (quote); and various clippings in folder 695, Poteat Papers.

57. *OGB,* March 7, 1924.

58. Speech manuscript dated January 29, 1924, in notebook in folder 823; and clipping labeled *Monroe Journal,* May 6, 1924, in folder 1150, Poteat Papers. See also clipping from *Greenville (S.C.) Baptist Courier,* March 15, 1923, in folder 612, Poteat Papers.

59. Clipping from *N&O,* labeled February 21, 1924, folder 606, Poteat Papers.

60. WLP to EMP, June 26, 1924, folder 1163 (quotes); clipping from *Durham Morning Herald,* March 13, 1924, folder 605; clipping labeled April 16, 1924, folder 614; clipping labeled *BR,* May 7, 1924, folder 615; clipping from *Nashville Baptist and Reflector,* April 10, 1924, folder 601; clipping dated March 24, 1924, folder 600, Poteat Papers; and minutes of the board of trustees, June 3, 1924. The *Morning Herald* criticized Norris and his supporters: "Their tactics would do credit to the days of Salem, Mass., when witches were tied to the stake, and when religious intolerance ruled. They would sacrifice knowledge upon the altar [of] narrowness and prejudice. Norris, down in Texas where the K.K.K. flourishes; where the cactus grows; where the greaser thrives, where tarantulas crawl, and rattlesnakes hiss; where coyotes howl, jackasses bray, and jackrabbits run, is in good company for propagating such stuff as he hurls at the head of a man who is his superior in every respect." Clipping from March 13, 1924, folder 605, Poteat Papers.

61. Webb, *Evolution Controversy,* 70–104; Thompson, *Tried As by Fire,* 79, 117, and 137–38; Numbers, *Creationists,* 47–48; Richard H. King, *A Southern Renaissance: The Cultural Awakening of the American South, 1930–1955* (Oxford, 1980), 42 and 53; clipping from December 1921 in folder 584; and clipping from *Atlanta Christian Index,* October 16, 1924, in folder 602, Poteat Papers. Howard K. Beale found that "between 1921 and 1929, . . . thirty-seven anti-evolution bills were introduced into twenty state legislatures" around the nation (*Are American Teachers Free? An Analysis of Restraints upon the Freedom of Teaching in American Schools* [New York, 1936], 227).

62. Gatewood, *Preachers, Pedagogues, and Politicians,* 114–23; and Singal, *War Within,* 122 and 126–28.

63. Gatewood, *Preachers, Pedagogues, and Politicians,* 125–26.

64. WLP to Robert W. Winston, August 25, 1937, folder 437, Poteat Papers (first quote); Gatewood, *Preachers, Pedagogues, and Politicians,* chap. 5 (Chase quotation on p. 129); and Cameron, "William Louis Poteat," 57–65.

65. Gatewood, *Preachers, Pedagogues, and Politicians,* 111–14 and 122–23.

66. Notes in notebook in folder 944; clipping from *N&O* in folder 557 (first quote); and clipping from *Greensboro Daily News* in folder 553 (last quote), Poteat Papers.

67. Poteat, *Can a Man Be a Christian To-day?,* 1–41 (quote on 2).

68. Ibid., 13, 21–22, and 35.

69. Ibid., 47, 53, 65, 60, and 70–71.

70. Ibid., 100.

71. Clipping from *Greensboro Daily News,* folder 553 (quotes); and clipping from *N&O* in folder 557, Poteat Papers.

72. Clipping labeled *Greensboro News,* May 23, 1925 (quote); clipping labeled *Charlotte Observer,* May 23, 1925; and clipping labeled *N&O,* May 20, 1925, all in folder 626, Poteat Papers.

73. Clipping from *N&O,* labeled May 31, 1925, folder 625, Poteat Papers.

74. Clipping from *Greensboro Daily News,* June 4, 1925, in clipping file of North Carolina Collection (first quote); clipping from *N&O,* June 4, 1925, folder 626 (last quote); clipping from *N&O,* June 5, 1925, folder 538; and clipping from *Winston-Salem Journal,* folder 630, Poteat Papers.

75. *BR,* July 1, 15, and 29, and August 5, 1925; clipping from *New York World,* folder 555; William T. Couch to WLP, August 25 and December 9, 1925, folder 551, Poteat Papers; and Singal, *War Within,* 265–73. Thomas Dixon assured Poteat that the book was "a stirring reaffirmation of the real faith of our fathers." Dixon to WLP, August 5, 1925, folder 552, Poteat Papers.

76. S.J. Betts, *Criticism of Dr. Poteat's Book Recently Published Entitled "Can a Man Be a Christian Today?"*(Raleigh, 1925), 1–12 (first quote on 6); and James R. Pentuff, *Christian Evolutionists Answered and President W.L. Poteat's Utterances Reviewed* (n.p., 1925). The *Nashville Baptist and Reflector* reviewed the book and concluded, "We brand him [Poteat] not only as an evolutionist, but as an anti-Baptist disturber of our Southern Baptist Zion . . ." August 20, 1925, clipping in folder 550, Poteat Papers.

77. Clipping labeled *Norfolk (Va.) Virginian-Pilot,* October 17, 1925, folder 625; and clipping labeled *Charlotte Observer,* October 12, 1925, folder 618, Poteat Papers.

78. Clipping labeled *Greensboro News,* September 6, 1925, folder 621 (first quote); clipping labeled *N&O,* July 22, 1925, folder 557 (last quote); variety of clippings from the *Boston Evening Transcript,* early August 1925, folder 555; and Edwin Mims, "Why the South is Anti-Evolution," labeled *The Forum* (September 1925), 550, in folder 554, Poteat Papers.

79. WLP to EMP, August 18, 1925, folder 556, Poteat Papers.

80. WLP to W.W. Barnes, August 26, 1925, folder 550, Poteat Papers. Poteat had "no idea of withdrawing under fire." WLP to Laurence Stallings, August 29, 1925, folder 557, Poteat Papers.

81. Clipping from October 23, 1925, labeled *Charlotte Observer,* folder 621; clipping from *BR,* September 2, 1925, folder 550; clipping labeled *N&O,* August 26, 1925, folder 555; clipping from *Asheville Citizen,* August 13, 1925, folder 551; George Pennell to WLP, August 14, 1925, folder 556; WLP to Pennell, August 18, 1925, folder 556; resolution dated August 29, 1925, folder 628; clipping from *N&O,* [September 1925], folder 624; clipping dated September 17, 1925, folder 624; and clipping from *Charlotte Observer,* labeled October 1, 1925, folder 551, Poteat Papers.

82. Clipping labeled *Greensboro Daily News,* September 17, 1925, folder 559; clipping labeled *Winston-Salem Journal,* September 18, 1925, folder 630; WLP to Edwin Mims, September 5, 1925, folder 554; and J.A. McKaughan to WLP, September 14, 1925, folder 223, Poteat Papers.

83. Clippings labeled *Charlotte Observer,* September 28, 1925, folder 626; and November 17, 1925, folder 618 (quotes), Poteat Papers.

84. Clipping labeled *Charlotte Observer,* October 31, 1925, folder 551, Poteat Papers.

85. Baptist State Convention, *Annual . . . 1925,* 28–30.

86. Poteat, "Alumni Banquet Address," November 18, 1925, typewritten manuscript in folder 746 (first quote); clipping labeled *Norfolk (Va.) Ledger-Dispatch,* November 19, 1925, folder 625; clipping labeled *Winston-Salem Twin City Sentinel,* November 19, 1925, folder 626, Poteat Papers; and Baptist State Convention, *Annual . . . 1925,* 31–32.

87. Clipping labeled *N&O,* November 20, 1925, folder 618 (quote); clipping labeled *N&O,* November 19, 1925, folder 617; and clippings from *Charlotte Observer,* November 19, 1925, folders 538, 617, and 630, Poteat Papers. On Bradbury see Numbers, *Creationists,* 47–48; Thompson, *Tried As by Fire,* 117; and Poteat, report of the president, May 1925, 3.

88. Clipping labeled *Greensboro Daily News,* November 21, 1925, folder 621 (first quote); clipping labeled *Charlotte Observer,* November 20, 1925, folder 630; and WLP to D.P. McGeachy, December 14, 1925, folder 554 (second quote), Poteat Papers.

89. Gatewood, "Politics and Piety in North Carolina: The Fundamentalist Crusade at High Tide, 1925–1927," *North Carolina Historical Review* 42 (summer 1965): 275–90; and clipping from *Greensboro Daily News,* [May 1926], folder 624, Poteat Papers.

90. Notes in notebook in folder 944 (first quote); and "Liberty and Restraint," March 4, 1927, typewritten speech manuscript in folder 925 (second quote), Poteat Papers.

91. WLP to EMP, April 7, 1931, folder 1165, Poteat Papers.

92. Eighmy, *Churches in Cultural Captivity,* 126–27 n. 9.

93. Edwin Mims, *The Advancing South: Stories of Progress and Reaction* (Garden City, N.Y., 1926), 14–16 and 305–10 (first quote on 14); Virginius Dabney, *Liberalism in the South* (Chapel Hill, 1932), 300–301 (last quote on 301); and Dabney to WLP, May 19, 1931, folder 83, Poteat Papers (second quote).

94. Poteat, "Liberal Movements in the South," *Yale Review* 16 (January 1927): 389–91 (quotes on 390); and WLP to Dabney, June 15, 1931, folder 83, Poteat Papers.

95. Clipping from *Charlotte News,* November 8, 1925, folder 554 (Mencken); clipping labeled *Thomasville Charity and Children,* May 13, 1926, folder 633 (last quote); and clipping from the *New Republic,* May 12, 1926, folder 555, Poteat Papers; and clipping from *Greensboro Daily News,* December 5, 1926, North Carolina Collection (Johnson).

6. Spokesman for Another Lost Cause

1. Newspaper clippings in scrapbook in folder 1238, Poteat Papers.

2. *OGB,* May 14 (quote), March 27, April 30, and May 8, 1926. See also clipping, "College Heads Hotly Criticized," folder 734, Poteat Papers.

3. Clipping, "Kitchin Resigns after Row at Wake Forest," folder 734, Poteat Papers. See also *OGB,* April 10 and May 8, 1926.

4. *OGB,* May 14, 1926. See also clipping, "College Heads Hotly Criticized," folder 734, Poteat Papers.

5. Clipping, "Kitchin Resigns after Row at Wake Forest" (quote); Kitchin to WLP, May 15, 1926; Walter F. Taylor to WLP, May 17, 1926; F.W. Carroll to WLP, May 26, 1926; and WLP to Gilbert T. Stephenson, June 16, 1926. All in folder 734, Poteat Papers. See also R.T. Vann to L.B. Moseley, May 26, 1926; and draft of Moseley to board of trustees of Wake Forest, undated, both in Lilburn Burke Moseley Petitions, Special Collections, Reynolds Library. Hubert Poteat felt the criticism heaped on him was unjust. See Hubert Poteat to Francis P. Gaines, August 21, 1927, folder 15, Francis P. Gaines Correspondence, President's Office Papers, Special Collections, Reynolds Library.

6. WLP to Kitchin, May 20, 1926, folder 734, Poteat Papers.

7. Walter F. Taylor to Gilbert T. Stephenson, July 28, 1926; and WLP to Stephenson, June 16, 1926. Both in folder 734, Poteat Papers.

8. Poteat, "Interview with Mr. Gilbert T. Stephenson, Raleigh, June 26, 1926" (quotes); WLP to Stephenson, June 16, 1926; and Stephenson to WLP, June 21, 1926. All in folder 734, Poteat Papers.

9. Walter F. Taylor to WLP, June 1, 1930, folder 413, Poteat Papers.

10. Paschal, *Wake Forest*, 3:133.

11. WLP to Edwin Mims, September 6, 1926, box 2, Edwin Mims Papers.

12. G.E. Lineberry to Lilburn B. Moseley, August 21, 1926, Moseley Petitions.

13. Clipping from *Asheville Citizen,* June 17, 1927, in folder 538, Poteat Papers (quote); and Paschal, *Wake Forest,* 3:133–34.

14. WLP to E.A. Harrill, February 14, 1928, folder 143, Poteat Papers.

15. WLP to Judge Johnson J. Hayes, December 16, 1927, folder 155 (quote); Poteat, "Impressions of the Near East," speaking notes, folder 903; WLP to EMP, March 31, 1927, folder 1163; WLP to John Arch McMillan, June 12, 1927, folder 285a; WLP to R.C. Lawrence, November 12, 1927, folder 223; WLP to W.L. Foushee, November 12, 1927, folder 121; W.L. Foushee to WLP, November 25, 1927, folder 121; "Statement of Account of Contributions to the W.L. Poteat Trip to Europe, Summer of 1927," folder 121; and clipping, "President Emeritus," scrapbook, folder 1238, Poteat Papers. See also *BWFC* 22 (July 1927): 39.

16. WLP to M. Leslie Davis, October 14, 1927, folder 83 (quote); Gilbert Stephenson to WLP, November 7, 1927, folder 346; G.E. Lineberry to WLP, November 18, 1927, folder 223; and minutes from "Convention Meeting of Board," November 16, 1927, folder 105, Poteat Papers.

17. WLP to J.C. Shelburne, May 13, 1933, folder 360 (first quote); WLP to Hamilton Holt, October 25, 1935, folder 182 (second quote); WLP to Coy Muckle, March 18, 1933, folder 252; WLP to Mrs. L.D. Bulluck [*sic*], February 3, 1928, folder 15; WLP to Judge I.M. Meekins, August 15, 1933, folder 262; WLP to Mary S. Covington, June 20, 1928, folder 71; WLP to W.B. Saunders Company, August 10, 1937, folder 364; and clipping "Poteat Goes On Teaching after 57 Crowded Years," scrapbook, folder 1238, Poteat Papers.

18. Statistics on Wake Forest grades, folder 436; and class lecture notes from 1927–28, folder 769, Poteat Papers.

19. WLP to Kyle M. Yates, March 30, 1934, folder 470 (first quote); WLP to Walter F. Taylor, December 15, 1927, folder 413 (second quote); clipping, "Dr. Poteat, Nearing 81, Says Repeal Will Be Short-Lived," scrapbook, folder 1239 (third quote); WLP to Ben L. Rose, November 26, 1928, folder 357; WLP to *Harpers Magazine,* November 5, 1934, folder 143; and WLP to the *New Republic,* January 28, 1929, folder 288. For science books see his orders for books. WLP to Standard Book Company, November 17, 1928, folder 361; WLP to the Baker & Taylor Company, July 3, 1936, folder 17; WLP to the Baker & Taylor Company, December 1, 1927, folder 14; WLP to Ethel Crittenden, March 13, 1929, folder 77; and WLP to the Missouri Store Company, September 7, 1936, folder 251. On election as an AAAS fellow see Henry B. Ward to WLP, August 26, 1933, folder 442. On correspondence with other scientists see WLP to Percy L. Johnson, June 19, 1931, folder 198; WLP to Bert Cunningham, September 19, 1931, folder 82; and W.C. Coker to WLP, October 5, 1928, folder 47. All in Poteat Papers. On activities with the academy see WLP to H.R. Totten, April 4, 1928, folder 418, Poteat Papers; "Proceedings of the Twenty-Seventh Annual Meeting of the North Carolina Academy of Science," *JEMSS* 44 (September 1928): 12; "Proceedings of the Twenty-Eighth Annual Meeting of the North Carolina Academy of Science," *JEMSS* 45 (November 1929): 11; "Proceedings of the Twenty-Ninth Annual Meeting of the North Carolina Academy of Science," *JEMSS* 46 (November 1930): 7; "Proceedings of the Thirtieth Annual Meeting of the North Carolina Academy of Science," *JEMSS* 47 (January 1932): 7, 9, and 10; and "Proceedings of the Thirty-First Annual Meeting of the North Carolina Academy of Science," *JEMSS* 48 (October 1932): 1, 4, and 12.

20. Thomas Dixon to WLP, March 27, 1934, folder 98 (first quote); EP to WLP, May 13, 1936, (second quote); WLP to EP, August 13, 1936, (third quote); EP to WLP, [February 1928] (picture on shelf); and various letters between 1928 and 1936 demonstrating visits to and from children and grandchildren, as well as showing Emma's frequent sickness and reliance on her husband, all in folder 1167; Walter Lippmann to WLP, October 26, 1936, folder 244; Poteat, "Memoirs"; WLP to Leroy Allen, December 19, 1933, folder 3; WLP to J.M. Culbreth, July 11, 1929, folder 80; and Mack Grogan to WLP, December 28, 1932, folder 125. Pride in their children is obvious in "To our wandering children," a short letter dated May 23, 1935, from

"Mother and Father," folder 314; and in WLP to Mrs. Ashcraft, August 6, 1932, folder 3. Poteat even bought a share of stock for grandson Wheeler Martin Jr. (WLP to Mrs. Vella A. Wynne, January 31, 1930, folder 468). Hubert Poteat, a graduate of Columbia University, also had connections in New York that helped his father and mother do such things as hear Harry Emerson Fosdick preach. ([James F. Hoge] to Hubert Poteat, December 17, 1935, folder 144). For five grandchildren see WLP to W.T. Jordan, February 5, 1932, folder 198. All in Poteat Papers.

21. WLP to Frank H. Leavell, September 18, 1933, folder 236, Poteat Papers.

22. EP to WLP, [August 1934], folder 1167; WLP to J.M. Culbreth, July 11, 1929, folder 80; and WLP to W.D. Weatherford, July 8, 1930, folder 446, Poteat Papers.

23. On Forest Home's dilapidation see C.A. Martin to Caswell Insurance & Realty Co., March 6, 1928, folder 251; on Poteat's lack of attachment to his Caswell County property see Douglass Poteat to WLP, July 12, 1937, folder 335; on tenant using the home see WLP to W.H. Mise, February 14, 1928, folder 267; on preparations for the sale see WLP to Atwood and Nash, December 3, 1927, folder 3; and on Poteat's assessment that the restored home was "one beautiful place" see WLP to W.T. Jordan, February 5, 1932, folder 198. Poteat's pleasure in visiting Helen there is obvious in "Memoirs"; and in Laurence Stallings, "Sunday Visitor," typescript labeled as from *New York Sun,* May 13, 1932, folder 536. On Forest Home rebuilding see "Stallings' Home Nears Completion," clipping in scrapbook, folder 1238. See also WLP to Baker & Taylor Company, February 16, 1929, folder 14; and for Poteat's summary of Stallings's career see WLP to Jeannette C. Gregory, February 16, 1935, folder 125. All in Poteat Papers.

24. WLP to Robert H. McNeill, May 9, 1928, folder 287 (quote); and Poteat, "Memoirs." Poteat's reflective mood is apparent in that he even found time to write "a little slave-time story" for a friend. WLP to Tom Henderson, March 13, 1937, folder 148. All in Poteat Papers.

25. Poteat, "An Intellectual Adventure: A Human Document," *American Scholar,* 280–86; and Chase to WLP, January 15 and 25, 1935, folder 46, Poteat Papers. In his usual confident, fastidious way, Poteat negotiated even the slightest change in his wording by the editor. Ruth E. Campbell to WLP, March 18, 1935; and WLP to Campbell, March 21, 1935, folder 9, Poteat Papers.

26. WLP to Mrs. L.D. Bullock, February 24, 1928, folder 15 (first quote); WLP to Frederick Lent, February 23, 1929, folder 238 (second quote); "General Education Board: Study of Faculty Salaries in Colleges and Universities," survey completed by Poteat, folder 3 (third quote); WLP to W.B. Edwards, July 9, 1934, folder 107 (fourth quote); WLP to Minerva Jones, January 29, 1930, folder 198 (fifth quote); WLP to the sixth grade, January 5, 1929, folder 436; Mrs. William Speas to WLP, September 18, 1936, folder 392; T.B. Attmore to WLP, May 22, 1929, folder 3; H.B. Branch to WLP, May 1, 1933, folder 15; King D. Brown to WLP, February 12, 1935, folder 15; WLP to Mrs. J.R. Bennett, March 16, 1929, folder 14; F.B. Bishop to WLP, January 16, 1930, folder 14; W.S. Allen to WLP, April 8, 1937, folder 8; and T. Wingate Andrews to WLP, June 8, 1928, folder 12, Poteat Papers.

27. Poteat, untitled typescript of his "impressions" of the trip, folder 83 (first quote); poem, "An Itinerary," July 23, 1931, folder 682 (quoted lines); clipping, "Dr. W.L. Poteat Fifty Years Wed," scrapbook, folder 1238; and for trip plans see correspondence with John J. Wicker of Wicker Tours, Inc., in folder 457, Poteat Papers.

28. Baxter Durham to WLP, September 22, 1933, folder 84; Jay Anderson to WLP, October 26, 1932, folder 3; E.B. Earnshaw to WLP, June 7, 1928, folder 106; E.B. Earnshaw announcement of delegates, November 14, 1932, folder 106; "Mrs. John F. Lanneau: A Minute Adopted by the Wake Forest Missionary Society," folder 664; and WLP to Wade D. Bostic, March 30, 1934, folder 28a. See also clippings "Deserved Rest" and "Members of Choir for Half a Century," scrapbook, folder 1238. All in Poteat Papers.

29. The annuals of the Baptist State Convention list the membership of the boards of trustees for the denomination's institutions.

30. WLP to [E.?]C. Simpson, October 8, 1927, folder 360 (first quote); WLP to Lee M. White, January 16, 1928, folder 436 (second quote); WLP to J.L. Jones, March 5, 1928, folder 198 (third and fourth quotes); speaking notes, "Centennial Program," October 9, 1927, folder 785 (fifth quote); Poteat, "Growth of Education, 1830–1930," in *BR,* April 2, 1930, clipping in

folder 891 (final quote); W.R. Cullom and others to Wake Forest faculty, October 4, 1927, folder 81; W.C. Barrett to WLP, July 20, 1927, folder 14; Walter M. Gilmore to WLP, December 12, 1929, folder 130; "Report of the Centennial Committee to the Baptist State Convention," folder 784; M.A. Huggins to WLP, January 25, 1928, folder 187; and "News Letter No. 1," N.C. Baptist Centennial Campaign, October 7, 1927, folder 1233. Meredith College continued to be troubled by debts well into the depression. See for example "To the Members of the Board of Trustees of Meredith College," September 18, 1931, folder 191. All in Poteat Papers. See also Baptist State Convention, *Annual . . . 1927,* 45–46, and *1928,* 35–38.

31. Chapel speaking notes dated May 22, 1928, folder 1131; J.M. Broughton to WLP, February 15, 1930, folder 37; WLP to Mrs. A.E. Tate, February 25, 1928, folder 406; WLP to Louis R. Wilson, November 7, 1931, folder 460; WLP to J.A. McKaughan, January 2, 1928, folder 278; WLP to E.F. Upchurch, July 21, 1930, folder 301; WLP to Meta Glass, November 7, 1931, folder 125; WLP to Fellow Alumnus, August 1, 1930, folder 3; WLP to E.B. Earnshaw, August 1, 1933, folder 106; Earnshaw to WLP, September 27, 1933, folder 106; WLP to Claude Gore, July 14, 1933, folder 125; WLP to Thurman D. Kitchin, May 11, 1935, folder 218; Poteat, "Greetings to Guilford College on its Hundredth Anniversary, May 24, 1937," folder 890; Poteat, "Inauguration of President Lingle, Davidson College, Greetings from the Church Colleges," folder 930; clipping, "Seventy-fifth Anniversary of Mars Hill," folder 940; John R. Sampey to WLP, February 26, 1929, folder 362; WLP to Sampey, May 6, 1931, folder 362; WLP to Rufus W. Weaver, December 19, 1927, and April 13, 1928, folder 449; draft report, "Junior Colleges," folder 449; Charles E. Johnson to WLP, February 6, 1933, folder 198; Charles E. Maddry to WLP, November 14, 1931, folder 253; and Charles E. Maddry to Fellow Burden Bearer, undated, folder 253, Poteat Papers; and Baptist State Convention, *Annual . . . 1933,* 29–35.

32. Francis P. Gaines to Every Alumnus of Wake Forest College, February 26, 1930, folder 126, Poteat Papers.

33. Arthur S. Link, "The First Century of Medical Education at Wake Forest," draft typescript in author's possession. Quoted on p. 41 (first quote) and p. 40 (second quote).

34. Link, "First Century," 30.

35. WLP to Walter F. Taylor, January 1, 1929, folder 413, Poteat Papers.

36. WLP to Frank Hobgood, June 14, 1930, folder 144, Poteat Papers.

37. WLP to T.F. Pettus, June 19, 1930, folder 327, Poteat Papers.

38. WLP to W.L. Foushee, June 14, 1930, folder 121, Poteat Papers.

39. Hudson, "Interview."

40. WLP to Walter F. Taylor, July 3, 1930, folder 411, Poteat Papers.

41. WLP to Kitchin, July 2, 1930, folder 218, Poteat Papers.

42. WLP to Hubert Poteat, July 14, 1930, folder 1171 (quote); WLP to John E. White, July 29, 1930, folder 452; WLP to Lester P. Martin, July 8, 1930, folder 257; and WLP to Carroll R. Holmes, July 8, 1930, folder 180, Poteat Papers.

43. J.S. Farmer to WLP, August 21, 1936, folder 114 (first and second quotes); D.B. Bryan to WLP, July 11, 1936, folder 42 (third and fourth quotes); and WLP to D.B. Bryan, July 13, 1936, folder 42, Poteat Papers.

44. Poteat, "A Friendly Private Word to the Editor," August 7, 1936, folder 15, Poteat Papers.

45. Irving Carlyle to WLP, September 3, 1936, folder 52 (first quote); WLP to Frank P. Hobgood, September 17, 1936, folder 173 (second quote); Hobgood to WLP, August 25, 1936, folder 173; J.S. Farmer to WLP, August 21, 1936, folder 114; and H.T. Hunter to WLP, August 13, 1936, folder 190, Poteat Papers.

46. As historian Paul Harvey notes, "In the 1920s, denominational conservatives perceived that they had lost the culture war to preserve an America dominated by a conservative Protestant morality. But they in fact had won the struggle to define their own denomination. In future years, voices for progressive change often went unheard" (*Redeeming the South*, 226).

47. Nell Battle Lewis, "North Carolina's Leading Liberal: The Odyssey of William Louis Poteat of Wake Forest," *Winston-Salem Journal,* July 3, 1927.

48. On southern Progressivism see Tindall, *Emergence of the New South*; Grantham, *Southern Progressivism*; and Link, *Paradox of Progressivism*.

49. M.C.S. Noble Jr. to WLP, November 26, 1930, folder 298 (first quote); WLP to Edwin Bjorkman, February 8, 1936, folder 14 (second quote); John J. Blair to WLP, October 6, 1927, folder 14; Eric M. North and George W. Brown to WLP, September 9, 1935, folder 15; "Prospectus of *The Golden Age*, A New Magazine for Children," pamphlet, folder 125; Oscar Haywood to WLP, March 1, 1928, folder 143; WLP to Governor O. Max Gardner, July 21, 1930, and April 24, 1931, folder 128, Poteat Papers; and WLP to Mrs. Gregory, January 10, 1930, Edwin Clarke Gregory Papers, Special Collections, Perkins Library, Duke University (third quote).

50. WLP to [?]B. Jeffries, December [?], 1931, folder 198; J.J. Moore to WLP, October 20, 1934, folder 252; William R. Kanarr to WLP, October 8, 1934, folder 208; and C.N. Sisson to WLP, January 14, 1930, folder 223, Poteat Papers.

51. Draft of telegram from WLP to Hinsdale written on telegram from R.L. Randolph and J.O. Purnell to WLP, March 12, 1931, urging him to action on the issue, folder 143 (first quote); WLP to J.W. Bailey, June 10, 1933 (other quotes), and July 11, 1933, folder 17; and Leroy Martin to WLP, July 7, 1933, folder 251, Poteat Papers.

52. WLP to Frank Porter Graham (hereafter cited as FPG), October 27, 1928 (quote), and FPG to WLP, October 29, 1928, Frank Porter Graham Papers, Southern Historical Collection; FPG to WLP, October 25, 1928, and August 7, 1928, folder 136; and Frank P. Hobgood to Co-Worker, April 25, 1934, folder 173, Poteat Papers.

53. FPG to WLP, January 21, 1929, box 12, NCCSS Papers; Harriet L. Herring to Friends of Social Service, January 9, 1929, folder 143 (first quote); FPG to WLP, June 5, 1928, and April 3, 1930 (last quote), folder 136; WLP to FPG, January 14 and 25, 1929, folder 136; Gertrude Weil to WLP, January 29, 1929, folder 451; S.H. Hobbs Jr. to WLP, October 20, 1932, folder 144; WLP to Mrs. W.T. Bost, January 19, 1938, folder 15; and Bulus B. Swift to WLP, July 7, 1930, folder 405, Poteat Papers. For Poteat and League of Women Voters see letterhead on Bulus B. Swift to FPG, July 2, 1930, Graham Papers. On shift toward industrial problems see Gulledge, *North Carolina Conference*, 36. For list of presidents and their terms see *Proceedings of the Golden Anniversary Meeting: North Carolina Conference for Social Service* (Raleigh, 1962), 84. See also "Frank Porter Graham," q.v. Powell, ed., *Dictionary of North Carolina Biography*, 2:332–33.

54. Branson to WLP, December 6, 1931, folder 15, Poteat Papers.

55. FPG to WLP, October 28, 1936, folder 136, Poteat Papers (quote); and WLP to FPG, November 6, 1936, Graham Papers. On football see WLP to FPG, September 25, 1930, and September 24, 1931; and FPG to WLP, November 8, 1933, Graham Papers.

56. "Report of the Monday Session of the Chapel Hill Conference," November 9, 1936, Graham Papers.

57. Unlabeled speaking notes, folder 1160, Poteat Papers.

58. "The Citizen and His City," undated speech notes from the 1920s, folder 820, Poteat Papers.

59. "The Economic Use of Public Funds," typed speech manuscript, November 11, 1926, folder 852; and untitled speech notes on Blue Ridge stationery, folder 1160 (quotes in sentence with "shallow theory"), Poteat Papers.

60. "Independence Day," speech manuscript, July 4, 1929, folder 872, Poteat Papers.

61. Poteat, *Can a Man Be a Christian To-day?*, 28–29.

62. "What North Carolina Needs," clipping, folder 958, Poteat Papers.

63. WLP to Lucy Hays Furman, November 25, 1929, folder 113, Poteat Papers. They were likely referring to W.J. Cash's article, "The Mind of the South," in H.L. Mencken's *American Mercury* 18 (October 1929): 185–92.

64. WLP to Dean Addison Hibbard, June 27, 1929, folder 164, Poteat Papers.

65. Typed abstract of address, "The Young Man of Nazareth," May 31, 1936, folder 1156 (last quote); and typed address, "Presenting the Mayflower Cup," December 2, 1932, folder 942 (other quotes), Poteat Papers.

66. WLP to Alex Seawell, January 11, 1935, folder 360, Poteat Papers.

67. Clipping from *Jacksonville Florida Times-Union*, June 10, 1925, folder 873, Poteat Papers.

68. Clipping labeled *N&O*, November 19, 1931, titled "Morning Tonic," folder 958, Poteat Papers.

69. WLP to Charles G. Rose, October 20, 1928, folder 357 (quote); Aubrey A. Perkins to WLP, October 25, 1928, folder 313; "Christian Ethics," notes in notebook dated July 1928, folder 922, Poteat Papers; and Poteat, *The Way of Victory* (Chapel Hill, 1929), [v].

70. WLP to Lippmann, May 13, 1929, folder 244, Poteat Papers.

71. Poteat, *Way of Victory*, 4 (first quote) and 2 (second quote).

72. Ibid., 8 (first and second quotes), 11 (third quote), 22 (fourth quote), and 44 (fifth and sixth quotes).

73. *Richmond Religious Herald*, November 28, 1935, clipping in folder 1015, Poteat Papers.

74. Poteat, *Way of Victory*, 63.

75. Clipping, "Poteat Heard at Tabernacle," folder 538 (first quote); and speech notes, "The Jesus Way," folder 911 (other quotes), Poteat Papers.

76. *BR*, December 9, 1931. See also WLP to Alexander W. McAlister, December 3, 1931, folder 395, Alexander W. McAlister Papers, Southern Historical Collection.

77. Speech notes, "Christianity and Business," August 6, 1930, folder 809, Poteat Papers.

78. *BR*, July 1, 1931.

79. Full text of speech in *Winston-Salem Journal*, clipping labeled November 6, 1931, folder 1081; and Edgar W. Knight to WLP, September 17, 1931, folder 220, Poteat Papers.

80. *Richmond Religious Herald*, November 28, 1935.

81. Poteat, *The Prophet Confronts His World*, pamphlet reprint from the January 1937 issue of the *Review and Expositor* (copy in Special Collections, Reynolds Library), 10.

82. Harriet L. Herring to WLP, January 28, 1929, folder 136; and FPG to WLP, January 31, 1929, folder 136, Poteat Papers.

83. John A. Salmond, *Gastonia 1929: The Story of the Loray Mill Strike* (Chapel Hill and London, 1995), esp. chaps. 2 and 5; and Egerton, *Speak Now*, 71–72.

84. Salmond, *Gastonia 1929*, 77–78; Lewis to WLP, July 13, 1929, folder 242; and WLP to Lewis, July 15, 1929, folder 242 (quote), Poteat Papers.

85. Clipping from *N&O*, labeled October 27, 1929, folder 538 (quote); and telegram from the *N&O* to WLP, October 26, 1929, folder 288, Poteat Papers.

86. Harry F. Ward to friends of civil liberty in North Carolina, October 9, 1929, folder 442 (quotes); and Harry F. Ward, Roger N. Baldwin, and Forrest Bailey to our friends, December 1929, folder 442, Poteat Papers.

87. Poteat's November 9, 1929, draft of reply written on Harry F. Ward to friends of civil liberty in North Carolina, folder 442 (quote); Ronald J. Tambly to WLP, November 18, 1929, folder 406; and WLP to FPG, December 13, 1929, folder 136, Poteat Papers.

88. Baptist State Convention, *Annual . . . 1929*, 47–48 (quotes); clipping, "Their House in Order," reprinted from *Charlotte News* and labeled *BR*, November 27, 1929, folder 1018; and FPG to WLP, January 14, 1930, folder 136, Poteat Papers. See also WLP to John W. Clark, November 25, 1929, folder 46, Poteat Papers.

89. FPG to WLP, December 12, 1929 (first quote), and January 10, 1930; and WLP to FPG, December 13, 1929 (second quote), all in folder 136, Poteat Papers.

90. FPG to Roger N. Baldwin, January 4, 1930, copy in folder 136 (quote); FPG to WLP, December 16, 1929, folder 136; and FPG to the Four Hundred Signers of the Statement, April 3, 1930, folder 136, Poteat Papers. Mrs. T.W. Bickett introduced a resolution to the NCCSS endorsing the statement. See report of resolutions committee, 1930, in box 1, NCCSS Papers.

91. FPG to WLP, January 10, 1930 (first quote); and "Statement in final, revised form" (other quotes), both in folder 136, Poteat Papers.

92. WLP to Senator F.M. Simmons, July 17, 1929, folder 377 (first quote); and WLP to the editor of the *World*, September 2, 1929, folder 436 (second quote), Poteat Papers.

93. *N&O*, February 4, 1934 (first three quotes); clipping, "Educators Chose as Assistants to Utility Director," scrapbook, folder 1238 (last quote); Ehringhaus to WLP, January 12, 1934, folder 108; WLP to Ehringhaus, January 9, 1934, and February 12, 1934, folder 108; WLP to Richard E. Reeves, February 6, 1933, folder 192; WLP to Fred. W. Reebals, October 26, 1927, folder 346; and WLP to Mr. Lumsden [?], October 19, 1928, folder 223. See also various clippings in folder 710. All in Poteat Papers.

94. Thomas R. Pegram, "Temperance Politics and Regional Political Culture: The Anti-Saloon League in Maryland and the South, 1907–1915," *Journal of Southern History* 63 (February 1997): 57–90; and Link, *Paradox of Southern Progressivism*.

95. Whitener, *Prohibition in North Carolina*, 182–92 (quote on 184).

96. Ibid., 193–96.

97. C.A. Upchurch to WLP, September 6, 1927, folder 301, Poteat Papers.

98. WLP to Senator Royal S. Copeland, January 7, 1928, folder 68, Poteat Papers.

99. WLP to Tyree C. Taylor, October 5, 1928, folder 406 (first quote); and WLP to J.W. Bailey, January 30, 1929, folder 17 (second quote), Poteat Papers. See also WLP to the editor of the *New York Times,* February 23, 1932, folder 288, Poteat Papers.

100. Special to *New York Times,* May 1928, clipping titled "Discounts Bolt in South," folder 538, Poteat Papers.

101. Poteat's notes written on Butler Pruette to WLP, March 24, 1930, folder 314, Poteat Papers.

102. Speech abstracts, "The Tenth Anniversary of Prohibition," January 26, 1930, Winston-Salem, N.C., at Auditorium Theater (first quote), and same title and date at Home Moravian Church (other quotes), folder 685; and C.A. Upchurch to WLP, January 29, 1930, folder 301, Poteat Papers.

103. WLP to Thomas H. Steele, February 20, 1931, folder 361, Poteat Papers. See also WLP to Joshua Levering, February 20, 1931, folder 240, Poteat Papers.

104. J.A. Hartness to WLP, January 23, 1931; Memorandum by C.A. Upchurch, January 19, 1931; and W.T. Shaw to WLP, January 7, 1931, all in folder 301, Poteat Papers.

105. WLP to F. Scott McBride, January 15, 1931 (quote); and McBride to WLP, December 17, 1930, folder 278, Poteat Papers.

106. Clipping, "Morrison's Stand for Dry Laws Is Praised," labeled *N&O,* June 19, 1932, folder 259 (quote); "An Appeal to the Moral Forces of North Carolina to Give Their Support to Hon. Cameron Morrison, In the Democratic Primary on July 2nd 1932," folder 275; campaign leaflet, "To Your Tents, O Israel!," signed by Poteat and others, folder 251; WLP to A.J. Barton, April 21, 1932, folder 20; clipping from January 1932 titled "Dr. W.L. Poteat," folder 65; George J. Burnett to WLP, September 15, 1932, folder 301, Poteat Papers; and Whitener, *Prohibition in North Carolina,* 195–97.

107. Speech abstract, "The Challenge," September 13, 1932, folder 786, Poteat Papers.

108. WLP to the editor, June 29, 1932, folder 689 (quote); and clipping labeled *N&O,* June 17, 1932, "Dr. W.L. Poteat Issues Prohibition Challenge," folder 687, Poteat Papers.

109. Clipping labeled November 7, 1932, titled "Baptists Reiterate Prohibition," folder 252; C.B. Deane to WLP and others, November 23, 1932, folder 84; WLP for the committee to the President, December 3, 1932, folder 184; WLP for the committee to Robert R. Reynolds and others, December 3, 1932, folder 17 and folder 689; and WLP for the committee to Roosevelt, December 3, 1932, folder 356, Poteat Papers.

110. Typescript, folder 685; WLP to friend, June 8, 1933, folder 406, Poteat Papers; and Whitener, *Prohibition in North Carolina,* 200–201.

111. WLP to J.W. Bailey, January 24, 1933, folder 17, Poteat Papers.

112. Poteat, "The Old Beak and Claws," typescript, folder 685 (first quote); WLP to James M. Northington, August 7, 1933, folder 302 (second quote); clipping, "Drys Are Ready for Stiff Fight," labeled June, 23, 1933, folder 687; clipping, "United Dry Forces Lay Intensive Campaign Plan," labeled July 12, 1933, folder 687; Cale K. Burgess to WLP, August 14, 1933, folder 709; Dorothy Evans to WLP, August 25, 1933, folder 105; and Burgess to WLP, October 4, 1933, folder 44, Poteat Papers.

113. Cale K. Burgess to WLP, October 16, 1933, folder 44; "United Dry Forces Weekly Release No. 6," October 23, 1933, folder 709; and S.L. Morgan to WLP, October 26, 1933, folder 273, Poteat Papers.

114. Burgess to Zeno Wall, November 14, 1933, folder 44, Poteat Papers (quote); and Whitener, *Prohibition in North Carolina,* 205.

115. WLP to G.W. Crabbe, December 16, 1933, folder 72, Poteat Papers.

116. Cale K. Burgess to friend, January 2, 1934, folder 44 (quote); Burgess to county chairmen, January 22, 1934, folder 428; and "Meeting of Board of Trustees and Meeting of Executive Committee of the United Dry Forces, March 20, 1934," typed minutes, folder 709, Poteat Papers.

117. Speech manuscript, "North Carolina To Maryland," January 21, 1934, folder 685, Poteat Papers.

118. Poteat, "The Proposed Liquor Referendum," February 9, 1935, folder 685 (quote); Cale K. Burgess to WLP, February 21 and March 4 and 22, 1935, folder 44; and WLP to Carroll W. Weathers, February 3, 1935, folder 447, Poteat Papers.

119. WLP to A.J. Barton, January 29, 1935, folder 20, Poteat Papers.

120. Whitener, *Prohibition in North Carolina,* 208–14.

121. WLP to I.N. Carr, November 28, 1933, folder 46 (first quote); WLP to John L. Hill, January 7, 1935, folder 167 (second quote); WLP to Hill, October 8, 1934, folder 167; Jaques Cattell to WLP, September 26, 1934, folder 46; royalty statement, May 22, 1936, folder 690; WLP to Hill, November 16, 1935, folder 167; and various review clippings in folder 1089, Poteat Papers. Poteat tried to use the influence of his daughter and her husband in New York to get the manuscript published by a national press but to no avail. In pleading for their help, he noted, "I do not forget that you and L[aurence] have a different attitude toward the control of liquor traffic from mine but you might at least look at my statement. You will not be embarrassed to write me frankly about my suggestion" (WLP to Helen Stallings, October 2, 1934, folder 1179, Poteat Papers).

122. Poteat, *Stop-light* (Nashville, 1935), 7 (first quote), 8 (second quote), and 49 (fourth quote); and review clipping labeled *Journal of the American Medical Association,* May 1936, folder 1089, Poteat Papers (third quote).

123. Poteat, *Stop-light,* 81 (first quote) and 88 (second quote).

124. Cale K. Burgess to WLP, May 21, 1936, folder 709 (first quote); clipping labeled *N&O,* April 11, 1936, "Poteat Summons Drys to Battle," folder 709 (second quote); WLP to Burgess, December 19, 1936, folder 44 (third quote); and Burgess to WLP, April 23 and May 8, 1936, folder 709, Poteat Papers.

125. WLP to Richard Lloyd, January 7, 1937, folder 223 (first quote); *Rockingham Post-Dispatch,* December 31, 1936, clipping in folder 709 (second quote); WLP to Wade H. James, February 13, 1937, folder 198 (third quote); WLP to Cale K. Burgess, December 30, 1936, folder 44; WLP to James M. Northington, January 1, 1937, folder 302; speech notes, "The Liquor Issue," January 28, 1937, folder 931; speech notes, "Hearing before Senate Committee," February 11, 1937, folder 1014; Burgess to WLP, February 12, 1937, folder 44; WLP to Governor Clyde R. Hoey, February 15, 1937, folder 177; WLP to J. Clyde Turner, February 13, 1937, folder 423, Poteat Papers; and Whitener, *Prohibition in North Carolina,* 214–20.

126. WLP to Luther Little, February 19, 1937, folder 223 (quote); "Wake County and Liquor Stores, Radio Talk by William Louis Poteat," June 21, 1937, folder 1111; and speech notes, "Wet or Dry," June 20, 1937, folder 1140, Poteat Papers.

127. Clipping, "Dr. Poteat, Nearing 81, Says Repeal Will Be Short-Lived."

128. Clipping, "Dr. Poteat's Address at Duke," labeled February 16, 1928, folder 764, Poteat Papers.

129. Typescript of press release, Wake Forest, July 23, 1924, folder 715 (1924 quotes); and clipping, "Brotherhood Urged As Means of Solving International Strife," labeled March 20, 1927, folder 909, Poteat Papers.

130. "Danger of Forgetting Is Seen by Dr. Poteat," *Greensboro Daily News,* November 13, 1927, clipping in folder 753 (first three quotes); WLP to William B. Umstead, October 26,

1927, folder 429 (other quotes); and clipping, "For Militarist-Pacifist Extremes, Happy Mean Is Advocated by Dr. Poteat," folder 764, Poteat Papers.

131. *Winston-Salem Journal,* November 18, 1927, clipping in folder 251, Poteat Papers.

132. Clipping, "Baptists Would Outlaw War and Curtail Training," with Poteat's marginalia indicating that he wrote the resolution, folder 909, Poteat Papers.

133. WLP to Arnold Jenny, November 18, 1927, folder 198, Poteat Papers.

134. "Sherwood Eddy Answers Legion," clipping from *N&O,* January 18, 1928, folder 922; and J.A. Ellis to Edward E. Spafford, January 31, 1928, copy in folder 215, Poteat Papers.

135. Speech abstract, "The Big Naval Program," February 9, 1928, folder 764 (first quote); and "Forward Observation Post," clipping in folder 764 (other quotes), Poteat Papers.

136. WLP to Helen Flemming, March 2, 1929, folder 113 (first quote); WLP to F.M. Simmons, February 18, 1928, folder 377 (second and third quotes); Simmons to WLP, March 7, 1928, folder 377; WLP to Calvin Coolidge, December 2, 1928, folder 66 (fourth quote); clipping from *Morning Post* (London), January 12, 1929, "Aloof from Intelligence," folder 538 (fifth quote); and WLP to J.W. Bailey, February 16, 1935, folder 17, Poteat Papers; and Baptist State Convention, *Annual . . . 1929,* 51. See also Baptist State Convention, *Annual . . . 1931,* 51–52.

137. WLP to Ralph E. Mollner, June 7, 1936, folder 299, Poteat Papers.

138. Clipping, "Labels," from *BR,* September 16, 1931, folder 917, Poteat Papers.

139. Paul Kern and Elbert Russell to WLP, February 29, 1936, folder 208, Poteat Papers.

140. Abstract of speech, "The Threat of War," May 5, 1936, folder 1099 (quotes); Allan Knight Chalmers to WLP, May 15, 1936, folder 46; Chester M. Tobin to WLP, March 16, 1937, folder 406; and WLP to Ray Newton, December 18, 1937, folder 288, Poteat Papers.

141. "The Influence of Public Health and Education upon the Development of the Human Race," *Southern Medicine and Surgery* 92 (June 1930): 396–99 (quotes on 397 and 398). This is Poteat's best statement of his support of eugenics. He presented similar ideas numerous times.

142. Ibid., 398–99.

143. Ibid., 399.

144. Ibid.

145. Clipping labeled *Raleigh Times,* February 27, 1929, folder 538, Poteat Papers.

146. Ibid.

147. Clipping labeled *Raleigh Times,* February 16, 1928, folder 993, Poteat Papers.

148. "Isn't Race Improving?," clipping from *Greensboro Daily News,* labeled May 3, 1930, folder 538, Poteat Papers.

149. Mabel L. Haynes to WLP, March 6, 1929, and WLP to Haynes, March 16, 1929, both in folder 146, Poteat Papers.

150. Speech notes, "Relation of Sexes," May 1, 1927, folder 1077, Poteat Papers.

151. Clipping labeled *Raleigh Times,* February 27, 1929, folder 538, Poteat Papers.

152. Speech abstract, "The Plasticity of Youth," April 18, 1928, folder 1006, Poteat Papers.

153. Speech notes, "Science and Public Affairs," October 11, 1933, folder 1059, Poteat Papers.

154. Clipping, "Dr. Poteat Speaker at Final Exercises Durham High School," labeled May 29, 1926, folder 972, Poteat Papers.

155. Speech manuscript, "Fearfully and Wonderfully Made," December 18, 1936, folder 868, Poteat Papers.

156. Speech abstract, "The Standard Man," October 5, 1928, folder 1086, Poteat Papers.

157. Speech abstract, "The Plasticity of Youth" (quote); and A.W. McAlister to WLP, September 18, 1931, folder 279, Poteat Papers.

158. WLP to James M. Parrott, January 21, 1932, folder 313; Parrott to WLP, January 22, 1932, folder 672; WLP to Guion G. Johnson, February 9, 1932, folder 198; Johnson to WLP, February 12, 1932, folder 672; W.A. Mickle to WLP written on WLP to Sir, March 2, 1932, folder 672; and Mrs. Eva W. Floyd to WLP on WLP to Sir, March 2, 1932, folder 672, Poteat Papers.

159. Poteat, "Marriage and Divorce," presented at the NCCSS, April 26, 1932, folder

939. Poteat also cooperated with a member of the school of law at Chapel Hill who was charged with the duty of writing conference ideas into legislation to be proposed. See WLP to Frank W. Hanft, February 11, 1933, folder 148, Poteat Papers.

160. WLP to George M. Cooper, March 21, 1936 (quote), and Cooper to WLP, March 19, 1936, both in folder 67; and Harry W. Crane to WLP, February 4, 1934, and December 31, 1936, folder 47, Poteat Papers. See also Ethel M. Speas, *Voluntary Mental Health Movement*, 11–13 (Copy in NCMHA Papers.

161. E.S. Gosney to WLP, December 29, 1931, folder 134 (quote); and Gosney to WLP, November 5, 1932, folder 125, Poteat Papers.

162. Poteat, "Reformers," clipping labeled *BR,* April 27, 1932, folder 1033, Poteat Papers.

163. Santford Martin to WLP, June 25, 1930, folder 258, Poteat Papers.

164. WLP to Martin, July 4, 1930, folder 258, Poteat Papers. On Parker see WLP to Lee S. Overman, April 12, 1930, folder 310, Poteat Papers. The NAACP vigorously and successfully opposed Parker's confirmation by the Senate. Poteat wrote, "Another consideration urged by Negroes, I believe, is even less impressive. If they should carry their point and upon that particular point should defeat Judge Parker, I wonder if it would not accentuate the race issue in politics and otherwise react unfavorably upon them. Besides, Judge Parker is an honorable and fair-minded man, and I cannot bring myself to believe that in any sense or degree he is unfriendly to the Negroes of our State or country, or would deny them their rights under the Constitution." Organized labor also opposed Parker because of his opinions that favored corporations, but Poteat revealed again his deep sympathy with corporate values when faced with the alternative of mass activism. Poteat wrote, "I have wondered how many lawyers of distinction in the country have not at some time appeared for corporations, and whether corporations never have standing or rights in court, and so must invariably look for nothing in their favor except as they are able to 'influence' the trial judge." See Kenneth W. Goings, *"The NAACP Comes of Age": The Defeat of Judge John J. Parker* (Bloomington and Indianapolis, 1990), chap. 2; and Richard L. Watson Jr., "The Defeat of Judge Parker: A Study in Pressure Groups and Politics," *Mississippi Valley Historical Review* 50 (September 1963): 213–34.

165. WLP to A.H. George, February 23, 1928, folder 125 (quote); Governor John C.B. Ehringhaus to WLP, January 5, 1937, folder 108; [Albon?] L. Holsey to WLP, June 26, 1929, folder 252; and George E. Haynes to WLP, March 18, 1929, folder 157, Poteat Papers.

166. C.E. Wilson to WLP, November 4, 1931, folder 544; draft, "Report on Racialism," folder 340 (first quote); and WLP to Wilson, September 23, 1933, folder 437 (other quotes), Poteat Papers.

167. Clipping from *N&O,* January 23, 1933, titled "Sounds Call to Brotherhood," folder 538, Poteat Papers.

168. Poteat's notes written on Will W. Alexander to members, December 23, 1933, folder 5, Poteat Papers.

169. WLP to Charles Clayton Morrison, June 18, 1931, folder 275, Poteat Papers. That Poteat capitalized *Negro* was itself a liberal statement at this time.

170. W.C. Jackson to WLP, January 7, 1930 (first quote), and December 26, 1929 (second quote), folder 199; list of commission members 1934–35, folder 662; list of members of the stabilization fund, folder 662; "An Announcement," folder 196; L.R. Reynolds to WLP and others, March 28, 1931, folder 349; Will W. Alexander, Henry S. Barnes, Robert R. Moton, and George Foster Peabody to WLP, February 15, 1930, folder 5; and Will W. Alexander to friend, May 5, 1936, folder 5, Poteat Papers.

171. "Annual Meeting . . . 1934: Report of North Carolina and Virginia," folder 359 (first quote); "Annual Meeting . . . 1933: Report of Executive Director," folder 662 (second quote); executive committee to members, June 26, 1929, folder 199 (third quote); W.C. Jackson to WLP, January 17, 1929 (with enclosure), June 16, 1930, and March 14, 1932, folder 199; L.R. Reynolds to WLP, February 17, 1938, folder 349; Howard W. Odum to WLP, February 24, 1933, folder 307; N.C. Newbold and others to members and friends, [Dec. 1932], folder 199; L.R. Reynolds to WLP and others, March 28, 1931, folder 349; pamphlet, "A Message to the Governor's Committee of Five Hundred Citizens," folder 662; and pamphlet, "Some Recent

Trends in Race Relations," 13–14, folder 662, Poteat Papers. See also L.R. Reynolds, "The Commission on Interracial Cooperation of North Carolina and Virginia," *Southern Workman* 63 (1934): 244–48; and "Annual Meeting, Commission on Interracial Cooperation, April 18–19, 1934: Report of North Carolina and Virginia," CIC Records, reel 53. By 1938 membership was about 1800. See *Going Forward Together through Conference and Cooperation: A Program to Improve Human Relations* (Raleigh, 1938), 4, pamphlet in CIC Records, reel 53. For more on the accomplishments of the state commission in the thirties see "Source Book of Information, Feb. 6, 1928–April 30, '42," North Carolina Commission on Interracial Cooperation Papers.

172. Poteat, "The Inter-racial Commission," September 13, 1931, folder 340, Poteat Papers.

173. Will W. Alexander to WLP, November 30, 1928, folder 5 (first quote); "Report of the Inter-racial Commission, Presented to Shelby Convention, Nov. 14, 1929," folder 910 (other quotes); W.C. Jackson to WLP, October 16, 1928, and March 22, 1929, folder 199; WLP to Jackson, November 27, 1928, folder 199; Will W. Alexander to WLP, November 8, 1928, folder 5; L.R. Reynolds to WLP, December 21, 1928, folder 349; WLP to Reynolds, March 16, 1929, folder 349; Reynolds to WLP, March 19, 1929, folder 349; Jackson to members, July 9, 1929, folder 199; and Walter M. Gilmore to WLP, October 7, 1929, folder 130, Poteat Papers.

174. I. Harding Hughes to friend, September 8, 1930 (with enclosure titled "Some Objectives ..."), folder 199 (first quote from letter, rest from enclosure); Hughes to WLP, February 21, 1930, folder 144; W.C. Jackson to members, July 8, 1929, February 14, 1930, and October 15, 1930, folder 199; and Jackson and Hughes to WLP, January 27, 1930, folder 199, Poteat Papers. See also Baptist State Convention, *Annual . . . 1930,* 35–36.

175. Newspaper clipping, [October 1937], folder 538; and on golf see also WLP to EMP, March 24, 1935, folder 1163; George Blanton to WLP, November 6, 1929, folder 14; James Boyd to WLP, April 29, 1930, folder 31; Maurie B. Cree to WLP, [1928], folder 75; and H.M. Vann to members of the Wake Forest Golf Club, April 1, 1932, folder 433, Poteat Papers.

176. "The Hospital Nightshirt," folder 898 (second and third quotes); scrapbook clipping, folder 1238 (first quote); clipping from *BR* labeled March 6, 1935, folder 538; WLP to J.L. Kesler, March 24, 1935, folder 212 (last quote); and WLP to Dr. Johnston, March 24, 1935, folder 198, Poteat Papers.

177. WLP to Thurman D. Kitchin, July 7, 1935, folder 218 (quote); WLP to M.A. Huggins, December 12, 1936, folder 187; and Huggins to WLP, June 25, 1936, folder 187, Poteat Papers.

178. Poteat, "Memoirs"; telegram from Charles S. Troutman to WLP, folder 406; and clipping from *Winston-Salem Journal,* June 1936, folder 1239, Poteat Papers.

179. Douglass Poteat to WLP, July 10, 1936, folder 335; and "The Rendezvous," folder 682, Poteat Papers.

180. B.W. Fassett to WLP, December 16, 1936, folder 113; and car invoice from Service Chevrolet Company, July 20, 1936, folder 540. For glaucoma see Donnie H. Jones Jr., "Memories of Doctor William Louis Poteat," folder 1253. For student chauffeur see WLP to Rev. C.H. Dicky, March 16, 1929, folder 83; David Morgan to WLP, April 24, 1934, folder 272; and WLP to Rev. William Way, April 5, 1928, folder 436, Poteat Papers.

181. Newspaper clipping, [October 1937], and other clippings, [November 1936], folder 538, Poteat Papers. See also Baptist State Convention, *Annual . . . 1936,* 40.

182. *Winston-Salem Journal,* November 14, 1936, clipping in folder 436, Poteat Papers.

183. Obituary clipping, folder 538, Poteat Papers.

184. Nathan C. Brooks Jr. to WLP, January 20, 1937, folder 35; WLP to E. Norfleet Gardner, July 22, 1937, folder 127 (for session titles); and Poteat's remarks at the funeral of Edwin McNeill Poteat, clipping from the *Baptist Courier,* July 29, 1937, folder 1164, Poteat Papers.

185. WLP to Baptist State Convention, November 15, 1937, folder 14, Poteat Papers.

186. *BR,* March 16, 1938.

187. J.L. Kesler to WLP, November 7, 1937, folder 212; WLP to R.C. Lawrence, October 1, 1937, folder 223; WLP to F. Clyde Tuttle, January 19, 1938, folder 406; undated newspaper clipping from *Richmond Times-Dispatch* and clipping from *Winston-Salem Journal,* November

2, 1937, both in folder 538; and clippings in scrapbook, folder 1239, Poteat Papers. See also *N&O,* October 20, 1937.

188. Robert N. Simms to WLP, November 23, 1937, folder 379, Poteat Papers (quote); Baptist State Convention, *Annual . . . 1937,* 15; and minutes of Wake Forest College faculty meeting, September 6, 1895.

189. See notes on "Christian Brotherhood," December 1927, in notebook, folder 944; and WLP to Dr. Madry [*sic*], April 30, 1931, folder 253, Poteat Papers.

190. All quotes from Poteat, "Christ and Race," published in unpaginated pamphlet form by the Baptist State Convention (Raleigh, 1938), copy in folder 794, Poteat Papers.

191. Letter of reference for Hayward Poole, December 17, 1937, folder 314 (first quote); WLP to Ben Geer, December 4, 1937, folder 129 (second quote); WLP to Raleigh [?], January 4, 1938, folder 340 (third quote); WLP to Heriot Clarkson, Christmas Eve 1937, folder 46; and clipping on Victrola Recording, scrapbook, folder 1239, Poteat Papers.

192. Obituary from *N&O,* clipping in folder 538; and "Address . . . on the occasion of the Funeral of Mrs. John A. Oates," February 29, 1928, pamphlet in folder 978, Poteat Papers.

193. Newspaper clipping, folder 538, Poteat Papers; and *OGB,* March 18, 1938.

194. Clipping, folder 538; *Winston-Salem Journal,* March 14, 1938, clipping in scrapbook, folder 1240; and clipping from *Asheville Times* in scrapbook, folder 1240, Poteat Papers.

195. Josiah Bailey to EP, April 7, 1938; H.L. Blomquist to EP and family, June 1, 1938; Josephus Daniels to EP, March 21, 1938; George W. Truett to EP, March 21, 1938; resolution of United Dry Forces; and various clippings. All in scrapbook, folder 1240. See also folder 570. All in Poteat Papers.

196. Clipping labeled *Richmond Times* and various clippings, folder 1240, Poteat Papers.

Conclusion

1. Egerton, *Speak Now.*

2. Tindall, *Emergence of the New South,* 562.

3. Tindall, *Emergence of the New South,* 636–37; and Singal, *War Within,* 292–93.

4. Wright, *Old South, New South,* 199.

5. Bruce J. Schulman, *From Cotton Belt to Sunbelt: Federal Policy, Economic Development, and the Transformation of the South, 1938–1980* (Durham and London, 1994), 3 (quote) and 53–54.

6. Thomas Dixon to WLP, February 4, 1938, folder 96, Poteat Papers.

7. The great argument for continuity is of course W.J. Cash, *The Mind of the South* (New York, 1941), but extremely valuable for the period of Poteat's life is Howard N. Rabinowitz's recent evidence for some continuity in *The First New South, 1865–1920* (Arlington Heights, Ill., 1992).

8. Boles, *Great Revival,* 125.

9. Numan V. Bartley, *The New South, 1945–1980* (Baton Rouge and London, 1995), Graham quoted on 276 and 275.

10. David Stricklin has published a study tracing a group of Southern Baptist radicals involved in social protest. The group originated with Walter N. Johnson, a Wake Forest graduate of 1899 who found some inspiration in the liberal example of William and Edwin Poteat. See *A Genealogy of Dissent.*

11. Clayton, *Savage Ideal,* 3; Singal, *War Within,* 5; Michael O'Brien, *The Idea of the American South, 1920–1941* (Baltimore and London, 1979); and King, *Southern Renaissance,* chap. 2.

12. Short life sketch by Poteat dated April 22, 1936, folder 538, Poteat Papers.

13. For man on train see Poteat's marginalia on p. 59 of William James, *Selected Papers on Philosophy* (New York, Toronto, and London, 1918), Poteat's copy signed October 1920, in possession of family.

14. Poteat, "Memoirs."

Bibliography

Primary Sources

Manuscript Collections

The bulk of the primary material used in this study is from Special Collections, Reynolds Library, Wake Forest University, Winston-Salem, North Carolina. The William Louis Poteat Papers are an exceptional source containing correspondence, extensive notes and manuscripts for speeches, and a wonderful collection of newspaper and magazine clippings from both secular and denominational publications. Additional material on William Louis Poteat's family is in the McNeill-Poteat Family Papers. I also consulted the Euzelian Society Records, the F.M. Jordan Papers, the Lilburn Burke Moseley Petitions, and the Francis P. Gaines Correspondence in the President's Office Papers. On Poteat's activities within Wake Forest College, I used various college records and publications in the Special Collections department of Reynolds Library, including minutes of the meetings of the board of trustees, minutes of the faculty meetings, printed annual reports of the president of the college, the yearly catalogs of the college, the student magazine (the *Wake Forest Student*), a magazine published by the president's office (the *Bulletin of Wake Forest College*), and the college newspaper, the *Wake Forest Old Gold and Black*. The *Student* and the *Bulletin* contain dozens of short articles by Poteat. At this same rich repository, I also used the published minutes of the Beulah Association, the Central Baptist Association, the North Carolina Baptist State Convention, and the Southern Baptist Convention. I also consulted the microfilmed minutes of the Yanceyville First Baptist Church. In Reynolds Library (but not in the Special Collections department), I consulted various issues of the *Journal of the Elisha Mitchell Scientific Society* (for information on the Mitchell society and the North Carolina Academy of Science), the *North Carolina Teacher* (for the activities of the North Carolina Teachers' Assembly), and the annual proceedings of the Conference for Education in the South during the first decade of the twentieth century. Also in Reynolds Library are several programs from the annual meetings of the North Carolina Teachers' Assembly.

 At the Southern Historical Collection in Wilson Library at the University of North Carolina at Chapel Hill, I used the Eugene C. Branson Papers, the Charles L. Coon Papers, the Frank Porter Graham Papers, the Alexander W. McAlister Papers, the North Carolina Commission on Interracial Cooperation Papers, and the Howard W. Odum Papers. Also in Wilson Library, I used the clipping file of the North Carolina Collection. At the North Carolina Division of Archives and History in Raleigh, I used the Willis G. Briggs Collection, the Herbert Hutchinson Brimley Papers, the North Carolina Conference for Social Service Papers, and the North Carolina Mental Health Association Papers. In Special Collections, Perkins Library, Duke University, Durham, North Carolina, I used the Benjamin N. Duke Papers, the Edwin Clarke Gregory Papers, the James Poteat Hotel Register, the William C. Powell Papers, and the William Cornelius Tyree

Papers. At the Duke University Archives, also in Perkins Library, I consulted the William Preston Few Papers and the John Carlisle Kilgo Papers.

Other collections used include the Edwin Mims Papers, Special Collections, Heard Library, Vanderbilt University, Nashville, Tennessee; and microfilm reels 20 and 53 from the microfilm edition of the Commission on Interracial Cooperation Records, Atlanta University Library, Atlanta, Georgia. The archivists in special collections at Boyce Library, Southern Baptist Theological Seminary, Louisville, Kentucky, supplied me by mail with copies of letters from the Edgar Young Mullins letter files; and the staff of the special collections department of Joyner Library, East Carolina University, Greenville, North Carolina, supplied me with copies of material from the North Carolina Academy of Science Records. At the public library in Yanceyville, North Carolina, I consulted microfilm copies of "Caswell County Tax Book, 1823–1824," "List of Taxable Property for the Year 1805," and "A List of Taxable Property in Caswell County for the Year 1838. . . ." Also there, I used a copy of a family genealogical newsletter, *Poteat Newsletter (Also Allied Families)* 1 (July 1988). Diana P. Hobby and Sylvia S. Lowe, granddaughters of William Louis Poteat, gave me access to diaries written by Poteat that are held by the family.

Selected Published Writings by William L. Poteat, Arranged Chronologically

"North Carolina Desmids—A Preliminary List." *Journal of the Elisha Mitchell Scientific Society (JEMSS)* 5 (January–June 1888): 1–4.
"A Tube-Building Spider: Notes on the Architectural and Feeding Habits of Atypus Niger Hentz(?)." *JEMSS* 6 (July–December 1889): 132–47.
"Notes on the Fertility of Physa Heterostropha Say." *JEMSS* 8 (July–December 1891): 70–73.
"The Effect on the College Curriculum of the Introduction of the Natural Sciences." *Science* 21 (March 31, 1893): 170–72.
"The Child As Teacher." *North Carolina Journal of Education* 1 (November 1897): 13–17.
"Rural Libraries." *North Carolina Journal of Education* 1 (May 1898): 14–17.
"Leidy's Genus Ouramoeba." *Science*, n.s., 8 (December 2, 1898): 778–82.
"The People's Bible." In *Eighty-Sixth Annual Report of the Bible Society of Virginia . . .*, 7–15. Richmond, 1900.
Laboratory and Pulpit: The Relation of Biology to the Preacher and His Message. Philadelphia, 1901.
"The Correlation of Social Forces." *Social Service Quarterly* 1 (April, May, June 1913): 30–32.
Putting the Kingdom First (pamphlet). Raleigh, 1913.
"The Social Task of the Modern Church." In *The South Mobilizing for Social Service: Addresses Delivered at the Southern Sociological Congress, Atlanta, Georgia, April 25–29, 1913*, ed. James E. McCulloch, 534–40. Nashville, 1913.
The New Peace: Lectures on Science and Religion. Boston and Toronto, 1915.
"The Old Method for the New World." *Bulletin of the North Carolina State Board of Charities and Public Welfare* 3 (April–June 1920): 6–11.
Can a Man Be a Christian To-day? Chapel Hill and London, 1925.
"Liberal Movements in the South." *Yale Review* 16 (January 1927): 389–91.
The Way of Victory. Chapel Hill, 1929.
"The Influence of Public Health and Education upon the Development of the Human Race." *Southern Medicine and Surgery* 92 (June 1930): 396–99.
Stop-light. Nashville, 1935.
"An Intellectual Adventure: A Human Document." *American Scholar* 5 (summer 1936): 280–86.
Christ and Race (pamphlet). Raleigh, 1938.
Youth and Culture. [Wake Forest, N.C.], 1938.

Newspapers

Greensboro Daily News
Milton (N.C.) Chronicle

Raleigh Biblical Recorder
Raleigh News and Observer
Wake Forest Old Gold and Black

Other Published Primary Sources

Arnold, Matthew. *Culture and Anarchy.* Ed. J. Dover Wilson. 1869. Reprint, Cambridge, England, 1969.

Betts, S.J. *Criticism of Dr. Poteat's Book Recently Published Entitled "Can a Man Be a Christian Today?"* Raleigh, 1925.

Biennial Report of the Superintendent of Public Instruction, of North Carolina, for the Scholastic Years 1896–'97 and 1897–'98. Raleigh, 1898.

Cherrington, Ernest Hurst, ed. *Anti-Saloon League Year Book.* . . . Westerville, Ohio, 1924–32.

Dabney, Virginius. *Liberalism in the South.* Chapel Hill, 1932.

Drummond, Henry. *The Ascent of Man.* New York, 1894.

Herron, George D. *The Christian State: A Political Vision of Christ.* . . . New York and Boston, 1895.

Holden, W.W. *Answer to the Articles of Impeachment.* . . . [Raleigh], 1870.

House, R.B., ed., and Santford Martin, comp. *Public Letters and Papers of Thomas Walter Bickett, Governor of North Carolina, 1917–1921.* Raleigh, 1928.

Kendall, Katharine Kerr. *Caswell County, 1777–1877: Historical Abstracts of Minutes of Caswell County, North Carolina.* Raleigh, 1976.

———. *Caswell County, North Carolina, Deed Books, 1777–1817.* Easley, S.C., 1989.

———. *Caswell County, North Carolina, Deed Books, 1817–1840.* Franklin, N.C., 1992.

———. *Caswell County, North Carolina: Land Grants, Tax Lists, State Census, Apprentice Bonds, Estate Records.* Raleigh, 1977.

———. *Caswell County, North Carolina, Marriage Bonds, 1778–1868.* Raleigh, 1981.

———. *Caswell County, North Carolina, Will Books, 1814–1843.* . . . Raleigh, 1983.

———. *Caswell County, North Carolina, Will Books, 1843–1868.* Raleigh, 1986.

Kidd, Benjamin. *Social Evolution.* London and New York, 1894.

Lyman, Robert Hunty, ed. *The World Almanac and Book of Facts for 1927.* New York, 1927.

Manuscript Census Returns, Fifth Census of the United States, 1830. Caswell County, North Carolina, Population Schedules. National Archives Microfilm Series M-19, roll 119.

Manuscript Census Returns, Seventh Census of the United States, 1850. Caswell County, North Carolina, White and Free Colored Population. National Archives Microfilm Series M-432, roll 623.

Manuscript Census Returns, Eighth Census of the United States, 1860. Caswell County, North Carolina, Schedule 1. National Archives Microfilm Series M-653, roll 891.

Manuscript Census Returns, Eighth Census of the United States, 1860. Caswell County, North Carolina, Schedule 2, Slave Population. National Archives Microfilm Series M-653, roll 921.

Manuscript Census Returns, Ninth Census of the United States, 1870. Caswell County, North Carolina, Population Schedule. National Archives Microfilm Series M-593, roll 1128.

"The Marine Biological Laboratory at Woods Hall [*sic*], Mass." *American Naturalist* 27 (June 1893): 594–98.

Martin, Thomas T. *Three Fatal Teachings.* N.p., [1920].

McCulloch, James E., ed. *Battling for Social Betterment: Southern Sociological Congress, Memphis, Tennessee, May 6–10, 1914.* Nashville, 1914.

———, ed. *The Call of the New South: Addresses Delivered at the Southern Sociological Congress, Nashville, Tennessee, May 7 to 12, 1912.* Nashville, 1912.

———, ed. *The New Chivalry—Health: Southern Sociological Congress, Houston, Texas, May 8–11, 1915.* Nashville, 1915.

Mencken, Henry L. *Prejudices: Sixth Series.* New York, 1927.

Miles, R.W. "The North Carolina Inter-Racial Committee." *Journal of Social Forces* 1 (January 1923): 154–55.

Mims, Edwin. *The Advancing South: Stories of Progress and Reaction.* Garden City, N.Y., 1926.

[Neal, Margaret]. "The North Carolina Conference for Social Service: The Record of Twenty-Five Years, 1912–1937." Bound carbon copy of typescript in the North Carolina Collection, University of North Carolina at Chapel Hill.

Pearson, C. Chilton. "Race Relations in North Carolina: A Field Study of Moderate Opinion." *South Atlantic Quarterly* 23 (January 1924): 1–9.

Pentuff, James R. *Christian Evolutionists Answered and President W.L. Poteat's Utterances Reviewed.* N.p., 1925.

[Phillips, H.C.], ed. *Report of the Seventeenth Annual Lake Mohonk Conference on International Arbitration....* Mohonk Lake, N.Y., 1911.

Proceedings of the First Annual Session of the Southern Educational Association ... 1890. Raleigh, 1890.

Proceedings of the Golden Anniversary Meeting: North Carolina Conference for Social Service. Raleigh, 1960.

Rauschenbusch, Walter. "The Social Program of the Church." In *The South Mobilizing for Social Service: Addresses Delivered at the Southern Sociological Congress, Atlanta, Georgia, April 25–29, 1913,* ed. James E. McCulloch, 504–11. Nashville, 1913.

[Report of the Select Committee of The Senate to Investigate Alleged Outrages in the Southern States], *Senate Reports.* 42 Cong. 1st Sess. [1871] No. 1. Serial 1468.

Reynolds, L.R. "The Commission on Interracial Cooperation of North Carolina and Virginia." *Southern Workman* 63 (1934): 244–48.

Rose, Ben L. *Thomas McNeill of Caswell County, North Carolina: His Forebears and Descendants.* Richmond, 1984.

Southern Educational Association, *Journal of Proceedings and Address of the Ninth Annual Meeting ... 1899.* N.p., 1899.

Stallings, Helen Poteat. "Ida Isabella Poteat, 1859–1940." *Meredith College Bulletin* 34 (November 1940): 6–7.

Taylor, Charles E., [comp.]. *General Catalogue of Wake Forest College, North Carolina, 1834–5—1891–2.* Raleigh, 1892.

Wilson, Edmund B. "The Mosaic Theory of Development." In *Defining Biology: Lectures from the 1890s,* ed. Jane Maienschein, 66–80. Cambridge, Mass., and London, 1986.

The World Almanac and Encyclopedia, 1905. New York, 1905.

The World Almanac and Encyclopedia, 1915. New York, 1914.

Secondary Sources

Ahlstrom, Sydney E. *Theology in America: The Major Protestant Voices from Puritanism to Neo-Orthodoxy.* Indianapolis and New York, 1967.

Aiken, John R., and James R. McDonnell. "Walter Rauschenbusch and Labor Reform: A Social Gospeller's Approach." *Labor History* 11 (spring 1970): 131–50.

Anderson, Benedict. *Imagined Communities: Reflections on the Origin and Spread of Nationalism.* 1983. Rev. ed., London and New York, 1991.

Appel, Toby A. "Organizing Biology: The American Society of Naturalists and Its 'Affiliated Societies,' 1883–1923." In *The American Development of Biology,* ed. Ronald Rainger, Keith R. Benson, and Jane Maienschein, 87–120. Philadelphia, 1988.

Ayers, Edward L. *The Promise of the New South: Life after Reconstruction.* New York and Oxford, 1992.

———. *Vengeance and Justice: Crime and Punishment in the 19th-Century American South.* New York and Oxford, 1984.

Bailey, Kenneth K. *Southern White Protestantism in the Twentieth Century.* New York, Evanston, and London, 1964.

Banks, Charles Edward. *The History of Martha's Vineyard, Duke's County, Massachusetts.* 3 vols. 1911. Reprint, Edgartown, Mass., 1966.

Barefield, James P. "The Wake Forest Curriculum: A Brief History." Unpublished paper in author's possession.

Bartley, Numan V. *The New South, 1945–1980*. Baton Rouge and London, 1995.

Bauman, Mark K. "Confronting the New South Creed: The Genteel Conservative As Higher Educator." In *Education and the Rise of the New South*, ed. Ronald K. Goodenow and Arthur O. White, 92–113. Boston, 1981.

Beale, Howard K. *Are American Teachers Free? An Analysis of Restraints upon the Freedom of Teaching in American Schools*. New York, 1936.

Beaty, Mary D. *A History of Davidson College*. Davidson, N.C., 1988.

Benson, Keith R. "From Museum Research to Laboratory Research: The Transformation of Natural History into Academic Biology." In *The American Development of Biology*, ed. Ronald Rainger, Keith R. Benson, and Jane Maienschein, 49–83. Philadelphia, 1988.

Bledstein, Burton J. *The Culture of Professionalism: The Middle Class and the Development of Higher Education in America*. New York, 1976.

Bode, Frederick A. "The Formation of Evangelical Communities in Middle Georgia: Twiggs County, 1820–1861." *Journal of Southern History* 60 (November 1994): 711–48.

Boles, John B. "The Discovery of Southern Religious History." In *Interpreting Southern History: Historiographical Essays in Honor of Sanford W. Higginbotham*, ed. John Boles and Evelyn Thomas Nolen, 510–48. Baton Rouge and London, 1987.

———. "Evangelical Protestantism in the Old South: From Religious Dissent to Cultural Dominance." In *Religion in the South*, ed. Charles Reagan Wilson, 13–34. Jackson, Miss., 1985.

———. *The Great Revival: Beginnings of the Bible Belt*. 1972. Reprint, Lexington, Ky., 1996.

———. *Religion in Antebellum Kentucky*. Lexington, Ky., 1976.

———. *The South through Time: A History of an American Region*. Englewood Cliffs, N.J., 1995.

———, ed. *Masters and Slaves in the House of the Lord: Race and Religion in the American South, 1740–1870*. Lexington, Ky., 1988.

Boswell, Ron. *The Blessing of Beulah*. Roxboro, N.C., 1984.

Bowler, Peter J. *Evolution: The History of an Idea*. 1983. Rev. ed. Berkeley, Los Angeles, and London, 1989.

Bridges, Hal. "D.H. Hill and Higher Education in the New South." *Arkansas Historical Quarterly* 15 (summer 1956): 107–24.

Brittain, James E., and Robert C. McMath Jr. "Engineers and the New South Creed: The Formation and Early Development of Georgia Tech." *Technology and Culture* 18 (April 1977): 175–201.

Bruce, Robert V. *The Launching of Modern American Science, 1846–1876*. New York, 1987.

Bryan, George McLeod. "The Educational, Religious, and Social Thought of William Louis Poteat as Expressed in His Writings, Including Unpublished Notes and Addresses." Masters thesis, Wake Forest College, 1944.

Burrows, Edward Flud. "The Commission on Interracial Cooperation, 1919–1944: A Case Study in the History of the Interracial Movement in the South." Ph.D. diss., University of Wisconsin, 1954.

Cameron, Harriet Suzanne. "William Louis Poteat and the Evolution Controversy." Masters thesis, Wake Forest College, 1962.

Cash, W.J. "The Mind of the South." In *W.J. Cash, Southern Prophet: A Biography and Reader*, ed. Joseph L. Morrison, 182–98. New York, 1967, First published in *American Mercury* (October 1929).

———. *The Mind of the South*. New York, 1941.

Clayton, Bruce. *The Savage Ideal: Intolerance and Intellectual Leadership in the South, 1890–1914*. Baltimore and London, 1972.

———. *W.J. Cash: A Life*. Baton Rouge and London, 1991.

———. "W.J. Cash: A Mind of the South." In *W.J. Cash and the Minds of the South*, ed. Paul D. Escott, 9–22. Baton Rouge and London, 1992.

Conkin, Paul K. *Gone with the Ivy: A Biography of Vanderbilt University*. Knoxville, 1985.

Coulling, Sidney. "Matthew Arnold and the American South." In *Matthew Arnold in His Time and Ours: Centenary Essays*, ed. Clinton Machann and Forrest D. Burt, 40–56. Charlottesville, Va., 1988.

Crocker, Ruth Hutchinson. *Social Work and Social Order: The Settlement Movement in Two Industrial Cities, 1889–1930.* Urbana and Chicago, 1992.

Crow, Jeffrey J. "Thomas Settle Jr., Reconstruction, and the Memory of the Civil War." *Journal of Southern History* 62 (November 1996): 689–726.

Crowe, Karen, [ed.]. *Southern Horizons: The Autobiography of Thomas Dixon.* Alexandria, Va., 1984.

Crowther, Edward R. "Holy Honor: Sacred and Secular in the Old South." *Journal of Southern History* 58 (November 1992): 619–36.

Curtis, Susan. *A Consuming Faith: The Social Gospel and Modern American Culture.* Baltimore and London, 1991.

Davis, Edward B. "Fundamentalism and Folk Science between the Wars." *Religion and American Culture* 5 (summer 1995): 217–48.

Dennis, Michael. "Educating the 'Advancing' South: State Universities and Progressivism in the New South, 1887–1915." Ph.D. diss., Queen's University, 1996.

———. "Reforming the 'Academical Village': Edwin A. Alderman and the University of Virginia, 1904–1915." *Virginia Magazine of History and Biography* 105 (winter 1997): 53–86.

Doyle, Don H. *New Men, New Cities, New South: Atlanta, Nashville, Charleston, Mobile, 1860–1910.* Chapel Hill and London, 1990.

Dunbar, Anthony P. *Against the Grain: Southern Radicals and Prophets, 1929–1959.* Charlottesville, 1981.

Dyer, Thomas G. "Higher Education in the South Since the Civil War: Historiographical Issues and Trends." In *The Web of Southern Social Relations: Women, Family, and Education,* ed. Walter J. Fraser Jr., R. Frank Saunders Jr., and Jon L. Wakelyn, 127–45. Athens, Ga., 1985.

———. *The University of Georgia: A Bicentennial History, 1785–1985.* Athens, Ga., 1985.

Dykeman, Wilma. *Prophet of Plenty: The First Ninety Years of W.D. Weatherford.* Knoxville, 1966.

Dykeman, Wilma, and James Stokely. *Seeds of Southern Change: The Life of Will Alexander.* Chicago and London, 1962.

Eaton, Clement. *The Mind of the Old South.* Baton Rouge, 1964.

———. "Professor James Woodrow and the Freedom of Teaching in the South." *Journal of Southern History* 28 (February 1962): 3–17.

Egerton, John. *Speak Now against the Day: The Generation before the Civil Rights Movement in the South.* New York, 1994.

Eighmy, John Lee. *Churches in Cultural Captivity: A History of the Social Attitudes of Southern Baptists.* 1972. Rev. ed., Knoxville, 1987.

Ellis, Ann Wells. "The Commission on Interracial Cooperation, 1919–1944: Its Activities and Results." Ph.D. diss., Georgia State University, 1975.

Escott, Paul D. *Many Excellent People: Power and Privilege in North Carolina, 1850–1900.* Chapel Hill and London, 1985.

Fairbanks, George R. *History of the University of the South. . . .* Jacksonville, Fla., 1905.

Flynt, J. Wayne. *Alabama Baptists: Southern Baptists in the Heart of Dixie.* Tuscaloosa and London, 1998.

———. "'Feeding the Hungry and Ministering to the Broken Hearted': The Presbyterian Church in the United States and the Social Gospel, 1900–1920." In *Religion in the South,* ed. Charles Reagan Wilson, 83–137. Jackson, 1985.

Ford, Charlotte A. "Eliza Frances Andrews, Practical Botanist, 1840–1931." *Georgia Historical Quarterly* 70 (spring 1986): 63–80.

Foster, Gaines M. *Ghosts of the Confederacy: Defeat, the Lost Cause, and the Emergence of the New South, 1865 to 1913.* New York and Oxford, 1987.

Fox-Genovese, Elizabeth. *Within the Plantation Household: Black and White Women of the Old South.* Chapel Hill and London, 1988.

Gaston, Paul M. *The New South Creed: A Study in Southern Mythmaking.* Baton Rouge, 1970.

Gatewood, Willard B., Jr. Introduction to *Controversy in the Twenties: Fundamentalism, Modernism, and Evolution,* ed. Willard B. Gatewood, 3–46. Nashville, 1969.

———. "Politics and Piety in North Carolina: The Fundamentalist Crusade at High Tide, 1925–1927," *North Carolina Historical Review* 42 (summer 1965): 275–90.

———. *Preachers, Pedagogues, and Politicians: The Evolution Controversy in North Carolina, 1920–1927.* Chapel Hill, 1966.

Genovese, Eugene D. *Roll, Jordan, Roll: The World the Slaves Made.* New York, 1974.

Gilmore, Glenda Elizabeth. *Gender and Jim Crow: Women and the Politics of White Supremacy in North Carolina, 1896–1920.* Chapel Hill and London, 1996.

Grantham, Dewey W. *Southern Progressivism: The Reconciliation of Progress and Tradition.* Knoxville, 1983.

Gross, Paul R. "Laying the Ghost: Embryonic Development, in Plain Words." *Biological Bulletin* 168 (supplement, June 1985): 62–79.

Gruber, Carol S. *Mars and Minerva: World War I and the Uses of the Higher Learning in America.* Baton Rouge, 1975.

Gulledge, Virginia Wooten. *The North Carolina Conference for Social Service: A Study of Its Development and Methods.* N.p., 1942.

Handy, Robert T. *A Christian America: Protestant Hopes and Historical Realities.* New York, 1971.

———. Introduction to *The Social Gospel in America, 1870–1920,* ed. Robert Handy. New York, 1966.

———. "The Social Gospel in Historical Perspective." *Andover Newton Quarterly* 9 (January 1969): 170–80.

Hankins, Barry. *God's Rascal: J. Frank Norris and the Beginnings of Southern Fundamentalism.* Lexington, Ky., 1996.

Harlan, Louis R. *Separate and Unequal: Public School Campaigns and Racism in the Southern Seaboard States, 1901–1915.* Chapel Hill, 1958.

Harland-Jacobs, Jessica. *Balancing Tradition and Innovation: The History of Botany at Duke University, 1849–1996.* [Durham], 1996.

Harper, Keith. *The Quality of Mercy: Southern Baptists and Social Christianity, 1890–1920.* Tuscaloosa and London, 1996.

Harvey, Paul. *Redeeming the South: Religious Cultures and Racial Identities among Southern Baptists, 1865–1925.* Chapel Hill and London, 1997.

Haskell, Thomas L. *The Emergence of Professional Social Science: The American Social Science Association and the Nineteenth-Century Crisis of Authority.* Urbana, Chicago, and London, 1977.

———. Introduction to *The Authority of Experts: Studies in History and Theory,* ed. Haskell, ix–xxxix. Bloomington, 1984.

Hawkins, Hugh. *Pioneer: A History of the Johns Hopkins University, 1874–1889.* Ithaca, 1960.

Haygood, Tamara Miner. *Henry William Ravenel, 1814–1887: South Carolina Scientist in the Civil War Era.* Tuscaloosa and London, 1987.

———. "Henry William Ravenel (1814–1887): Views on Evolution in Social Context." *Journal of the History of Biology* 21 (fall 1988): 457–72.

Hays, Samuel P. *The Response to Industrialism, 1885–1914.* Chicago, 1957.

Hill, Samuel S., Jr. *The South and North in American Religion.* Athens, Ga., 1980.

———. *Southern Churches in Crisis.* New York, 1966.

Hobson, Fred. Introduction to *South-Watching: Selected Essays by Gerald W. Johnson,* ed. Hobson, vii–xxxi. Chapel Hill and London, 1983.

Hofstadter, Richard, and Walter P. Metzger. *The Development of Academic Freedom in the United States.* New York, 1955.

Hopkins, Charles Howard. *The Rise of the Social Gospel in American Protestantism, 1865–1915.* New Haven and London, 1940.

Hudson, Winthrop S. "Walter Rauschenbusch and the New Evangelism." *Religion in Life* 30 (summer 1961): 412–30.

Johnson, Gerald W. "Billy with the Red Necktie." In *South-Watching: Selected Essays by Gerald W. Johnson.* Ed. Fred Hobson, 191–99. Chapel Hill and London, 1983.

Johnson, Mary Lynch. *A History of Meredith College*. 2nd ed. Raleigh, 1972.

Kevles, Daniel J. *In the Name of Eugenics: Genetics and the Uses of Human Heredity*. 1985. Reprint with a new preface, Cambridge, Mass., and London, 1995.

Kimball, Bruce A. *The "True Professional Ideal" in America: A History*. Cambridge, Mass., and Oxford, 1992.

King, Richard H. *A Southern Renaissance: The Cultural Awakening of the American South, 1930–1955*. Oxford, 1980.

Kirby, Jack Temple. *Darkness at the Dawning: Race and Reform in the Progressive South*. Philadelphia, New York, and Toronto, 1972.

Kissell, Richard M. "Politics and Prohibition in North Carolina, 1880–1882." Masters thesis, Wake Forest University, 1974.

Kohlstedt, Sally Gregory. "Museums on Campus: A Tradition of Inquiry and Teaching." In *The American Development of Biology*, ed. Ronald Rainger, Keith R. Benson, and Jane Maienschein, 15–47. Philadelphia, 1988.

Kuykendall, John W. *Southern Enterprize: The Work of National Evangelical Societies in the Antebellum South*. Westport, Conn., and London, 1982.

Larson, Edward J. *Sex, Race, and Science: Eugenics in the Deep South*. Baltimore and London, 1995.

Leloudis, James L. *Schooling the New South: Pedagogy, Self, and Society in North Carolina, 1880–1920*. Chapel Hill and London, 1996.

Lemmon, Sarah McCulloh. "North Carolina in the Twentieth Century, 1913–1945." In *Writing North Carolina History*, ed. Jeffrey J. Crow and Larry E. Tise, 172–90. Chapel Hill, 1979.

Lillie, Frank R. *The Woods Hole Marine Biological Laboratory*. Chicago, 1944.

Linder, Suzanne Cameron. "William Louis Poteat and the Evolution Controversy." *North Carolina Historical Review* 40 (April 1963): 135–57.

———. *William Louis Poteat: Prophet of Progress*. Chapel Hill, 1966.

Link, Arthur S. "The First Century of Medical Education at Wake Forest." Draft in author's possession.

———. "The Progressive Movement in the South, 1870–1914." *North Carolina Historical Review* 23 (April 1946): 172–95.

Link, William A. *The Paradox of Southern Progressivism, 1880–1930*. Chapel Hill and London, 1992.

Little-Stokes, Ruth, comp. *An Inventory of Historic Architecture, Caswell County, North Carolina: The Built Environment of a Burley and Bright-leaf Tobacco Economy*. [Raleigh], 1979.

Loveland, Anne C. *Southern Evangelicals and the Social Order, 1800–1860*. Baton Rouge and London, 1980.

Maienschein, Jane. "Agassiz, Hyatt, Whitman, and the Birth of the Marine Biological Laboratory." *Biological Bulletin* 168 (supplement, June 1985): 26–34.

———. Introduction to *Defining Biology: Lectures from the 1890s*, ed. Maienschein, 3–50. Cambridge, Mass., and London, 1986.

———. "Shifting Assumptions in American Biology: Embryology, 1890–1910." *Journal of the History of Biology* 14 (spring 1981): 89–113.

———. *Transforming Traditions in American Biology, 1880–1915*. Baltimore and London, 1991.

Marsden, George M. *Fundamentalism and American Culture: The Shaping of Twentieth-Century Evangelicalism, 1870–1925*. New York and Oxford, 1980.

Martin, Robert F. *Howard Kester and the Struggle for Social Justice in the South, 1904–77*. Charlottesville, Va., and London, 1991.

Mathews, Donald G. *Religion in the Old South*. Chicago and London, 1977.

May, Henry F. *The End of American Innocence: A Study of the First Years of Our Own Time, 1912–1917*. 1959. Reprint, Chicago, 1964.

McCandless, Peter. *Moonlight, Magnolias, and Madness: Insanity in South Carolina from the Colonial Period to the Progressive Era*. Chapel Hill and London, 1996.

McDonough, Julia Anne. "Men and Women of Good Will: A History of the Commission on

Interracial Cooperation and the Southern Regional Council, 1919–1954." Ph.D. diss., University of Virginia, 1993.

McDowell, John Patrick. *The Social Gospel in the South: The Woman's Home Mission Movement in the Methodist Episcopal Church, South, 1886–1939.* Baton Rouge and London, 1982.

Midgette, Nancy Smith. "The Alabama Academy of Science and the Maturing of a Profession." *Alabama Review* 37 (April 1984): 98–123.

———. "In Search of Professional Identity: Southern Scientists, 1883–1940." *Journal of Southern History* 54 (November 1988): 596–622.

———. *To Foster the Spirit of Professionalism: Southern Scientists and State Academies of Science.* Tuscaloosa and London, 1991.

Miller, Robert Moats. "Fourteen Points on the Social Gospel in the South." *Southern Humanities Review* 1 (summer 1967): 126–40.

Mintz, Steven. *Moralists and Modernizers: America's Pre–Civil War Reformers.* Baltimore and London, 1995.

Minus, Paul M. *Walter Rauschenbusch: American Reformer.* New York and London, 1988.

Morgan, David T., Jr. "The Great Awakening in North Carolina, 1740–1775: The Baptist Phase." *North Carolina Historical Review* 45 (summer 1968): 264–83.

Noll, Steven. *Feeble-Minded in Our Midst: Institutions for the Mentally Retarded in the South, 1900–1940.* Chapel Hill and London, 1995.

Novick, Peter. *That Noble Dream: The "Objectivity Question" and the American Historical Profession.* Cambridge, 1988.

Numbers, Ronald L. *The Creationists.* New York, 1992.

Numbers, Ronald L., and Janet S. Numbers. "Science in the Old South: A Reappraisal." *Journal of Southern History* 48 (May 1982): 163–84.

Numbers, Ronald L., and Todd L. Savitt, eds. *Science and Medicine in the Old South.* Baton Rouge and London, 1989.

O'Brien, Michael. *The Idea of the American South, 1920–1941.* Baltimore and London, 1979.

Olsen, Otto H. "The Ku Klux Klan: A Study in Reconstruction Politics and Propaganda." *North Carolina Historical Review* 39 (summer 1962): 340–62.

Orr, Oliver H., Jr. *Saving American Birds: T. Gilbert Pearson and the Founding of the Audubon Movement.* Gainesville, Fla., 1992.

Ownby, Ted. *Subduing Satan: Religion, Recreation, and Manhood in the Rural South, 1865–1920.* Chapel Hill and London, 1990.

Paschal, George Washington. *History of North Carolina Baptists, 1663–1805.* Vol. 1. Raleigh, 1930.

———. *History of Wake Forest College.* 3 vols. Wake Forest, N.C., 1935–43.

Pauly, Philip J. "The Appearance of Academic Biology in Late Nineteenth-Century America." *Journal of the History of Biology* 17 (fall 1984): 369–97.

———. "Summer Resort and Scientific Discipline: Woods Hole and the Structure of American Biology, 1882–1925." In *The American Development of Biology*, ed. Ronald Rainger, Keith R. Benson, and Jane Maienschein, 121–50. Philadelphia, 1988.

Pegram, Thomas R. "Temperance Politics and Regional Political Culture: The Anti-Saloon League in Maryland and the South, 1907–1915." *Journal of Southern History* 63 (February 1997): 57–90.

Porter, Earl W. *Trinity and Duke, 1892–1924: Foundations of Duke University.* Durham, N.C., 1964.

Powell, Ruth Gilliam. "History of the Southern Commission on Inter-Racial Cooperation." Masters thesis, University of South Carolina, 1935.

Powell, William S. *When the Past Refused to Die: A History of Caswell County, North Carolina, 1777–1977.* Durham, 1977.

———, ed. *Dictionary of North Carolina Biography.* 6 vols. Chapel Hill and London, 1979–96.

Quist, John W. *Restless Visionaries: The Social Roots of Antebellum Reform in Alabama and Michigan.* Baton Rouge and London, 1997.

———. "Slaveholding Operatives of the Benevolent Empire: Bible, Tract, and Sunday School

Societies in Antebellum Tuscaloosa County, Alabama." *Journal of Southern History* 62 (August 1996): 481–526.

Rabinowitz, Howard N. *The First New South, 1865–1920.* Arlington Heights, Ill., 1992.

Raleigh, John Henry. *Matthew Arnold and American Culture.* Berkeley and Los Angeles, 1957.

Ramage, James A. "Thomas Hunt Morgan: Family Influences in the Making of a Great Scientist." *Filson Club History Quarterly* 53 (January 1979): 5–25.

Reagan, Alice Elizabeth. *North Carolina State University: A Narrative History.* Ann Arbor, 1987.

Reid, Alfred Sandlin. *Furman University: Toward a New Identity, 1925–1975.* Durham, N.C., 1976.

Rudolph, Frederick. *Curriculum: A History of the American Undergraduate Course of Study Since 1636.* San Francisco, 1977.

Russell-Hunter, W.D. "An Evolutionary Century at Woods Hole: Instruction in Invertebrate Zoology." *Biological Bulletin* 168 (supplement, June 1985): 88–98.

Salmond, John A. *Gastonia 1929: The Story of the Loray Mill Strike.* Chapel Hill and London, 1995.

Schmidt, Jean Miller. *Souls or the Social Order: The Two-Party System in American Protestantism.* New York, 1991.

Schulman, Bruce J. *From Cotton Belt to Sunbelt: Federal Policy, Economic Development, and the Transformation of the South, 1938–1980.* Durham and London, 1994.

Simpson, Marcus B., Jr., and Sallie W. Simpson. "Moses Ashley Curtis (1808–1872): Contributions to Carolina Ornithology." *North Carolina Historical Review* 60 (April 1983): 137–70.

Singal, Daniel Joseph. *The War Within: From Victorian to Modernist Thought in the South, 1919–1945.* Chapel Hill, 1982.

Smiley, David L. "Educational Attitudes of North Carolina Baptists." *North Carolina Historical Review* 35 (July 1958): 316–27.

Sosna, Morton. *In Search of the Silent South: Southern Liberals and the Race Issue.* New York, 1977.

Spain, Rufus B. *At Ease in Zion: Social History of Southern Baptists, 1865–1900.* Nashville, 1961.

Speas, Ethel M. *History of the Voluntary Health Movement in North Carolina.* N.p., 1961.

Steelman, Joseph Flake. "The Progressive Era in North Carolina, 1884–1917." Ph.D. diss., University of North Carolina at Chapel Hill, 1955.

Stephens, Lester D. "Darwin's Disciple in Georgia: Henry Clay White, 1875–1927." *Georgia Historical Quarterly* 78 (spring 1994): 66–91.

———. *Joseph LeConte: Gentle Prophet of Evolution.* Baton Rouge and London, 1982.

Stetar, Joseph M. "In Search of a Direction: Southern Higher Education after the Civil War." *History of Education Quarterly* 25 (fall 1985): 341–67.

Stokes, Durward T. "North Carolina and the Great Revival of 1800." *North Carolina Historical Review* 43 (Autumn 1966): 401–12.

Storey, John W. *Texas Baptist Leadership and Social Christianity, 1900–1980.* College Station, Tex., 1986.

Stricklin, David. *A Genealogy of Dissent: Southern Baptist Protest in the Twentieth Century.* Lexington, Ky., 1999.

Stroupe, Henry S. "The Beginnings of Religious Journalism in North Carolina, 1823–1865." *North Carolina Historical Review* 30 (January 1953): 1–22.

Summerville, James. "Science in the New South: The Meeting of the AAAS at Nashville, 1877." *Tennessee Historical Quarterly* 45 (winter 1986): 316–28.

Thompson, James J., Jr. *Tried As by Fire: Southern Baptists and the Religious Controversies of the 1920s.* Macon, Ga., 1982.

Tilley, Nannie May. *The Bright-Tobacco Industry, 1860–1929.* Chapel Hill, 1948.

Tindall, George Brown. *The Emergence of the New South, 1913–1945.* Baton Rouge, 1967.

Trachtenberg, Alan. *The Incorporation of America: Culture and Society in the Gilded Age.* New York, 1982.

Trelease, Allen W. *White Terror: The Ku Klux Klan and Southern Reconstruction.* 1971. Reprint, Baton Rouge and London, 1995.

Trent, James W., Jr. *Inventing the Feeble Mind: A History of Mental Retardation in the United States*. Berkeley, Los Angeles, and London, 1994.

Tyler, Pamela. *Silk Stockings and Ballot Boxes: Women and Politics in New Orleans, 1920–1963*. Athens, Ga., and London, 1996.

Wagoner, Jennings L. "Higher Education and Transitions in Southern Culture: An Exploratory Apologia." *Journal of Thought* 18 (fall 1983): 104–18.

Walters, Jeffrey Kirk. "'Though the Heavens Fall': Liberal Theology and the Southern Baptist Theological Seminary, 1894–1925." Masters thesis, Auburn University, 1992.

Webb, George E. *The Evolution Controversy in America*. Lexington, Ky., 1994.

Whitener, Daniel Jay. *Prohibition in North Carolina, 1715–1945*. Chapel Hill, 1945.

Whitlow, Jeannine D., ed. *The Heritage of Caswell County, North Carolina, 1985*. Winston-Salem, 1985.

Wiebe, Robert H. *The Search for Order, 1877–1920*. New York, 1967.

Williams, Thomas R. "The Development of Astronomy in the Southern United States, 1840–1914." *Journal for the History of Astronomy* 27 (February 1996): 13–44.

Williamson, Joel. *A Rage for Order: Black/White Relations in the American South Since Emancipation*. New York and Oxford, 1986.

Wilson, Charles Reagan, and William Ferris, eds. *Encyclopedia of Southern Culture*. Chapel Hill and London, 1989.

Woodard, John R. "North Carolina." In *Religion in the Southern States: A Historical Study*, ed. Samuel S. Hill, 215–37. Macon, 1983.

Woodward, C. Vann. *Origins of the New South, 1877–1913*. Baton Rouge, 1951.

Wright, Gavin. *Old South, New South: Revolutions in the Southern Economy Since the Civil War*. New York, 1986.

Wyatt-Brown, Bertram. "The Antimission Movement in the Jacksonian South: A Study in Regional Folk Culture." *Journal of Southern History* 36 (November 1970): 501–29.

———. *Southern Honor: Ethics and Behavior in the Old South*. New York and Oxford, 1982.

Index

✦